Feminism After Bourdieu

A selection of previous *Sociological Review* Monographs

The Sociology of Death: theory, culture, practice*
ed. David Clark
The Cultures of Computing
ed. Susan Leigh Star
Theorizing Museums*
ed. Sharon Macdonald and Gordon Fyfe
Consumption Matters*
eds Stephen Edgell, Kevin Hetherington and Alan Warde
Ideas of Difference*
eds Kevin Hetherington and Rolland Munro
The Laws of the Markets*
ed. Michael Callon
Actor Network Theory and After*
eds John Law and John Hassard
Whose Europe? The turn towards democracy*
eds Dennis Smith and Sue Wright
Renewing Class Analysis*
eds Rosemary Cromptom, Fiona Devine, Mike Savage and John Scott
Reading Bourdieu on Society and Culture*
ed. Bridget Fowler
The Consumption of Mass*
ed. Nick Lee and Rolland Munro
The Age of Anxiety: Conspiracy Theory and the Human Sciences*
eds Jane Parish and Martin Parker
Utopia and Organization*
ed. Martin Parker
Emotions and Sociology*
ed. Jack Barbalet
Masculinity and Men's Lifestyle Magazines
ed. Bethan Benwell
Nature Performed: Environment, Culture and Perfermance
eds Bronislaw Szerszynski, Wallace Heim and Claire Waterton
After Habermas: New Perspectives on the Public Sphere
eds Nick Crossley and John Michael Roberts

*Available from Marston Book Services, PO Box 270, Abingdon, Oxon OX14 4YW.

The Sociological Review Monographs

Since 1958 *The Sociological Review* has established a tradition of publishing Monographs on issues of general sociological interest. The Monograph is an edited book length collection of research papers which is published and distributed in association with Blackwell Publishing. We are keen to receive innovative collections of work in sociology and related disciplines with a particular emphasis on exploring empirical materials and theoretical frameworks which are currently under-developed. If you wish to discuss ideas for a Monograph then please contact the Monographs Editor, Rolland Munro, at *The Sociological Review*, Keele University, Newcastle-under-Lyme, North Staffordshire, ST5 5BG.

Feminism After Bourdieu

Edited by Lisa Adkins and Beverley Skeggs

Blackwell Publishing/The Sociological Review

Blackwell Publishing
9600 Garsington Road, Oxford OX4 2DQ, UK

and

350 Main Street, Malden, MA 02148-5018, USA

First published 2004 by Blackwell Publishing Ltd

Library of Congress Cataloging-in-Publication Data applied for

ISBN 1-4051-2395-8

A catalogue record for this title is available from the British Library.

Printed and bound in the United Kingdom by Page Brothers, Norwich.

The publisher's policy is to use permanent paper from mills that operate a sustainable forestry policy, and which has been manufactured from pulp processed using acid-free and elementary chlorine-free practices. Furthermore, the publisher ensures that the text paper and cover board used have met acceptable environmental accreditation standards.

For further information on Blackwell Publishing, visit our website:
http://www.blackwellpublishing.com

Contents

Acknowledgements

Thanks to the University of Manchester Small Grant Scheme who assisted with funding the initial workshop on which this volume is based and to Danielle Griffiths for editorial assistance.

Figure 1 (page 141) 'If Only Every Child Was Born With a Silver Spoon' reprinted with the kind permission of Barnardo's.

Chapter 10 reprinted by permission of Sage Publications Ltd from Lisa Adkins, 'Reflexivity: Freedom or Habit of Gender', Theory Culture and Society 20(6): 21–42, © Sage 2003.

Introduction, Context and Background

Introduction: Feminism, Bourdieu and after

Lisa Adkins

Introduction: feminism and contemporary social theory

How might Bourdieu's social philosophy and social theory be of use to feminism? And how might it relate to – or possibly even fruitfully reframe – the ongoing problematics and current theoretical issues of feminism? It is very well recognized that Bourdieu's social theory had relatively little to say about women or gender (although see Bourdieu, 2001) with most of his writings framed pre-eminently in terms of issues of class (Moi, 1991). Yet the premise of this volume is that this substantive omission should not be taken to mean that Bourdieu's theoretical apparatus does not necessarily have relevance for feminism. Other key contemporary social theorists such as Foucault and Habermas have also – substantively speaking – had little to say about women and gender or indeed feminism but this, of course, has not stopped feminists deploying, rethinking and critically developing the theoretical resources offered by these theorists to produce some of the most influential, compelling and productive forms of contemporary feminist theorizing (see eg Butler, 1993; Fraser, 1997). In this volume contributors will use, critique, critically extend and develop Bourdieu's social theory to address some of the most pressing issues of our times. And in so doing they will address both ongoing and key contemporary problematics in contemporary feminist theory. These include the problematic of theorizing social agency (and especially the problematic of social versus performative agency); the issue of the relationship of social movements (and especially women's movements) to social change; the politics of cultural authorization; the theorization of technological forms of embodiment (that is the theorization of embodiment post bounded conceptions of the body); the relations of affect to the political; and the articulation of principles of what might be termed a new feminist materialism which goes beyond Bourdieu's own social logics.

In critically extending Bourdieu's social theory to illuminate contemporary socio-cultural issues, the contributors in this volume therefore attest to the powerful tools that Bourdieu's social theory may offer contemporary feminist theory, tools which are increasingly recognized by feminists working across both the humanities and social science disciplines (see eg Butler, 1997, 1999; Fowler, 2003; Krais, 1993; Lawler, 2000; Lovell, 2000, 2003; McNay, 1999, 2000; Moi,

1991; Reay, 1998; Skeggs, 1997; Woolf, 1999). These tools are legion, from a theory of modernity drawing on a heady mixture of phenomenology and elements of Marxism – or as it is sometimes termed Bourdieu's constructivist structuralism (Fowler, 2000) – through the drawing together of both cultural and economic space, to the centrality given to embodiment in his non-idealist theory of practice. And it is these tools that contributors to this volume have mobilized to produce both compelling analyses of contemporary issues and new directions in feminist theory.

Yet while this is so, it is worth reflecting on just how and why the contributors to this volume have found Bourdieu's contemporary social theory such a productive ground for feminist analyses, that is, on how and why the contributors to this volume have found a social theorist who had little interest in gender or feminism a central tool for feminist theory. In this context it worth pointing out, as Gerhard (2004) has argued, that *classical* social theory had an 'elective affinity' with both feminism and feminist issues whereby the object of social theory – the social – was in part conceived and defined by questions of gender (see also Evans, 2003; Felski, 1995).[1] In contemporary social theory, however, 'theories of gender difference play no role' (Gerhard, 2004:129). And this is the case from Luhmann's system theory, through Habermas's critical theory, to Foucault's genealogies of power/knowledge. Such contemporary social theory is also marked, Gerhard argues, by a general tendency towards a lack of appreciation of feminist theory.

In his general lack of attention to gender problematics and to feminist theory Bourdieu must therefore be located as typical of his contemporaries. But while the disavowal of feminist theory on the part of Bourdieu is to be lamented, nonetheless on the evidence of this volume, and perhaps counter intuitively, an understanding of the social which is not conceived with reference to a gender difference defined in the registers of social theorizing should not necessarily be read as limiting the possibilities of a dynamic engagement between contemporary feminist and social theory (although see Witz, this volume). Indeed, given the weight of critiques that the (sociological) concept of gender now carries, especially the problems that contemporary feminists have identified as inhering in the concept (see eg Barrett, 1992; Gatens, 1995; Grosz, 1990; Haraway, 1991), and how feminism itself no longer posits the sex/gender distinction as one of its key objects,[2] a social theory which does not place the concept of gender as central to its vision of the social – and particularly one which has at its core a critique of idealist thinking – precisely opens itself out to contemporary feminism.

What is important here, and as is very widely recognised, is that while social theory was once a rich resource for feminist theory, the past two decades or more have seen feminists generally disengage with social theory and move towards various forms of cultural theory. And this move was made precisely because of the exposure of the limits of sociological concepts such as gender or social structure for feminist analysis (Barrett, 1992). In their engagement with Bourdieu's contemporary social theory, the chapters in this volume are therefore suggestive

4

of the emergence of a renewed relationship between feminist and social theory. This however is a relationship which does not cohere around a single concept, nor is it one of an elective affinity vis-à-vis the social and gender, but a relationship which is far more dispersed. Thus it is notable that very few of the chapters in this volume are centrally concerned with a sociologically defined gender. Instead they have a range of diverse concerns as their central foci, ranging from embodiment, through temporality, to symbolic violence. These concerns have emerged as central to feminist inquiry post sociological gender, and it is around these concerns where Bourdieu has purchase for feminist theory. In the theorization of social action as always embodied (of the social as incorporated into the body), of power as subtly inculcated through the body, of social action as generative, and in his emphasis on the politics of cultural authorization, recognition and social position taking, Bourdieu's social theory offers numerous points of connection to contemporary feminist theory.

These connections are increasingly being recognzsed by contemporary feminists. Thus, and to name some well-known examples, Judith Butler (1997, 1999) has elaborated the relations between performative utterances and Bourdieu's understanding of social position taking and social space; Moi (1991, 1999) and Woolf (1999) have mobilized the resources of Bourdieu to think through the gendered dynamics of the field of cultural production; Lovell (2000) has made use of Bourdieu's social theory to rethink some of the key objects of feminism; McNay (2000) has drawn on Bourdieu's emphasis on practical action to retheorize agency for feminist theory and Skeggs (1997) and Lawler (1999, 2000) have made use of Bourdieu's concept of capitals to theorize classed femininity and motherhood respectively. Such writers have opened up a space between feminist theory and Bourdieu's social theory which this volume both contributes towards and further articulates. In so doing it marks, as I have already alluded to, a renewed synergy between feminist and social theories. But while, as I have suggested, this synergy cannot be conceived as an affinity regarding gender and the social (as Gerhard has identified to be operative for classical social theory) neither is it a synergy which can simply be characterized as a 'return to' an already known social on the part of feminists. For this is a turn to the social post critiques of the concept of gender; of social structure; of the bounded human subject; and of the dualisms of mind and body, nature and culture, subject and object. In short, this volume is not simply an engagement with, extension, or further elaboration of the work of Bourdieu, for the various contributors are reworking and redefining the contours of the social as a new ground for feminist theory.

Appropriating Bourdieu?

This reworking has taken place along a number of axes but what has characterized the contributions to this volume still further is a refusal simply to place the historical objects of feminism within a Bourdieusian frame. Thus the contributors have not asked whether gender, sexual difference, sexuality or the sexed body constitute a field, or whether or not gender has a discernable habitus, or whether or not masculinity and femininity can be conceived as different forms of capital. They have not sought therefore simply to modify Bourdieu's social theory to accommodate the objects of feminism or literally to ask if the objects of feminism translate into Bourdieu's theoretical world. Considering the possibilities (and limits) of appropriating Bourdieu's social theory for feminist purposes, and in her seminal *New Literary History* essay of nearly fifteen years ago, Moi (1991, 1999) explicitly warned against this starting point. Focusing on the object of gender and especially the question of whether or not gender can be understood as a (Bourdieusian defined) field of action, Moi argued that rather than a specific, autonomous field, gender is far better conceptualized as *part of* a field. This field is not one of Bourdieu's autonomous fields (such as the legal or educational field) but is Bourdieu's general social field. Gender is best conceptualized in this way, Moi argued, since gender is extraordinarily relational, with a chameleon-like flexibility, shifting in importance, value and effects from context to context or from field to field. Thus, much as Bourdieu himself defined social class as structuring social fields, Moi suggested that gender should also be understood in these terms, that is as dispersed across the social field and deeply structuring of the general social field. Such a conceptualization leads to an understanding of gender not as an autonomous system but as a 'particularly combinatory social category, one that infiltrates and influences every other category' (Moi 1999:288).

It is this kind of critical interrogation of Bourdieu's social theory of the sort performed by Moi which characterizes the contributions to this volume. Indeed, and echoing the concerns of Moi, the continuing need to destabilize the assumption that gender is associated with particular social fields or sites within both general and Bourdieusian inspired social theory has been further underscored in this volume. In my own contribution, for example, I explore the problems inhering in the assumption that femininity has a 'home' – the domestic sphere – and that current social change vis-à-vis gender concerns a movement of femininity from the domestic to the economic field. I suggest that working with this assumption can cause all sorts of problems, not the least of which is a tendency towards an idealized (and liberal) account of progress through time vis-à-vis gender relations. And in Terry Lovell's contribution, following Moi's Bourdieusian feminist work (and echoing McCall 1992), Lovell asks 'does gender fit' Bourdieu's social field? This leads Lovell directly into the thorny and disputed territory of the relations between class and gender, but in novel re-thinking of these relations, Lovell draws attention to the relations between feminism as a social movement and to Bourdieu's understanding of class formation.

Specifically, Lovell proposes that 'women' might be considered as a 'social group'. While, historically speaking, within feminism questions of this character have generally been framed by discussions of the axes of commonality and difference, the universal and the particular, Lovell reframes this issue by drawing upon Bourdieu's ideas regarding class formation and especially his view that social classes and groupings are constructed through successful bids for cultural and political authorization and recognition. Lovell suggests further vis-à-vis women that a process of group formation has occurred whenever women's movements as social and political movements have arisen. In short, her claim is that women's movements do the work of creating recognized representatives who in turn create a system of recognition and authorization, which allows 'women' as a group to come into being. In this formulation 'women' do not (and cannot) exist as a class 'in itself' (as has so often been posited within certain modes of feminist theorizing) but will only become a practical group through a process of authorization. 'Women' in other words *become* a socio-political category. What is so interesting about this formulation for feminism is that, rather than an external 'out there' phenomenon which is left more or less unaccounted for, Lovell's analysis brings feminism as a political movement right into the heart of feminist social theory. In so doing Lovell practises the art of Bourdieu's reflexive sociology. She is aware, like Bourdieu, that there is no point outside of a system from which an emancipatory politics or social movement can simply emerge, and that all social movements attempt strategies of authorization. Lovell herself recognizes that acknowledging feminist social movements as an actor in a field in this way may raise some uneasy questions for feminists but, nonetheless, this is a move which must be made if contemporary social phenomena are to be addressed; not least in the form of increasing class inequalities between women.

Symbolic violence and social change

The issue of increasing class inequalities between women is a major if not central point of concern in a number of chapters in this volume, including not only Lovell's, but also Stephanie Lawler's, Angela McRobbie's and Diane Reay's. Drawing on Bourdieu's understanding of symbolic power or symbolic violence as a key vehicle for the social reproduction of classed divisions, McRobbie suggests that the large scale movement of women into the labour market, the detachment of women from traditional family roles, and subsequent female individualization, has heralded new forms of class distinction and classification. More specifically, McRobbie holds that the (post-feminist) production and reproduction of social divisions is now increasingly *feminized*. Thus McRobbie notes how in the British context classed forms of social categorization are now inseparable from the female body. Moreover, these new forms of classification are increasing (and autonomously) circulated by and through the mass media, or as Bourdieu might have it, through the cultural and media field. McRobbie's chapter therefore underscores two crucial points for contemporary feminist social and cultural theory. First, it highlights the widening of class divisions between women (and the increasing articulation of class divisions *through* the bodies of women, that is the increasing feminization of class divisions), and second (and also in line with the arguments put forward by Lawler in her chapter) it underscores the increasing significance of the media field for these new forms of classification. Thus and in line with other recent commentators sympathetic to Bourdieu's social theory, McRobbie's chapter suggests that the media field is one of the most powerful and important in the contemporary world (Lash, 1995).

The significance of the media for new forms of social classification is also at issue in the chapter presented by Nicole Vitellone. Analysing recent child poverty campaigns in Britain, the crack-baby crisis in the US and recent British social realist films focusing on the use of heroin, Vitellone shows how these texts figure poverty in new ways, and in particular how they move away from what might be thought of as a sociological explanation of poverty (where for instance, economic exclusion is understood to lead to or cause poverty) to a model of poverty which centres on embodiment, where the embodiment of pharmacological substances produces notions of social suffering as well as forming the basis of new systems of social classification particularly as they relate to the problematic use of the category of the 'underclass'. In so doing Vitellone suggests that the now relatively established social science tool for understanding social suffering – the ethnography – is unable to address the ways in which the cultural field is now central to the articulation of poverty. Vitellone therefore adds fuel to McRobbie's (2002) critique of the Bourdieusian methodology employed in the *Weight of the World* (Bourdieu *et al,* 1999), namely that it remains untouched by the insights of Cultural Studies. But Vitellone takes her critique further to argue that her analysis of the embodiment of pharmacological substances has implications for the notion of the habitus. First, she argues that Bourdieu's habitus excludes the matter of substances and must be extended if the concept is to have any purchase for the contemporary world. Second, Vitellone questions universalistic notions of the future orientation of the habitus – for as she shows, the pharmacological habitus has a temporality which breaks with such a future orientation, involving a *suspension* of time. Finally and crucially, Vitellone demonstrates how Bourdieu's habitus is increasingly the subject of cultural production. She thus confirms Lash's (1995) claim that the real world increasingly resembles Bourdieu's theoretical world – particularly in the field of cultural production.

The importance of the cultural field for feminist social theorizing is also underscored by Bridget Fowler in her chapter on the obituary as a form of collective memory. In her historical account of the obituary Fowler documents a shift in biographies away from criteria of blood towards criteria of occupations defined and dominated by cultural capital. While Fowler notes that a common reading of this shift is one of a narrative of change through time or of an unfolding democratization of the obituary, this she argues is a selective reading which will ignore how the obituary involves a continuing *reproduction* of the class order through specific narrative strategies. Fowler writes of the how the modern meritocratic obituary is typically marked by its reliance on notions of a transformative future orientated agency, a form of agency which the modern obituary genre so often denies to women. This leads Fowler to reflect on the issue of cultural survival and in particular on the issue of literary survival value for women. Here Fowler wants to rethink agency outside of the registers of the obituary. Drawing on the work of Ricoeur (see also McNay, 2000 and Lawler, 2002), and in a parallel move to that made by Vitellone, in her chapter, Fowler argues for a notion of agency in which the future does not simply unfold as part of the logic of the habitus (as it does, for example, in Bourdieu's *State Nobility*, 1996) but one which may be typified by *suspensions of effort*, a temporality which Fowler claims typifies women's engagement in the work of cultural production. Such an understanding of agency will not only break with the illusio of cultural work as a heroic life or death struggle, but also with notions of transformative agency on which the modern obituary typically draws. Indeed this temporal horizon may durably transform the habitus of cultural production.

Yet while this is may be so, Fowler's chapter as well as McRobbie's raise a perennial question in regard to the social theory of Bourdieu, namely that of social change (Calhoun, 1995; Fowler, 2000). For while Fowler's and McRobbie's accounts are most definitely Bourdieusian, at their heart is a narrative of social change, namely an account of women's (or at least some women's) increasing individualization (see also McNay, 1999). But, as is well documented, Bourdieu's social theory has consistently been reproached for its lack of attention to social change, that is, for its overwhelming focus on social reproduction. In a twist to this storyline, neither McRobbie's nor Fowler's accounts seek to rectify this problem via a focus on change through resistance, as is so commonplace within sociological discourse, but *both locate change in regard to a shift in the conditions of social reproduction itself*. In Fowler's case this is a shift in narrative strategies, while in McRobbie's it concerns the reproduction of classed distinctions through the bodies of women. Both of these chapters, therefore, refuse an easy story line of women's resistance to gender norms, and refuse to see individualization as a release from such norms. Instead, both understand how individualization may bring new social divisions into being (see Adkins, 2002).

In my own chapter, too, I problematize accounts which will see the decomposition of the norms, traditions and expectations associated with modernity as a simple freedom or release from gender. Here I take issue with an increasingly mobilized Bourdieusian inspired account regarding gender transformation. Very briefly put, this argument runs as follows: that the large-scale movement of women into the labour market (or a feminization of public spheres of action) involves a clash of habitus and field, which leads to a critical reflexivity on the part of men and women vis-à-vis gender norms and to a detraditionalization of those norms. What I find problematic about this account is that while in late modern societies gender may certainly be said to be characterized by reflexivity, this reflexivity concerns not a freedom from gender but is actively reworking the social categories of gender – a reworking which has significant implications for the very spheres in which women are now so often heralded to be free, especially the economic field. But I take this further to ask why is it that there is an elision of reflexivity and freedom within the contemporary theoretical imaginary even for those who work with and through Bourdieu – a social theorist who after all was so keen to undo the determinism/freedom binary. I locate this problem in Bourdieu's writings on social change. Here Bourdieu will always break with his main theoretical principles and will see the possibilities for social change when a conscious or thinking mastery of the principles of the habitus can be gained.

Working both with and against the social theory of Bourdieu (Lovell, 2000), the chapters in this volume therefore offer up important challenges to current tendencies within social and cultural theorizing with their analyses clearly warning against idealized readings of the processes and dynamics which are so often cited as driving the contemporary world. They also work towards suggesting a research agenda for feminism or, as McRobbie might put it, a research agenda post-feminism. Specifically, they place the issues of social change, of social reproduction and the rethinking of classificatory systems as central to the concerns of contemporary feminism. If these issues sound familiar, it is worth underlining that they have not been framed in terms of the traditional registers of sociology and/or social theory, for instance, of social reproduction as an issue of the reproduction of labour power or the recursive reproduction of social structures; of social change as an outcome of resistance to traditions and norms; or of social hierarchy as the outcome of the exploitation of labour power. Instead the very terms and contours of these processes have emerged as fundamentally transformed, with for example, social reproduction understood as centrally concerned with shifting forms of (increasingly media mediated) female embodiment, social change as concerning these very shifting conditions of social reproduction, and processes of individualization as involving complex new modes of gendered and classed differentiation and division.

Reconceptualizing identity

Further lines of research potentials have been drawn in this volume via critical engagements with the emphasis in Bourdieu's theorizing on the subject as always a subject of praxis or the subject of practical reason. Drawing on and extending the phenomenological tradition (especially the work of Merleau-Ponty), Bourdieu will always see the subject as engaged in practical action, action which is always embodied and which (for the most part) is not necessarily consciously known. The consequence of this understanding is that the social will always be understood not as an external law, set of rules or representations which the subject will somehow blindly follow, learn or incorporate since, and as Lawler puts it in her contribution, the social will always be literally incorporated in the subject. This notion of the subject as not simply engaged with the world, but *in* the world is one which has great appeal to feminists. It breaks for example with idealist tendencies found in certain forms of feminist structuralist thinking, where gender or sexual difference always tend to end up being a product of the mind or of consciousness, for instance as a product of ideology or a loosely conceived 'discourse'. It thus breaks with the Cartesian traditions of social theorizing (which of course have been named by feminists as both exclusionary and normative) in insisting that mind and body, thought and action, are indissolvable.

In Lois McNay's chapter, Bourdieu's phenomenological ontology of the social is extended to cut through an ongoing impasse in feminist theorizing. Specifically, Bourdieu's focus on the subject as a subject of practice, and more particularly Bourdieu's phenomenology of social space, is invoked to break through the stand-off between, on the one hand, feminist structuralist analyses and, on the other, feminist cultural analyses. In both these approaches, McNay argues, there is a tendency to reduce gender to an abstract structural position – for example as a location intersecting with class relations, or as a location in symbolic or discursive structures (see also the chapter by Lovell). Focusing particularly on the latter forms of analyses (and especially the work of Judith Butler), McNay then extends Boudieu's social theory to understand gender as a *lived* social relation (an understanding which has parallels with de Beauvoir's notion of 'women's situation'). Such an analysis will, as McNay recognizes, force us onto the ground of experience, but – and following Bourdieu – this experience will not be foundational but always relational. Social being in this form of analysis cannot be reduced to experience but will reveal itself through experience vis-à-vis broader contexts. Such a relational phenomenological analysis will, in other words, allow the illumination of the complex relations between the immediacy of experience and abstract systems of power. Put in more familiar terms such a phenomenological analysis will allow an exploration of the links between identity and overt and covert forms of power relations. Gender in this analysis can never be understood as an abstract position but as an always lived social relation which will always involve conflict, negotiation and tension.

While McNay certainly does a lot of work to rescue the category of experience from a barrage of feminist critique (see eg Scott, 1992), nonetheless her emphasis on social being raises the spectre of a metaphysics of meaning and specifically the issue of the meaning of human being-ness which may be seen to pull against a phenomenological understanding. Indeed we may trace this tension back to the social theory of Bourdieu. In their philosophical excavation of Bourdieu, Dreyfus and Rabinow (1995) identify that in Bourdieu's social theory the 'motor' or meaning of human being-ness is social advantage (that is, the maximization of capitals), both material and symbolic. Yet this positing of a universal motivation vis-à-vis human action leaves Bourdieu, Dreyfus and Rabinow argue, with a problem. Specifically he is operating with a contradictory ontology of the social. On the one hand Boudrieu will tell us that (phenomenological) agents are situated or stuck in their embodied life-worlds, which (and in line with the phenomenological tradition) means that even if you recognize you are situated as such, does not mean that you can get out of or transcend this life-world. On the other, Bourdieu seeks to explain the motivations of subjects in their life-worlds in terms of capital accumulation strategies or game-playing. Yet surely this is a contradiction. How can the social scientist stand outside of her or his social habitus? If the motivation of human action is advantage, how then can the actions of the social scientist (who will attempt, for example, to expose social injustice) be explained? For Dreyfus and Rabinow, Bourdieu's science of existential structure and social meaning therefore does not convince. It should not, however, be abandoned; rather it needs to be modified. Specifically, Bourdieu's research programme would not be compromised (his social ontology would not be contradictory) if the scientific search for a universal meaning (the search for an explanatory principle) was abandoned, that is, if the claim towards a scientific sociology was discarded. Thus Dreyfus and Rabinow suggest that weaker and non-scientific explanations would not be at odds with Bourdieu's research agenda (see also Latour, 1991). Dreyfus and Rabinow raise serious issues around whether or not Bourdieu overcomes the objectivist/subjectivist divide in the manner that Bourdieu himself actually claimed, that is whether his mixture of Marxism and phenomenology does the methodological work it is so often credited with. Thus it raises some important questions as to whether or not, for feminist theory, a critical elaboration of Bourdieu's ontology of the social will perform the methodological work of breaking down the impasse between structuralist and culturalist thinkers.

In an important move made by Lawler in her chapter, an attempt is made to avoid universal meaning by a focus not on social being via a retrieval of experience (or as she terms it a focus on experienced subjectivities) but on how identities are *conferred* on subjects. Lawler achieves this through the use and extension of Bourdieu's writings on cultural authorization to media representations of two recent political protests by women in Britain. Demonstrating how one of these protests was framed in disgusted and horrified tones and how this particular protest was culturally de-authorized, Lawler suggests that these representations may be fruitfully understood in terms of the operations of the habitus. Specifically, the actions of the women protesters were condemned through the markers of their (classed and gendered) habitus – their clothes, homes, bodies and so on. Put differently these women were not seen to be legitimate actors in the field of political protest.

Two points stand out as significant from this chapter. First, Lawler extends this analysis to think through current controversies regarding assimilation and political resistance or structure and agency, and especially the differences in analyses of Bourdieu and Butler (1997). While Bourdieu would see that it is one's social authority (social positioning) which enables the cultural recognition of political resistance (the ability to speak and to be heard), Butler would question this relentless social logic seeing that recognition does not necessarily follow social positioning. This is so since dominant or authorized discourse may be expropriated: it may be appropriated and resignified by those who have been denied social power. Thus dominated groups may seize and rework those very terms which mark such groups as dominated and in the process potentially destabilise that authorized discourse. For Lawler, however what this account negates is attention to the *reception* to forms of cultural resistance. The protesting women she discusses were disallowed from speaking with authority because their speech was not authorized in the field of political protest. But this was not because these women's actions were somehow socially overdetermined (or that they were not political) but because their actions were invalidated through (as Lawler puts it) 'a reassertion of the doxic understandings of their persons that "forbade" their action in the first place'. For Lawler, therefore, neither domination nor resistance can be mapped simply or neatly onto the axes of social determinism and performative agency, for even when one may be resisting with authority this does not necessarily mean one will be heard or recognized (see also Fraser, 1999). In Lawler's hands, the debates regarding assimilation and resistance, redistribution and recognition or (as McNay might have it) the debates between structuralists and culturalists shift ground: they shift to the political field itself and the politics of authorization operative within that field. Moreover, Lawler's analysis reminds us that it cannot be assumed in advance what this field consists in, for hers is an analysis driven by kind of sociology of which Bourdieu would approve: a theoretically informed empirical sociology.

The second major point of interest in Lawler's chapter is that in the class contestation that she describes, visceral emotions are at issue. Specifically in the representations Lawler describes middle class disgust is at work. While not explicitly the focus of her discussions, nonetheless the implication of this is that such emotions play an important part of the habitus and (hence) of contemporary class politics. The importance of emotions for the latter is also described in the chapter presented by Beverley Skeggs. Skeggs claims that emotions such as rage, pain, frustration, fear, anger and resentment are, so often, not heard or recognized by social theorists and researchers interested in contemporary class politics. She argues, for example, that Bourdieu's theoretical world cannot grasp these emotions as his understanding of the habitus is driven by notions the accrual of value – a model which Skeggs claims will always exclude such emotions even as they are now central to contemporary forms of class struggle.

Emotions, affect and the habitus

The issue of emotions and their part in the strategic game of class advantage is tackled head on by Reay in her chapter on family strategies and education. Reay documents a complex relationship between what she terms emotional capital (which she identifies as primarily gendered labour generated in the mother child interaction vis-à-vis schooling) and cultural capital. On the basis of extensive empirical investigation she suggests that the concept of emotional capital 'disrupts neat links between profit, or what Bourdieu calls increases in capital, and educational success'. For instance educational success (the accumulation of cultural, social and often economic capital) is often at the cost of emotional well being, and conversely, emotional well being (the generation of emotional capital in the specifically gendered mother-child interaction around schooling) is often as the cost of educational success. What is important about this finding is, of course, that it problematizes what Dreyfus and Rabinow have identified as Bourdieu's motor of the meaning of human being-ness, namely that humans will endlessly attempt to optimize their capital accumulation strategies: that strategic game-playing governs human action. In Reay's analysis, educational success, for example, does not emerge as an unmitigated social 'good' nor is emotional capital a form of accumulated labour which can simply be accrued by individuals or groups for straightforward advantage. This is so because (as Reay puts it) emotional capital is 'all about investment in others rather than the self – [it is] the one capital that is used up in interaction with others and is for the benefit of others'.

While Reay certainly does not want to abandon the Bourdieusian project, nonetheless her analysis is suggestive of the ways in which this project (and in particular Bourdieu's understanding of the meaning of human action as the accrual of advantage) can be derailed not only by philosophical excavation of the sort performed by Dreyfus and Rabinow but also by detailed empirical investigation. It also suggests that in understanding human action primarily as strategic action or game play Bourdieu's social theory may be missing out on some key aspects of contemporary sociality, particularly those which are not always instrumental. That is, Bourdieu's social theory, or at least that part which seeks to name the meaning of human action, neglects to consider those aspects of action which exist outside of, cannot be reduced to and/or exceed the domains of exchange and instrumentality, forms of action which of course have historically been central to feminist inquiry. Emotions in Reay's analysis are exactly a case in point, for if emotions are part of the classed and gendered habitus yet their operations cannot be reduced to advantage, where does this leave Bourdieu's social theory?

In Elspeth's Probyn's chapter on the affective habitus emotions are also at issue. Here the issue is not capital or capital-accumulating strategies but on the body. In its emphasis on the subject as in the world, where mind and body, thought and action are as one, Bourdieu's social theory locates the body as a fully fledged component of social action, or rather – and more correctly stated – for feminists following the social theory of Bourdieu, embodiment emerges as a key topic of investigation (Hayles, 1999). But Bourdieu's body is never *only* a body in action. This is because, for Bourdieu, embodied action concerns sedimented or accumulated – but usually forgotten – history. Embodiment is therefore both generative and practical, but is also the product of history: it is an enactment of the past. As Probyn notes, in his interest in how bodies are produced materially, Bourdieu brings together the worlds of both objective and subjective sociality. But Probyn wants to extend this further and think through what Bourdieu may have to say regarding the relation between emotion and the body or, rather, what Bourdieu may have to say about the feeling body. Carefully teasing out Boudrieu's somewhat cloudy statements on emotion, Probyn concludes that for Bourdieu. emotion is part of the body's knowledge and, as such, is probably more correctly identified not as emotion but as affect, where following Massumi (2002) affect is 'irreducibly bodily and autonomic'. Yet while this may be so, Probyn notes a tendency in Bourdieu's work to sidestep the significance of the feeling body by a particular ordering of the relation between emotions and the body. Bourdieu will say the body mimes grief and it weeps, but is this always the case asks Probyn? Is this not to assume, Probyn asks, that affect is always an outcome of the social – the habitus? After all, for Bourdieu the function of emotions seems pre-eminently to concern a reining in of the body to the habitus. Does this *social* logic actually close off the very possibilities for the body that his theory seems to open out? Probyn claims that a fuller conception of the feeling body can be found in the work of Marcel Mauss, who always wanted to see the physicality of the social, indeed of the habitus. Via Mauss, Probyn develops the notion of the *affective habitus*, a habitus charged with physicality, and in so doing opens out the possibility that social theory may finally begin to address the relations between the physical and the social – relations which Probyn herself animates via a compelling discussion of shame.

So in Probyn's hands, and against the grain of dominant interpretations, Bourdieu becomes an impoverished theorist of the material, physical body. But Probyn is doing a great deal more than developing an affective dimension to the habitus, for this intervention must be located in terms of what might be termed a new feminist materialism. Frustrated with analyses which will always end up seeing power and other phenomena – including the body – as only ever discursive or cultural, for instance as representational or symbolic, this new materialism wants literally to rethink matter – and not just social or cultural matter but the brute force of the world and the weight of it, including the body and its sheer physicality. And this is a project which has some urgency, for as Probyn herself shows as well as Lawler and McRobbie in their contributions, *affects have interests and interests that matter*.

If in this volume Probyn warns against taking Bourdieu at face value vis-à-vis embodiment and the habitus, then perhaps Witz has provided the strongest statement warning of the dangers of Bourdieu's ontology of the social for feminist theorizing. While Dreyfus and Rabinow have identified the contradictory logic of attempting to hold on to a phenomenological approach to the social *and* positing a universal meaning of human action, Witz identifies a further contradictory logic in Bourdieu's theoretical apparatus, particularly in regard to the concept of the habitus. This contradiction relates to how the notion of the habitus combines both a phenomenological *and* a structuralist anthropological understanding of embodiment. While as Witz argues, in discussions of Bourdieu's habitus, the structural anthropological elements are usually ignored (with the focus almost exclusively on its phenomenological construction), this is to overlook how its structural anthropological components raise serious doubts as to the utility of the notion of habitus. This is particularly the case for feminist theory but also in regard to the general claims made for Bourdieu's social theory, including the claims that it is a productive force for the theorization of agency and for the project of embodying sociology. Witz shows this to be the case, since Bourdieu will invoke a structural anthropological imaginary whenever he turns to the specific issue of *gendered* embodiment. Thus, Witz argues, in *Masculine Domination* (2001) Bourdieu's notion of the androcentric unconscious derives from his (structural) anthropological study of Kabyle society, a 'well preserved androcentric society'. Bourdieu therefore bases his (allegedy socio-logical) understanding of gender relations in contemporary differentiated, het-erodox societies on an outdated anthropological study of an undifferentiated society. This leads to a predisposition to overstate the doxic order of gender, indeed it is this anthropological labour which drives the general idea found *repet-itively* across Bourdieu's works that gender is particularly deeply and durably invested in bodies. It is therefore crucial, Witz argues, that caution is exercised in relation to Bourdieu's concept of the habitus, particularly as appropriating this concept may inadvertently entail the instatement of an structural anthro-pological notion of gender which will always overplay the doxic gender order, indeed embody gender so durably that the body and gender practices become interchangeable.

Both Probyn and Witz therefore warn against a straightforward appropria-tion of the notion of the habitus by feminist theorists, for this may be not only to risk failing fully to theorize the body and its affects but also to invoke an understanding of the social which relies on a deeply obfuscated but nonetheless efficacious system of binary thinking which will always raise problems for fem-inist theorists. But it is not only the habitus which in this volume has emerged as problematic in Bourdieu's theoretical repertoire. Also at issue have been his concepts and understandings of reflexivity, of capital accumulating strategies, of emotions, of the body and embodiment, of social change and of the subject. Thus, and as I have already suggested, none of the contributors have assumed that feminist theoretical and conceptual concerns can be easily mapped onto the social theory of Bourdieu or vice-versa, rather they have critically engaged with, interrogated and excavated Bourdieu's social theory. This volume may therefore be understood to fall into the now long tradition of feminist texts which have sought to redefine the relationship between social and feminist theory (see eg Bologh, 1990; Evans, 2003; Felski, 1995, 2000; Fraser, 1989; Marshall, 1994; Marshall and Witz, 2004; Smith, 1987; Sydie, 1987; Witz and Marshall, 2004; Wolff, 2000). And in seeking to rewrite this relationship this collection has not simply reproduced Bourdieu's understanding of the social but has transformed it, a transformation which we hope marks new territories not just for feminist inquiry, but for the social and cultural theory fields in general.

Notes

1 Or put differently, the social question (or the crisis of modernity) was in part defined by the woman question.
2 See Lloyd, 2003 for a discussion of the shifting objects of feminism.

References

Adkins, L. (2002) *Revisions: Gender and Sexuality in Late Modernity.* Buckingham and Philadelphia: Open University Press.

Barrett, M. (1992) 'Words and Things: Materialism and Method in Contemporary Feminist Analysis' in M. Barrett and A. Phillips (eds) *Destabilizing Theory: Contemporary Feminist Debates*. Cambridge: Polity.

Bologh, R. (1990) *Love or Greatness: Max Weber and Masculine Thinking – A Feminist Inquiry*. London: Unwin Hyman.

Bourdieu, P. (1996) *The State Nobility*. Cambridge: Polity.

Bourdieu, P. (1999) *Weight of the World: Social Suffering in Contemporary Society*. Cambridge: Polity.

Bourdieu. P. (2001) *Masculine Domination*. Cambridge: Polity Press.

Butler, J. (1993) *Bodies That Matter: On the Discursive Limits of 'Sex'*. London: Routledge.

Butler, J. (1997) *Excitable Speech: A Politics of the Performative*. London: Routledge.

Butler, J. (1999) 'Performativity's Social Magic' in R. Shusterman (ed.) *Bourdieu: A Critical Reader*. Oxford: Blackwell.

Calhoun, C. (1995) 'Habitus, Field and Capital: The Question of Historical Specificity' in C. Calhoun, E. LiPuma and M. Postone (eds) *Bourdieu: Critical Perspectives*. Cambridge: Polity Press.

Dreyfus, H. and Rabinow, P. (1995) 'Can There Be a Science of Existential Structure and Social Meaning?' in C. Calhoun, E. LiPuma and M. Postone (eds) *Bourdieu: Critical Perspectives*. Cambridge: Polity Press.

Evans, M. (2003) *Gender and Social Theory*. Buckingham and Philadelphia: Open University Press.

Felski, R. (1995) *The Gender of Modernity*. Cambridge, MA: Harvard University Press.

Felski, R. (2000) *Doing Time: Feminist Theory and Postmodern Culture*. New York: New York University Press.

Fraser, N. (1989) *Unruly Practices: Power, Discourse and Gender in Contemporary Social Theory*. Cambridge: Polity Press.

Fraser, N. (1997) *Justice Interruptus: Critical Reflections on the 'Postsocialist' Condition*. London: Routledge.

Fraser, M. (1999) 'Classing Queer: Politics in Competition' *Theory, Culture and Society* 16(2): 107–131.

Fowler, B. (2000) 'Introduction' in B. Fowler (ed.) *Reading Bourdieu on Society and Culture*. Oxford: Blackwell.

Fowler, B. (2003) 'Reading Pierre Bourdieu's Masculine Domination: Notes Towards an Intersectional Analysis of Gender, Culture and Class' *Cultural Studies* 17: 3–4: 468–494.

Gatens, M. (1995) *Imaginary Bodies: Ethics, Power and Corporeality*. London: Routledge.

Gerhard, Ute (2004) '"Illegitimate Daughters": The Relationship Between Feminism and Sociology' in B. L. Marshall and Witz A. (eds) *Engendering the Social: Feminist Encounters with Sociological Theory*. Maidenhead and New York: Open University Press.

Grosz, E. (1990) 'Inscriptions and Body-Maps: Representations and the Corporeal' in T. Threadgold and A. Cranny-Francis (eds) *Feminine/Masculine/Representation*. St Leonards: Allen and Unwin.

Haraway, D. (1991) *Simians, Cyborgs and Women: The Reinvention of Nature*. London: Routledge.

Hayles, N. K. (1999) *How We Became Posthuman: Virtual Bodies in Cybernetics, Literature, and Informatics*. Chicago, Ill.: The University of Chicago Press.

Krais, B. (1993) 'Gender and Symbolic Violence: Female Oppression in the Light of Pierre Bourdieu's Theory of Social Practice' in C. Calhoun, E. LiPuma & M. Postone (eds) *Bourdieu: Critical Perspectives*. Cambridge: Polity Press.

Lash, Scott (1995) 'Pierre Bourdieu: Cultural Economy and Cultural Change' in C. Calhoun, E. LiPuma and M. Postone (eds) *Bourdieu: Critical Perspectives*. Cambridge: Polity Press.

Latour, B. (1991) 'The Politics of Explanation: An Alternative' in S. Woolgar (ed.) *Knowledge and Reflexivity: New Frontiers in the Sociology of Knowledge*. London: Sage.

Lawler, S. (1999) 'Getting Out and Getting Away: Women's Narratives of Class Mobility' *Feminist Review* 63(1): 3–24.

Lawler, S. (2000) *Mothering the Self: Mothers, Daughters, Subjects*. London: Routledge.

Lawler, S. (2002) 'Narrative in Social Research' in T. May (ed.) *Qualitative Research in Action.* London: Sage.

Lloyd, M. (2003) 'Mourning as Becoming' *Feminist Theory* 4(3): 343–347.

Lovell, T. (2000) 'Thinking Feminism With and Against Bourdieu' *Feminist Theory* 1(1): 11–32.

Lovell, T. (2003) 'Resisting with Authority: Historical Specificity, Agency and the Performative Self' *Theory, Culture and Society* 20(1): 1–17.

Marshall, B. L. (1994) *Engendering Modernity: Feminism, Social Theory and Social Change.* Cambridge: Polity.

Marshall, B. L. and A. Witz (2004) (eds) *Engendering the Social: Feminist Encounters with Sociological Theory.* Maidenhead: Open University Press.

McCall, L. (1992) 'Does Gender Fit? Bourdieu, Feminism and Conceptions of Social Order' *Theory and Society* 21: 837–867.

McNay, L. (1999) 'Gender, Habitus and the Field: Pierre Bourdieu and the Limits of Reflexivity' *Theory, Culture and Society* 16(1): 175–193.

McNay, L. (2000) *Gender and Agency: Reconfiguring the Subject in Feminist and Social Theory.* Cambridge: Polity.

McRobbie, A. (2002) 'A Mixed Bag of Misfortunes?: Bourdieu's Weight of the World' *Theory, Culture and Society* 19(3): 129–138.

Massumi, B. (2002) *Parable for the Virtual: Movement, Affect, Sensation.* Durham: Duke University Press.

Moi, T. (1991) 'Appropriating Bourdieu: Feminist Theory and Pierre Bourdieu's Sociology of Culture' *New Literary History* 22(4): 1017–1049.

Moi, T. (1999) *What Is A Woman?* Oxford: Oxford University Press.

Reay, D. (1998) *Class Work: Mothers' Involvement in Children's Schooling.* London: University College Press.

Scott, Joan (1992) 'Experience' in J. Butler and J. Scott (eds) *Feminists Theorize the Political.* London: Routledge.

Skeggs, B. (1997) *Formations of Class and Gender.* London: Sage.

Smith, D. (1987) *The Everyday World as Problematic: A Feminist Sociology.* Milton Keynes: Open University Press.

Sydie, R. A. (1987) *Natural Women, Cultured Men: A Feminist Perspective on Sociological Theory.* Milton Keynes: Open University Press.

Witz, A. and Marshall B. L. (2004) 'Introduction: Feminist Encounters with Sociological Theory' in B. L. Marshall and A. Witz (eds) *Engendering the Social: Feminist Encounters With Sociological Theory.* Maidenhead and New York: Open University Press.

Wolff, J. (1999) 'Cultural Studies and the Sociology of Culture' *Invisible Culture: An Electronic Journal for Visual Studies* Issue 1: http://www.rochester.edu/in_visibleculture/issue1/wolff/wolff.html.

Wolff, J. (2000) 'The Feminine in Modern Art: Benjamin, Simmel and the Gender of Modernity' *Theory Culture and Society* 17(6): 33–53.

Context and Background: Pierre Bourdieu's analysis of class, gender and sexuality

Beverley Skeggs

Introduction

Pierre Bourdieu died in January 2002, leaving a huge legacy of work, across a range of topics and disciplines. Although institutionally established as Professor of Sociology at the prestigious College de France his first substantive research was anthropological – on the Kabliya in Algeria (*The Algerians* 1962). From this he developed his 'theories of practice' in *Outline of a Theory of Practice* (1977) and *The Logic of Practice* (1990a) moving to education: *The Inheritors* (1964), *Reproduction in Education, Culture and Society* (1977), *Homo Academicus* (1988), and *The State Nobility* (1996a). His concerns then led to culture more generally: *Distinction* (1986) a critique of the judgement of taste, *Photography: A Middle Brow Art* (1990b) on art and its institutions, *The Love of Art* (1966), *On Television* (1998a) and quantitative analysis of museums and *The Rules of Art* (1996b) on literature. Interested throughout in the institutional structures and methods of knowledge: *The Craft of Sociology* (1991) and *Pascalian Meditations* (2000) develop his theory of 'bodily knowledge' on dispositions and recognition. *Masculine Domination* (2001) is a study of the power of masculinity. His more polemical and political writings, include searing critiques of neo-liberal globalization: *Acts of Resistance* (1998b) and *Firing Back* (2003). *The Weight of the World* (1999) is a jointly produced empirical study that documents the economic and moral poverty in contemporary France. Bourdieu was also a dedicated teacher as well as a public intellectual, organizing '*Reasons to Act*' as a political grouping and a radical publishing house. He has not always been loved as Mottier (2001) points out: Jeannine Verdes-Leroux published a volume on Bourdieu with the subtitle 'Essay on the Sociological Terrorism of Pierre Bourdieu', and Roger Debray described his work on TV as 'banal'.

But what is striking in all this output is its lack of attention to feminist theory, even though Bourdieu does explore gender relations in his work: in *Outline of a Theory of Practice* and in the *Logic of Practice*, where he focuses on how a structured sexual division of labour generates a sexually differentiated perspective on the world. In *Distinction* he examines the gendering of taste and *Masculine Domination* is devoted to exploring sexual difference. Why then has

Bourdieu ignored so much feminist work, making us ask how appropriate is Bourdieu for feminist analysis? For Leslie McCall (1992) Bourdieu is useful because of the parallels between feminist approaches to epistemology and methodology, in which theoretical frameworks and political programmes are always embedded in social relations. In this chapter I will begin the answer to this question, examining the parallels and challenges from and to feminism.

Bourdieu has been particularly useful for enabling feminists to put the issue of class back onto the feminist agenda. His analysis of capitals provide a route to be mapped between the two major strands of class theory that proved mostly infertile for feminist analysis. Firstly, that of 'political arithmetic' class analysis, which involves fitting people into pre-ordained classifications, in which the debates focused on the accuracy of the classifications or the accuracy of the fit, so that some feminists showed that measuring people through their father's occupations with no account of mother's labour was inadequate to say the least (Crompton 1993; Stanworth 1984 and Lovell Chapter 1, this volume). Secondly, the traditional and then less traditional Marxist analysis of class, in which class is conceptualized as a relationship of exploitation, primarily based on the division of labour. Feminists argued long and hard for the inclusion of women's labour into the analysis, culminating in the long and heated 'domestic labour debate' in the 1970s and 80s (see Hartmann and Sargent, 1981 and Barrett, 1998) but eventually abandoned the struggle for the more fruitful explorations of power and difference more generally. These traditional paths of class analysis and the 'new' engagement with other forms of difference such as race, nation, and sexuality, led to a period of neglect of class in feminist theory.[1] Although it has never disappeared from the areas of education and social policy, where it would make less sense to ignore it when it so obviously impacts upon their central objects of analysis: in the early 1980s attempts were being made by feminists such as Madeline Arnot (1979) to use Bourdieu to weave together class and gender in relation to education. This education legacy consistently pursued by Arnot was taken up in the late 1990s by Diane Reay and developed throughout her work (see Chapter 2). In the discipline of Sociology, Bourdieu was taken up through a variety of routes: through studies of 'theory' more generally (e.g. by Richard Jenkins, 1982; Axel Honneth 1986; Craig Calhoun *et al*, 1993 and Derek Robbins, 1999) more specifically in understandings of race and nation in Ghassan Hage (1998) and in feminist theory via Toril Moi (1991), Leslie McCall (1992), Bridget Fowler (1997), Beverley Skeggs (1997), Lois McNay (1999), Terry Lovell (2000) and Lisa Adkins (2003).

There has been a range of responses to Bourdieu from feminists. In this volume we see evidence of those who are Bourdieu 'scholars', who work closely with his texts and develop his theories (e.g. Lois McNay and Bridget Fowler), and those who work against and through Bourdieu to put his theories to different uses, reformulating and using them eclectically (often combined with other theories). This is not as messy as it sounds, as Bourdieu himself argued for the flexibility of his theories and the necessity of inconsistency (Bourdieu and Waquant, 1992).

So what does Bourdieu offer? Primarily *explanatory power* that is not offered elsewhere. He has consistently worked with three major strands. Firstly, the linking of objective structures to subjective experience (necessity and will, or structure and agency), an issue that has dogged feminists, philosophers and sociologists for some time. Secondly, his metaphoric model of social space in which human beings embody and carry with them the volumes and compositions of different capitals enables us to think through different types of values and mobility. Thirdly, his methodological insights, in which reflexivity, as a prerequisite to knowledge, provides us with a way of examining the positions from which we speak; a requirement that has always been at the heart of feminists critiques of masculine-dominated research agendas. This chapter is organized into three sections, firstly an analysis of Bourdieu on gender, secondly an exploration of Bourdieu on sexuality and emotions and thirdly a brief exploration of Bourdieu on taste and culture.

Gender and culture

Based on an understanding of the Kabyle in Algeria, Bourdieu conceptualizes gender primarily as sexual difference, an 'understanding of the objective structures and cognitive structures' which are often hidden (Bourdieu, 2001: vii). For Bourdieu social identity is first made from sexual identity, from the experience of the mother's and father's bodies. But to this he adds the sexual division of labour in the home; the experience of the parental body is always shaped by this sexual division formed by the wider sexual division of labour. The body experienced is always a social body made up of meanings and values, gestures, postures, physical bearing, speech and language. It is through the body that the child learns intimately to experience wider structural features, which are never *just* an experience of the structural but always entwined with the child's physical and sexual presence, with its bodily relation to others. This is a dialectical process involving objectification in which some features become objectified over time and form the habitus. The strongest elements of the habitus are those that occur in early childhood for the habitus requires a long period of inculcation for practice to unfold (Bourdieu, 1990a). The child also impacts upon its parents and the organization of the sexual division of labour. The logic of practice is thus based on a chain of attributes. For instance, the sexual division of labour, although dialectical, becomes objectified in the caring labour of femininity, which is institutionalized beyond the family (state welfare, education, labour market) and impacts upon household organization.

Just like many feminists, Bourdieu sees the family as a fiction and a social artefact, a well founded illusion because it is produced and reproduced with the guarantee of the state and operates as a central site of normalization and naturalization. Yet as Elizabeth Silva (2004) notes, this illusory identification does not save Bourdieu from normalizing his own conception of the family by defining it as *the* universal norm, in a similar way to how he defines working-class women as closer to nature. He argues that the family functions as a field in which normalcy or the ability to constitute oneself as the universal is the capital. This enables normalcy to be both a kind of capital within the field of the family and a form of symbolic capital that represents accumulated privilege in other fields.

In an analysis of schooling Bourdieu and Passeron (1977) suggest that the process of gender attribution to students and academic disciplines is similarly dialectical and universal. The transference of femininity from the student to the school subject and back again to the student exemplifies the dialectic of objectification and embodiment, formed via an 'elective affinity' shaping the habitus. Yet here the normalcy of gendered reproduction works very differently for boys and girls. For girls it can only offer a limited form of capital if they conform to gender normalcy. For boys it offers masculine power, institutionalized in the school as a form of symbolic capital that (as with the family) represents accumulated privilege in other fields. Yet the failure to draw attention to how normalcy *works differently* through gender as a form of capital leads to significant problems.

Embodiment is the product of the composition and volumes of capital that can be accrued and carried by the body and the fit between the habitus (the disposition organizing mechanism) and the field. Embodiment also provides us with a way of recognising authority in its physical dispositions. The embodied entitlement to space (physical and aural) is often a statement of social entitlement.

For Bourdieu, the embodied gendered dialectic is strongly structured through hierarchical relations of difference, symbolized by binary oppositions (high/low culture; strong/weak fields; dominant/dominated classes; masculine/feminine; public/private), by which in a very traditional manner, masculinity exists in the public (via the economic) and femininity in the private (via forms of cultural reproduction; in which women's bodies are 'sign bearing' carriers of taste: see later). It is the logics of these dichotomies that structure and underpin the different social fields, and hence inform how embodiment takes place. For Bourdieu, these structures, logics and positions are 'fundamental' (McCall, 1992). Yet the analysis of gender within these logics as a form of capital is not very clear. As noted earlier, Bourdieu links social identity to sexual identity, shaped through early experience in the family. When comparing Bourdieu's analysis of gender to that of ethnicity, McCall charts the emergence of a significant contradiction. In relation to economic and cultural capital, Bourdieu identifies ethnicity as a 'secondary principle' that reinforces the structure of capital since it is relatively independent of economic or cultural properties (ethnicity distributes its members into social classes according to its location in the hierarchy of the ethic group). Stratification therefore functions as a secondary *vertical* overlay on the stratification of social classes. This is in contrast to gender:

> . . . in every relationship between educational capital and a given practice, one sees the effect of the dispositions associated with gender which help to determine the

logic of the reconversion of inherited capital into educational capital (Bourdieu, 1986:105).

As McCall points out, the initial capital here appears to be gender neutral, acting as a distributing mechanism *within* the social group defined by the volume and composition of the initial capital. Gender is shaped in the reconversion process by 'dispositions associated with gender' (McCall, 1992:842) resulting in a gendered form of cultural capital, but still essentially defined by the associated field of occupation. But for Bourdieu a field is the product of the basis of the interest and stakes implicitly shared by its members. Gender becomes a *mediating dimension* of the position in social structure, distinguishing class locations:

> Sexual properties are as inseparable from class properties as the yellowness of a lemon is from its acidity; a class is defined in an essential respect by the place and value *it gives* to the two sexes and to their socially constituted dispositions (Bourdieu, 1986:106, emphasis added).

But why then, asks McCall, are not forms of gender forms of capital if they exist as indices of the class structure, as capital?

She shows how Bourdieu attempts to deal with this by suggesting that the 'secondary' criteria of gender – *within* rather than *vertical* – is 'hidden'. Although forms of capital correspond to occupational fields such as literary, scientific, managerial, they have gendered meanings because they are given form by gendered dispositions which are misrecognized. As McCall points out embodied gender capital is symbolic according to Bourdieu because it is the most hidden and universal form of capital: 'therefore, gender as a principle of division is secondary because it is hidden and it is hidden because it appears to be universal and natural' (McCall, 1992:844). Gender operates as a hidden form of cultural capital, but also as a disposition, an asymmetric form of capital. As McCall notes:

> An attractive woman who must interact with men at work may be perceived by heterosexual men as a distraction at best, incompetent at worst, or even a potential legal threat if she were to charge sexual harassment or sex discrimination. An attractive man however escapes connotations of incompetence and may even consider it his duty to enliven the workplace with his stimulating presence (McCall, 1992:846).

Gendered dispositions are hidden behind the nominal construction of categories, enabling the misrecognition of gender. For Bourdieu, gender is hidden under the surface of categories (hence leading to his critique of Judith Butler for her emphasis on the surface level of the symbolic, what he calls 'naming', which he believes blocks any recognition of what lurks below).[2] For Bourdieu, misrecognition occurs when symbolic capital has been acquired by a successful act of legitimation which itself veils the social processes and structures that are necessary to existence, so femininity is misrecognised as a natural, essentialised personality disposition.

Whilst recognizing that gender is often hidden in the structuring of categories (such as occupations, forms of art, types of education), I'd also argue that gender can be a form of cultural capital but only *if* it is symbolically *legitimated* (historically, for instance via class, as a particular version of middle-class moral femininity). Gendered dispositions can be used by those of a different gender to Bourdieu's traditional fields. As Adkins and Lury (1999) have shown men are able to turn the use of feminine dispositions to their advantage in a way that women cannot because they are perceived to have those dispositions 'naturally'. Even though femininity is symbolically ubiquitous, it is not symbolically dominant in the same way as particular versions of masculinity (although see Connell, 1989, for an understanding of the class-based hierarchies of masculinity), rarely operating as symbolic capital (except when used by men and when it amalgamates with other dispositions of privilege and power). Gender, in this case femininity, can be a range of things; it can be a resource, a form of regulation, an embodied disposition and/or a symbolically legitimate form of cultural capital. Because, for Bourdieu, cultural capital is always associated with high cultural practices and classifications, it is also difficult to see all the different variants of femininity as a form of cultural capital (although upper middle-class femininity would work). It is however possible to re-work cultural capital not just as high culture if we think more generally about culture as a resource or a use-value which can be separated from the fields and means by which it is *exchanged*.

So how can we use Bourdieu to think through gender? Both Lois McNay (Chapter 8) and Bridget Fowler (Chapter 7) argue that gender is not a field at all but a form of symbolic violence in the cultural field that produces transmogrifications (changes into a different shape). Symbolic violence exposes the temporal differences between types of femininity, the practice of femininity and the different values attached to different forms. We speak about femininity as if it is a bounded entity that can be known, yet it is inherently ambiguous, indeterminate, contradictory and unstable. The fact that it works as a term to describe selfless social practices such as caring, highly regulated domestic practices and appearance, based on the attribution of worth means that the terms of symbolic violence are constantly shifting. That the appearance of femininity is a constantly transformable act based on attachment and detachment of practices and objects in a circuit of exchange, a wilful playfulness, performative and performing, means that it needs careful empirical attention, not just an understanding of mis-recognition.

In a previous ethnography I showed how white working-class women did not and could not inhabit the category of femininity (Skeggs, 1997). It was a sign under which they did not belong because it had been developed historically in opposition to Black and working-class women, carrying with it qualities of docility and fragility, dispositions not associated with the working-class who were defined as robust, masculine, dangerous and contagious. The working-class women of the research performed femininity because they had to and did not have any alternatives that could hold value within their local space, making their performances as painless as possible, often with good collective fun. These women were aware of the perspective of the dominant which was always filtered though class judgements, constantly alert to the way they were judged as sexually excessive, pathologized as fecund and read as bad mothers; they were also critically reflexive about their practice. Their experience was not an unconscious pre-reflexive gendered experience based on misrecognition, but a specifically classed-gendered experience, one of which they were highly critical and highly attuned; they strongly refused the perspectives of the powerful. Other feminist work also shows how the experience of judgement and its refusal, make motherhood a highly conscious class-based experience (Lawler, 2000; Reay, 1998), as does the pathologization of the sexual desire of working-class women (Walkerdine and Lucey, 1989). In this sense the women of these empirical analyses are the authors of their experience of femininity, without being symbolically authorized. This difference, to which Butler (1993) draws attention, is different from Bourdieu's binary dichotomy of dominated or dominating. De Certeau (1988) asks, how do we authorize ourselves? My research suggests authorization can be produced at a local level by taking a different perspective and re-valuing the positions we are expected to inhabit without value: the women who were de-valued gave themselves value and authorized their existence as valuable people through the practice of respectability; a respectability defined in opposition to the middle-class. This was not a taking-on of the views of the dominated but an entire reworking of perspective and value: they contested middle-class, symbolically dominant values of respectability, especially motherhood (Lawler, 2000; Reay, 1998; Walkerdine, 2002).

The idea that gender is pre-reflexive and unconscious or a desire for the dominant or a form of misrecognition (as Bourdieu would suggest) just does not work. The ubiquitous reinforcement of femininity on a daily basis should alert us to the fact that it cannot be purely performative, pre-reflexive or unconscious, that the habitus may not be working for those for whom accruing positive value is not possible. There is one thing we know for certain about gender and that is its ambivalent nature. And post-colonial theorists on race have shown very clearly it is precisely ambivalence, always amenable to change and adaptability, which guarantees the survival of anything of a dispersed, repetitive and ambivalent nature (Bhabha, 1994).

In the UK, at least, the conscious enactment of dispersed gender, in which there are few alternatives and which, to some extent, women have learnt to enjoy ('to make the most of a bad job' as my respondents said of doing femininity) is also accompanied by an almost scathing lack of respect for traditional male power. So whilst institutionalization of certain forms of masculinity occur, this is not always authorized by women. There is a difference between processes of legitimation and authorization. For Bourdieu this would be seen as a good example of resistance, when the 'fit' between positions and dispositions breaks down. Yet this is how gender is done daily. Bourdieu would argue that dominated groups are more likely to be resistant because they are less invested in the games of power. Yet women often tolerate men when they don't need to, at the same time often reducing them metaphorically to powerless children 'he's just another child in the family'. Women stay with men in the face of domestic violence because they see no alternative. Again, all of this is well documented in feminist research. We know that women often do not take masculinity seriously and are aware of the weakness and vulnerability of the contradictions within masculinity – of force and weakness. The ambiguity of femininity has enabled them to adapt. Women can often easily produce a perfect critique of masculine traits and dispositions, yet this does not lead to resistance or change as Bourdieu would predict; rarely do women take on the 'view of the dominant on the dominant on themselves' (Bourdieu, 2001:42).

Sexuality and emotions

This is why we need to think against Bourdieu's assumption that gender and sexuality are reproduced by the take-up of norms; rather, it is precisely the inversion of norms that is the product of feminist and queer struggles. As David Halperin (2003) points out, lesbians and gay men have learnt not to just to occupy positions of ambiguity but also to *deploy* ambiguity to resist the forces of power and violence by making oneself unrecognizable, difficult to read, or making oneself abject in a non-pathological way. Rather than taking on the view of the dominant, queers have been copiously involved in reworking what it means to be dominated and refusing the value that is attributed to domination. Some of the most interesting theories of power to emerge from queer theory play and experiment with power and domination (see Califia, 1994; Warner, 1993). As long as the heterosexual family is positioned as the norm, encompassing the sexual division of labour, as it is by Bourdieu, then others can only ever be read against it, hence concepts of 'pretend' families and 'families of choice'.

Queer theorists have tried to think through the workings of gender *and* sexuality, such as Judith Butler's heterosexual matrix, or challenged gender *with* sexuality, such as Monique Wittig's (1992) refusal as a lesbian to 'be a woman', or Biddy Martin's (1996) attention to femininity played straight, or Ann Tyler's (1991) study of passing and drag, or Judith Halberstam's (1998) critique of female masculinity. These analyses take us far beyond the traditional sex/gender distinction[3] enabling us to think through power in ways that do not rely on traditional structures of the sexual division of labour and other binary dichotomies.

For Bourdieu (2001) queers reproduce gender divisions, in which there is always (surprise . . .) a masculine dominant. This enables him to normalize any challenge to traditional gender roles; queer families become normal, for Bourdieu, because they always reproduce heterosexual gender roles. Yet, as queer theorists have shown, in the coming together of gender *and* sexuality in the figure of the femme, traditional relations of power and gender are brought into question; it is the masculine butch who has to fulfil the femme's needs: the masculine is no longer a position of dominance. The femme also complicates judgements of gender based on appearance, for the value of femininity becomes

26

reworked in its enactment; femme appearance can have both negative and positive value, be legitimate or illegitimate, dominant or dominating depending on its instantiation. Because femininity is an amalgam of practice and appearance it can be simultaneously negative and positive, making an easy understanding of gender and gender values difficult. Halberstam's (1998) analysis of female masculinity, for instance, complicates perspective – how we know by what we see as gender and sexuality. The complexities of these manoeuvres and perspectives cannot be encompassed by Bourdieu's analysis of simply gender and domination. Bourdieu's terribly well organized habitus cannot encompass all the practices between gender and sexuality, the contradictions, plays, experimentations, swappings, ambiguities and passings both within gender and between gender and sexuality (which, of course, are always informed by class, race and age).

We may also wonder how Bourdieu would account for all the techniques identified by Foucault in the production of sexuality. The confession, a technique used for administration produces what we think of as selves, channels our desires and energies into bodily pleasures and pain that are often *not* to our advantage. For Foucault (1979) there is no exchange-value accruing self or habitus. Whereas Foucault identifies the specific techniques that produce personhood through sexuality, Bourdieu has a much more generalized habitus. Some may prefer Bourdieu's attempt to formulate a self with some agency – although the agency is also produced through domination, and habit, with an interest in accrual – to Foucualt's docile bodies. Yet paradoxically, Bourdieu appears to reproduce the sexual difference model favoured by French psychoanalysts such as Lacan who attempted to 'rescue' sexual polarization from the 'virile protests of feminism', and who also works with an external symbolic division of labour that produces sexual difference. Didier Eribon (2003) exposes Lacan and Bourdieu's approach as deeply conservative with its emphasis on external sexual symbolic structures in which 'the other is always the other' (2003:11). For Eribon argues we can see Lacan (and most of psychoanalysis) on the side of transcendence and Foucault, Deleuze and Guattari and Bourdieu on the side of immanence. But Bourdieu's insistence on a traditional sexual division of labour means that he reproduces the traditional model within immanence offering him no potential to move beyond traditional gender divisions. His gendered and sexed habitus can only ever be reproductive[4] because it is locked within that which produces it. Bourdieu's own analysis is performative of the categories it seeks to critique.[5]

Taste and judgement

In *Distinction* (1986) Bourdieu demonstrates how the aesthetic disposition is inseparable from a specific cultural competence. Cultural competence can be known by the tastes held by people, especially their relationship to, and knowledge of, objects and practices. Central to the development of 'high' culture was the Kantian aesthetic based on the judgement of pure taste, which distinguished that which pleases from that which gratifies, 'to distinguish disinterestedness, the sole guarantor of the specific aesthetic quality of contemplation, from the interest of reason' (Bourdieu, 1986:5).[6] The purifying, refining and sublimating of primary needs and impulses defines taste. The different ways of *relating* to objects and practices marks out the systems of dispositions and, as Bourdieu's classic comment notes: 'Taste classifies, and it classifies the classifier' (1986:6):

> In matters of taste, more than anywhere else, any determination is negation; and tastes are no doubt first and foremost distastes, disgust provoked by horror or visceral intolerance ('sick-making') of the taste of others (Bourdieu 1986:56).

Cultural practice takes its social meaning and its ability to signify social difference and distance, not from some intrinsic property, but from the location of *cultural practice* in a system of objects and practices (Waquant, 2000). It is not just a matter of obtaining objects and knowing how to use, play, experiment with them; rather, what matters is how they are conceptualized (objectified) by relations to others. This is not dissimilar to Marilyn Strathern's (1992) critique of theories of exchange underpinned by commodity logic. As an exemplar she critiques Arjun Appadurai's (1986) analysis of the 'commodity potential of things'. Appadurai argues that the social life of any 'thing' [can] be defined as . . . its exchangeability (past, present or future) for 'some other thing' (1986:13). He refers to this as the 'tournament of value' by which participation in exchange measures the strategic skills and standing of the people involved. In the moment of exchange, characterized by Appadurai as the 'flow' of things, value is made visible. Thus the cultural value of exchange determines their value. Part of the problem with this form of analysis, Strathern argues, is that it contains the idea that relationships and value can be reduced to units that can be counted. For Strathern, counting is not what is important in understanding exchange, but rather *the relationships* that enable exchange to take place and the perspective that is taken on the exchange. Bourdieu straddles the position between Appadurai and Strathern, for even when he states that it is the relationships that determine the value of things, he is more interested in their objectification. In *Distinction* he reduces relationships and value to units that can be counted. In fact his model of correspondences depends on making culture into units that can be counted. Bourdieu also relies on culture to produce gender: women are nature, men are culture, not dissimilar to the working-class having base emotions whilst the middle-class develop refinement and disinterest. The problem with these forms of dichotomous abstraction is that if they exist without any empirical understanding of how they are put into effect and their effects, they appear only to reproduce the very categories that they set out to critique.

For instance, it is in the process of objectification, Bourdieu argues, that women are the predominant markers of taste. It is women's role to convert economic capital into symbolic capital for their families through the display of tastes. As Lovell (2000) has argued, for Bourdieu, women's status is as *capital bearing objects*, whose value accrues to the primary groups to which they belong (for him, the family), rather than as capital-accumulating subjects in social space. Women's strategic circulation plays a key role in the enhancement of the symbolic capital held by men, rarely having capital-accumulating strategies of their own; they are repositories. This is most clearly shown in the diagram in *Distinction* on 'the space of social positions', in which to include women would be to include them twice. Lovell argues that Bourdieu's attempts to understand gender in *Masculine Domination* are premised upon women as objects, in a similar way to how Levi-Strauss described women – as the basis of exchange.

In contrast, feminist analysis has revealed that women can be subjects with capital-accumulating strategies (Adkins, 2000; Lawler, 2000; Moi, 1991; Munt, 1995; Reay, 1998; Skeggs, 1997; Walkerdine and Lucey, 1989). Feminists have also shown how gender struggles over the boundaries of taste and design have been significant to understandings of what actually counts as contemporary taste (e.g. Sparke, 1995). What is significant is how Bourdieu's emphasis on exchange, accrual and interest lead again to structural reductions with emphasis on objectification. This ignores the affectual impact of matters of taste, which produce class relations beyond the structural (e.g. Steedman, 1986) in the intimate moments and spaces of everyday life.

Conclusion

One of the most important things that feminist research has shown is how ambivalence is at the heart of many forms of gender and sexuality reproduction. What feminists have shown consistently over a long period of time is that norms do not work, or are not taken up; identities are a limited resource, a form of cultural capital that are worked and uncomfortably inhabited. In a recent study of sexuality, law and violence, Moran and Skeggs (2004) show how a great deal of effort and energy goes into producing forms of 'comfort' (via home, estrangement, boundary maintenance) or ontological security to overcome the ambivalence that beats at the heart of being human. Bourdieu cannot account for that ambivalence, as Adkins (2003) shows, because he places ambivalence outside of the realm of practice, he understands norms to be incorporated, where an agreement exists between the dispositions of subjects and the demands of a field, and more importantly, where he assumes that the field is a precondition of the habitus and the habitus will always submit to the field (see also Butler, 1999).

By ignoring all the things that do not 'fit' Bourdieu ignores a significant amount of social life. Values such as altruism, integrity, loyalty and investment in others are all missing (although described in *Weight of the World*), the use-values that we have in everyday life are of minimal value to Bourdieu's analysis. But from the basis of many ethnographies (informing many of the analyses in this book) I would argue that these non-accumulative, non-convertible values are central to social reproduction, especially gendered reproduction. As is the behaviour of 'doing nothing'. The TV programme *The Royle Family* perfectly encapsulates how social reproduction proceeds by doing nothing but how this inactivity (not action, nor habit) is the social glue that holds the family, gender relations, race and class together.

This chapter and the remainder of this book explore how Bourdieu can be put to use but with limits. There are many things he cannot account for, particularly gender and sexuality. But there are also many things for which he is very useful, such as understanding the middle-class, their authorization, exchange and use of distinction. He is especially good at understanding how the middle-classes operate as a 'class for themselves', something that has become increasingly apparent on a global scale (see Harvey, 1993, 2003). He can show how the bourgeois perspective is put into effect, how interests are protected and pursued and how authorisation occurs, but although he works with a theory of practice (see Bourdieu, 1977) he cannot account for the nuanced practices of those who do not operate from a dominant position.

For some Bourdieu is considered to have produced a theory of subjectivity – the habitus – firmly located in the social, yet it is this location that restricts what can be understood beyond the social: an unconscious that may have an energy of its own, or may, as Foucault has suggested, be the limit to our social understanding. By assuming an unconscious that works as a 'structuring mechanism', the contradictions and ambiguities identified by psychoanalysts or post-structural theorists are ignored. As in most of Bourdieu's work, the emphasis is on order and structure. Within the habitus is an implicit theory of intention and interest, in which the unconscious habitus accrues practices that work in its own interest. When finally Bourdieu asks people about how they experience the positions to which they are ascribed, their accounts are left without analysis (in *Weight of the World*) (see McRobbie, 2002). Yet, it is in these accounts that we finally see ambiguity and contradiction breaking through.

Notes

1 See Skeggs (2000) for an introduction to the debate on sociology and class and Skeggs (2004) for a more general overview.
2 This is similar to the classic Marxist methodological take which draws on depth metaphors to insist that 'real' knowledge lurks behind surface knowledge, e.g., commodity fetishism.
3 In the early 1970s feminists drew a division between sex as biology and gender as social or cultural. This was challenged from the 1980s by feminists who showed that biology was just as much a cultural product as social roles of gender (see Franklin, Lury and Stacey, 1991).
4 In contrast Barthes works with the concept of 'neuter' because he notes: 'Just like jeans, love is unisex', asserting the universal nature of love.
5 A problem of which Bourdieu is aware (see Bourdieu, 1987).
6 Cook (2000) argues that Bourdieu's critique of taste is itself marked by its own aesthetic moments. The 'anti-Kantian' aesthetic is not simply presented as one further datum in an enterprise of the social critique of taste. Bourdieu prefers it to what he presents as the emotionally cold formalisms of high bourgeois taste. He invites his readers to give new value to a mode of judgment, which

is presented as socially despised. He, therefore, Cook argues, makes a judgment of taste between judgments of taste.

References

Adkins, L. (2000) 'Objects of Innovation: Post-Occupational Reflexivity and Re-traditionalizations of Gender' in S. Ahmed, J. Kilby, C. Lury, M. McNeil and B. Skeggs (eds) *Transformations: Thinking Through Feminism*. London: Routledge.
Adkins, L. (2003) 'Reflexivity: Freedom or Habit of Gender?' *Theory, Culture and Society* 20(6): 21–42.
Adkins, L. and Lury, C. (1999) 'The Labour of Identity: Performing Identities, Performing Economies' *Economy and Society* 28(4): 598–614.
Appadurai, A. (ed.) (1986) *The Social Life of Things*. Cambridge: Cambridge University Press.
Arnot, M. (1979) 'Cultural Reproduction: the Pedagogy of Sexuality' *Screen Education* 32/33: 141–153.
Barrett, M. (1988) *Women's Oppression Today: The Marxist Encounter*. London: Verso.
Bhabha, H. (1994) *The Location of Culture*. London: Routledge.
Bourdieu, P. (1962) *The Algerians*. Boston: Beacon Press.
Bourdieu, P. (1964) *Les Heritiers*. Paris: Les Editions de Minuit.
Bourdieu, P. (1966) *L'Amour de L'art*. Paris: Les Editions de Minuit.
Bourdieu, P. (1977) *Outline of a Theory of Practice*. Cambridge: Polity Press.
Bourdieu, P. (1979) 'Symbolic Power' *Critique of Anthropology* 4: 77–85.
Bourdieu, P. (1983) 'The Forms of Capital' in J. G. Richardson (ed.) *Handbook of Theory and Research for the Sociology of Education*. New York: Greenwood Press.
Bourdieu, P. (1986) *Distinction: A Social Critique of the Judgement of Taste*. London: Routledge.
Bourdieu, P. (1987) 'What Makes a Social Class?' *Berkeley Journal of Sociology* 1–17.
Bourdieu, P. (1988) *Homo Academicus*. Cambridge: Polity.
Bourdieu, P. (1990a) *The Logic of Practice*. Cambridge: Polity.
Bourdieu, P. (1990b) *Photography: A Middle Brow Art*. Cambridge: Polity.
Bourdieu, P. (1991) *The Craft of Sociology*. New York: Walter de Gruyter.
Bourdieu, P. (1992) *Language and Symbolic Power*. Cambridge: Polity Press.
Bourdieu, P. (1996a) *The State Nobility*. Cambridge: Polity.
Bourdieu, P. (1996b) *The Rules of Art*. Cambridge: Polity.
Bourdieu, P. (1998a) *On Television and Journalism*. London: Pluto.
Bourdieu, P. (1998b) *Acts of Resistance*. Cambridge: Polity.
Bourdieu, P. (2000) *Pascalian Meditations*. Cambridge: Polity.
Bourdieu, P. (2001) *Masculine Domination*. Cambridge: Polity Press.
Bourdieu, P. (2003) *Firing Back*. New York: The New Press.
Bourdieu, P. and Passeron, J-C. (1977) *Reproduction in Education, Society and Culture*. London: Sage.
Bourdieu, P. and Waquant, L. (1992) *An Invitation to Reflexive Sociology*. Chicago: University of Chicago Press.
Bourdieu, P. *et al* (1999) *Weight of the World: Social Suffering in Contemporary Society*. Cambridge: Polity.
Bourdieu, P. and Waquant, L. (2001) 'NewLiberalSpeak: Notes on the Planetary Vulagate' *Radical Philosophy* 105: 1–6.
Butler, J. (1993) *Bodies That Matter: On the Discursive Limits of 'Sex'*. London: Routledge.
Butler, J. (1999) 'Performativity's Social Magic' in R. Shusterman (ed.) *Bourdieu: A Critical Reader*. Oxford: Blackwell.
C. Calhoun, E. LiPuma and M. Postone (eds) (1993) *Bourdieu: Critical Perspectives*. Chicago: Chicago University Press.
Califia, P. (1994) *Public Sex: The Culture of Radical Sex*. San Francisco: Cleis Press.

Connell, R. W. (1989) 'Cool Guys, Swots and Wimps: The Interplay of Masculinity and Education' *Oxford Review of Education* 15(3): 291–303.

Cook, J. (2000) 'Culture, Class and Taste' in S. Munt (ed.) *Cultural Studies and the Working Class: Subject to Change*. London: Cassell.

Crompton, R. (1993) *Class and Stratification: An Introduction to Current Debates*. Cambridge: Polity.

De Certeau, M. (1988) *The Practice of Everyday Life*. London: University of California Press.

Eribon, D. (2003) 'Towards an Ethic of Subjectification: The 1970s as Resistance to Psychoanalysis' paper presented at *Sexuality after Foucault* conference, University of Manchester, November 28–30.

Foucault, M. (1979) *The History of Sexuality, Volume One*. Harmondsworth: Penguin.

Fowler, B. (1997) *Pierre Bourdieu and Cultural Theory: Critical Investigations*. London: Sage.

Franklin, S., Lury, C. and Stacey, J. (eds) *Off-Centre: Feminism and Cultural Studies*. London: Harper Collins.

Hage, G. (1998) *White Nation: Fantasies of White Supremacy in a Multicultural Society*. Annandale: Pluto Press.

Halberstam, J. (1988) *Female Masculinity*. Durham and London: Duke University Press.

Halperin, D. (2003) 'Sexuality after Foucault' Plenary address *Sexuality after Foucault* conference, University of Manchester, November 28–30.

Hartmann, H. and Sargent, L. (1981) *The Unhappy Marriage of Marxism and Feminism*. London: Pluto.

Harvey, D. (1993) 'Class Relations, Social Justice and the Politics of Difference' in M. Keith and S. Pile (eds) *Place and the Politics of Identity*. London: Routledge.

Harvey, D. (2003) *The New Imperialism*. Oxford: Oxford University Press.

Honneth, A. (1986) 'The Fragmented World of Symbolic Forms: Reflections on Pierre Bourdieu's Sociology of Culture' *Theory, Culture and Society* 3(3) 55–66.

Jenkins, R. (1982) 'Pierre Bourdieu and the Reproduction of Determinism' *Sociology* 31: 270–281.

Lawler, S. (2000) *Mothering the Self: Mothers, Daughters, Subjects*. London: Routledge.

Lovell, T. (2000) 'Thinking Feminism With and Against Bourdieu' *Feminist Theory* 1(1): 11–32.

Martin, B. (1996) *Femininity Played Straight: The Significance of Being Lesbian*. London: Routledge.

McCall, L. (1992) 'Does Gender Fit? Bourdieu, Feminism and Conceptions of Social Order' *Theory and Society* 21: 837–867.

McNay, L. (1999) 'Gender, Habitus and the Field: Pierre Bourdieu and the Limits of Reflexivity' *Theory, Culture and Society* 16(1): 95–117.

McRobbie, A. (2002) 'A Mixed Bag of Misfortunes?: Bourdieu's Weight of the World' *Theory, Culture and Society* 19(3): 129–138.

Moi, T. (1991) 'Appropriating Bourdieu: Feminist Theory and Pierre Bourdieu's Sociology of Culture' *New Literary History* 22(4): 1017–1049.

Moran, L. and Skeggs, B. (with P. Tyrer and K. Corteen) (2004) *Sexuality and the Politics of Violence and Safety*. London: Routledge.

Mottier, V. (2002) 'Masculine Domination: Gender and Power in Bourdieu's Writings' *Feminist Theory* 3(3): 345–359.

Munt, S. (1995) 'The Lesbian Flaneur' in D. Bell and G. Valentine (eds) *Mapping Desire*. London: Routledge.

Reay, D. (1998) *Class Work: Mother's Involvement in their Children's Primary Schooling*. London: UCL Press.

Robbins, D. (1999) *Bourdieu and Culture*. London: Sage.

Skeggs, B. (1997) *Formations of Class and Gender: Becoming Respectable*. London: Sage.

Skeggs, B. (2000) 'Rethinking Class: Class Cultures and Explanatory Power' in M. Haralambos (ed.) *Developments in Sociology: An Annual Review*. Ormskirk, Lancs: Causeway Press.

Skeggs, B. (2004) *Class, Self, Culture*. London: Routledge.

Sparke, P. (1995) *As Long as it's Pink: The Sexual Politics of Taste*. London: Harper Collins.

Stanworth, M. (1984) 'Women and Class Analysis: A Reply to Goldthorpe' *Sociology* 18(2): 153–171.

Steedman, C. (1986) *Landscape for a Good Woman: A Story of Two Lives*. London: Virago.

Strathern, M. (1992) 'Qualified Value: The Perspective of Gift Exchange' in C. Humphrey and S. Hugh-Jones (eds) *Barter, Exchange and Value: An Anthropological Approach*. Cambridge: Cambridge University Press.

Tyler, C-A. (1991) 'Boys Will Be Girls: The Politics of Gay Drag' in D. Fuss (ed.) *Inside Out: Lesbian Theories/Gay Theories*. London: Routledge.

Walkerdine, V. (2002) *Growing Up Girl*. London: Macmillan.

Walkerdine, V. and Lucey, H. (1989) *Democracy in the Kitchen: Regulating Mothers and Socialising Daughters*. London: Virago.

Waquant, L. (2000) 'Durkheim and Bourdieu: the Common Plinth and its Cracks' in B. Fowler (ed.) *Reading Bourdieu on Society and Culture*. Oxford: Blackwell.

Warner, M. (ed.) (1993) *Fear of a Queer Planet: Queer Politics and Social Theory*. Minneapolis: University of Minnesota Press.

Wittig, M. (1992) *The Straight Mind*. Hemel Hempstead: Harvester Press.

Section I:
Rethinking class and gender

Bourdieu, class and gender: 'The return of the living dead'?

Terry Lovell

Introduction

Class analysis has been staple fare of the discipline of sociology. There have always been disputes about how class is to be defined and theorised, but its centrality to sociological thought was common ground across these disputes until well into the second half of the 20th century. Its pre-eminence began to be challenged in the second half of the 20th century with the thesis of the separation of ownership from control of the means of production (see for example Dahrendorf, 1957). The renewal of Marxist sociology from the 1960s stayed this challenge to some extent, but it has returned with renewed vigour with the decline of Marxist and other left-leaning sociologies from the 1990s. Among its modern heirs must be counted the various architects of the thesis of the individualization of society that in some versions[1] envisages a capitalism without class.

Those who would continue to speak of class must engage with questions concerning the units of class analysis that have troubled many feminists insofar as these are collectivities such as families and households rather than individuals. Those who theorize 'individualization' often align themselves with some aspects of feminism, and detect in the process of individualization in the context of global capitalism, not only the demise of class but also of patriarchy; they point to changes that have improved the position of women, and achieved some at least of the goals of feminism. Conversely, the sociological defence of class analysis is sometimes associated with a (muted) critique of feminism, often on the grounds of the neglect of social class.

In the first section of this chapter I shall look at the defence of conventional approaches to class mounted against feminist critics and also against 'culturalist' analyses by those that argue the necessity of speaking of a 'family/household system' that is pivotal in the processes of production, reproduction and transformation of class and gender privilege in the modern social world. The second section looks at 'women' as a category. Are social constructionists correct in maintaining a strict division between (biological) 'sex' and (socio-cultural) 'gender', or in gathering sexual difference itself into the domain of socio-cultural construction? What is the case for theorizing 'women' as a class, as do French materialist feminists? Should we rather understand gender group-ings in terms of 'status'? Is 'seriality' a useful alternative concept? The third section brings what has been established in the first two sections into a discus-sion of gender in Bourdieu's 'social field', the central concern of this chapter.

Section 1. Conflicts over class and gender

The individualization thesis: its promise for gender analysis

Some of the theorists of modern individualization have drawn from the resources offered by postmodernism, although not necessarily from the post-structuralist 'linguistic turn', and in doing so, have been willing to give culture and consumption a central position in the analytical frame. They detach socio-economic class from particular cultural formations, and culture, increasingly mediated by consumption, is held to be more formative of the social identities and allegiances of individuals than social class. Ulrich Beck has gone so far as to speak not only of a 'capitalism without class', but of 'class', alongside 'family', 'neighborhood' and other furniture of classical sociology as 'zombie categories' (Beck and Beck-Gersheim, 2001:203): the living dead of sociological discourse drained of their earlier vitality in the processes of identity-formation and purposive social action in modern society.

Individualization theory has certain attractions for feminists over more tra-ditional structural sociologies. For in extending the social status of 'individual' to women, unlike the classical individualism that has been the target of numer-ous feminist critiques (see for example Pateman, 1988), it appears to afford a greater recognition of agency.

Secondly, the emphasis on consumption rather than rather than production in relationship to the formation of subjectivities and identities also puts gender into the foreground, given the responsibility for certain aspects of consumption that women have traditionally carried.

Thirdly, in locating the main source of women's oppression in the nature of these 'zombie' collectivities and in the secondary position of women within the labour market, individualization theory echoes and honours much 1970s feminist sociological analysis. Anthony Giddens (1992) posits a 'transformation of intimacy';[2] Manuel Castells attributes some of the characteristics of 'the network society', including the fragmentation of the patriarchal family and the emergence of new family forms, the changes in reproduction patterns and the increasing participation of women in the labour market, in part to the effects of the women's movements and feminism (Castells, 1997). The global 'network society' heralds, he claims, 'the end of patriarchalism'. Beck and Beck-Gersheim's version of the individualization thesis analyses the effects of the transformation of the family and personal life. As primary collectivities are drained of life, so the ties that have bound women are correspondingly loos-ened, permitting a shift among young women away from the value of 'living for others' to the aspiration for a little bit of 'a life of one's own' (Beck & Beck-Gernshein, 2001). How could women, feminists or not, fail to feel the seduction of this hope and this promise?

In this chapter I shall focus not on the evidence that these 'benefits' are unequally distributed across lines of class and 'race', but on the charge that the 'liberation' achieved by (some) women may have masked, for feminists, an associated deepening of *class* inequalities (Fowler, 2003).

The renewal of class analysis

The reserve which feminists, since the advent of the WLM and the re-emergence of feminism in the late 1960s, have increasingly shown towards the more structural approaches that locate the units of social life in mixed sex collectivities, particularly those that are based on institutionalized heterosexuality – collectivities that have been imagined as 'birth communities' (Yuval Davis, 1997) – has served to enhance the seductions of the individualization thesis. For these collectivities are typically internally differentiated in unequal power relations that disadvantage women, an inequality that tends to be lost from view in those forms of analysis that take them as the units of social life. Women seem to disappear into them without remainder, even where the focus of analysis is on the capitalist labour market into which women are recruited as individuals. There is a tacit assumption that the interests that women share in the fortunes of the family/household to which they belong override in importance those that are specific to their gender.

This was one of the main points at issue in the debate that took place in the 1980s in the pages of the journal *Sociology*. John Goldthorpe's paper in 1983 threw down the gauntlet to feminist critics of the conventional view, claiming that it was able to give a superior, more realistic, empirically-grounded and methodologically sound account of the position of women than did those that had argued that due attention to the position of women within class analysis had destabilised and even undermined traditional sociological approaches to class (Delphy, 1984; Oakley, 1981, and others. See also the response to Goldthorpe by Stanworth, 1984).

Feminist sociologists had mounted an extensive critique of sociological methods that measured social class in terms of the occupational status of 'heads of households', presumptively male. Women's own class status by virtue of their labour market participation is made invisible in this classing of the family/household. Goldthorpe gives a lengthy and in many ways impressive 'defence of the conventional view'. He characterizes both views with lucidity:

i) [I]t is the family rather than the individual which forms the basic unit of social stratification; ii) particular families are articulated with the system of stratification essentially via the position of their male 'head' – which, in modern societies, can be most adequately indexed by reference to their occupational category or grade. This view is typically attacked on two rather different levels. First, it is argued that such a view entails a disregard of certain increasingly important features of contemporary 'social reality': most obviously, the proportion of families that do not have a male 'head'; and the proportion of even 'normal' families in which the wife as well as husband is found in gainful employment – and perhaps in a different occupational category or grade to that of her husband. Secondly, though, and more fundamentally, it is held that the conventional view effectively precludes examination of what should be recognized as one major feature of the stratification system as a whole: that is, sexual stratification, which, of course, cuts directly through the conjugal family. It follows, then, that not only are women rendered largely 'invisible' within the study of stratification, but furthermore that the existence of sexual inequalities becomes more or less disregarded (Goldthorpe, 1983:465).

Goldthorpe argues that the conventional view provides the basis for a realistic appraisal of the position of women within social structures. On the increase in married women's labour market participation, he comments that 'although the degree of women's economic dependence on their husbands may in this be somewhat mitigated, such employment *typically forms part of a family strategy*, or at all events, takes place within the possibilities and constraints of the class situation of the family as a whole' (1983:469, emphasis added). For Goldthorpe women have a stake and often a voice in the development of 'family strategies' regarding their own labour-market participation. He puts the point succinctly: 'lines of class division and potential conflict run between, but not through, families' (Goldthorpe, 1983:469).

The position articulated by Goldthorpe may be taken here as the baseline: a robust defence of the conventional view that has, traditionally, informed sociological analysis of gender and class. There have been other less traditionalist defences. In a collection entitled *Renewing Class Analysis* (Crompton *et al*, 2000) a range of these are surveyed and sampled. Yet social class, across all the various attempts to renew class analysis that are represented in this collection, remains, fundamentally, a socio-economic category. The issues that dominated the mainstream sociological approach survive and are as troubling as they ever were in a world in which inequality is deepening, both within 'western' societies and globally: the ways in which class positions and relations are reproduced across generations, the ways in which it affects life chances, including life-expectation, health, access to education, educational attainment, employment trajectories, command of resources and so on. But the 'renewals' exemplified in this particular volume do not depart very far from the world of work and of economic practice, in spite of the fact that relatively neglected questions have emerged in the process: class *processes* in employment and the effects of the entry of women onto the labour market, especially married women, and gendered access to consumer services in the world of banking and finance.[3]

The relative separation of 'the economic' from 'the cultural' is common across the conventional view and the various renewals of class analysis. I do not have space to develop this point here, but it is notable that feminist scholarship has been very often interdisciplinary, feeling the pull of the domain of 'the cultural' as critical in the analysis of forms of gender domination that cannot be wholly attributed to social structural factors.

Pierre Bourdieu was one of the 20th century's most prominent heirs to the classical sociological tradition, in which class is central, but his work is also distinguished by the attempt to construct a systematically integrated account of class and culture, and a distinctive inflexion of the concept of 'class', that I shall examine below. Because of this, his influence has been felt not only within the discipline of sociology but also that of cultural studies, including film and television studies, as well as upon sociology and its sub-disciplines, especially the sociology of education and the sociology of art. His influence upon feminism was slow to develop, but has grown among those who wish to contribute to 'the renewal of class analysis' especially those who have also been more deeply influenced by cultural studies than have most, though by no means all, of those who have centred their concerns exclusively on the world of work (Adkins and Skeggs, 2004).

Bourdieu's reflexive sociology has attracted a belated but growing, if critical, interest among feminists only in part because of his integrated approach to socio-economic class and culture. Dispersed throughout his massive oeuvre is a good deal of interesting comment on gender in the social field. With his publication of his work on masculine domination (Bourdieu, 1990, 2001) he has entered the lists in a more concentrated form, but has, paradoxically, attracted a good deal of sharply critical comment, especially from feminists in France (see Armangaud *et al*, 1993). So, to quote the title of an essay by Leslie McCall, 'does gender fit?' (McCall, 1992). Or perhaps *how* does gender fit into Bourdieu's reflexive sociology? Before turning to this question, the issue of 'women' as a category must be addressed.

Section 2. Women: biological sex, social class, status category or series?

Women and biology

The manner in which women's biology has been used to rationalize women's subordination (Sayers, 1982) has created within feminism, and not only sociological feminism, a strong commitment to social constructionist understandings of gender (see Witz, 2000). In the case of certain forms of contemporary feminist philosophy, sexual difference itself is understood to be socially constructed rather than biologically given (Butler, 1990, 1993). The nature and consequences of biological differences between the sexes have been fiercely contested within feminism. The 'biological essentialist card' is often too easily played whenever biological sexual difference is given any place at all within feminist analysis (see for example, the exchange over the working-class family between Barrett (1984, 1988) and Brenner and Ramas (1984)).

The feminist literary theorist Toril Moi, in her study of Simone de Beauvoir, borrowed the question posed by Beauvoir for her title. 'What is a woman?' Moi asks, with Beauvoir. She answers with a very simple, common sense definition: 'a woman is . . . a person with a female body' (Moi, 1999:8). Like the woman on the Clapham omnibus, Moi recognizes and begins with embodied biological sexual difference. She engages in an extended critique of Judith Butler, and argues that the existence of a variety of undecidable types of body does not in and of itself deconstruct the category of sexual difference. Neither does the fluidity and lack of fixity of 'the biological'. She mounts a strong case against the distinction that circulates widely within feminist discourse between (biological) sex and (socio-cultural) gender. Whilst recognizing its usefulness in some contexts, these are strictly limited:

> When it comes to thinking about what a woman is . . . the sex/gender distinction is woefully inadequate. Many critics appear to believe that a sexed human being is made up of the sum of sex plus gender. From such a perspective it does look as if everything in a woman or a man that is not sex must be gender and vice versa (Moi, 1999:35).

Moi further argues that feminists, including Butler, who have interpreted Beauvoir's work in terms of the sex/gender opposition, have misread it (Butler, 1986). She argues against the move of either incorporating biological sexual difference within gender, as Butler does, or reducing gender to biological sexual difference, the latter fuelling an understanding of women in terms of their biology as in the evolutionary psychology that is hegemonic in the media and popular understandings. For Moi, nobody who has a female body can be denied the title of 'woman' but women cannot be reduced to their female bodies: sexual difference does not permeate a woman through and through. So biological sexual difference remains in place in Moi's thinking. She finds an alternative to the sex/gender distinction in Beauvoir's concept of *the body as situation*: 'For Beauvoir, a woman is someone with a female body from beginning to end, from the moment she is born until the moment she dies, but that body is her situation, not her destiny' (1999:76). Moi argues for a context-dependent, historically located answer to Beauvoir's question.

Although Moi is not a sociologist, this contextually situated approach gives her a certain stake in the discipline. Feminist theory since the 1980s has followed a trajectory away from sociology and towards philosophy and cultural/literary studies in seeking its theoretical/conceptual frame (Barrett and Phillips, 1992; Smart, 1994). Moi was part of 'the psychoanalytical turn' in feminist literary studies, but she combined it with Bourdieu's sociology at a time at which his work had little circulation within feminism. She was responsible for introducing to feminist literary theorists some of the major organizing concepts of Bourdieu's reflexive sociology, arguing that his work was ripe for feminist 'critique and appropriation' (Moi, 1991).

Materialist feminism: do women constitute a social class?

> Philosophical materialism is the view that all that exists is material or is wholly dependent upon matter for its existence . . . human beings . . . [are] . . . fundamentally bodily in nature. (Urmson and Rée, 1989:194, *The Concise Encyclopaedia of Western Philosophy and Philosophers.*)

The premises from which we begin are not arbitrary ones, not dogmas, . . . but real individuals, their activity and the material conditions under which they live, both those which they find already existing and those produced by their activity. . . . Men can be distinguished from animals by consciousness, by religion or anything else you like. They themselves begin to distinguish themselves from animals as soon as they begin to *produce* their means of subsistence, a step which is conditioned by their physical organization. By producing their means of subsistence men are indirectly producing their actual material life. (Marx and Engels, 1965:31, *The German Ideology*.)

Beauvoir has many followers, particularly within the school of French materialist feminism: in France, Christine Delphy, Michèle Le Doeuff, Claudette Guillaumin and others, and in Britain, those feminists who have located themselves in relation to this school (Lisa Adkins, Stevi Jackson, Diana Leonard and others). Materialist feminism comes in diverse forms, and I shall follow Jackson in distinguishing those that emanated from the French school and that remained firmly located on the domain of 'the social' (Jackson, 2001) from those, very often emanating from philosophy, cultural, or literary studies: Rosemary Hennessy (1993), Donna Landry (Landry and MacClean, 1993) and others (see Hennessey and Ingraham, 1997) who have remained within the tradition of Marxist feminism in seeking some kind of synthesis of Marxist/socialist analysis with 'the cultural turn' associated with psychoanalysis and the poststructuralist theory of language, and who are therefore more influenced by the other major school of French feminism dominated by Hélène Cixous, Luce Irigaray and Julia Kristeva that was hostile towards Beauvoir (see Moi, 1987). French materialist feminism is distinctive in conceptualising sexual divisions and relationships as (antagonistic) *class* relationships in their own right in the Marxist sense. Materialist feminism in France originated with the group that was associated with the journal *Questions féministes*, (with which Beauvoir herself was associated). This materialist feminism represented a fusion of radical feminism with elements of Marxist feminism that in the process extended the meaning of 'materialism' beyond the primacy given within Marxism to the capitalist mode of production.

The early writings of Christine Delphy demonstrate the extent of that initial (highly critical) engagement. Delphy, like British Marxist feminists of the same period, located her materialism within the concept of the 'production of material life' and 'the social relations of production and reproduction'. But the Marxian paradigm was problematic for Marxist and French feminist materialists alike in its relegation of human sexuality and reproduction to the realm of nature:

The maintenance and reproduction of the working class is, and must ever be, a necessary condition of the reproduction of capital. But the capitalist may safely leave its fulfilment to the labourer's instinct of self-preservation and of propagation (Marx, 1970:572).

Engels' work became a critical resource for a Marxist theory of the social relations of reproduction (Sayers *et al*, 1987) but Engels wrote of the family rather than sexuality. Both materialist feminisms drew attention to the unpaid labour undertaken by women in the home. Both participated in the extended debate over domestic labour that had almost run its course by the beginning of the 1980s (Malos, 1980). Delphy resolved the problem of sexuality together with that of domestic labour by positing two parallel modes of production, the first pertaining to capitalism, the second to 'family', or 'patriarchal production', and by assimilating women's sexuality to the category of exploited labour. For Delphy then, the mode of production of 20th century Western society could not be described exclusively as capitalist. For only the first mode, she argued, is properly so described, centring as it does on the exploitation of labour to produce surplus value in commodity production. The unpaid domestic labour of women may have benefited capitalism but, Delphy argued, it was labour that was more immediately exploited by men rather than by the capitalist class. 'The main enemy' so far as women as a class were concerned, was patriarchy – a system of male power over women.[4]

Delphy considered not the relationship of women to the capitalist means of production as the chief determinant of women's class position, but their position within exploitative relations of family production, whose linchpin was marriage: institutionalized compulsory heterosexuality:

> Even though a marriage with a man from the capitalist class can raise a woman's standard of living, it does not make her a member of that class. She herself does not own the means of production. Therefore her standard of living does not depend on her class relationship to the proletariat; but on her serf relations of production with her husband (Delphy, 1984:71).

It was male-female sexual relations, especially marriage that tied women into unequal, servile relationships with men. However while heterosexuality presupposed biological sexual differences, biology did not found the unequal relations of men and women, nor define them as 'classes'. For Delphy men and women are *socially* constituted groups structured around antagonistic *gender* class relations and interests.

In drawing attention to very significant aspects of the production of material life that took place outside the capitalist mode of production, French materialist feminism remained strictly materialist. But the designation of women as a full social class by virtue of their position within the social relations of *family* rather than capitalist production, structured by institutionalized heterosexuality, took them well beyond any semblance of Marxist orthodoxy. This was a step too far for many Marxist feminists, and the two materialisms separated with some acrimony (Barrett and McIntosh 1979; Delphy, 1984).

As is clear in this quote from Delphy, working-class women were presented as subject to a double exploitation of their labour through their participation in both modes of production. But bourgeois women were not considered to be full members of their prima facie social class.

Both the definitions at the head of this section emphasize the physical and bodily nature of 'material life'. Marx and Engels do not separate off the physical, the embodied, from formative *social* activity: 'The writing of history must always set out from these material bases and their modification in the course of history through the actions of men' (Marx and Engels, 1965:31). French materialist feminists locate gender classes entirely within the realm of the social, a realm screened off from the biological. They have in the main relatively little to say about the specificity of women's biological bodies, in spite of their great debt to Beauvoir, who has much to say on this topic with which she opens her study of 'woman's situation'. They were scrupulously social constructionist in their theories. The distinction between (biological) sex and (socially constructed) gender retained some circulation – Delphy continued to use the distinction although critically – but French materialist feminists were among the earliest to suggest that sex, too, and not just gender, was fully social; sexual difference could not be distinguished from gender on the grounds that one belonged to 'nature', the other to 'culture'. In this move they anticipated in all but one respect the position taken in the 1990s by Judith Butler, who famously declared:

> this construct called sex is as culturally constructed as gender; indeed perhaps it was always already gender, with the consequence that the distinction between sex and gender turned out to be no distinction at all (Butler, 1990:7).

The key remaining difference was that where Butler spoke of 'cultural construction' of sex and gender, the materialist feminists spoke of 'social construction'. Butler, unlike the majority of the French (and associated British – see Jackson, 2001) materialist feminists, had taken 'the cultural/linguistic turn' with a vengeance, and unlike most of the school of French materialist feminism, also draws on psychoanalytic theory, a resource eschewed explicitly by Jackson, for example, along with 'the cultural turn' (Jackson, 1999).

Among those who brought the sexual entirely into the realm of the social was Monique Wittig. The social relationship that generated sexual difference, created hierarchical and oppressive classes with opposed interests, was (reproductive) heterosexuality, imposed on females whether they wished or no, to make of them an oppressed class, 'women'. Wittig's answer to Beauvoir's question, in her writings from the 1970s, is very different to that of Moi. The meaning of 'woman' is brought into sharp focus for Wittig by the figure of the lesbian:

> [T]he lesbian *has* to be something else, a not-woman, a not-man, a product of society, not a product of nature, for there is no nature in society (Wittig, 1992:13).

The practice of heterosexuality organizes and creates the (social) distinction between men and women:

> The category of sex is the product of a heterosexual society in which men appropriate for themselves the reproduction and production of women, and also their physical persons by means of a contract called the marriage contract (Wittig, 1992:6).

The recurrent theme of sexuality and sexual reproduction as work is significant, as this redefinition as 'work' enabled the French materialists to take sex into the domain of the social, even in the case of biological reproduction (Tabet, 1996). Sexual and reproductive work has a product: the child. It is alienated labour however, for the product does not belong to its producer; indeed it is a species of 'slave-labour' because it is obligatory.[5]

Incorporating heterosexual practice and human reproduction into the category of work may not generate an account of (hetero)sexuality with much nuance. It hardly allows acknowledgement of the deep investments that many women make in their reproductive bodies, in pregnancy, reproduction, children as that which was opened up by the engagement with psychoanalysis. But one very promising avenue was created with the shift from sex as work to sexual work – paid work that takes place within the frame of commodity exchange (Adkins, 1995; Adkins and Merchant, 1996; Pateman, 1988). It brought into the frame not only directly 'sexual work' such as prostitution, but also to the way that labour is gendered and sexualized within the economic division of labour.[6]

Gender as status

Max Weber famously distinguished between class, status and party in his study of power in society. Sociological stratification theory, especially as developed in the US, tends to conflate class with status (Crompton *et al*, 2000; Goldthorpe, 1983; Savage, 2000). French materialist feminism in France and Britain, as it was developed in the 1970s and 1980s, placed the weight of emphasis as we have seen upon the production of 'women' as a gender *class*, one constituted through the social relations of domestic production, including sexuality, rather than upon the participation of women in the capitalist labour market.

As we have seen, the argument was that while working class women are full members of *both* the working class, and the subordinate *gender* class, 'bourgeois' women who do not have 'bourgeois' positions in the labour market are classed only through their gender, and they share their *gender* class, of course, with their working-class sisters. Delphy, however, acknowledges that their respective standards of living may be very different. I want to raise the question whether the differences that Delphy acknowledges here do not take us into the arena of 'status power' rather than class power,[7] forms of power that women have held over other women. For the wives and daughters of capitalists and the secretaries of powerful men may exercise status power, even though their status is relational and the power whose exercise it enables may be more precarious than that of their husbands or their bosses. If we make this move, we need to do so in full consciousness of the fact that this form of power is very real. We should not underestimate its capacity to inflict injury, as Bourdieu, and Iris Marion Young, and Nancy Fraser all recognize (Bourdieu, 2001; Fraser, 1997, 1998; Young, 1990).

We might follow Young at this point, and speak of 'social groups', without differentiating status groups from class groups (Young, 1990). This lack of specificity allows her to raise the issue of forms of oppression that various subordinated groups are characteristically vulnerable to, including racialized groups, gender groupings, social classes, and others. These are of course cross cutting. We are all members of more than one social group. Fraser, in her exchanges with Young (Fraser, 1997; Young, 1997), and later with Butler (Butler, 1998; Fraser, 1998) emphasizes the distinction between status and class, using an explicitly Weberian frame. But 'the economic' and 'the cultural' or the 'status order' that is structured by the dominant culture, are for Fraser analytical rather than substantive categories. She classifies groups according to whether they are structured primarily by the economic or the status order, although she recognizes, importantly, that some groups may be 'bivalent' and that, substantively, the two are closely imbricated, so that injustices that have their root, analytically, in one, may require 'remedies' in the other, or in both sets of power relations (Fraser and Honneth, 2003).

Gender as seriality

Under the broad head of 'postmodernism', Young, among others, has floated the idea of a different kind of political mobilization that may be contingent and shifting, formed for specific and limited purposes. She distinguishes between 'groups' and 'series', drawing on Sartre: 'not all structured social action takes place in groups' (Young, 1995, 198). Series are collectivities that are transient, amorphous, forming in the course of everyday life and habitual actions. The bus queue affords Sartre's example. Series, unlike groups such as social classes, do not need or usually intend to become, solidified. Young argues that gender may be understood profitably as seriality (Young, 1995). I do not have space in this chapter to give this concept and Young's argument the attention they deserve but I shall be returning to it subsequently. It is interesting that Juliet Mitchell also proposes a distinctive account of gender as seriality in her work on siblings (Mitchell, 2003).

In the next section I shall consider Bourdieu's account of gender in the social field, in terms of sex/genders as social groups, whether in terms of social class in the manner in which this is affirmed by French materialist feminism, or in terms of status.

Section 3. Bourdieu and the social field: 'does gender fit?'

Bourdieu is often accused of base/superstruture reductionism, but this does not protect him from the opposite charge, that he has no adequate model of 'the economic' (Callinicos, 1999). But Bourdieu engages neither in economic reductionism nor in the elevation of everything into the realm of 'the cultural'. Bourdieu's 'social field' is doubly articulated. The maps of social space that Bourdieu produces in *Distinction* are structured around two related hierarchies that measure, respectively, holdings of economic and of cultural capital and their composition in relation to the occupants of those positions. The positions themselves denote labour-market occupations. Women may be entered into this general field in terms of *either* their labour-market participation, *or* the status of the *households* to which they belong. Thus far Bourdieu is at one with Goldthorpe and the conventional view. For Goldthorpe, class position generates class-consciousness, class struggle and the creation of class institutions, class politics. Bourdieu does not disagree, but in his classic paper on social class, gives this basic model a rather different inflexion:

> A 'class', be it *social, sexual, ethnic or otherwise*, exists when there are agents capable of imposing themselves as authorized to speak and to act officially in its place and in its name, upon whom, by recognizing themselves in these plenipotentiaries, by recognizing them as endowed with full power to speak and act in their name, recognize themselves as members of the class, and in doing so, confer upon it the only form of existence a *group* can possess (Bourdieu, 1987:15, emphasis added).

On this definition, there exist sexual classes, and *sexual* classes do indeed 'cut directly through the conjugal family' (Goldthorpe, 1983:469). For Bourdieu, social classes/groupings are constructed through successful bids for authorization by 'agents capable of imposing themselves' – in the case of the historical formation of the English working class, by the political societies and movements documented by E.P. Thompson (1963). They are not 'pre-given' in social space: rather positioning in social space may predispose an answering recognition and authorization by those addressed as the socio-political category in question (see Lovell, 2003). There are therefore no social classes or sexual classes per se – no classes 'in themselves' – until this process of representation and recognition has begun to occur. They are the outcome of political and cultural work:

> Constructed classes theoretically assemble agents who, being subject to similar conditions, tend to resemble one another, and, as a result, are inclined to come together as a practical group (Bourdieu, 1987:6).

It follows firstly, that gender categories may be addressed (by 'feminist plenipotentiaries?') as distinct 'social groups', to become over time through this two-way process of authorization, 'practical groups'. This process of group formation has occurred whenever women's movements have arisen. Bourdieu's definition is commensurable with the French materialist feminist claim that women constitute a social class, although for the latter, this class does indeed exist 'in itself' prior to its mobilization *as* a gender class. Bourdieu's proviso however is that such classes are made and not given. And French materialist feminism could no doubt be accommodated to this view, though there would be protest over the concept of 'plenipotentiaries'.[8] Bourdieu considers that 'the working class as we perceive it today . . . is a well-founded historical construction' (Bourdieu, 1987:9). Can we say the same about the class (or 'group' – notice Bourdieu's equivocation between these two terms) of 'women'?

There is an immediate problem in that women and men occupy very different positions in social space, depending on their socio-economic class, their marital status, 'race'. 'Objectively', the sociologist may monitor and note the gendered characteristics of women and men, both in terms of their positioning

48

within the labour market, their holdings of cultural capital, their gender-habitus, and so on. Interestingly, Bourdieu limits himself to this level of analysis by and large, in his book length study of masculine domination – to women as occupants of positions among the dominated in social space and as bearers of a feminine habitus that signifies subjection (Bourdieu, 2001). But their status as the dominated gender does not cluster them together within his map of social space. We might usefully compare women with Bourdieu's category of 'cultural producers', those whose holdings of cultural capital are high. In terms of *class* hierarchies, he refers to them as 'the dominated fraction of the dominant class'. Cultural producers, however, have their own dedicated position within social space, as a differentiated sub-field of power (Bourdieu, 1993). But because gender, and gender-hierarchies of domination occur at every level of the general social field, we cannot speak as readily of 'the dominated gender of the dominant class'. There is no sub-field of gender: of gender-domination, gender power.

Bourdieu touches only in passing the forms of mobilization, or 'gender class formation', achieved through feminism and the various women's movements. Most of his book documents instead the characteristic forms of symbolic violence that women suffer. He characterizes features of 'the feminine habitus'[9] and documents the effects that this habitus trails in the lives of women, including feminists, who are trying to escape from or ameliorate this form of domination.[10]

Bourdieu is reserved at best about the status of feminism and the women's movement. Possibly he considers, perhaps with good reason, that the 'class' or status group of women would have to be understood to be but weakly founded, unlike the English working class that provides his paradigm case. If the 'classing' of women as a gender group rests upon the work of creating recognized plenipotentiaries or representatives, in Bourdieu's terms, then there is little in Bourdieu to suggest that he considers that this work of representation has been taken very far as yet.

Bourdieu has little to say about feminism as a political movement, then, but quite a lot to say about the positioning of women in social space, in relation both to the labour market (used as an *indicator* of holdings of economic capital), and of the 'economy of symbolic goods' (cultural and symbolic capital). Leslie McCall (1992) discusses the reservation that many feminists have expressed concerning Bourdieu, in particular, that he perceives gender to be only secondary as a structuring principle of the social field. She offers an interesting reading of this: that gender is 'hidden', 'unofficial', 'real'. On this reading its 'secondary' status does not diminish and possibly even enhances its significance. It is dispersed across the social field, but its organizing principle is pervasive and, as Bourdieu insists, naturalized, doxic, and deeply structuring.

It is important to note that Bourdieu is at least as close to Max Weber as he is to Marx in his account of the double articulation of social space. The economy of symbolic goods is a field of *power* relations. Position holders, whether individuals, families, or other joint units, struggle to increase their overall holdings of cultural and symbolic capital, and high holdings enable the exercise of power over those with less, as well as resources to provide some defence, however circumscribed, against domination, against symbolic violation. 'Culture', in other words, is not superstructural, but is a resource in power relationships, power struggles that are specific to this particular 'economy'. Bourdieu's whole discussion of women and men as 'gender classes' focuses on the economy of symbolic goods, and this would suggest that he sees genders as status groups rather than as classes. However the two 'economies' are connected, as they were for Max Weber. In the economy of symbolic goods, women play a critical role. Bourdieu follows Lévi-Strauss in identifying women as bearers in their persons of embodied cultural capital, prizes that circulate in the exchanges of the marriage market, and therefore cultural *objects*, but also sees them as key functionaries and agents in the capital holding strategies of families, kin, ethnic group, etc, as regards cultural, social, and symbolic capital, and it is here that his work on women and gender is most interesting.

Bourdieu makes some cautious comments on the political struggle for sex equality towards the close of his study of masculine domination, and these reveal, perhaps, why Bourdieu is so reserved about feminism and women's movements:

> [T]hese struggles are liable to reinforce the effects of another form of fictitious universalism, *by favouring firstly women drawn from the same regions of social space as the men who currently occupy the dominant positions* (Bourdieu, 2001:117, emphasis added).

Bridget Fowler spells out what is implied here in a series of cautionary 'what ifs':

> What if we have become so mesmerized by stories of *women's* progress or its limits that we fail to notice the increasing polarization of class inequalities going on behind our backs, and the indirect contribution of women's work to this, through the combining of high salaries at the service class level? (Fowler, 2003:482).

Fowler views the evidence that the women's movement and feminism may have accrued 'profits' not only to those women best positioned to reap the benefits, but also for the dominant class as a whole, viz-a-viz their relationship to the dominated socio-economic class. Inequalities of social class have deepened and widened. The view that the 'advance' of women has been the advance of women of the dominant class and of the class to which they belong, and that it has been achieved at the expense of the working class as a whole, but especially working class men, is one that is being voiced with increasing frequency (Coward, 1999). And Fowler also draws attention to the uncomfortable facts of female-female domination across the lines of class, drawing here on the work of Bridget Anderson (2000) on the new class of female domestic labourers (see also Ehrenreich and Hochschild, 2003).

'Materialism' always carries the danger of representing the power that is rooted in economic relations as somehow 'more real' than symbolic power. But if Bourdieu establishes anything it is the deep power of *symbolic* violence to inflict harm, pain, injury. For Bourdieu, there is a close relationship, though not one of dependency, between economic power and symbolic power, although it is true that he does not place them face to face on a level playing field so to speak, in his 'social field': there are hierarchical relationships from left to right[11] on Bourdieu's map of social space (Honneth, 1986) – with the holders of economic capital identified as 'the dominant fraction of the dominant class', and holders of cultural capital as 'the dominated fraction of the dominant class'. But symbolic violence, the currency that circulates in the economy of symbolic goods, structures relationships of *domination*. It is important to remember this when rehearsing the manner in which changes that have altered the balance of power in relation to gender in that other (dominant) economy, mainly through the enhanced access of women to the labour market, may have increased the inequities that structure social class relationships in social space, when class is reckoned in terms of *household* or family, rather than individual holdings of economic capital.

We should not lose sight of the symbolic violence – leaving aside the physical violence whose toll in suffering and deprivation in the lives of women shows no sign of abating – that is inflicted on women by virtue of their sexed identity. While the slogan of 'sisterhood' notoriously papered over the differences that separate women from one another, there are still striking examples (as Bourdieu himself argues in his study of masculine domination) of similarities across great differences of class, space and history. I want to end by placing side by side two testimonies that may be read in terms of these similarities in the strategies used by the dominant and by the dominated 'gender classes', one from a middle-aged contract worker in the Colombian flower industry towards the close of the 20th century whose father was a peasant share-cropper, the other an older professional woman whose father was a successful small businessman, each speaking of their childhood experiences:

Amaranta's testimony

> My father used to say 'even if we have our clothes stitched in pieces, even if we don't have two pairs of shoes, the important thing in life is to eat well', and he didn't give us clothes or was concerned about us studying, nothing like that, everything he got was to be spent on food. My mother used to sell our food to buy us clothes and school books, and everything to study. It was funny because he didn't realise how she managed to get all these things for us. She used to take little by little from the bean and maize sacks until she had her own sack and then she would give it to sell in the market in somebody else's name (Madrid, 2003:143).

Ann's testimony

> My father had many close friends in Germany, and after WWII he wished to help them. But clothing was rationed and required coupons. My mother, with eight children at that time, was entirely dependent on my father to feed and clothe all of us. He greatly relished his food, and as a result, we never wanted in this respect. But there

was never enough money for new clothes. As the fifth child, and the third in a series of 5 girls, hand-me-downs were the norm. Rich in clothing coupons she could not afford to use, my mother sold them to my father, telling him they had been acquired on the black market. So he unwittingly bought his own children's clothing coupons, enabling my mother to replenish our meagre collective stock (Personal communication).

While access to the labour market, or to the 'public patriarchy' of the welfare state, would have given these two women additional resources for resistance in their struggle against gender domination, differences of class would channel the forms of employment open to them, leaving, still, a gulf between them. But across vast differences of class, 'race' and ethnicity, time, geographical location, culture and language then, there are striking similarities in these two stories: in the exercise of domestic patriarchal power, and of maternal resistance using the weapons of stealth and subterfuge. Bourdieu recognizes the weapons that women use to fight their corner and to get some little room for manoeuvre, but he cites the familiar saw that 'the weapons of the weak are weak weapons' (Bourdieu, 2001:32). Indeed they are, if we are willing to count only the power of radical transformation. But they were powerful enough in both cases to ensure that these mothers' daughters had access to some small, basic share of 'cultural capital'. It remains true nevertheless that to relieve this form of gender domination may have unintended consequences from the point of view of social class inequalities.

Conclusion

In conclusion I want to draw attention to a problem that troubles me. Whether conceptualized as class, status group, or series, the analyses offered by all of the social constructionist feminists, and by sociologists such as Bourdieu, run into difficulties insofar as they do not include in the equation the sharp sexual division of labour in human reproduction. Moi comes closest to opening up the space for this, but she scarcely touches on this issue. And while I agree with her that biological differences between the sexes do not have any necessary and relentless *consequences*, no categorical imperatives for the way in which social relations and institutions are organized, I would want to make the point the other way round: the manner in which we organize those institutions and social relations has powerful effects upon the situation of many women. It follows that the feminist project ignores sexual difference and the social relations of reproduction at its peril. If women constitute a class, it is a class differentiated not only along the lines of 'race', socio-economic class, sexuality – the three 'differences' that are most commonly recognized – but also differentiated by those who become, willy nilly or by choice, the mothers of children and those that do not.

Attention to the level of 'biological exigencies' is critical, then, for an effective feminist politics and scholarship, and I do not find much evidence of this attention within the militantly social constructionist approaches which have formed my own thinking and with which I have great sympathy. Taking these social relations into account, the analyses offered here might have to change. For example, the concept of 'gender as seriality', at least as developed by Young (1995) does not seem to account for the phenomenon noted earlier by Young herself, the 'thrown-ness' of social groups, (a concept borrowed from Heidegger) and the identities they carry (Young, 1990:46). We are 'thrown' by our sexed bodies into our gender identity. Anyone with a female body, as Moi insists, following Beauvoir, is a woman 'from the moment she is born until the moment she dies'. Our female bodies are our 'situation'. Whether we are 'called' into gendered identities/politics through being constituted as groups or on the basis of transient seriality, only *women* can be 'called' *as* women. But women may become part of a gender-series or status group on a differential basis: mothers, 'childfree', professional women, unpaid carers, intellectual women, etc. *Pace* the concerns of materialist feminism, and of Bourdieu, it probably remains true that the impulse behind the WLM was broader than these more limited forms of mobilization, therefore more akin to class mobilization. Short of this, whether we opt for a 'politics of recognition' or a 'politics of redistribution', we shall be obliged to weigh very carefully the consequences of any transformations in either the economic order or the status/cultural order in terms of the differential effects such transformations may have for different categories of women.[12]

To re-centre the discussion on the social relations of reproduction is to introduce an actor that has been described by John O'Neill as an implausible candidate for the status of 'the individual': the child (O'Neill 1994). O'Neil is passionate in his commitment to 'the civic commons', to a 'thick' form of sociality. But his discussions of women and feminism illustrate only too well the problem of more collective subjectivities, from which this paper started.

Notes

1 Mike Savage (2000) has argues that the individual, and the individualization thesis do not have to be specified in a manner which makes the concept of social class redundant, but rather that social class has its effects through individuals and individualization. In this he is in important part influenced by Bourdieu.

2 Giddens centres the quest, dating as far back as the idea of romantic love, for 'the pure relationship'. It is interesting to compare this concept with Bourdieu's footnote encomium to love in *Masculine Domination* (2002:109–112). I added a somewhat caustic footnote on this to my 2000 paper, and must remain sceptical in the face of Fowler's claim of great significance for this encomium, on the grounds that it provides an alternative to the systematic and relentless presentation of social relations in terms of hierarchy and domination, of which he is often accused.

3 Savage, one of the editors of the Crompton *et al* collection, articulates elsewhere a position that attempts to keep together in the same frame both class analysis *and* 'the cultural' (Savage, 2000).

4 It is interesting that the radical political lesbian slogan 'sleeping with the enemy', was taken as the title for a popular film starring Julia Roberts in 1991. In a forthright and contentious attack on heterosexual feminists, this was one accusation that was levied at them (Leeds Revolutionary Feminists, 1981). Heterosexual feminists were in effect, (gender)-class traitors.

5 The figure of the handmaid in Margaret Attwood's novel, *The Handmaid's Tale*, might stand as exemplar for the position of the heterosexual woman engaged in heterosexual exchanges in the account offered by Wittig.
6 The literature on 'body-work' is by now extensive, and is informed by other approaches: by Foucault and by poststructuralist theories of the body. But French and associated materialist feminism made a distinctive contribution to this line of analysis that still informs this whole enterprise, often in conjunction with other approaches.
7 Interestingly, Delphy speaks of women as a *caste*, which for Weber was a status rather than a class category.
8 The WLM had a different concept of 'leadership' and this is perhaps best expressed by *Beyond the Fragments* (Rowbotham, Segal and Wainwright, 1979).
9 Often it must be said in terms that will be very familiar to those who have worked over a longer span of time in this field.
10 The habitus encompasses embodied femininity, and there has been some discussion among feminists using Bourdieu as to whether femininity ought to be counted as a form of 'cultural capital'. Moi (1999) thinks that *sexual status* should and does count in the struggles within the economy of symbolic goods and within labour-market struggles, but it usually counts as *negative* cultural capital. Skeggs understands femininity to be 'cultural capital', something that may be cultivated to yield certain 'profits', but in a manner that is deeply problematic for its holders (Skeggs, 1997).
11 In Bourdieu's work on cultural production (1993) these are transposed, so that 'economic capital' is on the right, cultural capital on the left.
12 Fraser's 'thought experiment' using Weberian ideal types, comprises a systematic consideration of a whole range of political strategies that feminists need to consider 'after the family wage'. One of her principles is that, at least when we are considering this matter in principle rather than pragmatically, we need to identify strategies that do not involve trading off one gain for a loss or compromise elsewhere (Fraser, 1997).

References

Adkins, L. (1995) *Gendered Work: Family, Sexuality and the Labour Market*. Buckingham: Open University Press.
Adkins, L. and Merchant, V. (eds) (1996) *Sexualizing the Social*. Basingstoke: Macmillan.
Adkins, L. and Skeggs, B. (eds) (2004) *Feminism After Bourdieu*. Oxford: Blackwell/The Sociological Review.
Anderson, B. (2000) *Doing the Dirty Work: the Global Politics of Domestic Labour*. London: Zed Books.
Armangaud, F. and Ghaïss, J. (1993) 'Pierre Bourdieu: Grand Temoin?' in *Nouvelle Questions Féministes* 14(3): 83–88. (Abridged English translation with C Delphy, 'Liberty, Equality . . . but most of all Fraternity' *Trouble and Strife* 31: Summer 1995.)
Barrett, M. (1988) *Women's Oppression Today: The Marxist Encounter*. Second Edition. London: Verso.
Barrett, M. (1984) 'Rethinking Women's Oppression: A Reply to Brenner and Ramas' *New Left Review* 146: 123–128.
Barrett, M. and McIntosh, M. (1979) 'Christine Delphy: Towards a Materialist Feminism' *Feminist Review* 1: 95–105.
Barrett, M. and McIntosh, M. (1980) 'The "Family Wage": Some Problems for Socialists and Feminists' *Capital and Class* 11: 51–72.
Barrett, M. and Phillips, A. (eds) (1992) *Destabilizing Theory: Contemporary Feminist Debates*. Cambridge: Polity Press.
Beck, U. and Beck-Gernsheim, E. (2001) *Individualization: Institutionalized Individualism and its Social and Political Consequences*. London: Sage.

Bourdieu, P. (1987) 'What Makes a Social Class? On the Theoretical and Practical Existence of Groups' *Berkeley Journal of Sociology* 32: 1–17.

Bourdieu, P. (1990) 'La domination masculine', *Actes de la Recherche en Sciences Sociales* 84: 2–31.

Bourdieu, P. (1993) *The Field of Cultural Production: Essays on Art and Literature*. Cambridge: Polity Press.

Bourdieu, P. (2001) *Masculine Domination*. Cambridge: Polity Press.

Brenner, M. and Ramas, M. (1984) 'Rethinking Women's Oppression' *New Left Review* 144: 33–71.

Butler, J. (1986) 'Sex and Gender in Simone de Beauvoir's Second Sex' *Yale French Studies* 72: 35–49.

Butler, J. (1990) *Gender Trouble: Feminism and the Subversion of Identity*. New York and London: Routledge.

Butler, J. (1993) *Bodies That Matter*. New York and London: Routledge.

Butler, J. (1998) 'Merely Cultural' *New Left Review* 227: 33–44.

Callinicos, A. (1999) 'Social Theory Put to the Test of Politics: Pierre Bourdieu and Anthony Giddens' *New Left Review* 236: 77–102.

Castells, M. (1997) *The Information Age: Economy, Society and Culture. Vol 11: The Power of Identity*. Oxford: Blackwell.

Coward, R. (1999) *Sacred Cows: Is Feminism Relevant to the New Millennium?* London: Harper Collins.

Crompton, R. et al (eds) (2000) *Renewing Class Analysis*. Oxford: Blackwell/The Sociological Review.

Dahrendorf, R. (1957) *Class and Class Conflict in Industrial Society*. Stanford, CA: Stanford University Press.

Delphy, C. (1984) *Close to Home: A Materialist Analysis of Women's Oppression*. London: Hutchinson.

Ehrenreich, C. and Hochschild, A. (eds) (2003) *Global Woman: Nannies, Maids and Sex Workers in the New Economy*. London: Granta.

Fowler, B. (2003) 'Reading Pierre Bourdieu's *Masculine Domination*: Notes Towards an Intersectional Analysis of Gender, Culture and Class' *Cultural Studies* 17(3/4): 468–494.

Fraser, N. (1997) *Justice Interruptus: Critical Reflections on the "Postsocialist" Condition*. New York and London: Routledge.

Fraser, N. (1998) 'Heterosexism, Misrecognition and Capitalism' *New Left Review* 228: 140–149.

Fraser, N. and Honneth, A. (2003) *Redistribution or Recognition? A Political-Philosophical Exchange*. London: Verso.

Giddens, A. (1992) *The Transformation of Intimacy*. Cambridge: Polity.

Goldthorpe, J. (1983) 'Women and Class Analysis: In Defence of the Conventional View' *Sociology* 17(4): 465–488.

Hennessy, R. (1993) *Materialist Feminism and the Politics of Discourse*. New York and London: Routledge.

Hennessy, R. and Ingraham, C. (eds) (1997) *Materialist Feminism: A Reader in Class, Difference, and Women's Lives*. New York and London: Routledge.

Honneth, A. (1986) 'The Fragmented World of Symbolic Forms: Reflections on Pierre Bourdieu's Sociology of Culture' *Theory, Culture and Society* 3(3) 55–66.

Jackson, S. (1999) *Heterosexuality in Question*. London: Sage.

Jackson, S. (2001) 'Why a Materialist Feminism is (Still) Possible – and Necessary' *Women's Studies International Forum* 24(3–4): 283–293.

Landry, D. and McClean, G. (1993) *Materialist Feminisms*. Oxford: Blackwell.

Leeds Revolutionary Feminists (1981) 'Political Lesbianism: The Case Against Heterosexuality' in Leeds Revolutionary Feminists *Love Your Enemy: The Debate Between Heterosexual Feminism and Political Lesbianism*. London: Onlywoman Press.

Lovell, T. (2000) 'Thinking Feminism With and Against Bourdieu' *Feminist Theory* 1(1): 11–32

Lovell, T. (2003) 'Resisting With Authority: Historical Specificity, Agency and the Performative Self' *Theory, Culture and Society* 20(1): 1–17.

Madrid, G. (2003) *Working with Flowers: An Analysis of the Social, Cultural and Ethical Relations in Colombia and the UK*. Warwick: University of Warwick. Unpublished PhD thesis.

Malos, E. (ed.) (1980) *The Politics of Housework*. London: Allison and Busby.

Marx, K. (1970) *Capital*. Volume 1. London: Lawrence and Wishart.

Marx, K. and Engels, F. (1965) *The German Ideology*. London: Lawrence and Wishart.

McCall, L. (1992) 'Does Gender *Fit*? Bourdieu, Feminism, and Conceptions of Social Order' *Theory and Society* 21: 837–67.

Mitchell, J. (2003) *Siblings: Sex and Violence*. Cambridge: Polity.

Moi, T. (1987) *French Feminist Thought: A Reader*. Oxford: Blackwell.

Moi, T. (1991) 'Appropriating Bourdieu: Feminist Theory and Pierre Bourdieu's Sociology of Culture *New Literary History* 22: 1017–1049.

Moi, T. (1999) *What is a Woman? And Other Essays*. Oxford: Oxford University Press.

Oakley, A. (1981) *Subject Women*. London: Martin Robertson.

O'Neill, J. (1994) *The Missing Child in Liberal Theory*. Toronto: University of Toronto Press.

Pateman, C. (1988) *The Sexual Contract*. Cambridge: Polity Press.

Rowbotham, S., Segal, L. and Wainwright, H. (1979) *Beyond the Fragments: Feminism and the Making of Socialism*. London: Islington Community Press.

Savage, M. (2000) *Class Analysis and Social Transformation*. Buckingham: Open University Press.

Sayers, J. (1982) *Biological Politics*. London: Tavistock.

Sayers, J. et al (1987) *Engels Revisited: New Feminist Essays*. London and New York: Tavistock.

Skeggs, B. (1997) *Formations of Class and Gender: Becoming Respectable*. London: Sage.

Smart, C. (1994) '*Transformations in Sociology: Who'd be a Feminist Sociologist in the 1990s?* Leeds: Leeds University.

Stanworth, M. (1984) 'Women and Class Analysis: A Reply to John Goldthrope' *Sociology* 18(2): 159–170.

Tabet, P. (1996) 'Natural Fertility, Forced Reproduction' in D. Leonard and L. Adkins (eds) *Sex in Question: French Materialist Feminism*. London: Taylor and Francis.

Thompson, E. P. (1963) *The Making of the English Working Class*. London: Gollancz.

Urmson, J. O. and Ree, J. (1989) *The Concise Encyclopaedia of Western Philosophy and Philosophers*. London: Unwin Hyman.

Wittig, M. (1992) *The Straight Mind and Other Essays*. New York and London: Harvester Wheatsheaf.

Witz, A. (2000) 'Whose Body Matters? Feminist Sociology and the Corporeal Turn in Sociology and Feminism' *Body and Society* 6(2): 1–24.

Young, I. M. (1990) *Justice and the Politics of Difference*. Princeton, NJ: Princeton University Press.

Young, I. M. (1995) 'Gender and Seriality: Thinking About Women as a Social Collective' in L. Nicholson and S. Seidman (eds) *Social Postmodernism: Beyond Identity Politics*. Cambridge: Cambridge University Press.

Young, I. M. (1997) 'Unruly Categories: A Critique of Nancy Fraser's Dual Systems Theory' *New Left Review* 222: 147–160.

Yuval-Davis, N. (1997) *Gender and Nation*. London: Sage.

Gendering Bourdieu's concepts of capitals? Emotional capital, women and social class

Diane Reay

Introduction

Although Bourdieu deals extensively with gender differences in his work, far less space is given to the emotions. This chapter attempts to address this lacuna by extending Bourdieu's concept of capitals to the realm of emotions. While Bourdieu never refers explicitly to emotional capital in his own work, he does describe practical and symbolic work which generates devotion, generosity and solidarity, arguing that 'this work falls more particularly to women, who are responsible for maintaining relationships' (Bourdieu, 1998:68). This chapter takes on-going research into mothers' involvement in their children's education as a case study for developing the concept of emotional capital. It describes the intense emotional engagement the vast majority of mothers had with their children's education. The chapter also explores the extent to which emotional capital may be understood as a specifically gendered capital, in particular, by examining the impact of social class on gendered notions of emotional capital.

The background: Bourdieu's concept of capitals

In this chapter I am attempting to unravel a number of feminist conundrums and at the same time develop a theoretical understanding of emotional capital. I am trying to extend Bourdieu's concept of capitals into the murky waters of the emotions. While Bourdieu himself never mentions emotional capital, he does develop an extensive theoretical understanding of other forms of capital. Cultural capital is Bourdieu's best known concept. It is primarily a relational concept and exists in conjunction with other forms of capital. Therefore, it cannot be understood in isolation from the other forms of capital, economic, symbolic and social capital, that together constitute advantage and disadvantage in society. Social capital is generated through social processes between the family and wider society and is made up of social networks. Economic capital is wealth either inherited or generated from interactions between the individual and the economy, while symbolic capital is manifested in individual prestige and personal qualities, such as authority and charisma (Bourdieu, 1985). In addition to the interconnection of the types of capital, Bourdieu envisages a process in which one form of capital can be transformed into another (Bourdieu, 1986). For example, economic capital can be converted into cultural capital, while cultural capital can be translated into social capital. These, however, are complex processes which are not straightforwardly achieved.

The overall capital of different fractions of the social classes is composed of differing proportions of the various kinds of capital (Bourdieu, 1993). It is mainly in relation to the middle and upper classes that Bourdieu elaborates this variation in volume and composition of the different types of capital. For example, individuals can be adjacent to each other in social space yet have very different ratios of economic to cultural capital. These differences are a consequence of complex relationships between individual and class trajectories. Moreover, the value attached to the different forms of capital are stakes in the struggle between different class fractions. Bourdieu uses the analogy of a game of roulette. Some individuals:

> those with lots of red tokens and a few yellow tokens, that is lots of economic capital and a little cultural capital will not play in the same way as those who have many yellow tokens and a few red ones. . . . the more yellow tokens (cultural capital) they have, the more they will stake on the yellow squares (the educational system). (Bourdieu, 1993:34).

For Bourdieu all goods, whether material or symbolic have an economic value if they are in short supply and considered worthy of being sought after in a particular social formation. He describes a process in which 'classes' invest their cultural capital in academic settings (Bourdieu, 1977). Because the upper, and to a lesser extent, the middle classes, have the means of investing their cultural capital in the optimum educational setting, their investments are extremely profitable. From this perspective educational establishments can be viewed as mechanisms for generating social profits (Bourdieu and Passeron, 1977). However, cultural capital is not just about the relationship of different social groupings to the educational system, it is also about the centrality of the family to any understanding of cultural reproduction (Reay, 1998a). Bourdieu, in his article co-authored with Boltanski, states 'the educational system depends less directly on the demands of the production system than on the demands of reproducing the family group.' (Bourdieu and Boltanski, 1981:142–3).

Cultural capital is primarily transmitted through the family. It is from the family that children derive modes of thinking, types of dispositions, sets of meaning and qualities of style. These are then assigned a specific social value and status in accordance with what the dominant classes label as the most valued cultural capital (Giroux, 1983). Integral, therefore to cultural capital, is the potential for a complex analysis of the interactions between home background, the processes of schooling and a child's educational career. According to Nash:

> Through Bourdieu's work we have been able to reconstruct a theory of the family and recover the centrality of family resources to educational differentiation within a

radical context which allays the fears of a retreat to cultural deficit theory (Nash, 1990:446).

Families, therefore, provide the link between individual and class trajectory and, as such Wilkes asserts, 'should be the units of study for class analysis' (Wilkes, 1990:127). However, while the concept of cultural capital implies the centrality of the family, Bourdieu also seems to be recognizing the centrality of the mother:

> It is because the cultural capital that is effectively transmitted within the family itself depends not only on the quantity of cultural capital, itself accumulated by spending time, that the domestic group possess, but also on the usable time (particularly in the form of mother's free time) available to it (Bourdieu, 1986:253).

Feminist research on the domestic division of labour would also point to the mother as the parent who expends the most time on childcare (Graham, 1993; Oakley, 1993; Lawler, 2000) and thus the parent most directly involved in the generation of cultural capital. Childcare is made up of a complex amalgam of practical, educational and emotional work (James, 1989; Oakley, 1993; Reay, 1998b). Within the sphere of parental involvement in education recent research has highlighted the gendered nature of parental involvement in terms of both the practical and educational work involved (David, 1993; David *et al*, 1993; Reay and Ball, 1998). However, very little consideration has been paid to emotional involvement, although a growing body of both sociological and psychological research points to the gendered nature of emotion work in personal relationships (Erickson, 1993; Duncombe and Marsden, 1993; Reay *et al*, 1998; Wharton and Erickson, 1995; Zajdow, 1995). This research shows that within families, women engage in emotional labour far more than most men, taking responsibility for maintaining the emotional aspects of family relationships, responding to others' emotional states and also acting to alleviate distress. As Nicky James (1989:27) asserts, managing the family's emotional life requires 'anticipation, planning, timetabling and trouble-shooting'. Bourdieu, in *Masculine Domination* (2001:77), writes that 'it has often been observed that women fulfil a cathartic, quasi-therapeutic function in regulating men's emotional lives, calming their anger, helping them accept the injustices and difficulties of life'. In this chapter, however, it is the quasi-therapeutic role women perform in relation to their children that I want to focus on. It was this emotional management aspect of mothers' involvement in their children's education that emerged time and again in the research projects that I have been involved in over the past ten years. As Steph Lawler (2000:125) points out, 'children's needs, and especially their emotional needs, are the point of motherhood'. Emotions within the family have traditionally been conceptualized as standing outside economic interpretations within both mainstream theorizing and feminisms. One of the few feminist exceptions is Diane Bell's work. Bell (1990) argues that an economy of emotion operates within families and that it is the responsibility of women. She equates mothering with book-keeping, arguing that one of the major roles of mothering is to balance the family's emotional budget.

The genesis of emotional capital

While Bourdieu never refers explicitly to emotional capital in his own work, he does highlight the key role of the mother in affective relationships. Writing of the practical and symbolic work which 'generates devotion, generosity and solidarity', Bourdieu argues that 'this work falls more particularly to women, who are responsible for maintaining relationships' (Bourdieu, 1998:68). It is only over the last twenty years that the view that emotions are somehow outside the remit of sociologists has begun to be challenged (Hochschild, 1983; Jackson, 1993; Duncombe and Marsden, 1993; Williams and Bendelow, 1997). One of the main challenges has come from Helga Nowotny. Nowotny, drawing on Bourdieu's conceptual framework, developed the concept of emotional capital. She saw emotional capital as a variant of social capital, but characteristic of the private, rather than the public sphere (Nowotny, 1981). Emotional capital is generally confined within the bounds of affective relationships of family and friends and encompasses the emotional resources you hand on to those you care about. According to Nowotny, emotional capital constitutes:

> knowledge, contacts and relations as well as access to emotionally valued skills and assets, which hold within any social network characterised at least partly by affective ties (Nowotny, 1981:148).

Unlike the other forms of capital – cultural, economic, social and symbolic which are invariably theorzsed in ungendered ways – Nowotny saw emotional capital as a resource women have in greater abundance than men. Linked to this gendered perspective, however, Nowotny saw emotional capital as developed in adverse circumstances – in response to barriers rather than possibilities. She asserts that the important question we need to ask about gender differences in capital is 'why women have been able to accumulate only certain kinds of capital and why they have been equally limited in converting the capital they have gained into certain other types' (1981:148). So Nowotny recognizes a key difference between emotional and other capitals. Emotional capital gained in the private sector lacks the direct convertibility of other capitals like cultural and economic capital. However, the main consequence of emotional capital's lack of value in the public sector is that it is 'largely used for further family investments in children and husbands' (1981:148). To an extent Nowotny could be seen to be endorsing Bourdieu's analysis of women in their capacity as wives and mothers as capital-bearing objects whose value accrues to the primary groups to which they belong. This, however, plunges us straight into the problematic Terry Lovell (2000) raises in relation to Bourdieu's theory. Such an analysis ties in with understandings that position women as objects rather than subjects in their own right; as means rather than ends! Clearly we have moved on considerably since Bourdieu was writing about masculine domination in the 1960s and 70s and Nowotny about the position of women in Austria in the early 1980s. The contemporary labour market provides many examples of 'women as subjects with capital-accumulating strategies of their own' (Lovell, 2000:38). However, Lovell also writes about 'the cultural housekeeping' undertaken by women of the symbolic, social and cultural capital of their families and their responsibilities for its transmission across generations.

Patricia Allatt has drawn on Nowotny's work in her research into families using the private schooling sector. Her research describes processes in which all the capitals are interwoven in the transfer of privilege – for example, economic capital augmenting social capital, emotional capital compounding cultural capital. She defines emotional capital as 'emotionally valued assets and skills, love and affection, expenditure of time, attention, care and concern'. Thus, emotional capital can be understood as the stock of emotional resources built up over time within families and which children could draw upon. Allatt lists support, patience and commitment as examples of such emotional resources (Allatt, 1993). Her empirical work described 'emotional capital' in the families studied 'particularly in the way mothers devoted their skills gained from their formal education to the advancement of their children' (Allatt, 1993:143).

Nowotny also cites examples of women for whom credentialism is first and foremost about furthering their children's educational advancement rather than their own. However, the most intensive feminist exploration of emotional capital in the domestic sphere is Eva Illouz's (1997) conceptualization of domination and capital as both gendered and classed and I refer to her work extensively in my own attempts to theorize emotional capital.

Difficult emotions: trying to understand mothers' emotional involvement in their children's schooling

In the rest of this chapter I try and work with case study data from three research projects in order to make links between emotional involvement, emotional capital and educational achievement. The first project on mothers' involvement in their children's schooling was carried out between 1993 and 1995, a second on black women and their involvement in supplementary schooling was conducted in 1996, and a third on transition to secondary school conducted between 1997 and 2001. I have referred to existing literature which examines mothering in terms of emotional management; a focus on the emotions of other family members. However, accompanying mothers' attempts to manage children's emotional life in the context of schooling in all three research projects were very powerful emotional responses of their own. One of the strongest impressions I have gained from fieldwork has been of the intense emotions, both positive and negative, permeating mothers' accounts of their children's schooling. Across all three research projects one of the few constants was mothers' emotional involvement in their children's education. The women experienced an extensive range of emotions in relation to their children's schooling. Guilt, anxiety and frustration, as well as empathy and encouragement were the primary motifs of mothers' involvement. Whereas within both Allatt's and Nowotny's conceptualization of emotional capital it is primarily positive emotions that generate profits for families, the first analytic problem I faced was that seemingly positive emotions could sometimes have negative repercussions for children, while apparently negative emotional involvement could spur children on academically.

So, while it would seem logical to view only positive attributes as constitutive of emotional capital, there was no simple correlation between positive emotions and emotional capital. Many of the emotions that mothers felt and communicated to children in the course of supporting their education could have both positive and negative efficacy. Cynthia Burack (1994) writes about how 'the disagreeable passions, and, in particular anger have been problematic for both feminisms and malestream theorizing, especially when they are embodied in women'. I found that anger could communicate to children that the mother had clear expectations of educational performance that she would back up with sanctions and this could result in the child making increased efforts. At other times, it could generate resistance, non-compliance and the break down of communication. Similarly, a mother's anxiety could produce an intense involvement in her child's schooling which communicated to the child the importance of educational success and led to educational progress. It could also result in the child becoming anxious alongside the mother. Some mothers, in particular working-class mothers, gave children positive feedback and support for their educational performance even when class teachers felt the children concerned were either making insufficient effort or were underperforming. Thus the data showed no single pattern of consequences from mothers' emotional involvement. This left me with a conceptual dilemma of how to theorize the relationship between emotional capital, emotional involvement and educational achievement when there appeared to be no clear cut pattern.

However, across differences of class and ethnicity it soon became clear, despite substantial areas of overlap, that emotional involvement was not always a process of transmitting emotional capital from mother to child, although all the mothers were involved in providing children with emotional capital at times. In particular, my research data indicated a very thin dividing line between empathy and over identification when children were experiencing difficulties in school. Many mothers talked poignantly of their concern at children's distress. However, while it was natural for mothers to share in children's feelings of anxiety and unhappiness, if they became too enmeshed in children's distressed feelings they were often left both unable to provide appropriate support and having to deal with a welter of negative feelings of their own. Working-class Maria talked of how difficult it was for her to separate out her extremely distressed feelings about her own educational experience from what was happening currently to Leigh. She felt this enmeshment made it particularly difficult to support Leigh through his own problems:

> When Leigh was having these problems with his reading I kept thinking maybe it's me, maybe it's ME. I think oh here we go again, doubting myself, thinking I'm stupid and I thought now what do I do about it. I find it really difficult helping Leigh with

his reading. . . . I'm the wrong person for it because I'm already angry in myself because of my education and how that sort of progressed, and all the problems I had to go through, all the embarrassment and humiliation. I have ended up screaming and shouting and we've had bad rows about it. I'd have put him off altogether so I've had to back off and let the school take it on. I'm the wrong person to teach him because of the emotional state I get into.

In the excerpt above, Maria's emotions, in particular her intense anxiety, can be seen to be inhibiting the acquisition of both emotional and cultural capital. She talked of a continuing feud between herself and Leigh over whether spellings should be corrected:

I've even got to the point of lying in bed worrying about it, then I'll be up at 1 o'clock in the morning crawling around looking for the tipex and going through the books in his rucksack, correcting his mistakes.

Illouz (1997:56) argues that 'the ability to distance oneself from one's immediate emotional experience is the prerogative of those who have readily available a range of emotional options, who are not overwhelmed by emotional necessity and intensity, and can therefore approach their own self and emotions with the same detached mode that comes from accumulated emotional competence'. She views such a disposition as classed and in particular a skill associated with the 'new' middle classes and their involvement in what Rose (1998) terms 'technologies of the self' and 'the psy industries'. Unsurprisingly, it was primarily working-class women, with negative personal experiences of schooling, who found it extremely hard to generate resources of emotional capital for their child to draw on if they experiencing difficulties in school. Negative emotions, however, did not always result in negative educational repercussions for children.

The efficacy of negative emotions was particularly evident in the project on Black mothers' and supplementary schooling (Reay and Mirza, 1998; Mirza and Reay, 2000) but was a feature of black women's accounts across all three studies. I've tried to bring black feminist theorising together with Bourdieu's concepts in order to make sense of the apparently paradoxical positive returns black mothers seemed to generate from a range of negative responses to mainstream schooling. In 'The Use of Anger: Women responding to Racism' Audre Lorde (1984) links the conceptual and political work of confronting racism with the capacity to be angry and to tolerate and use anger. It was this positive efficacy of anger that black mothers often demonstrated in relation to their children's mainstream schooling in the research on black supplementary schooling. Black mothers appeared to have learnt an awareness of enhancing ways of providing children with emotional support through their own experience of dealing with racism.

Below, I draw on the case study of Cassie, a mother in the Black supplementary school study, in order to illustrate this theoretical point:

Akin was having a crisis at school and it was a very difficult situation. He saw the other boy as being racist but his teacher felt he was provoking the situation. By Friday he just exploded and was really in a rage, crying with anger. For a long time I felt 'Oh my God', then I went up and said 'What's happened?' and he was being blamed by the teacher for something and the teacher didn't believe that he hadn't instigated it and Akin was really hurt. I spent a long time talking it through with him. It was complex because it had to do with racism as well.

Cassie goes on to talk about the intense emotional support she has to provide Akin with to help him deal with the problem, and also her own strong feelings of anxiety and anger when she went to discuss the incident with Akin's class teacher:

I was furious but I knew I couldn't explode. I had to be friendly but firm, make sure that I got across Akin's side of things.

There are parallels here with Gill Crozier's research into black parents involvement in their children's education where she found parents, and in particular mothers, were engaged in resisting discriminatory practices and thus defending their children, rescuing and comforting them in the face of abuse and humiliation (Crozier, 2002). In *In Other Words* Bourdieu writes that habitus 'can also be controlled through the awakening of consciousness and socio-analysis' (Bourdieu, 1990:116). It seems possible from Cassie's and the accounts of other black mothers that this awakening of consciousness and socio-analysis and the emotional capital it generates can be triggered in response to living in a racist society. Yet, there remain problematic issues around seeming to sanitize oppression and its dirty work, this time in relation to ethnicity and race rather than gender. Certainly, black mothers often articulated powerful, politicized understandings of racial oppression and its potential impact on their children, nearly always accompanied with strategies to support their children emotionally and educationally:

I suppose I see because of the National Curriculum that I have to support him in learning which he probably won't get at school which is actually to talk to him about his background, his own identity and the pitfalls that face him as a black boy (Cassie).

The emotional costs for mothers and children

Annette Lareau's research exemplifies the emotional costs to both child and mother of such intense involvement in children's schooling. She describes the symptoms of stress manifested by children, particularly low attainers, in the white middle-class school in her research study. In outlining the case study of Emily, she points out that Emily's mother, unlike her husband, found it impossible to achieve any emotional distance on Emily's underachievement. Instead she felt 'she had failed as a mother in her role of supervising, intervening and compensating for the weaknesses in her daughter's education' (Lareau, 1989:152). The vast majority of men in my research studies also operated in the background. As one father said 'fathers are involved – but at a distance'. Increasing numbers of men may be appropriating femininity and feminine ways of being in order to increase their mobility in the labour market (Adkins, 2002), but in the domestic sphere there seems to be more fixity around who does the mothering with women still taking responsibility for the majority of emotional involvement and emotional management. The women in my research approximated more to Giddens' (1992:200) 'emotional under-labourers of modernity' than to the women in Benjamin and Sullivan's study (1996) who were able to transform their affective role within the family.

While emotional involvement was gendered, however, it did not differ greatly by social class. Yet, as we can see from the example of Maria, working-class women found it more difficult to supply their children with resources of emotional capital than their middle-class counterparts because they were frequently hampered by poverty, negative personal experiences of schooling, insufficient educational knowledge and lack of confidence. We find the same dynamic relationship between the different forms of capital that Allatt writes about in relation to her privileged families but this time operating in a depreciating spiral rather than the one that Allatt describes in which the different forms of capital augment each other (Allatt, 1993). Working-class women were often caught up in a spiral in which low levels of dominant cultural capital, economic capital and social capital all made it relatively difficult to provide their children with the benefits of emotional capital. Class differences also played a part in determining whether mothers could divert their emotional involvement into generating academic profits for their children. Working-class women often lacked the right conditions or context for providing either emotional or dominant cultural capital. That is not the same, however, as saying that working-class mothers did not provide emotional capital through their involvement in schooling; rather it did not go hand in hand with cultural capital to anything like the extent middle-class women's did. Despite disadvantage, there were many examples of working class women's sensitivity, emotional support and encouragement all combining to enhance their children's emotional capital. (See Reay, 2002 for a case study of a white working-class boy whose educational successes in a failing comprehensive school were supported and encouraged by his mother.)

Across class boundaries there was regular marshalling of motivation with mothers encouraging and developing feelings of confidence and enthusiasm in children. Yet, as Maria's account demonstrates, it was far more difficult for the working-class mothers, often dealing with a personal history of academic failure, to generate the same levels of academic confidence and enthusiasm among their children as their middle-class counterparts. I have written about the impact of working-class habitus on mothers' relationships to their children schooling elsewhere (Reay, 1997). History is key here; I suggest that, in common with other forms of capital, there are generational aspects of emotional capital in that reserves are built up in families over time. While working-class Dawn talks in terms of a mother working long hours in the labour market who 'was never there for her and so I found primary school terrifying', middle-class

Lindsey talks of a mother who always encouraged and helped her with her school work: 'she was always certain all her daughters could do anything they set their minds to'.

Much of the data demonstrate the costs to mothers of their emotional involvement in their children's schooling. They are using up a lot of time and emotional energy in their support which, as I have demonstrated above, sometimes brings them into conflict rather than harmony with their children. They are often unsupported in this emotional work by male partners (David *et al*, 1994; Reay, 1995). Involvement in children's schooling generated intense class anxiety, in particular, for some of the middle class mothers who expressed fears that credential inflation and increased marketization within education was making it more difficult than in the past for children from middle-class backgrounds to attain appropriate jobs (Jordan *et al*, 1994; Brown, 1995). However, there were also costs for children and, in relation to emotional capital, if there are hidden costs for the child then emotional capital can be seen to be depreciated. A recurring theme throughout the elaboration of middle-class mothers' work in relation to schooling is maternal control. As Liliana told me:

> He is too tired even to do his homework. My husband said to me 'Just let him be', but I have to force him. I have to force him. I know it's awful but I have to and he hates it.

Virginia Morrow writes about the possible negative impacts on children's self-esteem of the current climate of increasing academic pressure in education, arguing that as a consequence schooling may enhance children's cultural capital while simultaneously depreciating their emotional capital (Morrow, 1999). In the research projects on mothers' involvement in schooling and secondary school transition there were numerous examples of familial strategies for enhancing cultural capital operating to deplete emotional capital. The middle-class mothers in the sample were far more likely than their working-class counterparts to see academic work in the home as an area which was not open to negotiation. Freedom was perceived to be a consequence of self actualization. One outcome was little apparent freedom in the lives of their school-aged children (Reay, 1998c). Freedom seldom went further than the freedom to choose between dance or drama classes, learning the piano instead of the violin, and socializing on a Friday rather than a Saturday. This lack of freedom can only be made sense of in connection with the notion of future 'choices' that educational credentials allow. Here we need to evoke the ideal of the 'free' bourgeois subject, a subject that must be intensely regulated as a child in order to achieve these 'freedoms' as an adult – a contradiction entirely hidden in discourses of mothering and child-rearing. We can see graphically this curtailment of freedom and the emotional costs for children in the case study of Sally, one of the middle-class children in the transitions project I carried out in collaboration with Helen Lucey (see Lucey and Reay, 2002). Sally's mother, herself extremely anxious about the local secondary school market, decided to enter Sally for four selective school exams without telling her:

> My mum said, 'Sally would you mind doing a couple of tests to get into a good secondary school?' and I'm like 'Okay but how many is a couple?' and she says 'four' and I'm like 'seriously?' At first I thought she must be joking. (Sally)

Sally actually gets a place in one of the four selective schools, the only one of the sixteen middle-class children in the sample who sat the test to do so. However, despite Sally's success her mother is aware that taking the tests and waiting for the decision has had emotional costs for Sally:

> I think it's taken its toll and I think she's expressing it physically; she's never had so many colds and whatever as this year. I think she's somatizing actually. But she can't feel that she can go along with all the kids at school and just be happy. She's got to think that she might go to Longfield House. She's in a very difficult position really. As a parent I could say well ok we'll settle for Hamlyn but I just don't think, taking a longer view, that I could feel happy with that decision so I'm prepared to sit with the anxiety (Sally's mother).

Sally's mother acknowledges that Sally is suffering and is sensitive to this. At the same time her 'longer view' allows her to deny the emotional costs to her daughter in the present. It is impossible to look at the relationship between emotional involvement and emotional capital without examining the ways in which mothers conceptualized children's happiness. Here there were key class differences. While all the working-class mothers talked frequently about their child's happiness in the present, apart from a small number of women with children with special educational needs, the middle-class mothers, like Sally's mother, were much more likely to be working with a conceptualization of future happiness. Their concept of happiness was not just based on children's current mental state but was also premised on a projection of what would constitute happiness in adulthood – this was seen to be highly dependent on educational success (Allatt, 1993; Jordan, Redley and James, 1994). But, with its clean, rational focus, the concept of deferred gratification misses out all the emotional messiness of the here and now. Instead it launders the emotional conflicts and costs that are occurring on a range of different levels: the mother-daughter conflict of desires, the anxiety, worry and fear Sally is having to carry and the internal psychic conflict being defended against by both mother and daughter. A year later Sally is having to get up at 6.30 to get to her prestigious secondary school and comments that 'I have to go so early and get back so late it's really stressful and tiring'. Her mother rationalizes this:

> I think it's an enormous waste of time and energy and it's an enormous shame, but I was prepared to contemplate enormous journeys for her if it meant she got into a school with a good offer academically. I felt the trade-off was so much better, that she'd get so much more out of it.

The term 'trade-off' is telling here because, through the lens of Bourdieu's concept of capitals, this is exactly what is happening – emotional capital is being forfeited in the pursuit of cultural capital. There is a further irony here. Sally's mother, a psychotherapist, may be marshalling 'the enhanced emotional competences of the new middle classes to achieve an educational profit' but lurking behind educational gains are emotional losses.

The problematic of emotional wellbeing

The case study of Sally and her mother suggest that emotional capital cannot be linked conceptually to educational success in any clear-cut way. A number of the mothers seem to pursue educational success at the expense of their child's emotional wellbeing. These women were primarily middle-class but also included a small but growing number of working-class mothers. As a consequence, in some of the mothers' accounts children's educational success carried an emotional cost rather than a profit, enhancing children's cultural capital while depreciating their emotional capital. In contrast, a majority of the working-class women and a few of the middle-class mothers made a distinction between children's emotional wellbeing and educational success, prioritizing the former. This distinction highlights a problem which permeates all of Bourdieu's concepts of capital; they are underpinned by an assumption of middle-class practices and attitudes as normative and within middle-class frames of reference, academic success is given primacy as a goal. The norm was for middle-class mothers to be working extremely hard on their child's educational attainment. Notions of voluntarism rarely entered their accounts. They all expressed intense anxiety about the increasingly competitive nature of the local secondary school market and the consequences in terms of extra educational work with children. This continuous pressure on children to succeed academically needs to be set against the positive impression of highly motivated conscientious pupils that the middle-class children gave in the classroom context. In contrast, we have working-class Lisa who sees her daughter's emotional wellbeing in terms of freedom from academic pressure:

> I don't approve of parents who put lots of pressure on their kids, you know telling them they should be a doctor or a solicitor. Who are they doing it for? Not the kid. They're doing it for themselves. What I want is for Lucy to be happy.

This data presented me with a second feminist conundrum. I was faced by extensive evidence of mainly middle-class mothers beavering away at the sort of practices sanctified and enshrined in government educational policy. There are similar processes at play here to those Lisa Adkins (2002) found in relation to sexuality and gender. In this case the idealization and normalization of the relations of privilege and exclusion are mobilised in relation to class and education. And all too often the flip side to this reification of middle-class practices as normative has been the relegation of working-class mothering to the realms of deficit and pathology. I have struggled with the problematic of how to theorize beyond middle-class norms as an academic researcher; of how to hold on to different ways of being and acting that are equally valid and appropriate for the context in which they are being enacted. I don't feel Bourdieu achieves this but neither does the vast amount of feminisms. Although Illouz (1997:52) is careful not to develop a classed binary of idealisation and deficit, she does argue that middle-class women with the emotional and verbal habitus necessary to achieve dominant definitions of intimacy are far more likely to attain emotional wellbeing for themselves and their families than their working-class counterparts.

My own analytic response has been twofold. Firstly, to argue that, unlike the other capitals, cultural, economic, social and symbolic, the concept of emotional capital disrupts neat links between profit, or what Bourdieu calls increases in capital, and educational success (ie, educational success generates increases in cultural, symbolic, social and often economic capital). The same relationship does not automatically exist between educational success and emotional capital. If emotional capital is to be viewed as inextricably linked to educational success and the acquisition of cultural capital then for substantial numbers of mothers and their children, it would perversely appear to be at the cost of emotional wellbeing. As I have demonstrated through my data, some of the middle-class children's academic success seemed to be at a cost to their emotional wellbeing and my understanding of the processes in play was that having to focus so intensely on academic achievement depreciated emotional capital while simultaneously augmenting cultural capital. In particular, as Walkerdine and Lucey found in their sample of middle-class, ten year old girls (Walkerdine and Lucey, 1989), a number of the high achieving middle-class girls were both very anxious about school work and negative about their own academic ability. Conversely, some mothers, predominantly working-class but including a small number of middle-class mothers, appeared to emphasize children's emotional wellbeing over and above educational achievement. High levels of emotional capital were being generated in the mother-child interaction around schooling but levels of cultural capital remained relatively low.

My second response has been to stress that what constitutes emotional capital seems to vary between different class contexts. Whilst recognizing that sensitive, sympathetic encouragement and support will always have positive efficacy regardless of class differences, in contradistinction to prevailing discourses of parental involvement (DFEE, 1994), what constitutes an optimal response to children's education appears to vary according to the very different class contexts of parents (Reay and Ball, 1997;1998). Positioning in the field is crucial. Middle-class emotional investments in education generate higher, more secure returns for the same level of investment compared to that of working-class parents for whom any level of emotional investment is relatively risky and insecure. Emotional wellbeing is more easily achieved in circumstances of privilege (Wilkinson, 1995). Economic security and high social status enhance individuals' sense of emotional wellbeing while poverty is not an environment in which emotional capital can normally thrive.

Many of the mothers on benefit and income support were emotionally preoccupied with surviving from day to day on inadequate resources. Some of the working-class mothers talked about sometimes getting so depressed about their financial situation they found it impossible to find the emotional space to support their children's education:

> Jalil: I know I should hear her every night but sometimes I'm not up to it. I just go to bed after tea so I can forget about everything.
> Diane: About what?
> Jalil: Come off it Diane, you'd get fed up never having enough money, worrying about bills. You try it.

A culture of survivalism and the anxieties and tensions it produces are not conducive to the transmission of emotional capital. As Jalil illustrates above, living in poverty constitutes an emotionally draining experience (Oppenheim and Harker, 1996; Smith and Noble, 1995).

The damage of middle-class normativity is most apparent in Maria's account. I have discussed earlier her intense emotional involvement in Leigh's schooling. This inability to separate out emotionally from what was happening in school left both Maria and Leigh feeling 'failures':

> I am a complete failure. I've lost so much sleep worrying about Leigh's education trying to work out what I need to do but nothing seems to work. I mean all those years of worrying myself silly and he's still going to be a failure.

Maria, extremely anxious about Leigh's academic performance, is locked into a negative interaction with him in which increased pressure from her results in a pattern of withdrawal and refusal where, as Leigh's teacher points out, 'he is terrified of getting anything wrong so basically has stopped trying'. Maria constantly measures herself against middle-class standards for parental involvement despite lacking middle-class resources. In contrast, Lisa has protected herself and her daughter from such invidious self labelling by consistently refusing 'shameful recognitions': what Bev Skeggs defines as 'recognition of the judgment of others and awareness of social norms' (Skeggs, 1997:123).

As a consequence, high levels of emotional capital are transmitted by very different practices according to mothers' past and current social class positioning. This class-based variability means that some working-class mothers would appear to be better able to pass on emotional capital to their children when they achieve a degree of disengagement from the educational pressurising common among the middle-class mothers. Intense emotional involvement in children's schooling often produced small returns for the working-class mothers relative to their middle-class counterparts because other key ingredients such as educational knowledge and confidence, material resources and social capital were not available. Emotional capital appears to have a much looser link with social class than Bourdieu's other capitals. It does not necessarily rise in parallel with increased social status and appears to be generated by different practices depending on the class contexts of mothers.

Conclusion

Within contemporary educational markets, class and gender continue to infuse attitudes and actions. As Beverley Skeggs (1997:167) asserts, 'there are potent signs of the unremitting emotional distress generated by the doubts and insecurities of living class that working-class women endure on a daily basis'. There is also a much more hidden, but equally visceral, emotional distress within middle class families where practices 'of doing the best for your child' and 'deferring gratification' can result in extensive negative emotional fall-out for middle class children, especially all those 'good, clever' girls like Sally. Eva Illouz (1997:61) argues that it is increasingly 'moral resources, the very sources and resources of the self, that are robbed by an increasingly expanding market that not only undermines the moral resources of the self but also restructures their allocation'. Although Illouz is writing about the labour market, her insights are equally relevant to the new developing markets in education. I suggest that the concept of emotional capital is useful for unravelling some of the confusing class and gender processes embedded in contemporary educational markets. The gendered practices which make up involvement in schooling are exemplified in the complex contradictions of 'a capital' which is all about investment in others rather than self – the one capital that is used up in interaction with others and is for the benefit of those others. We can also glimpse how uneven and uneasy processes of individualization have been for women. At the interface of home and school, processes of female individualization are rendered both complex and conflictual as contemporary notions of 'living your own life' clash with conventional expectations of 'being there for others' (McNay, 1999; Beck and Beck-Gernsheim, 2002). In particular, the processes through which emotional capital is generated highlight the costs for mothers of always being 'close-up', while men maintain their prerogative to remain 'at a distance'. Emotional capital also reveals some of the class specific intricacies of parental involvement. The concept problematizes prevailing values which uncomplicatedly identify academic success as uniformly positive; an unmitigated 'good'. It also uncovers a further feminist conundrum in which both middle-class mothers, in their pursuit of educational advantage for their children at the cost of their emotional well-being, and working-class mothers, constrained in ways which mitigate against the acquisition of both emotional and cultural capital, are at risk of disadvantaging their children, albeit in differing ways.

References

Adkins, L. (2002) *Revisions: Gender and Sexuality in Late Modernity.* Buckingham: Open University Press.

Allatt, P. (1993) 'Becoming Privileged: The Role of Family Processes' in I. Bates and G. Riseborough. (eds) *Youth and Inequality.* Buckingham: Open University Press.

Beck, U. and Beck-Gernsheim, E. (2002) *Individualisation.* London: Sage.

Bell, D. (1990) 'Doing Anthropology at Home: A Feminist Initiative in the Bicentennial Year' in N. Sirman and K. Ganesh (eds) *Anthropological Perspectives on Research and Teaching Concerning Women*. London: Sage.

Benjamin, O. and Sullivan, O. (1996) 'The Importance of Difference: Conceptualising Increased Flexibility in Gender Relations at Home' *The Sociological Review* 44(2): 225–251.

Bourdieu, P. (1977) 'Cultural Reproduction and Social Reproduction' in J. Karabel and A. H. Halsey (eds) *Power and Ideology in Education*. Oxford: Oxford University Press.

Bourdieu, P. (1985) 'Social Space and the Genesis of Groups' *Theory and Society* 14(6): 723–744.

Bourdieu, P. (1986) 'The Forms of Capital', in J. G. Richardson (ed.) *Handbook of Theory and Research for the Sociology of Education*. New York: Greenwood Press.

Bourdieu, P. (1990) *In Other Words: Essays Towards Reflexive Sociology*. Cambridge: Polity Press.

Bourdieu, P. (1993) *Sociology in Question*. London: Sage.

Bourdieu, P. (1998) *Practical Reason*. Cambridge: Polity Press.

Bourdieu, P. (2001) *Masculine Domination*. Cambridge: Polity Press.

Bourdieu, P. and Passeron, J.-C. (1977) 'Reproduction in Education' in P. Bourdieu and J.-C. Passeron *Reproduction in Education, Society and Culture*. London: Sage.

Bourdieu, P. and Boltanski, L. (1981) 'The Educational System and the Economy: Titles and Jobs', in C. Lemert (ed.) *French Sociology: Rupture and Renewal since 1968*. New York: Columbia University Press.

Bourdieu, P. and Waquant, L. (1992) *An Invitation to Reflexive Sociology*. Chicago: University of Chicago Press.

Brown, P. (1995) 'Cultural Capital and Social Exclusion: Some Observations on Recent Trends in Education, Employment and the Labour Market' *Employment and Society* 9: 29–51.

Burack, C. (1994) *The Problem of the Passions: Feminism, Psychoanalysis and Social Theory*. New York: New York University Press.

Burkitt, I. (1997) 'Social Relations and Emotions'. *Sociology* 31(1): 37–55.

Crozier, G. (2002) paper presented at the *Parental Choice Market Forces* seminar. London: King's College, June 2002.

David, M. E. (1993) *Parents, Gender and Education Reform*. Cambridge: Polity Press.

David, M. E. Edwards, R. Hughes, M. and Ribbens, J. (1993) *Mothers and Education: Inside Out? Exploring Family-Education Policy and Experience*. Basingstoke: Macmillan.

DFEE (1994) *Our Children's Education: The Updated Parents' Charter*. London: HMSO.

Duncombe, J. and Marsden, D. (1993) 'Love and Intimacy: The Gender Division of Emotion and 'Emotion Work' – A Neglected Aspect of Sociological Discussion of Heterosexual Relationships' *Sociology* 27(2): 221–241.

Erickson, R. J. (1993) 'Reconceptualising Family Work: The Effect of Emotion Work on Perceptions of Marital Quality' *Journal of Marriage and the Family* 55: 888–900.

Giddens, A. (1992) *The Transformation of Intimacy*. Cambridge: Polity Press.

Giroux, H. (1983) 'Theories of Reproduction and Resistance in the New Sociology of Education: A Critical Analysis' *Harvard Educational Review* 53(3): 257–293.

Graham, H. (1993) *Hardship and Health in Women's Lives*. London: Harvester Wheatsheaf.

Hochschild, A. R. (1983) *The Managed Heart: The Commercialisation of Human Feeling*. Berkeley/ Los Angeles: University of California Press.

Illouz, E. (1997) 'Who Will Care for the Caretaker's Daughter?: Towards a Sociology of Happiness in the Era of Reflexive Modernity' *Theory, Culture and Society* 14(4): 31–66.

Jackson, S. (1993) 'Even Sociologists Fall in Love: An Exploration in the Sociology of Emotions' *Sociology* 27(2): 201–220.

James, N. (1989) 'Emotional Labour: Skill and Work in the Social Regulation of Feelings' *The Sociological Review* 37(1): 15–42.

Jenkins, R. (1982) 'Pierre Bourdieu and the Reproduction of Determinism' *Sociology* 16(2): 270–281.

Jordan, B., Redley, M. and James, S. (1994) *Putting the Family First: Identities, Decisions, Citizenship*. London: UCL Press.

Lareau, A. (1989) *Home Advantage*. Lewes: Falmer Press

Lawler, S. (2000) *Mothering the Self: Mothers, Daughters, Subjects.* London: Routledge.

Lorde, A. (1984) *Sister/Outsider.* Freedom, CA: Crossing Press.

Lovell, T. (2000) 'Thinking Feminism with and Against Bourdieu', in B. Fowler (ed.) *Reading Bourdieu on Society and Culture.* Oxford: Blackwells.

Lucey, H. and Reay, D. (2002) 'Carrying the Beacon of Excellence: Social Class Differentiation and Anxiety at a Time of Transition' *Journal of Education Policy* 17(3): 321–336.

McNay, L. (1999) 'Gender, Habitus and the Field: Pierre Bourdieu and the Limits of Reflexivity' *Theory, Culture and Society* 16 (1): 95–117.

Mirza, H. and Reay, D. (2000) 'Spaces and Places of Black Educational Desire: Rethinking Black Supplementary Schools as a New Social Movement' *Sociology* 34(4): 521–544.

Morrow, V. (1999) 'Conceptualising Social Capital in Relation to Health and Well-Being for Children and Young People: A Critical Review' *The Sociological Review* 47(4): 744–765.

Nash, R. (1990) 'Bourdieu on Education and Social and Cultural Reproduction' *British Journal of Sociology of Education* 11(4): 431–447.

Nowotny, H. (1981) 'Women in Public life in Austria' in C. Fuchs Epstein and R. Laub Coser (eds) *Access to Power: Cross-National Studies of Women and Elites.* London: George Allen & Unwin.

Oakley, A. (1993) *Social Support and Motherhood: The Natural History of a Research Project.* London: Blackwell.

Oppenheim, C. and Harker, L. (1996) *Poverty. The Facts.* London: Child Poverty Action Group.

Reay, D. (1995) 'A Silent Majority: Mothers in Parental Involvement', in R. Edwards and J. Ribbens (eds) Women in Families and Households: Qualitative Research. *Women's Studies International Forum Special Issue* 18(3): 337–348.

Reay, D. (1997) 'Feminist Theory, Habitus and Social Class: Disrupting Notions of Classlessness' *Women's Studies International Forum* 20(2): 225–233.

Reay, D. (1998a) 'Bourdieu and Cultural Reproduction: Mothers' Involvement in Their Children's Primary Schooling' in M. Grenfell and D. James (eds) *Bourdieu and Education: Acts of Practical Theory.* London: Taylor and Francis.

Reay, D. (1998b) *Class Work: Mothers' Involvement in Children's Schooling.* London: University College Press.

Reay, D. (1998c) 'Engendering Social Reproduction: Mothers in the Educational Marketplace' *British Journal of Sociology of Education* 19(2): 195–209.

Reay, D. (2002) 'Shaun's Story: Troubling Discourses of White Working Class Masculinities' *Gender and Education* 14(3): 221–234.

Reay, D. and Ball, S. J. (1997) ' "Spoilt for Choice": The Working classes and Education Markets' *Oxford Review of Education* 23(1): 89–101.

Reay, D. and Ball, S. J. (1998) ' "Making Their Minds Up": Family Dynamics of School Choice' *British Educational Research Journal* 24(4): 431–448.

Reay, D., Bignold, S., Ball, S. J. and Cribb, A. (1998) ' "He Just Had a Different Way of Showing it": Gender Dynamics in Families Coping with Childhood Cancer' *Journal of Gender Studies* 7(1): 39–52.

Reay, D. and Mirza, H. (1998) 'Uncovering Genealogies of the Margins: Black Supplementary Schooling' *British Journal of Sociology of Education* 18: 477–499.

Rose, N. (1998) *Inventing our Selves: Psychology, Power and Personhood.* Cambridge: Cambridge University Press.

Skeggs, B. (1997) *Formations of Class and Gender: Becoming Respectable.* London: Sage.

Smith, T. and Noble, M. (1995) *Education Divides: Poverty and Schooling in the 1990s.* London: CPAG.

Walkerdine, V. and Lucey, H. (1989) *Democracy in the Kitchen: Regulating Mothers and Socialising Daughters.* London: Virago.

Wharton, A. S. and Erickson, R. J. (1995) 'The Consequences of Caring: Exploring the Links Between Women's Jobs and Family Emotion Work' *Sociological Quarterly* 36: 273–296.

Wilkes, C. (1990) 'Bourdieu's Class' in R. Harker, C. Mahar and C. Wilkes (eds) *An Introduction to the Work of Pierre Bourdieu.* London: Macmillan.

Wilkinson, R. G. (1995) *Unhealthy Societies: The Afflictions of Inequality.* London: Routledge.

Williams, S. and Benedelow, G. (1997) (eds) *Emotions in Social Life: Critical Themes and Contemporary Issues.* London: Routledge.

Zajdow, G. (1995) 'Caring and Nurturing in the Lives of Women Married to Alcoholics'. *Women's Studies International Forum* 18: 535–546.

Exchange, value and affect: Bourdieu and 'the self'

Beverley Skeggs

Introduction

This chapter examines the different formations of the self proposed in contemporary cultural and social theory including Bourdieu and his notion of habitus, showing how most formulations are premised upon the accrual of property and value in the self via various technologies. This self-accrual process conceives of culture as an exchangeable-value in which some activities, practice and dispositions can enhance the overall value of personhood; an example of which would be the cultural education of the middle-class child who is taken to galleries, museums, ballet, music lessons, etc, activities which are all assumed to be morally 'good' for the person but which will also have an exchange-value in later life such as the cultural capital necessary for employability and social networking. The intimate link between economic and moral value is explored.

I'll begin with an outline of the foundational archaeology that underpins the different concepts of the self proposed in contemporary theory. When compiling these different formulations I was surprised by how many concepts assume the possibility that property can be made from cultural practices which can then be stored in the self, or in Bourdieu's case, corporeal dispositions generated and organized via the habitus. Considering we are in a period when class is denied as an issue on a regular basis it is significant that assumptions proliferate about how individuals have equal access to the cultural resources for self-making, as if the self can be entirely divorced from the conditions which make it possible. I argue the cultural resources for self-making and the techniques for self-production are class processes and making the self makes class. I then explore the concepts of self and Bourdieu's habitus in some depth asking how do we conceptualize those experiences that do not fit within an exchange-value model of self and culture.

What was also interesting (to me) in mapping the different concepts of self was how similar they were to the old notion of possessive individualism that Macpherson (1962) identifies as the cornerstone of seventeenth century political theory. The 'possessive individual' was/is a person who is defined through *his* capacity to own property in *his* person (Lury, 1998; Strathern, 1999) and to have the capacity to stand outside of him/self, to separate from 'his body' and then to have a proprietal relation to him/self as bodily property (Pateman, 1988). Possessive individualism was predicated on the relational capacity to draw to the self objects (and for the purposes of this chapter I'd argue, *the dispositions of other persons*) personalized through acts of appropriation or consumption (Strathern, 1999). *His* property was premised upon *his* experiences and how these were taken and promoted as the proper and highly moral, later protected by law, property relations and concepts of rights-bearing individuals (see Davies, (1994, 1998) for an examination of how the proper is the basis of law).

The possessive individual developed from the perspective of a small elite group, with access to circuits of symbolic distribution who were able to legitimate their own perspectives, interests and authority by defining themselves against the 'mass', who they represented as the constitutive limit for what an individual could be. The *he* consolidated through law and other means of institutionalization (such as welfare and education) enabled the experiences of a powerful minority to determine what constituted a person and was eventually conceptualized through various other discursive routes extending beyond elite men into the middle-class more generally, yet similarly institutionalized and authorized through the proper, the good, the norm and the attribution of moral value to particular practices in the making of the self (see Skeggs, 2004, for an account of this complex history).

Central to the reproduction of the possessive individual was how particular techniques such as confession, narrative, biography and scientific discourse were used to legitimate interests and generate authority through the promotion of particular perspectives which established the perspective of *the possessive individual as the norm, the natural, the good and the proper through the attribution of moral value to themselves*. In institutionalizing themselves through different systems of knowledge, possessive individuals came to consolidate their interests across a variety of fields. What is significant for this chapter and for contemporary concepts of self is how much the possessive individual still underpins how we conceptualize selves and class relations.

What I also found to be significant when outlining the different models of the self was how they propose different relationships to objects, and how these relationships (be they acquiring, playing-with, knowing and assessing) shape the formations of self and class relations. Peter Stallybrass (1998) charts the legacies within the imperial history of European personhood. Beginning with an analysis of the concept of the fetish, he details how the fetish was used to demonise the supposedly arbitrary attachment of West Africans to material objects. From this the European subject was constituted in opposition to arbitrary attachments. Hence, he charts how central to Marx's analysis of the fetish was the formation of different subjects known through their relationships to objects: those defined as 'primitive' supposedly imbued their objects with history, memory, even personality (Mauss, 1990[1925]). Whilst the European colonialist, defined in opposition, generated and only saw the value of 'things' in exchange.

Kopytoff (1986) argues that this contrast between individualized persons and commodified things was a central ideological plank of colonialism that served to divorce use from exchange-value, but also significantly, served to associate certain forms of self *with* use and exchange-values. The 'civilized' exercised a relationship to things based on a specific perspective on value which was always about exchange: the value of labour was/is generated by what it can produce for exchange. As Stallybrass observes about the formation of European colonial subjects, they were:

> . . . [a] subject unhampered by fixation upon objects, a subject who, having recognised the true (i.e. market) value of the object-as-commodity, fixated instead upon transcendental values that transformed gold into ships, ships into guns, guns into tobacco, tobacco into sugar, sugar into gold, and all into an accountable profit (Stallybrass, 1998:186).

What therefore becomes significant for the purpose of this chapter is how the European colonial self, premised on understanding only the exchange-value of things and not imbuing things with meaning, memory and history, enables different self formations via relationships to things (including knowledge and dispositions as commodities to be acquired in self-making). Lash (1990) maintains that the contemporary middle-class use symbols as substitutes for things, leading Baudrillard (1983) to argue that value is only ever produced symbolically.

The legacy of this colonial formation of personhood generates the possibility of a self that can conceive of a *future* in which value can be realised: a specific exchange-value perspective, one that transforms leisure into employability and cultural into symbolic and/or economic capital, enabling future profit to inhere in the self. Practice and relationships to objects and people therefore become central in how value can be realized. Where once the relationships of exchange were premised on labour (the relations of production), now I argue, they are also premised on the use of culture from which a value can be generated: the exchange relations of culture which are central to self and class-making.[1]

I'll now outline the different models of the self proposed in contemporary theory.

Different models of the self

These brief outlines offer a framework for unpacking the foundational assumptions at work in a range of theories:

A. *The aesthetic self* was proposed by Michel Foucault (1979) as an imperative of modernity, particularly modern power, a project to be achieved via the inculcation of technologies of subjectivity, in which selves are formed through the productive power of discourse. The self, Foucualt demonstrates, is a category that does not pre-exist the discourses that constitute it. Through technologies of subjectivity, such as confession, bio-power and therapy, the self generates its own governance, hence transferring power from direct repression. In Foucault's earlier works (e.g., 1979) the self is produced solely by techniques, yet in later works Foucault struggles with concepts of agency and consciousness.

Foucault's theories of self have been extensively developed by Nick Rose (1989) to explore techniques of governance via self-formation. Emphasis here is not on accrual or exchange-value as a strategic practice but on how techniques produce the self as governance within power relations. Central to governance are the knowledges promoted as 'expertise' by the professions that work on the psychological production of the self (the 'psy' sciences) often used and translated through management, child development, therapeutic and social work techniques. The extensive deployment of power via technologies of self-governance is well described by the concept of the 'enterprising self' by Paul du Gay (1996) in which rather than just being an aesthetic project, the self has to become an enterprising subject, acquiring cultural capital in order to gain employment; hence making the responsibility for un/employment an individual responsibility rather than a capitalist demand for labour and exploitation.[2] The emphasis in these Foucauldian developments is on how particular techniques of subjectivity promote positive production (rather than repression and control), pervading numerous sites of social life, including work, law (Valverde, 1998); mothering (Lawler, 2000) and policing (Garland, 2001), generating extra-ordinary subjectivity (Dovey, 2000); compulsory individuality (Taylor, 1989; Strathern, 1992); intimate citizenship (Berlant, 1997) and DIY citizenship (Hartley, 1999).

Whilst Foucault was at pains to describe the history of modern 'civilization', knowledge, modes of governance and power, sociologists have been able to extract aspects of this analysis and subject them to theoretical and empirical scrutiny. Deleting the Foucaudian emphasis on technologies and sexualities, and inserting some form of agency into the pursuit of symbolic practices and aesthetic activities, social theorists such as Mike Featherstone (1991) and Mike Savage *et al* (1992) identify another version of the aesthetic self as a practice specifically associated with the professional sector of the middle-classes. They show how the aesthetic middle-class self is reliant upon access to and appropriation of other cultures in its own formation, a process institutionalized by cultural intermediaries, who locate, evaluate and incorporate working-class cultures attempting to break new markets and provide greater resources for the middle-class to access and enjoy. These cultural intermediaries, who define which cultural knowledge and practice is worth knowing and acquiring, institutionalize judgements that can be used as arbiters of taste-making in self-formation. The self is perceived as a 'project' to be worked upon, accruing its value over space and time.

This model of accruing self becomes more specific in the figure of the **Cultural Omnivore:** the omnivore is a particular self-formation, documented by Erickson (1991, 1996); Peterson and Kern (1996) and Peterson and Simkus (1993) to show how traditional class distinctions are being broken down as the middle-class plunder and re-evaluate cultural forms that were traditionally associated with the working-class. US country music, for example when used by 'rednecks' has little cultural value. Erickson and Peterson are interested in how cultural boundaries are being redrawn as the middle-class draws culture to itself. They suggest that this leads to the breaking down of class divisions, yet other theorists such as Warde *et al* (2000) suggest that omnivorousness only enhances class divisions more clearly. The figure of the omnivore is a traditional model of appropriation, accumulation and exchange-value whose focus is on culture. The cultural omnivore has been well examined and promoted as a marketing strategy, used by advertising agencies to open up new markets and generate a particular bourgeois subject. Brooks (2001), for instance, identifies 'Bobos': as a category of bourgeois urban bohemians who are specifically targeted and produced through 'edge' activities, experiences and products. Note how both the omnivore and the sociological aesthetic self rely on attachments to practices and objects in which value is generated by being attached to the self. Exchange value is generated from the symbolic value of both the practice/object and by the relations by which they are attached (e.g., entitlement, exploitation and appropriation).

B. A more recent version of Foucault's aesthetic self has been proposed by Celia Lury (1998): *the prosthetic self*. Instead of attaching and detaching cultural objects and practices to the self for the accrual of value in the project of aesthetic self-making, the prosthetic self is instead based on *experimentation*, on playing with knowledge, objects and culture. This is a technique of the self, in which aspects that previously seemed (naturally or socially) fixed, immutable, beyond will or self-control are increasingly made sites of *strategic decision-making*. The prosthesis, which can be either perceptual or mechanical, Lury argues, makes self-extension by experimentation possible. In adopting/adapting a prosthesis, the person creates (or is created by) a self-identity that is no longer defined by the edict 'I think therefore I am'; rather, he or she is constituted in the relation 'I can, therefore I am' (Lury, 1998). Absolutely central to this 'doing', experimental self is, Strathern (1992) argues, (like the aesthetic self) having the right knowledge and perspective, hence being able to make the 'right judgement'. Strathern (1999) shows how, not only is the self crafted from reified, objectified relations, but also how property claims are then made from these. She argues that where things already appear to exist in the world then establishing 'property' is a question of creating personal claims in them:

> When the 'thing' that becomes property through the claims that people make on it is then perceived as the product of social relations in the first place, that fresh perception may itself be perceived as a product of social effort for it requires and constitutes knowledge (Strathern, 1999:18).

We need to ask who can make claims on cultural practices, who can establish their perspectives as knowledge, how do we know which cultural practices are worth experimenting with and how are property claims established?

In her study of prosthesis, Strathern (1991, 1992) points out that the opportunity for forms of self-extension come not only from the choosing and putting on of parts (prosthesis), but also from the notion of the part as dramatic, as performative (Munro, 1996). The addition of a part (object) extends the possibilities for cultural performance as 'part' (subject). Her point is that the middle-classes move from figure to figure, attaching and detaching in their self-performance, and crucially, as Munro suggests, perception of the second figure involves forgetting parts of the first figure. There is never a whole, selves are always in extension.[3] Munro warns against reading this in a realist way, as if a core self appropriates a range of identities, assuming that there is a true self to which one can return. He argues that, in the process of extension, one never travels out of place (that is the core self), rather the only movement is ever circular, from one figure to another. One figure picks up on what the other excludes. Thus, he maintains, we are always in extension: 'Indeed extension is all we are ever in' (1996:264). But who can extend and how far becomes a central issue. The whole process is predicated on the power and ability to move, to *access* others, *to mobilize* resources. Yet we do not have equal access and ability to mobilize resources. The prosthetic self must *know* which practices, knowledge and objects to strategise about and play with. As a model it is reliant on exchange-value but is less corporeal and accumulative as the body attaches and detaches its prosthesis rather than storing it in or on the body as self-value. It is the ability to play with other objects and people that is the source of value. Discarding practices as not worth experimentation inserts them into the circuit of judgements of value. Acquiring knowledge and perspective through the technique of experimentation for strategic decision-making places the emphasis on knowledge above owning but, nonetheless, it is still about judgement and value and crucially about the *relationships that enable entitlement* to others and things. The prosthetic self continues the tradition of the colonial European subject who rejects meaningful attachments, but rather than seeing objects directly generating transcendent exchange-value, it is the process of experimentation and the relations which enable it that generates value. Prosthetic playfulness takes place within a dominant symbolic so that the values are already established but the practice of play (if by cultural intermediaries who can influence value systems) can enable revaluation to take place.

Decision-making also presents the middle-class with constant dilemmas according to Strathern (1992) who shows how discourses of choice are central to the Western production of ideas of 'individuality', providing what she calls 'proscriptive individualism'. Thus, forms of control are manifested in inner-directed technologies of the self, which in consumerism are expressed as technologies of choice. An individual is defined by the 'innate' capacity of 'free choice' and this choice expresses the inner authentic individuality of that person. The abstracted notion of 'choice' becomes an inherent ideal as well as the route to the expression of individuality. Yet, as Anne Cronin (2000) demonstrates, the modern self, who can will itself to be (through consumption), is not freely accessible to all, and women as well as other marginalized groups remain excluded. She documents how the gendering address of consumerist imagery via femininity is used to restrict the access of women to the individuality it offers, making individuality an unequal resource.

C. The reflexive self offers aspects of the above models but, rather than being reliant upon the self as an aesthetic project or a space for strategic experimentation, it is a self produced through the technique of biography and the ability to understand and reflect upon the risks that surround the self. The reflexive self is promoted by Anthony Giddens (1991) and Ulrich Beck (1992) as a model of the universal self. Individuals, Beck maintains, although unable to escape structural forces in general, can decide on which forces to act and which to ignore. This, he argues, does not create a 'free' individual, rather, it creates individuals who live out, biographically, the complexity and diversity of the social relations which surround them. It is this self, this biographical production, that Beck calls 'reflexive modernity'. Giddens sees institutional reflexivity as fundamental to the development of a new universal 'life politics' where (like Beck) individuals search to create a coherent biography in a fractured world. Here the self becomes a project on which to be worked in order to produce some sense of coherence, premised upon a dual model of the self which (similar to Adam Smith, 1757) requires a self that reflects upon itself; simultaneously externalising the self from social relations, so that the former can reflect and plan its future actions, then reinsert itself back into society through internalisation: it is a self that therefore knows its self. This is not a technique of the self, in which aspects previously considered to be fixed, immutable, beyond will or self-control are increasingly made sites of strategic decision-making   the prosthetic self   where the edict 'I can, therefore I am' constitutes the self rather it relies upon the old edict 'I think therefore I am'. The emphasis is on the ability to 'think' drawing on elements of possessive individualism that rely upon the ability to stand outside of that which one considers to be a self and to separate from the body in order to have a (we can insert 'thinking/reflecting') proprietal relation to him/self as bodily property.

And again it is a him, as Adkins (2002) has shown: a particular reproduction of modern masculinity unhinged from the conditions of its own production, a self that is proposed as detached from structure, but in fact reproduces his own structural position. He is also of a particular class, as Savage (2000) demonstrates, a privileged individual who requires access to particular knowledge and techniques in order to deploy them in a way that can be recognized as reflexive. Just like the possessive individual the reflexive self condenses an individual's experience, turns it into a perspective and proposes it as a universal category (Skeggs, 2002). Again, this is a self which assumes that *access* to particular forms of knowledge *can* be acquired. This assumption is much more pernicious than the other models of self because by proposing the universality of this self, other forms of self-making are pathologized; people who do not display the requisite reflexivity are seen to be lacking, not fully formed selves, and this lack is moralized and individualized, a failure of the self to know its self, rather than being seen as a lack of access to the techniques and knowledge required to enable the display of the reflexive self (see Wood and Skeggs, 2004).

The reflexive self appears to be a modern version of the 'rational actor', the self who can know and assess its potential and make strategic decisions on what action to take and what to acquire on the basis of this rational reflection. This is an agency-overloaded self who has no difficulty accessing the knowledge required to make rational decisions. With a huge long historical baggage, premised upon the discourse of rationality and defined against femininity (de Groot, 1989), the rational actor has been hugely influential across a range of different sites, even class theory (e.g., Goldthorpe 1996). Fine (2001) charts the ubiquitous hold of the figure of the rational actor, particularly on contemporary understandings of economics. In order to understand its pervasiveness Valerie Walkerdine (1988) suggests the figure of the rational actor represents a particular masculine desire for knowledge and control made into a theory. She draws on Rotman's (1980) critique of the semiotics of mathematics to show how it is a fantasy of both discourse and practice, in which the world becomes what is wanted by the theorist: regular, ordered, controllable. It is a tautological desire producing what it requires, defining ways that are logically ordered and predictable, then executed within those discursive practices as truth. 'Reason's Dream', as Rotman calls it, is seductive for it offers to its desirer power over others, one's 'self', and the prediction and control of events. This is very much about all-encompassing agency and self-governance generating exchange-value; the rational-actor self knows how to optimize self-value: 'I strategise therefore I am'. It is the direct opposite to the non-agenic technologies of subjectivity proposed by Foucaudians.

D. Coming from a much more cynical perspective and located within a critique of French contemporary thought, Kroker (1992) identifies a ***Possessed Individual***. No longer 'possessive individualism' under the sign of private property and contract law, but possessed individualism under the sign of what he identifies as abused-value. According to Kroker, in the French mind there is no subject capable of appropriation, no acquisitive self, only a possessed subject which exists with such intensity that it disappears into its own simulacra. Kroker argues possessed individualism is the condition of modern freedom because it involves perfect forgetfulness; 'of history, of sexuality, of the memorized self' (1992:5). This forgetfulness of meaningfulness continues the legacy of colonial European personhood suggesting again that it is the *relationship to things* (including other people and in this case no-thing) that is a crucial defining feature in concepts of the self. This concept of non-self conceives of technology as a form of cynical power producing subjects, not as strategic, acquiring or reflexive, but as subjects of random and unpredictable forces. The non-self is forced to become a subject through the different forces of its production:

> [S]ometimes possessed by the imminently reversible language of seduction (Baudrillard); sometimes possessed by technologies of cynical power tattooing the flesh and colonising the imaginary domain of psychoanalytics (Foucault); sometimes

possessed by cynical rhetoric without a subject (Barthes) and sometimes possessed by the strategical language of a dromocratic war machine (Virilio). All that remains is a series of cold abstractions: Baudrillard's 'simulacrum', Lyotard's 'driftworks', Virilio's 'chronopolitics' and Foucault's 'technologies of the self' (1992:13).

The subject is inscribed and passive. This is subjectivity to the point of aesthetic excess and implosion so that 'the self no longer has any real existence, only a perspectival appearance as a site where all the referents converge and implode' (1992:5). Whilst Kroker admits to this as a particular French theoretical formation,[4] he proceeds to argue that it describes most perfectly American subject formation. Kroker's analysis is a movement from 'I think therefore I am', to 'I can therefore I am' to 'technologies are us'. The will to technique, Kroker argues, is invested by the logic of the cynical sign in which there is no reflexive consciousness, no strategic decision-making or self-project to be worked upon; the subject is seduced and disciplined in an indifferent game of chance and probability. The subject is subject-to as it is in most French philosophy; it is abused rather than generated by itself (and this sets up the contradictions which we will observe later in relation to Bourdieu).

Underpinning most of these models is a particular formulation of how the self is formed through its relationship to objects, a relationship made through history and memory (even if it is history and memory that are erased). It is significant how possibly the most sophisticated form of middle-class personhood (the prosthetic self) envisages a relationship of experimentation, moving, playing and discarding the objects, persons and practices used, making knowledge of objects and relationships to them as that which constitutes exchange-value. This suggests that theories of consumption which focus on objects themselves are missing the crucial point, namely that it is in the relationship that value is made or not.

Habitus

We now finally make it to Bourdieu's theory of *habitus*. Whilst Bourdieu does not directly figure a self, and is opposed to the concept of self, which he considers to be a bourgeois fabrication, he instead transposes habit to decentralize the self, making it opposite to conscious action and will-power. But the concept of habitus offers us a model of self in a very French and contradictory way. Habitus offers both a model of disciplined bodies (as in *Pascalian Meditations*) in which the habitus is the product of strategies objectively co-ordinated by mechanisms unknown to the individual, but also the future-projected, strategizing, accruing, exchange-value self. The habitus is similar to all the other French theorists who propose technologies (or mechanisms) also unknown to those who are subject to them: for instance technology as pure spin (Virilio), technology as simulation (Baudrillard), the rhetoric of technology (Barthes), technology as a desiring machine (Deleuze and Guattari), technology, as aesthetics (Lyotard) and technologies of subjectivity (Foucault). The habitus is a technology of strategic game-playing accrual.

Bourdieu argues that individuals are always placed in situations in which they will be uncertain of the outcomes, thereby they have to draw on strategies to operate in particular situations; these strategies are objectively co-ordinated without the individual's consciousness, enabling the analogical transfer of schemes permitting the solution of similarly shaped problems. Therefore, for Bourdieu the habitus is 'a system of lasting, transposable dispositions which, integrating past experiences, functions at every moment as a matrix of percep-tions, appreciations, and actions' (Boudieu, 2000:82–3). Bourdieu's desire to oppose the bourgeois mode of wilful, agenic self leaves him with a very specific technology: structured and structuring. Habitus is the:

> [p]roduct of a chronologically ordered series of structuring determinations, which at every moment structures in terms of the structuring experiences which produced it the structuring experiences which affect its structure, brings about a unique integra-tion, dominated by the earliest experiences, of the experiences statistically common to the members of the same class (2000:86–7).

The habitus operates to a relatively coherent logic – what Bourdieu calls the logic of practice – which begins in childhood but which thereafter structures the experiences contained by it. As he notes in *Outline of a Theory of Practice*:

> The habitus, the durably installed generative principle of regulated improvizations, produces practices which tend to reproduce the regularities immanent in the objec-tive conditions of the production of their generative principle, while adjusting to the demands inscribed as objective potentialities in the situation, as defined by the cog-nitive and motivating structures making up the habitus. It follows that these practices cannot be directly deduced either from the objective conditions, defined as the instan-taneous sum of the stimuli which may appear to have directly triggered them, or from the conditions which produced the durable principle of their production. These prac-tices can be accounted for only by relating the objective structure defining the social conditions of the production of the habitus which engendered them to the conditions in which this habitus is operating, that is, to the conjuncture which, short of a radical transformation, represents a particular state of this structure (Bourdieu, 1977:78).

The habitus is an 'immanent law' laid down by each agent in their earliest upbringing by the internalisation of objective structures. This is how individu-als embody, in the form of dispositions the marks of social position and social distance (see also Diane Reay and Steph Lawler in this volume). We can see how habitus reproduces the tradition of French technologies, especially when we learn that Bourdieu took the term from Mauss (1979) who in his definition of habitus notes:

> These 'habits' do not just vary with individuals and their imitations; they vary between societies, educations, properties and fashion, prestiges. In them we should see the *tech-niques* and work of collective and individual practical reason rather than, in the ordi-nary way, merely the soul and its repetitive faculties (1979:101, emphasis added).[5]

In this sense it is remarkably similar to the tradition of French philosophers who premise personhood on the experience of forces beyond the control of the subject. Another significant trajectory in Bourdieu's concept of habitus is his debt to phenomenology. Nick Crossley (2001) notes the echoes from Husserl:

> This lived experience itself, and the objective moment constituted in it, may become 'forgotten'; but for all this it in no way disappears without a trace; it has merely become latent. With regard to what has become constituted in it, it is *a possession in the form of a habitus*, ready at any time to be awakened anew by an active association (Husserl, 1972:122, emphasis in original).

We therefore have a combination of technology and property housed within a body that lives its traces, not dissimilar to the exchange-value self originally proposed in the discourse of possessive individualism in the seventeenth century; the central difference is the consciousness of the strategic agent.

It may be that Bourdieu works with the same double meaning of subjectivity that does not translate easily into English, as pointed out by Henriques *et al* (1984) whereby the French term *assujettir* means both to produce subjectivity and make subject. Yet Bourdieu does propose that the habitus impacts upon the structures that shape it, with the potential to change the formation of the field from whence it came (see Crossley, 2001; McNay, 1999, 2000).

Yet for Bourdieu the habitus is not just subject to external forces/structures which organize within and with sometimes reverse impact, it is also a very explicit model of accumulation, based on knowledge of the game and how to play it. The objective forces somehow shape a logic based on exchange-value in which the habitus always works with a perception of future value and accumulation, showing how practice never ceases to conform to economic calculation, even when it gives 'every appearance of disinterestedness by departing from the logic of interested calculation and playing for stakes that are non-material and not easily quantified' (1977:177). And even when Bourdieu tries to challenge accusations of rational action (the habitus that accrues in its interests) in *An Invitation to Reflexive Sociology* (Bourdieu and Waquant, 1992) his metaphors collapse him back into exchange-value models, and when he critiques the language of strategy (in *Pascalian Meditations*) he still continues to use it.

The habitus is the embodiment of the accumulation (or not) of value given by the volume and composition of the different forms of capital (economic, social, cultural, symbolic), displayed as dispositions, which sometimes for Bourdieu are aligned with social positions but sometimes are not. He notes:

> The habitus is the product of the work of inculcation and appropriation necessary in order for those products of collective history, the objective structures (e.g., of language, economy, etc) to succeed in reproducing themselves more or less completely, in the form of durable dispositions (Bourdieu, 2000:85).

Even though he argues that strategy cannot be fully known, he still veers between the objective logic of practice and the game play:

It is because subjects *do not*, strictly speaking, *know what they are doing* that what they do has more meaning than they know. The habitus is the universalizing mediation which causes an individual agent's practices, without either explicit reason or signifying intent, to be none the less 'sensible' and reasonable' (1977:79) (emphasis added).

The objective homogenizing of group or class habitus which result from the homogeneity of the conditions of existence is what enables practices to be objectively harmonized without any intentional calculation or conscious reference to a norm (1977:80).

It is this model of the habitus accruing value (composition and volume), in the conversion of its different forms of capital, be it consciously or unconsciously,[6] that I argue reproduces the properties of the exchange-value self. Bourdieu argues that the imperative to maximize value fuels the habitus and that value can be accrued and stored in the body (as opposed to the prosthetic self's experimental attachment and detachment). In contrast, however, the working-class habitus is shaped by necessity and resignation, an adapted habitus (as in *Distinction*). The working-class only enter a zero-sum game; yet as Diane Reay (1997) asks, how can the working-class feel entitled and hence take over spaces when they have no access to the structure of feelings of entitlement? Terry Lovell (2000) points to the numerous women who have not experienced the corporeal sedimentation of the habitus of masculinity who can 'pass' and strategically play (or even experiment) with masculinity in a man's world without being caught.

Bourdieu clearly notes the inequality and injustice involved in the production of the habitus, especially in the misrecognition of value, what he identifies as the arbitrary nature of value that is attributed to persons and objects:

This value is such as to induce investments and over-investments (in both the economic and psychoanalytic sense) which tend, through the ensuing competition and rarity, to reinforce the well-grounded illusion that the value of symbolic goods is inscribed in the nature of things (1977:183).

Here Bourdieu is remarkably similar to Marx's theory of commodity fetishism and Stallybrass' critique of how symbolic value inheres in objects that can be exchanged, hence obscuring the relationships that enable exchange. But for Bourdieu it is objective structures and forces that produce these relations. We have the French subject-to, but then in contradiction a strategic subject whose consciousness is both sedimented prior to experience who is also able to act upon these sedimented traces (but not necessarily as a conscious action) to enhance future investment by game-play and rational calculating decisions: this is a subject without subjectivity in which forces objectively and corporeally inhere to generate knowledge of the game. It is the corporeal nature of accumulation and exchange that marks Bourdieu out from the either non-accumulative or completely calculating. But it is this corporeal nature that limits Bourdieu's understanding of the working-class or feminists, or anybody whose positions are not legitimated by dominant symbolic relations. Objective forces force habitus to strategically game play, but what if you cannot enter the game, join the action or get on the field?

What about the working-class?

Whilst Bourdieu exposes how value-conversion occurs or not, how value is arbitrary, how we carry our history and how positions are crucial in the formation of bodies and knowledge, he presents a model of the working-class in *Distinctions* in a particularly quaint and romantic way but with dignity – but in *Weight of the World* as racist, pathetic, useless and abused. His analysis is similar to all the models presented above, providing a description of how the middle-class make themselves and how the game is established to middle-class advantage. But how do we understand working-class relations and subjectivity through Bourdieu or these other models? Are the working-class always lack, beyond value, without value, resigned and adjusted to their conditions, unable to accrue value to themselves? Where is the analysis of the daily class struggle that is reproduced on a daily basis and so well documented by ethnographies such as Simon Charlesworth (2000), in films such as *La Haine* (Haylett 2000) or by music such as *Eminen, The Streets* and a huge amount of rap?

If the working-class are only ever evaluated through the dominant symbolic and read both through methodology and theory as trapped by their habitus – positions embodied as value-less dispositions – then how do we represent them with value? And how do those trapped within the negative symbolic ever forge value for themselves? Is his theory performative? Are we as theorists who use Bourdieu also trapped inside the dominant symbolic? To which he would say yes, (see Bourdieu, 1989), but this leaves us with a need for an explanation, rather than having been brought into effect by one.

Bourdieu's model of resigned, adaptive working-class habitus both closes down the working-class possibility of playing the game but also closes off the positive, affective, justifiable experiences of anger and exclusion. Boyne (2002) argues that Bourdieu does not entertain the idea that there could be genuine social exclusion for such a thing would be a contradiction in terms. He notes how Bourdieu is reluctant to rehabilitate the notion of anomie for normless subjects cannot exist within his framework of social understanding. Bourdieu's response, however, Boyne argues, is based on his concept of shared suffering:

> I do not have to force myself to share in the feeling, inscribed in every word, every sentence, and more especially in the tone of their voices, their facial expressions and body language, of the *obviousness* of this form of collective bad luck that attaches itself like a fate, to all those that have been put together in those site of *social regulation*, where the personal suffering of each is augmented by all the suffering that comes from co-existing and living with so many suffering people together – and perhaps more importantly, of the destiny effect of belonging to a stigmatized group (Bourdieu *et al*, 1999:64).

Boyne notes how in *Weight of the World*, the experience of exclusion is unmediated. In contrast to the necessitarianism that Bourdieu examined in *Distinction*, the suffering is explained not by reflexivity but by the lack of a countervailing culture to impose and legitimate what is necessary (see also McRobbie, 2002). But as feminists know only too well, there is a significant difference between suffering and survival.

In *Weight of the World* the working-class habitus is absolute and complete lack, an adjustment with no possibility of change. But what about the elements of working-class culture that we know have value not just for the working-class: the creative hedonism; the anti-pretentious humour, the dignity, the high ethical standards of honour, loyalty and caring? And what about how practices such as respectability, assumed to be middle-class, are significantly reworked and re-valued when lived by the working-class: a complete ethical re-evaluation. What about all the working-class dispositions that the middle-class crave and appropriate whenever they can? These are the values beyond the dominant symbolic, often protected and beyond appropriation (Weiner, 1992). This is why I want to argue for a way of thinking beyond exchange-value, instead through use-values that do not rely either on a concept of the self (which has always been a dubious position for the working-class: see Steedman 1999, 2000), nor rely on a concept of accumulative subjectivity, which is always reliant on exchange-value.

We need to pay attention to the different value systems that exist outside of the dominant symbolic (for this we would need decent ethnography and a lack of attachment to the dominant symbolic value system or dominant theories of self to explore responses). We still need an analysis of middle-class entitlement: how to acquire, play and discard the working-class in its own making, something which I have explored elsewhere (Skeggs, 2004). But we also need to understand working-class relations to the dominant symbolic. We know from work on motherhood and caring (eg, Walkerdine and Lucey, 1989; Skeggs, 1997; Reay, 1998; Lawler, 2000) that working-class mothers operate with a very different ethical value system to the dominant symbolic. Just as studies of black men in the US by Duneier (1992) and Lamont (2000) show radically different values in place. We also know from Steedman (2000) and Vincent (1981) that the working-class learnt to tell themselves in a particular way (as redeemable and respectable) in order to have their voices heard by the middle-class or to receive poor relief, and we know this process of performing a respectable, proper self is still necessary in contemporary society in order to receive welfare. We also know from Bridget Byrne's (2003) research that the working-class tell themselves in a variety of ways which are often not recognized as self-narration. Bourdieu (2001) maintains that bodily dispositions are lived as a form of practical mimesis: 'the body believes in what it plays at: it weeps if it mimes grief' (2001:73). Yet we know from analyses of femininity that the body does not believe if it is a working-class one (see Fraser, 1999; Skeggs, 1997; Tyler, 1991); femininity for many working-class women is a performance, not performative. And we know that even when some of the working-class learn to play the game of the middle-classes this often generates a habitus that can rarely be comfortably inhabited.

An account of the de-authorization of the dominant exchange-value system is also required. The long history of anti-pretentious critique of the uptight, boring moral restraint of the middle-classes is one of the major critiques continually constructed against the middle-classes (Vicinus, 1974), of which the British TV comedy *The Royale Family* is a wonderful example. We also need to be able to understand the habitus of recalcitrance, of non-belonging, of no-caring, those who refuse to make a virtue out of necessity, the 'f*** off and 'so what' of utterances, the radical emptiness of the habitus, one that does not want to play the dominant symbolic game and accrue any value? (see Charlesworth, 2000). We need to know about the cramped spaces of politics where libidinal energies break through the processes of inscription that attempt to contain and govern (see Thoburn, 2002, 2003).

Gayatri Spivak (1990) shows how use-value is precisely that which disrupts the chain of value connections, because it is beyond value, understood in traditional economistic terms. Moreover, use-values can only be known when they are put to use, so they force a focus on the uses of culture, relations and practice. This means we can explore how something has different values in different relations, different contexts, enabling us to break through the dominant symbolic understandings premised on exchange. Spivak argues that value is a *catachresis*: contra to Marx, it has no literal origin or referent, because use-value will always exceed that which it claims to represent.

Affect may enable us to explore how use-values are experienced, expressed and known. It is interesting that Marx, alongside other theorists such as Marcuse, Debord, Deleuze and Guattari, have all represented humans as sensuous beings inhabiting a sensuous world, in which affect is highly significant. I think we can explore use-values through emotion. Pain, frustration and fear have been particularly well described, as has shame by Elspeth Probyn in this volume and elsewhere (Probyn, 2000). I'm not talking about the culture of restricted affect, as described by Lauren Berlant (2000) which she identifies as the containment of emotional expressivity, accompanied by a search for intense experiences and the emergence of new forms of corporate culture and state control. Nor am I talking about the way restricted affect is used as a marketing and branding strategy – so prevalent in the US that it has even been identified as a specific economy (Pine and Gilmore, 1999). And I am really *not* talking about the anger that is produced as an entertainment device on reality TV shows to captivate the audience and pathologize the working-class further with associations of excess and lack of self control (e.g. *Jerry Springer*). I'm talking about the ubiquitous daily experiences of anger and frustration which are carefully contained and not regularly expressed.

My ethnographic research (Skeggs, 1997) and even more so the ethnography of Charlesworth (2000) were fuelled by statements of class hatred: anger, rage, frustration, defiance, intransigence, envy, antagonism. These were not statements of adjustment or resignation, nor claims of wounded attachments made to make political claims (see Brown, 1995). Neither were they claims for victimhood made by those who felt victim only because their perceived entitlements had not been realised, or statements of resentment made to shore up privileges already held, which Cameron McCarthy (2000) identifies as the new middle-class politics of resentment. Rather they were expressions of sheer, unadulterated, non-strategic indignation, rage, anger and resentment. The daily comments of 'it's not right', 'it's not fair' cannot convey the futility and frustration contained within them; knowing that indeed things are not right and not fair (see also Rubin, 1972/1992). These statements come from a social position of future-blocked as opposed to a future that can be invested in.[7] We need to understand the complexity and the mixture of the humour, the anti-authoritarian critique, the statements of injustice and the sheer frustration and rage: all these emotions cohere in the one body and are usually spontaneously released.

Partly, I suspect the middle-classes rarely hear these comments because research respondents are unlikely to express them. Even in ethnographies, people are cautious about representing themselves as bundles of seething anger and resentment (although Charleswoth's work is an exception). The spontaneous nature of the expressions means that they are less easily accessible. Moreover respondents are sometimes rendered speechless by the symbolic violence enacted upon them, as shown by Lisa Taylor's (2004) research.[8] Also, most of the forms of resistance we recognize are middle-class (especially the defence mechanisms identified by psychoanalysis). We only find these working-class affects in the periperformative utterances, often not even directed to the object, or in the piss-take, in which others become the source of derision, but which can easily be turned against oneself (see Willis, 2002). Periperformative utterances are expressions that do not rely on the appropriation of the cultures of others in order to generate value; expressions that do not project into the future. Bourdieu (1990) argues that emotion is a presenting of the impending future, but I'd argue that negative affects are past, present and future – drawing on the history of inequality which is an accident of birth, the frustration that things are not fair and a knowledge that they are unlikely to change in the future.

I want to suggest it is by the emotions of affect that class struggle is being expressed, although not often heard. These utterances are however an expression of an alternative value system, one not easily recognized, often misrecognized, and certainly one that cannot be framed in the shape of a self that is in any way interested in accruing exchange-value to itself.

Conclusion

By outlining the different models of the self proposed in contemporary theory, I hope to have shown how whilst they work in their different ways both as analyses and constitutive of different aspects of middle-class experience, perspective and strategy, they do not leave us with the tools for understanding a great deal of working-class experience and value. In particular, Bourdieu's theory of the habitus, whilst explaining perfectly the middle-class and aspects of working-class inability to inhabit entitled dispositions, cannot account for that which is beyond abstraction, beyond the metaphoric model of exchange, investment and accumulation. Whilst cultural property can be stored in the self (as we see with aesthetic selves and cultural omnivores) or played with (as in prosthetic self) and whilst property claims can be made through the relations of entitlement and institutionalized in different self formations, we need to be able to understand how those who cannot or do not want to make property out of their relations to others live and move through social space. It is not enough to represent them as lack or the negative experience of the dominant symbolic for this always presents them in a zero sum game. But more importantly because exchange-value has always been associated with the proper and is imbued with morality, those who cannot accrue value in themselves by dominant symbolic techniques are therefore always/already read as immoral. Hence a refusal to play the game or the lack of knowledge to participate in middle-class taste culture is read back onto the working-class as an individualized moral fault, a pathology, a problem of bad-choice, bad culture, a failure to be enterprising or to be reflexive. This is why these dominant bourgeois models of the self are so dangerous; they always present the working-class as individualized moral lack. And instead of seeing this attribution of immorality to the working-class as part of a class struggle made from the relationship between people and objects, it is instead seen to be a property of the person, of the self. Class relations of cultural exploitation are presented as a failure of the self to know, play, do, think and/or repeat itself in the proper way. We have a repetition of the seventeenth century possessive individual where the powerful and privileged, with access to knowledge and law, define themselves as a self against the mass who only present the immoral constitutive limit; the immoral cannot inhabit a proper personhood and therefore cannot accrue value to themselves. The working-class are not allowed access to the resources and technologies required for self-production. This is why self-making is class-making. It is impossible to produce what the dominant symbolic (and academic theories) identify as a self if one does not have access to the techniques and means to do it; but it is not impossible to produce a subjectivity from alternative use-values, not just based on necessitarianism, suffering and subject-to forces, but on living life with a very different set of values.

Notes

1 Elsewhere (Skeggs 2004) I argue that these exchange relations of culture are new forms of exploitation, institutionalized via media production.

2 As Devine (1998) and Granovetter (1995) have shown cultural differences have come to play an increasingly significant role in making distinctions between prospective employees; the acquisition of certain forms of cultural capital enables employers to define the personal suitability and compatibility (often their similarity) to the company. In this sense the acquisition of and access to certain forms of cultural capital becomes more significant than qualifications alone.

3 Strathern does not use the concept of the self, which she argues assumes a Western model of coherence.

4 French thinkers, from Jean Baudrillard and Roland Barthes to Paul Virilio, Jean-Francois Lyotard, Deleuze and Guattari and Foucault have presented a description of technology as cynical power. Indeed, what might be called the key impulse of French 'bio-modernism' has been to explore the mutation of technology within a series of critical discourses (Krocker, 1992).

5 Thanks to Nick Crossley for drawing my attention to this and see Crossley (2001).

6 Bourdieu refuses the concept of the unconscious, which he believes is never anything other than the forgetting of history, in 'which history itself produces by incorporation the objective structures it produces in the second natures of habitus . . . in each of us, in varying proportions, there is part of yesterday's man; it is yesterday's man who inevitably predominates in us, since the present amounts to little compared with the long past in the course of which we were formed' (Bourdieu, 2000:78–79).

7 In the 1997 *Formations* ethnography the women worked to put a floor on their current circumstances rather than investing in the future; their struggle was to retain the past and the present rather than being able to envisage or project into the future.

8 Lisa Taylor (2004) notes how this symbolic violence is frequently visualized on 'make-over TV' when the recipients of the make-over are rendered speechless. She also notes how this silence is produced when a middle-class respondent unintentionally insults a working-class respondent with an offhand comment about working-class tastelessness. To challenge the comment, the working-class respondent would have to enter into an argumentative mode in a social exchange predicated on politeness.

References

Adkins, L. (2002) *Revisions: Gender and Sexuality in Late Modernity.* Buckingham: Open University Press.

Baudrillard, J. (1983) *Simulations.* New York: Semiotext(e).

Beck, U. (1992) *Risk Society.* London: Sage.

Berlant, L. (1997) *The Queen of America Goes to Washington City: Essays on Sex and Citizenship.* Durham and London: Duke University Press.

Berlant, L. (2000) 'The Subject of Feeling: Pain, Privacy, Politics' in S. Ahmed, J. Kilby, C. Lury, M. McNeil and B. Skeggs (eds) *Transformations: Thinking Through Feminism.* London: Routledge.

Bourdieu, P. (1977) *Outline of a Theory of Practice.* Cambridge: Polity Press.

Bourdieu, P. (1986) *Distinction: A Social Critique of the Judgement of Taste.* London: Routledge.

Bourdieu, P. (1989) 'Social Space and Symbolic Power' *Sociological Theory* 7: 14–25.

Bourdieu, P. (2000) *Pascalian Meditations.* Cambridge: Polity.

Bourdieu, P. (2001) *Masculine Domination.* Cambridge: Polity Press.

Bourdieu, P. and Waquant, L. (1992) *An Invitation to Reflexive Sociology.* Chicago: University of Chicago Press.

Bourdieu, P. *et al* (1999) *Weight of the World: Social Suffering in Contemporary Society.* Cambridge: Polity.

Boyne, R. (2002) 'Bourdieu: From Class to Culture' *Theory, Culture and Society* 19(3): 117–128.

Brooks, D. (2001) *Bobos in Paradise: The New Upper Class and How They Got There.* New York: Shuster and Simon.

Brown, W. (1995) 'Wounded Attachments: Late Modern Opposition Political Formations' in J. Rajchman (ed.) *The Identity in Question.* New York and London: Routledge.

Byrne, B. (2003) 'Reciting the Self: Narrative Representations of the Self in Qualitative Interviews' *Feminist Theory* 4(1): 29–49.

Charlesworth, S. (2000) *A Phenomenology of Working Class Experience.* Cambridge: Cambridge University Press.

Cronin, A. M. (2000) 'Consumerism and "Compulsory Individuality": Women, Will and Potential' in S. Ahmed, J. Kilby, C. Lury, M. McNeil and B. Skeggs (eds) *Transformations: Thinking Through Feminism.* London: Routledge.

Crossley, N. (2001) 'The Phenomenological Habitus and its Construction' *Theory and Society* 30: 81–120.

Davies, M. (1994) 'Feminist Appropriations: Law, Property and Personality' *Social and Legal Studies* 3: 365–391.

Davies, M. (1998) 'The Proper Discourses of Purity' *Law and Critique* IX: 147–173.

De Groot, J. (1989) ' "Sex" and "Race": The Constuction of Language and Image in the Nineteeth Century' in S. Mendus and J. Rendall (eds) *Sexuality and Subordination.* London: Routledge.

Devine, F. (1998) 'Class Analysis and the Stability of Class Relations' *Sociology* 32(1): 23–42.

Dovey, J. (2000) *Freakshow: First Person Media and Factual Television.* London: Pluto.

du Gay (1996) *Consumption and Identity at Work.* London: Sage.

Duneier, M. (1992) *Slim's Table: Race, Respectability and Masculinity.* Chicago: University of Chicago Press.

Erickson, B. (1990) 'What is Good Taste For?' *Canadian Review of Sociology and Anthropology* 28: 255–278.

Erickson, B. (1996) 'Culture, Class and Connection' *American Journal of Sociology* 102: 217–251.

Featherstone, M. (1991) *Consumer Culture and Postmodernism.* London: Sage.

Fine, B. (2001) *Social Capital versus Social Theory.* London: Routledge.

Foucault, M. (1979) *The History of Sexuality, Volume One.* Harmondsworth: Penguin.

Fraser, M. (1999) 'Classing Queer: Politics in Competition' *Theory, Culture and Society* 16(2): 107–31.

Garland, D. (2001) *The Culture of Control: Crime and Social Order in Contemporary Society.* Oxford: Oxford University Press.

Giddens, A. (1991) *Modernity and Self-Identity.* Cambridge: Polity.

Goldthorpe, J. (1996) 'Class Analysis and the Re-orientation of Class Theory' *British Journal of Sociology* 45: 211–233.

Granovetter, M. (1995) *Getting a Job: A Study of Contacts and Careers.* Chicago: Chicago University Press.

Hartley, J. (1999) *The Uses of Television.* London: Routledge.

Haylett, C. (2000) ' "This is about Us, This is Our Film!" Personal and Popular Discourses of "Underclass" ' in S. Munt (ed.) *Cultural Studies and the Working Class: Subject to Change.* London: Routledge.

Henriques, J., Hollway, E., Urwin, C., Venn, C. and Walkerdine, V. (1984) *Changing the Subject: Psychology, Social Regulation and Subjectivity.* London: Methuen.

Husserl, E. (1972) *Experience and Judgement.* Evanston: Northwestern University Press.

Kopytoff, I. (1986) 'The Cultural Biography of Things' in A. Appadurai (ed) *The Social Life of Things.* Cambridge: Cambridge University Press.

Kroker, A. (1992) *The Possessed Individual: Technology and the French Postmodern.* New York: St Martin's Press.

Lamont, M. (2000) *The Dignity of Working Men: Morality and the Boundaries of Gender, Race and Class.* Cambridge, Mass: Harvard University Press.

Lash, S. (1990) *The Sociology of Postmodernism.* London: Routledge.

Lawler, S. (2000) Mothering the Self: Mothers, Daughters, Subjects. London: Routledge.

Lovell, T. (2000) 'Thinking Feminism With and Against Bourdieu' *Feminist Theory* 1(1): 11–32.

Lury, C. (1998) *Prosthetic Culture: Photography, Memory and Identity.* London: Routledge.

Macpherson, C. B. (1962) *The Political Theory of Possessive Individualism.* Oxford: Oxford University Press.

Mauss, M. (1990[1925]) *The Gift: The Form and Reason of Exchange in Archaic Societies.* New York: Norton.

McCarthy, C. (2000) 'Reading the American Popular: Suburban Resentment and the Representation of the Inner City in Contemporary Film and TV' in D. Flemming (ed.) *Formations: A 21ˢᵗ Century Media Studies Textbook.* Manchester: Manchester University Press.

McNay, L. (1999) 'Gender, Habitus and the Field: Pierre Bourdieu and the Limits of Reflexivity' *Theory, Culture and Society* 16(1): 175–193.

McNay, L. (2000) *Gender and Agency: Reconfiguring the Subject in Feminist and Social Theory.* Cambridge: Polity.

McRobbie, A. (2002) 'A Mixed Bag of Misfortunes?: Bourdieu's Weight of the World' *Theory, Culture and Society* 19(3): 129–138.

Munro, R. (1996) 'The Consumption View of Self: Extension, Exchange and Identity' in S. Edgell, K. Hetherington and A. Warde (eds) *Consumption Matters.* Cambridge: Polity.

Pateman, C. (1988) *The Sexual Contract.* Cambridge: Polity.

Peterson, R. and Kern, R. (1996) 'Changing Highbrow Taste: From Snob to Omnivore' *American Sociological Review* 61: 900–907.

Peterson, R. and Simkus, A. (1993) 'How Musical Taste Marks Occupational Status Groups' in L. Lamont and M. Fournier (eds) *Cultivating Differences: Symbolic Boundaries and the Making of Inequality.* Chicago: Chicago University Press.

Pine, J. I. and Gilmore, J. H. (1999) *The Experience Economy: Work is Theatre and Every Business a Stage.* Boston: Harvard Business School Press.

Probyn, E. (2000) 'Shaming Theory: Thinking Disconnection: Feminism and Reconciliation' in S. Ahmed, J. Kilby, C. Lury, M. McNeil and B. Skeggs (eds) *Transformations: Thinking Through Feminism.* London: Routledge.

Reay, D. (1997) 'Feminist Theory, Habitus and Social Class: Disrupting Notions of Classlessness' *Women's Studies International Forum* 20(2): 225–233.

Reay, D. (1998) *Class Work: Mothers' Involvement in Children's Schooling.* London: University College Press.

Rose, N. (1989) *Governing the Soul.* London: Routledge.

Rotman, B. (1980) Mathematics: An Essay in Semiotics. Bristol: Bristol University.

Rubin, L. B. (1972/1992) *Worlds of Pain: Life in the Working Class Family.* New York: Basic Books.

Savage, M. (2000) *Class Analysis and Social Trasformation.* Buckingham: Open University Press.

Savage, M., Barlow, J., Dickens, P. and Fielding, T. (1992) *Property, Bureaucracy and Culture: Middle-Class Formation in Contemporary Britain.* London: Routledge.

Skeggs, B. (1997) *Formations of Class and Gender: Becoming Respectable.* London: Sage.

Skeggs, B. (2002) 'Techniques for Telling the Reflexive Self' in T. May (ed.) *Qualitative Research in Action.* London: Sage.

Skeggs, B. (2004) *Class, Self, Culture.* London: Routledge.

Smith, A. (1757) *Theory of Moral Sentiments.* London: Liberty Press.

Spivak, G. C. (1990) *The Post-Colonial Critic.* London: Routledge.

Stallybrass, P. (1998) 'Marx's Coat' in P. Spyer (ed.) *Border Fetishisms: Material Objects in Unstable Places.* London: Routledge.

Steedman, C. (1999) 'State Sponsored Autobiography' in B. Conekin, F. Mort and C. Waters (eds) *Movements of Modernity: Reconstructing Britain 1945–1964.* London: Rivers Oram.

Steedman, C. (2000) 'Enforced Narratives: Stories of Another Self' in T. Coslett, C. Lury and P. Summerfield (eds) *Feminism and Autobiography: Texts, Theories, Methods.* London: Routledge.

Strathern, M. (1991) *Partial Connections.* Maryland: Rowman and Little.

Strathern, M. (1999) *Property, Substance and Effect: Anthropological Essays on Persons and Things.* New Brunswick, New Jersey and London: Athlone.

Taylor, C. (1989) *Sources of the Self: The Making of Modern Identity.* Cambridge: Cambridge University Press.

Taylor, L. (2004) 'From Lifestyle Media to Lived Practice: an Ethnography of Class, Gender and Ordinary Gardening' PhD *Cultural Studies* University of Wolverhampton: Wolverhampton.

Thoburn, N. (2002) 'Difference in Marx: The Lumpenproletariat and the Proletarian Unameable' *Economy and Society* 31(3): 434–60.

Thoburn, N. (2003) *Deleuze, Marx and Politics.* London: Routledge.

Tyler, C.-A. (1991) 'Boys Will Be Girls: The Politics of Gay Drag' in D. Fuss (ed.) *Inside Out: Lesbian Theories/Gay Theories.* London: Routledge.

Valverde, M. (1998) 'Governing Out of Habit' Studies in Law, *Politics and Society* 18: 217–242.

Vicinus, M. (1974) *The Industrial Muse: A Study of Nineteeth Century British Working Class Literature.* London: Croom Helm.

Vincent, D. (1981) *Bread, Knowledge and Freedom: A Study of Working-Class Nineteeth Century Autobiography.* London: Europa.

Walkerdine, V. (1988) *The Mastery of Reason: Cognitive Development and the Production of Rationality.* London: Routledge.

Walkerdine, V. and Lucey, H. (1989) *Democracy in the Kitchen: Regulating Mothers and Socialising Daughters.* London: Virago.

Warde, A., Tomlinson, M. and McMeekin, A. (2000) 'Expanding Tastes? Cultural Omnivorousness and Social Change in the UK' CRIC Working Paper: University of Manchester.

Weiner, A. B. (1992) *Inalienable Possessions: The Paradox of Keeping-While-Giving.* Berkeley: University of California Press.

Willis, P. (2002) '"Taking the Piss": Double Consciousness and the Sensuous Activity of Manual Labour' *Labour Studies* conference, University of Manchester.

Wood, H. and Skeggs, B. (2004) 'Notes on Ethical Scenarios of Self on British Reality TV' *Feminist Media Studies* 4(2): 203–231.

Section II:
Symbolic violence and the cultural field

Notes on 'What Not To Wear' and post-feminist symbolic violence

Angela McRobbie

Pramface

In this cursory and at points, I am afraid, rather polemical engagement with aspects of Bourdieu's writing, I examine forms of female symbolic violence found in mid-evening television programmes given over to the so-called 'make-over' ie, the transformation of self with the help of experts in the hope or expectation of improvement of status and life chances through the acquisition of forms of cultural and social capital. The public denigration by women of recognized taste (the experts and presenters) of women of little or no taste, brings a new (and seemingly humorous) dimension to this kind of primetime television. The reprimands by the presenters span the spectrum from the school-marmish ticking off for poor grooming, bad posture and unattractive mannerisms, to the outright sneer, or classroom snigger directed towards the unkempt young, single mother wearing stained trousers as she drops off her child at school. Over the last few years this genre of popular television has achieved huge ratings and has attracted a great deal of publicity on the basis of a format which brings experts in taste and lifestyle together with willing victim in need of improvement.

My interest here is primarily in two BBC TV programmes *What Not To Wear* and *Would Like to Meet*, both of which have had series running through from 2002–2004 (for full details see BBC website at bbc.co.uk/). The format in WNTW comprises a victim/participant who wishes to be made over by the two presenters, Trinny Woodall and Susannah Constantine (whose book based on the series reached the number one slot for Christmas book sales in the UK December 2002, see Constantine and Woodall, 2002). The experts take a very close look at the victim, they ask her to show them her wardrobe, and she allows herself to be paraded for scrutiny, usually in her underwear (so that the girls can get an idea of shape and proportions) and then she is taught how to shop, what to look for, what colours would suit, how to buy a better fitting bra ('no more saggy boobs'), and so on. Then she is left on her own, with a budget, to buy new outfits. Under the watchful eye (hidden video camera) of the girls, she goes shopping and every time she tries to buy the bad old look, the girls guffaw and then pounce and stop her, guiding her towards more flattering purchases. WLTM comprises of three experts, two female, and one male, whose job it is to dissect the problems of a victim who is failing to find a partner, get dates or enjoy a lively social life. Here too the victim is scrutinized for body failings and also for unappealing characteristics including voice, manners, facial expression etc. The experts train the victim into new habits of self- presentation, arrange a dummy date and then expect the now confident victim to pluck up courage and ask someone out. Throughout the proceedings the experts spy on the victim from a van equipped with a hidden video camera. (As readers will, I am sure, be aware, there are also many other, hybrid, genres, in one series both gardener and interior designer team up to make over house and garden, in another two women cleaners shame a victim in the hope of encouraging him or her to become more clean and tidy, and in a recent and kinder US programme, *Queer Eye for the Straight Guy*, five gay men help a straight man each week to improve his home, self image and fashion sense.)

The programmes I am concerned with actively generate and legitimate forms of class antagonism particularly between women in a way which would have been socially unacceptable until recently. That is, the rules of television were such that public humiliation of people for their failure to adhere to middle-class standards in speech or appearance would have been considered offensive, dis-criminatory or prejudicial. Denigration, however, is now done with a degree of self-conscious irony, both the presenters and the audiences are assumed to know that no harm is intended and that, in post politically-correct times, this is just good fun. It is now possible, thank goodness, to laugh at less fortunate people once again. And the message is that the poor woman would do well to emulate her social superiors. While men are involved, as both experts and victims, this is largely a female genre of TV and the overall address is to women (see Brunsdon, 2003). Indeed the presence of men for such make-overs is normally so that they become more pleasing or palatable to women. This primarily female address corresponds to the changing identity of women in contemporary Britain. No longer defined in terms of husbands, fathers or boyfriends, women and in particular younger women have been set free to compete with each other, sometimes mercilessly. Public enactments of hatred and animosity are refracted at a bodily or corporeal level. But is this just girl against girl or are there specif-ically class dynamics? I would argue that there are clear class elements, re-drafted along the lines of the meritocratic model promoted by the Blair government. People are increasingly individualized, they are required to invent themselves, they are called upon to shape themselves so as to be flexible, to fit with the new circumstances where they cannot be passively part of the work-force but must, instead, keep themselves employable and adapt themselves and their skills for the rapidly changing demands of the labour market.

Thus, class makes a decisive re-appearance in and through the vectors of transformed gendered individualization. Walby has suggested that with full par-ticipation in the workforce, differences between women are actually becoming more marked. 'There are new divides opening up, between younger and older women. . . . older women . . . face an older life in poverty' (Walby, 1999:3) so that 'age inequalities can compound those of class' (Walby, 1999:6). There is an enormous disparity of income between younger and older women (with the latter much worse off). And although racial disadvantage weighs more heavily against black males than females, there are still marked inequalities of access in relation to education and careers between white and black women. Overall this scenario would suggest gender transformation including widespread fragmentation and dispersal but with younger, well-qualified, white women moving towards a more secure middle-class position. Change and movement are a feature of women's experience in recent years. How do these changes connect with the sharpness of the class antagonisms in these programmes? Of course, as Bourdieu and many others have shown, women have by no means been immune to the articulation of sharp and often cruel class distinctions (Bourdieu, 1984). Working class women have been very aware of the denigratory judgements made against them by their middle-class counterparts particularly in regard to their appearance and non-respectability (Skeggs, 1997). Middle-class women have played a key role in the reproduction of class society, not just through their exemplary role as wives and mothers but also as standard-bearers for middle-class family values, for certain norms of citzenship and also for safeguarding the valuable cultural capital accruing to them and their families through access to education, refinement and other privileges.

The question is, when women become more detached from traditional family roles as a result of movement into the labour market over a lifetime, how does this effect class society? What are the cultural forms and the wider repertoire of meanings which seek to give shape to and retain control over new gendered hierarchies? Is it the case that through the prism of individualization, class differences are re-invented, largely within the cultural and media field, so as to produce and re-produce social divisions now more autonomously feminized? Are women being more intensely re-classified on the basis that they now occupy positions of key importance in the wider political economy? Does the move into the workplace displace the masculine inflection of class values, with a wide range of more feminized meanings? (The reader need only peruse the pages of the right wing newspaper *The Daily Mail* to have this thesis quickly confirmed; here women under the age of 40 are new class subjects par excellence)[1]. Perhaps it was an easy mistake for feminists to make, to assume that the gains of feminist success in terms of the winning of certain freedoms (to earn your own living, to be entitled to equal pay etc) would bring with it, for women, an extension and enlargement of feminist values of collectivity and equality. Female individualization is, then, a social process bringing into being new social divisions through the denigration of low class or poor and disadvantaged women by means of symbolic violence. What emerges is a new regime of more sharply polarized class positions, shabby failure or well-groomed success. The pre-welfarist rough and respectable divide is re-invented for the 21st Century.

Let me consider briefly two illuminating journalistic moments, each of which is indicative of a social dynamic which re-iterates these specifically feminine modalities of symbolic violence, as processes of class differentiation now thoroughly projected onto and inseparable from the female body. From now on the young, single mother will be understood to be an abject person with a 'mismanaged life'. A social category, a certain type of girl whose bodily features and disposition betray her lowly status. This marks a reversal of the language of welfare liberal values for whom the teenage mother was someone to be provided with support. A new virulent form of class antagonism finds expression through the public denigration of the bodily failings of the girl who at a too young age embraces motherhood. Thus Christina Odone (Deputy Editor of the left-wing weekly *The New Statesman*) provides a more serious-minded (if inevitably laced with some irony) version of this recent form of boundary marking practice by writing that 'top range women . . . prefer to leave reproduction to the second eleven . . . a bump risks becoming as clear proof of a working-class background as the fag hanging from someone's lips'. She goes on to say that a teenage mother produces a 'socially autistic child with little expectation and even less talent' (Odone, 2000:21). In the same vein, but this time emerging from within the heartland of tabloid pop culture, one of the girl singers from the pop band Atomic Kitten (Kerry Catona), a blond girl with a wiry physique and who sports a strong tan, finds herself widely referred to on the Popbitch website as 'pramface' (which in turn circulates across the wider pop media). That is, she is deemed to look like the kind of poor, low class girl with a baby in pushchair. Other derogatory forms of female social classification include minger (or pig as *The Sun* newspaper labelled runner up for the Big Brother 2002 TV contest, Jade Goody).

What does pramface mean? A kind of girl. What kind of girl? Not dressed for work, therefore not earning an honest living. But not a student. With a baby but looks single, that is, not sufficiently attractive and presentable to attract a long term partner. She must be unmarried and dependent on benefits. As a seemingly recognizable social type it is assumed there must be many like her. The insult is thus indicative of a renewed and injurious practice of social re-ordering. The bodies of young women are now to be understood according to a scale running from welfare-dependent, single maternity, marking failure, to well-groomed, slim, sophistication, marking success. The pramface girl who is pinched and poor-looking, common and cheaply dressed, with a child in a buggy, is in sharp contrast to the 'A1' girls who can spend a disposable income on themselves and aspire to full participation in consumer culture. Through this differentiation class distinctions are now more autonomously (ie, these are all single girls) generated, within what Bourdieu might call the media or journalistic field and refracted through the youthful female body. This is a relatively recent phenomenon. Denigratory speech unashamedly and spitefully directed towards girls by other girls is associated with pre-feminist old-fashioned 'bitchiness'. Hurtful comments about body image, shape, style or poor taste would be considered as belonging to the school playground, and vociferously condemned by liberal-minded adults and teachers as a form of bullying. Likewise sniggers about living in a council estate or having a mother who does not look well off, might be expected to be met with a sharp reprimand. The prevalence, once again, of this kind of language is a mark of the cultural undoing of the social and liberal reforms which had an institutional life in the UK from the late 1960s until the mid 1990s.

'Needs and Norms' (Bourdieu, 1984)

Bourdieu's writing allows us to re-cast symbolic violence as a process of social reproduction, this time through a particular (post feminist) spatial and temporal framing of female individualization, the body, and the world of cultural objects. The victim of the make-over TV programme presents his or her class habitus (including home, family, friends and neighbours, and social milieu) for analysis and critique by the experts. That is, although the victim is individualized, he or she is also understood as embodying a social category of persons. These bodies on show display an 'incorporated history'. The programmes comprise of a series of encounters where cultural intermediaries impart guidance and advice to individuals ostensibly as a means of self-improvement. The experts guide the victims through various activities, from shopping, cooking and interacting with people, to flirting and going on dates. A key (entertainment) feature of the programmes (and one which most invites a Foucauldian analysis) involves observing the victims by means of hidden video cameras, as ethnographic technique, (ie, so that they can be seen *au naturel*). Usually the victims then have a chance to report back on their progress by making their own video diaries. Bourdieu is, I would argue, so useful here because he theorizes taste, while also understanding the body to be at the centre of what McNay calls 'modern strategies of social control' (McNay, 1999). McNay also reminds us that Bourdieu considers how social inequalities are perpetuated as power relations directed towards bodies and the 'dispositions of individuals'. Bourdieu focuses on constraint and injury, on practices of symbolic violence and their effectivity. The 'corporeal inculcation' of symbolic violence is, McNay argues, 'exercised with the complicity' of the individual. These programmes would not work if the victim did not come forward and offer herself as someone in need to expert help. On the basis of her own subordinate class habitus, the individual will have a 'feel for the game', a 'practical sense for social reality' which means that in the context of the programmes she will instinctively, and unconsciously, know her place in regard to the experts, hence the tears, the gratitude and the deference to those who know so much better than she does, and who are willing (temporarily) to share this knowledge and expertise.

In the two programmes WNTW and WLTM the habitual knowingness of the body is confronted with the demand of the dominant field that the victim/participant copies, or partake in a kind of mimesis, so that the habitus might be modified to conform with the requirement of good taste.[2] If, as Butler suggests, the habitus is the space for the generation of social belief in the obviousness of dominant social reality, then the cajoling, reprimanding and encouragement of the presenters and make-over experts provides clear insight into the operations of the field as it attempts to alter the habitus, while also inculcating the realism of the unachievable (Butler, 1999). Butler also suggests that the habitus and the field move towards congruence with each other insofar as the habitus is already inclined to submit to social authority. Butler does, however, take Bourdieu to task on the basis that with the habitus so easily capitulating to the demands of the field, she wonders how they can be conceptually understood as separate. Yes, I would agree, there is the real danger that field and habitus seem to suggest a set of binaries, one crudely of structure, the other of agency. On the other hand, the whole force of Bourdieu's writing is to avoid such an account. Butler does not accuse Bourdieu of such a mechanical distinction, indeed she seems impressed by the generative and formative capacities Bourdieu accords to the habitus. She does query however the over-dominative model marked out by the way in which the field invariably procures the submission of the habitus. There is '(t)he ideal of adaptation as the presiding norm of his theory of sociality' (Butler, 1999:118).

Unfortunately there is no space here to rehearse in more depth this lively critique by Butler. Perhaps habitus and field, flawed as they might be, are terms which are functional within certain limits. They allow, for example, an analysis such as the one I am presenting here, to move more rapidly towards sociological generalization (albeit with all the pitfalls that entails). Field and habitus allow me to suggest re-configuration by cultural means of the relations between class and gender in contemporary Britain. They help to explain how processes of social re-alignment take shape forcefully within the space of relaxation and enjoyment provided by media and entertainment. In a sense they allow a sociological rather than a textual reading. For instance, we can see quite clearly that the field and the habitus of the cultural intermediaries must remain separate (hence unachievable) from that of the victims and participants. There is no suggestion that the victims will ever truly belong to the same social group as their improvers. This is made clear in a multiplicity of small ways such as the consoling words and concluding comments on the part of the experts who retain an ever critical and sceptical eye. They also maintain monopoly over technical or professional vocabularies, they demonstrate their familiarity with a whole other world still out of reach of those who have now been made-over (often by name dropping or referring to exclusive shops, neighbourhoods, restaurants or art events). Among themselves they surmise that, once they, the experts, have departed, the victim is bound to return to her bad old ways. Thus we might say that what is happening in the programmes is that there is an attempt to transform the female working-class and lower middle-class habitus by means of shaming, instruction and the momentary celebrity glamour of being on television. The habitus is to be brought into line so as to conform with, as Bourdieu would say, the 'needs and norms' of the emergent consumer-dominated cultural field, and by these means women are both individualized and respectabilized. Now that women have decisively entered the labour force, female consumer culture has, in Blair's Britain, come to occupy a key site in regard to normative female identity and by this means the map of social class is re-drafted in gender terms. With the eradication of the old, traditional working class, these programmes and their equivalents across popular culture and in the tabloid press, construct a new, feminized, social space which is defined in terms of status, affluence and body image. More generally by these means women are subjected to more subtle practices of power directed to winning their consent to and approval of a more competitive, consumer-oriented, modernized, neo-liberal, meritocracy.

'Panic mingled with revolt' (Bourdieu, 1984)

Bourdieu's concepts of cultural capital and cultural intermediaries provide fine tools for understanding these programmes as a genre. It is only possible here however to provide a hasty sketch of how this might be done. In front of the camera, the cultural intermediaries flaunt or play up sometimes flamboyantly their own middle- or upper middle-class backgrounds by bringing these to bear, in the way in which they present the programmes, almost to the point of exaggeration or distortion. After all, everyone knows the British are obsessed with class and it makes for good television. These class locations are flagged up through their distinctive corporeal styles. Often the women are upper middle-class and 'loud' in voice and appearance and impart aspects of the cultural capital which they have accrued effortlessly. (The best example of this are the two older women who present the cooking programme *The Two Fat Ladies* (see bbc.co.uk/two fat ladies) and of course the glamorous and voluptuous Nigella Lawson who references the writing of Henry James while presenting the Channel Four *Nigella Bites* programme, see channelfour.co.uk/nigella bites and also Brundson forthcoming.) Their knowledge about good taste comes naturally because it is simply part of how they have been brought up. There is 'distance from necessity', there is nothing too urgent, too over enthusiastic, too *arriviste* about their expertise. They have had all the time in the world to learn about the kinds of things not taught at school and not on the academic curriculum. They simply know this stuff, they know how to put together an outfit without even thinking about it, they know which colours work, they know how to throw a wonderful dinner party and make it look as though there was no labour and no anxiety and no planning involved. They also know what 'not to wear'. They signal various degrees of disgust or repulsion, or extreme bodily displeasure at those who do not possess such good taste as themselves.

The two young women who present *WNTW* are well-connected young women of upper middle-class background (boarding school, mix with royalty etc). Their body language in the programmes indicates a leisurely approach to life and work, they sprawl over the sofa as they watch the video clips of the victims anxiously trying to choose an outfit and they laugh and giggle at their mistakes. It is not without irony that we now see so many upper class girls try to earn their own living successfully by drawing from and popularizing their own store of cultural capital, by in effect flogging it on the marketplace of populist television. (It is surely a bit like selling off the family silver.) Brundson has made a similar point, upper middle-class women now going out to work on the basis of providing instruction about how to look after the home (Brunsdon, 2003). Presumably there are those who might suggest that such programmes have also to be seen as possibly democratizing, in the sense that there is some re-distribution of cultural capital going on in them, with BBC television, in a post-modern Reithian mode, performing a national/domestic/educative function by kindly providing instruction on areas of everyday life not covered in the school curriculum. Bourdieu would, however, surely reply that by such means as these, deference and cultural goodwill to existing social hierarchies is inevitably con-firmed (Bourdieu, 1984).

Taking Bourdieu's analysis into account and adding my own comments above about gender changes, we could suggest that the two girls who present WNTW, (Trinny and Susannah) now find themselves in the workplace, since they, like most young women today, will no longer rely entirely on a male partner to look after them financially over a lifetime (in post-feminist times this is recognised as a high risk strategy). A career is a better investment. Therefore, upper middle-class young women will be competing against their extremely well educated, middle class counterparts in the labour market. There we have it, no longer 'gen-tlemen and scholars' as Bourdieu describes, but 'posh girls and educated girls'. Through this new matrix of gender and class, articulated most clearly in and through the fields of culture and media, new forms of class differentiation are being produced through processes of symbolic violence. It would be an impor-tant sociological exercise to track and analyse the role of insult and wounding comments or looks in these programmes. My own notes reveal comments such as 'what a dreary voice', 'look at how she walks', 'she shouldn't put ketchup on her chips', 'she looks like a mousy librarian', 'her trousers are far too long', 'that jumper looks like something her granny crocheted, it would be better on a table', 'she hasn't washed her clothes', 'your hair looks like an overgrown poodle', 'your teeth are yellow, have you been eating grass?' and 'Oh My God. . . . she looks like a German lesbian', this last insult was considered so hilarious that it was trailed as a promotion for the programme across the junctions of BBC TV for almost two weeks before it was broadcast.[3]

There is cruelty and viciousness often reminiscent of 1950s boarding school stories where the nasty snobbish girls ridicule the poor scholarship girl for her appearance, manners, upbringing, accent and shabbily dressed parents (however virtue usually wins out in these stories and the nasty girls come to grief). Pro-grammes like WLTM and WNTW are self-vindicating on the basis that the victims are young adults; they are willing participants and submit themselves to being made over with great enthusiasm. This is popular entertainment which uses irony to suggest that it is not meant to be taken literally. However, this does not mean that there is no humiliation. Participants frequently dissolve into tears and there is 'panic mingled with revolt' as they are put through their paces, unlearning what is considered unacceptable and unattractive about themselves.

My argument so far has been that this process of re-education marks out some of the sociological contours of change for women in contemporary Britain. This analysis emphasises the power of the field to re-direct the habitus so as to produce new class differences between women. I am aware however that I leave several strands hanging. Television scholars would surely point to the more complex production of meanings within these texts, such that there might, on occasion, be a victory by the participants over the presenters when the good taste proffered by the girls is ultimately refused. Sometimes the ordinariness and the unkempt image of the victim retains a resilience, dignity, self-respect and obstinacy, despite and against the efforts of the experts. Drawing on Butler others might point to the political strategies of re-territorialization which accrue from the performative effect of hateful words, there is plenty of website opposition to the denigratory dynamics of words like pramface or to its Scottish equivalent 'ned'. Sadly it seems there is little space for the resolutely unimproved woman to stake a political claim to remaining shabby.[4] Again, drawing on Butler, the repetition of such strings of insulting and injurious terms might be suggestive of much deeper anxieties precisely about the category of women in contemporary Britain as unstable, detached from the old, safe moorings of class, stable marriage and appropriate gender and sexual identity. With their own money in their pockets, who knows what might happen? If the return to marriage marks one popular cultural strategy (see McRobbie 2005) then this feminine re-invoking of class differences (by means of bitchiness/snobbishness) is surely another.

To conclude, readers might wonder why little has been said so far on how race figures in these televisual encounters. There are several black and Asian glamorous women presenting programmes like these across the channels but are ethnic minority women victims and participants treated with the same contempt as their white counterparts? And where gay men are so visible as experts in these programmes, how is lesbian identity interwoven with these processes of class rearrangement? One quick and easy answer to this lies in social approval being granted across the lines of sex and race on the basis of the desire for improvement and the capacity to conform to normative ideals of glamour and good looks which, in turn, consolidate a re-assuring, middle-class identity. In WNTW Trinny and Susannah are disparaging about a woman cab driver who is too 'masculine' and who is 'hiding her fab figure', but to date they do not appear to have offered their services to lesbian participants. And so far I have not come across a programme where the experts openly laugh at, or make denigratory comments about, black or Asian women; the tone is somehow softened when the subject of the make-over is black. This surely introduces dynamics for further analysis. It is not simply that this is only a matter of re-instating of old class prejudices, pitching white middle-class against white working-class women. More that the historical repertoires of traditional English class snobbishness and bitchiness find immediate expression in the denigratory comments about the image, appearance, voice and accent of white working-class people. These wounding words are still there in the habitus of middle-class life, even though they have been dormant. Black people have been understood as racialized subjects rather than class subjects historically, and so in effect they have not been included in this particular vocabulary of symbolic violence. Insults directed at them are invariably racialized. As Stuart Hall wrote, for black people in Britain 'class is lived through the modality of race' (Hall, 1978). More specifically to pursue such a line of analysis we would need to consider concretely the editorial codes and conventions in place as scripts are being written and victims selected and then briefed. There is then a good deal more work to be done on 'mundane texts' such as these (Rose, 1999). We might also ponder the narrowing of bodily norms and the strict limits on what constitutes acceptable sexual identity, on the part of young women, as a counter to earlier feminist and lesbian arguments and as a means of further excluding or repudiating those who find no comfort, indeed only pain, in the prescribed femininity as defined by Trinny and Susannah. But let me return to Bourdieu. My claim here is that his writing allows an understanding of how social re-arrangement along gender lines takes shape within media and popular culture by means of habitus adjustment to ensure conformity with the contemporary requirements of the fields of employment, consumer culture and sexuality.

Notes

1 The power of the right-wing *The Daily Mail* in the UK should never be under-estimated; it's the only daily newspaper with more than 50% of readers women. Cleverly, and without being noticed, it is devoted to re-defining the terrain of contemporary femininity.
2 One male victim in WLTM over-stepped the limits by over-enthusiastically copying every aspect of the male expert.
3 This is clearly non-systematic, however there are no claims being made in this chapter that I have carried out exhaustive research on the programmes, my intention is instead to open up areas of discussion.
4 Thanks to a Scottish MA student at Goldsmiths College London, who led me through the fight back against the slur of 'nedism' in the Scottish press and parliament.

References

Bourdieu, P. (1984) *Distinction*. London: Routledge.
Brunsdon, C. (2003) 'Lifestyling Britain: The 8–9 Slot on British Television' *International Journal of Cultural Studies* 6(1): 5–23.
Brunsdon, C. (forthcoming, 2004) 'Feminism, Post-Feminism: Martha and Nigella' *Cinema Journal*.
Butler, J. (1999) 'Performativity's Social Magic', in R. Shusterman (ed) *Bourdieu: A Critical Reader*. Oxford: Blackwell.
Constantine, S. and Woodall, T. (2002) *What Not To Wear*. London: Weidenfeld Nicolson Illustrated.
Hall, S. *et al* (1978) *Policing the Crisis*. London: Hutchinson.
McNay, L. (1999) 'Gender, Habitus and the Field' *Theory Culture and Society* 16(1): 95–119.

McRobbie, A. (2005) 'Post Feminism and Popular Culture' *Feminist Media Studies* 4(3): 255–64.
Odone, C. (2000) 'If High Flyers Refuse to Be Mums' *The New Statesman*, 3/4/2000: 21.
Rose, N. (1999) *Powers of Freedom*. Cambridge: Cambridge University Press.
Skeggs, B. (1997) *Formations of Class and Gender*. London: Sage.
Walby, S. (1999) 'Introduction' in S. Walby, S. *New Agendas for Women*. Basingstoke: Macmillan.

Rules of engagement:
Habitus, power and resistance

Steph Lawler

Identities are not ... reflections of objective social positions which is how class is often theorized (if at all). This ... would be to see identities always retrospectively. Nor are the social positions essential categories. Identities are continually in the process of being re-produced as responses to social positions, through access to representational systems and in the conversion of forms of capital (Beverley Skeggs, 1997:94)

[C]lass inequalities, which might be thought of as 'large scale' issues of social and economic justice (or injustice), give rise to 'real' social effects, one of which is classed subjectivities (Mariam Fraser, 1999:120).

Introduction

This chapter is about some of the ways in which class and gender become incorporated into embodied selves. Rather than focusing on (experienced) subjectivities, however, the argument will concentrate on the ways in which identities are *conferred* on subjects, so that they are marked as normal or abnormal, as wrong or right. I will argue that Bourdieu's insights into the ways in which class distinctions and divisions circulate around cultural and symbolic, as well as economic axes, enable a critical analysis of configurations of class that are not named as such. This is especially significant at a time when 'the death of class' is announced across a range of academic and political sites. However, as I will argue, class divisions, class distinctions and class inequalities have not 'died': neither has class ceased to be a meaningful category of analysis. Rather, the drawing of classed distinctions is displaced and individualized. It is displaced on to individual persons (or families) who are approved or disapproved, normalized or pathologized. And because class has conventionally been theorized in solely economic terms and around issues of redistribution, there is little critical language in which to analyse and oppose such moves.

Gender is central here, as one axis around which class distinctions are drawn and maintained (and, of course, vice-versa). That is, part of the different meanings attached to different forms of masculinity and femininity cohere around class. In the rest of this chapter, I want to use Bourdieu's concept of habitus to analyse representations of classed femininities – and in particular, to look at how classed and gendered identities become part of the stakes in political struggles. I also want to use his work to think about what this might say about issues of resistance and conformity.

The representations I am considering here are broadsheet press representations of two different protests. The protests in question took place in the summer of 2000 and in January of 2001. Both involved parents (mainly mothers) protesting against the housing of child sex abusers within their communities – an issue that came to the forefront of British political discussion following the highly-publicized disappearance and murder of eight-year-old Sarah Payne. Before I discuss press representations of these protests, however, I want to outline Bourdieu's conceptualization of habitus, and consider its usefulness for the analysis I am undertaking here.

Habitus and the subject

Bourdieu's concept of habitus is central to his analysis of social identity, and represents his attempt to theorize the ways in which the social is literally incorporated. Habitus is a 'socialized subjectivity' (Bourdieu and Wacquant, 2002:126); it is Bourdieu's way of theorizing a self which is socially produced. It is a way of analysing how social relations become constituted within the self, but also how the self is constitutive of social relations. It has been described as a 'second sense', 'practical sense' or 'second nature' (Johnson, 1993) that equips social actors with a practical 'know-how'. Habitus is manifest in styles of standing and moving, taking up space, in ways of speaking (idioms, as well as accent), in styles of dress, and so on (Bourdieu, 1986, 1990). It is not, however, confined to the body since it also consists of series of dispositions, attitudes and tastes. As such, habitus is a concept which cuts across conventional mind / body splits. It also cuts across conventional distinctions between conscious and unconscious, since much of its force derives from non-conscious elements:

> The process of acquisition [of habitus] – a practical *mimesis* (or mimeticism) which implies an overall relation of identification and has nothing in common with an *imitation* that would presuppose a conscious effort to reproduce a gesture, an utterance or an object explicitly constituted as a model- and the process of reproduction – a practical reactivation that is opposed to both memory and knowledge – tend to take place below the level of consciousness, expression and the reflexive distance which these presuppose. . . . [The body] does not represent what it performs, it does not memorize the past, it *enacts* the past, bringing it back to life. What is 'learned by the body' is not something one has, like knowledge that can be brandished, but something **that one is** (Bourdieu, 1990:73, italicized emphasis in original, bold emphasis mine).

As this quotation indicates, habitus carries the concept of history – both personal history and social, or collective, history. Elsewhere, Bourdieu defines habitus as 'embodied history, internalized as a second nature and so forgotten as history' (Bourdieu, 1990:56). For Bourdieu, 'the subject is not the instantaneous *ego* of a sort of singular *cogito*, but the individual trace of an entire collective history' (1990:91).

The emphasis on history can make the concept of habitus appear as the carrier of the weight of dead generations, a means of more or less straightforward reproduction. However, it is important to note that habitus is not determining, but generative. Although reproduction across generations does occur within this formulation, the dynamic character of the social world means that it will not occur perfectly: for example, more or less identical habitus can generate widely different outcomes. 'Practical sense' is bounded, rather than determined. It does not determine a pre-constituted subject: rather, it generates the human subject *qua* subject.[1] Certainly, this subject is agentic: s/he acts, decides and chooses: to do otherwise would be to not be a subject. In a sense, Euro-American social organization demands agentic subjects through its injunctions continually to 'choose' (Strathern, 1992). This does not mean that this agency is not 'real', simply that it is not foundational. To be forced to act does not nullify action (Fuller, 1988).

What is central here is the *relationality* of habitus. Habitus 'makes sense' only in the context of specific local contexts or 'fields'[2] – the 'games' for which 'the rules of the game' equip us:

> The motor – what is sometimes called motivation – resides neither in the material or symbolic purposes of action, as naïve finalists imagine, nor in the constraints of the field, as the mechanistic thinkers suppose. It resides in the relation between the habitus and the field, which means that the habitus contributes to determining what determines it (Bourdieu, 1994:194–5).

But habitus is also relational in another sense: habitus exist in relation to *each other*. Because habitus are profoundly social, they carry the traces of the lines of division and distinction along which the social is organized. That is, class, race, gender, sexuality, and so on, are all marked within the habitus. Further, and because these social distinctions are hierarchical, not all habitus are worth the same. Some are normalized, while others are pathological. In this sense, habitus clash, as well as class. Part of the 'second sense' embodied in habitus entails a judgment of other habitus. However, only some people have the authority to make such judgments stick. It is not, *pace* Dreyfus and Rabinow (1993), that Bourdieu sees everyone as simply endlessly accumulating social 'profits', but rather that 'profits' are made through the owners of some capitals being distinguished from the owners of others.

What gives habitus its particular force, in this context, is that power is conceptualized as working such that it is not what you do or what you have, that is marked as wrong or right, normal or pathological, but *who you are*. This is not to deny that subjects can resist such a positioning, nor that habitus may be imperfectly aligned with the field.[3] However, it is important to note that there are some people who, by virtue of their habitus, are able to pass judgment, implicitly or explicitly, on others, and to make that judgment count. Differences between habitus, then, come to be made into inequalities:[4]

[A] difference, a distinctive property . . . only becomes a visible, perceptible, non-indifferent, socially *pertinent* difference if it is perceived by someone who is capable of *making the distinction* – because, being inscribed in the space in question, he or she is not *indifferent* and is endowed with categories of perception, with classificatory schema, with a certain *taste*, which permits her to make differences, to discern, to distinguish (Bourdieu, 1998a:9, original emphases).

As Hannah, a white middle-class 16-year-old in Walkerdine *et al's* study, comments, class is 'also about taste and about dress and about interests. You can spot it a mile off even though it's not to do with money' (Walkerdine *et al*, 2001:38). And Walkerdine *et al* comment that:

If Hannah could 'spot it a mile off', it would be ridiculous to assume that the targets of her pejorative evaluations would not also be able to spot it in themselves and others, even if they could nòt theorise it in the way that Hannah's upbringing had taught her to do for many years. . . . [I]n this analysis class is in everything about the person, from the location of the home, to their dress, their body, their accent (Walkerdine *et al*, 2001:39).[5]

To summarize: I have argued that habitus constitutes a 'factor of social difference' (Fiske, 1992) which is also a factor of inequality. It is an important means through which 'large scale' social inequalities (such as class and gender) are made real, and are also made to inhere within the person, so that it is persons themselves who can be judged and found wanting, and persons themselves who can be made to bear the 'hidden injuries' of inequality. Bourdieu's attempt to cut through antinomies such as self/other, structure/agency and, in Nancy Fraser's (2001) terms, recognition/redistribution gives us a method for considering the ways in which inequalities can circulate culturally, as well as materially. Further, Bourdieu's highlighting of ultimately arbitrary character of social distinctions (so that, for example, what counts as 'tasteful' is an effect, not of intrinsic properties, but of social relations) gives us a way to challenge the taken-for-granted ('the doxic' in Bourdieu's terms). This is especially pressing in the case of classed inequalities, since class is largely silenced, reduced instead to a voluntaristic emphasis on ways to get the working classes to change (Roberts 1999; Lawler 2000).

Unspeakable subjects

I want now to return to the issue of press representations of the two sets of protests. My analysis here is not about the protestors themselves, but centres, rather, around the representation of the protests in 'broadsheet' newspapers.[6]

Hence, I am concerned, not with the (felt) subjectivities of the protestors, but with the (conferred) identities through which these protestors were constituted as personae within these representations. In particular, I want to consider the ways in which evaluations of classed femininity were used to constitute the two groups of protestors in wholly different ways. My contention here is that these representations constituted working-class and middle-class feminine identities in ways which normalized middle-class identities and pathologized working-class identities. Further, implicit references to the women's femininity were an important means through which the representations articulated classed distinctions. This reportage – produced for a mainly middle-class readership – reveals the relational and hierarchical character of habitus. This is not because the stories somehow 'reveal' the habitus of the writers, but because they are elements in much larger cultural configurations of class and femininity.

The first protests occurred in Paulsgrove, Portsmouth, on a working-class housing estate. They were part of a series of protests which took place in the wake of 'name and shame' campaign run by the British tabloid, *The News of the World*. This campaign involved the paper printing the photographs and personal details of 'known paedophiles' living in Britain. Protestors in Paulsgrove were demanding the removal from the area of men believed to have abused children.[7]

The second set of protests took place in the London suburb of Balham, and were mobilized against proposals to open a residential centre for serious ex-offenders, including those convicted of sexual offences against children. In both protests, press attention was focused on women protestors.

The difference between press representation of the two cases could not be starker. The Balham protests received minimal press coverage, in contrast to the enormous amount of coverage devoted to the Paulsgrove protests. In the former case, the women were represented as devoted mothers, vigilant, rather than vigilante;[8] and identification was invited, so that they became part of a fictive 'we' who are right to be worried about 'our' children. Press coverage was almost entirely sympathetic, with only two dissenting voices (local residents) reported as disapproving the protests. There were no references to these women's appearances, their homes, or their incomes. The only personal details reported were about their jobs (solidly professional),[9] the ages of their children and, in one case, their title (Lady Cosima Somerset). These protestors are 'not rioters, but QCs, bank managers and City traders' (Midgley, 2001).[10]

The Paulsgrove protests received massive press coverage, including numerous comment pieces. These women were consistently presented in disgusted and dismissive terms. With the exception of a single half-supportive story in *The Times*,[11] not a single broadsheet story presented their protest as a rational or understandable one. Instead, they were consistently represented as a 'mob' (and the trope of Salem was repeatedly invoked). Minute details of their lives – their income, their past relationships, the ways in which they furnished their homes – were reported. Their bodily appearance and their clothing were described in detail. It must be noted that the highly-charged negative tones which characterized these representations cut across conventional Left/Right distinctions within the broadsheets: the left-liberal *Guardian* and *Observer* were just as dismissive of the Paulsgrove women as the right-wing *Telegraph* and *Times*.

The vilification of these women took place across three main axes: their bodily appearance (assumed to mark a deeper, pathologized, psychology); their ignorance or lack of understanding; and their inadequacy as mothers.

Appearance

> Valerie Toovey is 55 and had 22 grandchildren. Her glass cabinet is filled with pictures of them all and her shelves are lined with hundreds of ornaments they have given her. . . . Valerie, large gold earrings rattling as she furiously shakes her tightly-permed head . . . (Gillan, *The Guardian*: 12/8/00).

> Each evening scores of mothers, all with their children, emerge from their homes clutching bags of crisps, fizzy drinks and bottles of alcopops, to gather round the spiky-haired, heavy-smoking Katrina Kessell. Demonstrators, ranging from mothers pushing prams to tattooed teenagers . . . (Martin, *The Telegraph*: 10/8/00).

> Mums set aside the disco Lycra essential for telegenic promotion of hanging and castration (Riddell, *The Observer*: 13/8/00).

> There on TV were the mums (no dads) faces studded, shoulders tattooed, too-small pink singlets worn over shell-suit bottoms, pallid faces under peroxided hair telling tales of a diet of hamburgers, cigarettes and pesticides (Aaronovitch, *The Independent*: 11/8/00).

Appearance, here as elsewhere, functions as a marker of the person. In the case of the Paulsgrove women, their bodies mark them as having a 'deeper', pathological, personality. To work on the body is usually coded as 'feminine' (Skeggs, 1997) but this work should be 'invisible'. The work done by these women on their bodies – in the form of piercings, tattoos, dyed hair and styles of dress – is foregrounded, and thus rendered visible. The work (presumably) done by the Balham women on *their* bodies is not. Hence the Paulsgrove women are pathologized by an emphasis on 'feminine' work.[12] Moreover, aesthetics here has been turned into morality, so that immorality and ignorance are read off from an aesthetic marked as 'facile' (Bourdieu, 1986) or 'common'.

The emphasis on the appearance of the Paulsgrove women (through textual description and accompanying photographs) provides a means of judging them through an aesthetic which is already classed. Bleached hair, tattoos and the rest are used to signify a form of femininity that itself signifies a lack of morality. Hence the moral demands made by the protestors (what they did) are shifted through an assumed immorality (who they were).

Ignorance . . .

The Paulsgrove women were repeatedly represented as ignorant. For example, Katrina Kessell (reportedly one of the primary organizers of the protests) is described as:

wrong-headed and self-deluding, and not given to lengthy discussion of such abstract concepts as irony, principle, or the Rule of Law (Ferguson *The Guardian*: 4/2/01).

More specifically, they were described as 'not understanding the difference' between (basically) sad old men who expose their genitals to children and child murderers. In *The Guardian*, for example:

Maybe they will even realize that paedophilia is not a single enemy: that there are some abusers whose behaviour, though indecent and vile, does not represent a homicidal threat to children (Leader: 11/9/00).

or, in *The Telegraph*:

[M]any sexual offences against children are not remotely of this severity or seriousness, nor are they of unique wickedness. Quite often . . . I meet pathetic old men who have merely exposed themselves to children in the park (Dalrymple: 13/8/00).

The women were also presented as 'cultural dupes' – whipped up into an unthinking frenzy by the *News of the World's* campaign. However, the most common manifestation of the women's alleged ignorance was represented as their assumed ignorance of the fact that the home is the riskiest place for children and that most children are abused by intimates.

It is worth considering this claim for a moment, since it is informed by feminist politics and it was frequently articulated in broadsheet coverage and in letters to the broadsheet press (Bell, 2002). Although available evidence indicates that children are indeed most at risk from family members, it is something of a leap from this to claim that they are *only* at risk from family members. There were, in fact, men convicted of sexual crimes against children, who were not family members, living on the Paulsgrove Estate. Moreover, many intimates were once strangers and many people with a sexual interest in children make it their business to cross the line from 'stranger' to 'intimate'. The rigid line between 'intimates' and 'strangers', drawn so starkly within the press, as well as by other commentators (see, eg, Haug, 2001), does not hold up. But in some ways, this is beside the point, because the argument, *in this context*, seems to be doing another kind of work – the work of drawing distinctions. First, it further renders the protestors' actions illegitimate and ignorant. Their anxieties are represented as paranoid fantasies. Second, it renders those who voice these claims as more knowing, more understanding – more *distinguished* – than those who are positioned as not knowing this. Finally, it positions some forms of family as much more 'risky' than others. None of the reports or commentaries on the Balham protests carried any suggestion that *these* children were more at risk within their families.

Drawing distinctions, of course, is a significant way in which class operates. Those 'in the know' are able to pronounce on, and disapprove, those 'not in the know'.[13] For Bourdieu, ignorance is an important means through which working-class 'lack' is signified:

Anglo-American ideology . . . [historically] distinguished the 'undeserving poor' . . . from the 'deserving poor' . . . Alongside or in place of this ethical justification there is now an intellectual justification. The poor are not just immoral, alcoholic and degenerate, they are stupid, they lack intelligence (Bourdieu, 1998b:43).

This, for Bourdieu, is part of the sociodicy of dominant groups – a theoretical justification for their privilege (no need to listen to the dominated if they are stupid anyway). Conversely, privileged groups are constituted as knowledge-able and understanding. It is noteworthy that the protestors in Balham were not vilified by being characterized as 'not understanding' the greater risk of the private sphere. Instead, their protests are presented as logical, since there is a high proportion of children living in the area. Peter Stanford, for example, comments:

> The Home Office . . . might just pause to ask whether Nappy Valleys[14] are the best place for [ex-offenders' hostels]. The presence of such a disproportionately high per-centage of children seems to cut across any therapeutic intent in the work that goes on within their walls. Perhaps paedophiles themselves are not well served by this plan (Stanford, 2001).

So here we have a unity of interests – a harmonious world in which everyone's interests are compatible. We have to ask why this argument was never used in the Paulsgrove case – why, for example, it was never suggested that the interests of those convicted of child sexual abuse there might not be best served by living among children. Through constituting the Paulsgrove women in terms of ignorance, reportage manages to avoid publicly condemning the cause for which the women were ostensibly fighting, while condemning them for fighting it.

Abusive motherhood . . .

Children were present in both protests, but were very differently portrayed. Pho-tographs accompanying reportage of the Balham protests show well-dressed, winsome children holding candles and posters inscribed with slogans such as, 'Ban the bad people from Balham' and 'Protect us'. These children closely approximate the figure of 'the child' which, like femininity, is a classed (and raced) sign. These children are unknowing – paedophiles are simply 'bad people'. Here we have the 'real' child instantiated: middle-class, white, unknow-ing, innocent and vulnerably dependent (Hockey and James, 1993). The Pauls-grove children are excluded from the apparently open and capacious category, 'child'. Since the responsibility for producing 'real' children rests firmly with mothers (Lawler, 2000), the Paulsgrove women's motherhood is rendered suspect through representations of their children as horrific. The women protesting in Balham were represented as concerned parents: theirs is described as a 'child-centred' community (Stanford, 2001); what is emphasized is their desire to protect their children. The Paulsgrove women are criticized for taking their children on protests. Carol Sarler writes of 'the mites in . . . Paulsgrove' holding banners 'whose words they would be better off not knowing' (Sarler, 2000).

The accusation of child abuse was a recurring one: the women were constituted as abusing their children by taking them on protests against child abusers. This assumed abuse was taken to obliterate the ostensible purpose of the protests. So comments like Aaronovitch's: 'And they'd taught their three-year-old kids (on whose behalf all this was *supposedly* being done) to chant slogans about hanging and killing' (Aaronovitch, *The Independent*: 11/8/00, my emphasis) were common.

This assumption is taken further in a comment column in the *Sunday Telegraph*. Here Dr. Theodore Dalrymple first, draws attention to the fact that most danger to children comes from intimates. But he then moves on to accuse the protestors at Paulsgrove of themselves being child abusers. They were 'demonstrating against themselves' he argues: the public protests were an example of the psychic defence mechanism of 'projection' since it was the protestors themselves who were child abusers. What is the basis for this assertion? According to Dalrymple, there are high levels of 'illegitimacy' and 'serial stepfatherhood'; and there are 'teenage pregnancies':

> It is precisely on such estates that teenage pregnancy is most frequent, where it is not uncommon to find mother and daughter to be each nurturing illegitimate babies of precisely the same age in the same household, where uncles are younger than their nephews, where full siblings are rare but half- and step-siblings are common, and where the age of consent to sexual relations has been completely abolished – as often as not under the complacent gaze of the supposedly responsible adults. Complete disorder in the relations between the sexes reigns, and the resultant violence is of a degree and severity of which the complacent middle classes have little idea (Dalrymple, *The Sunday Telegraph*: 13/8/00).

This depiction of working-class families as a chaotic threat to the established order is part of a long tradition (see, eg, Roberts, 1999) but it is given a specific spin here by turning the Paulsgrove women's protests against them. Dalrymple claims to know the 'true' motives of the protestors (projection as a reaction-formation to the knowledge of their own status as 'abusers') while the women themselves are represented as incapable of self-knowledge or self-reflection. Not only in this extract but everywhere in broadsheet representations of the Paulsgrove women, a gap is established between being and seeming: they seem to be (they pass themselves off as) concerned mothers, but this appearance is belied by their 'true' motives, which lie elsewhere (there were frequent suggestions that they participated in these protests as forms of attention-seeking; as an excuse to exercise violence; or simply because they enjoyed it). However, the gap itself is established (in part) through appearance. These women do not possess the 'right' bodies, or bodily dispositions, or forms of speech. In contrast, a perfect congruence is established between the appearance and the essence – between the seeming and the being – of the Balham women, who both appear to be, and are, concerned mothers.

118

Rules of engagement

The Paulsgrove protestors could be seen as claiming something to which they are not (considered to be) entitled – the right to choose those among whom one lives, even the right to expect political support for the protection of their children. In contrast, the Balham protestors are implicitly granted this right. The Paulsgrove women could also be seen as transgressing gender norms, in that the specular effect of their protests was one which transgressed the norm of the passive, quiet, 'sensitive' woman. Could their actions, then, be understood in terms of resistance? I ask this, not because I want to recoup their protests into a resistance theory, but because I think the protests – and especially their reception – raise important questions about how we conceptualize both assimilation and resistance.

It's clear that, within the press stories themselves, the women's actions were not framed in terms of resistance – in the way in which, for example, anti-globalization protests or even recent protests in the UK by the Countryside Alliance have been framed – as the more or less desperate attempts of 'ordinary people' to effect change. Even broadly Left newspapers, which might be expected to be sensitive to issues of class and gender, consistently represented the Pauls-grove women in disgusted and horrified tones. Indeed, the recent slippage from working-class to underclass might well grant legitimacy to a left-wing patholo-gizing of the working class. The 'working class' or 'underclass' is now further removed from 'the proletariat' who were only ever of interest to much of the Left because of their key role in relation to capital, and hence in revolutionary politics. Now that the proletariat is held not to exist, its place taken by a feck-less underclass, what possible worth could be attached to those who slip the net of the allegedly expanding middle classes?

Yet, whatever the nomenclature, this group is essential to the middle class because, without it, the middle class would be unable to define itself. Without an other against whom to mark a normalized identity, against whom to draw distinctions, the middle classes would be unable to draw the kinds of distinctions that establish them *as* middle-class (and therefore as occupying a normal and desirable position). Classes exist, in Bourdieu's terms, neither in terms of voluntary choices nor in terms of essential attributes but as divisions that are produced and reproduced (cf. Walkerdine and Lucey, 1989). 'Classes exist in some sense in a state of virtuality, not as something given but as something to be done' (Bourdieu, 1998a:12).

The Paulsgrove protestors' claims to authority were founded, not specifically on a class or gender politics (they did not explicitly mobilize under the signs of either 'class' or 'gender') but on claims to recognition as concerned parents. However, class politics is present here. The protestors' claims were *disqualified*, in the representations I am discussing here, through an invocation of the signi-fiers of a pathologized working-class existence. Hence class politics is at work through a *middle-class* disgust at what these women were (seen to be). Disgust works to invalidate the protest and to pathologize the persons taking part – precisely because it is the authority instantiated in a middle-class habitus that can make such judgments stick.

James Bohman (1999) argues that those authorized to speak and to judge the actions of others must obey certain formal rules, or they will find their own authority contested. For example, he argues:

> The judge can say 'I find you guilty!' not because it is backed up by any reasons, but because he is acting on behalf of a group of other agents and with the resource of institutions. . . . But for all his authority to do so, the judge must still give reasons which conform to practices of justification or have his decisions overturned in review (Bohman, 1999:139).

But what Bohman overlooks is that the practices of justification which must be conformed to are not necessarily the *overt* practices of justification which govern a specific field. In the case of crimes of sexual violence, for example, judges may well invoke, not the overt practice or process of law but social assumptions about appropriate male and female behaviour (Smart, 1989). So long as these pro-nouncements are not 'outlandish' – i.e. so long as they accord with doxic truths, judges lose none of their authority in making them (though they may be subject to criticism) since their authority is instantiated within the person. There is often more than one 'game' – and hence more than one set of rules – in play at a par-ticular moment.

There are no overt rules which would debar the Paulsgrove protestors from demonstrating. There are, of course, formal laws – under which some of them were charged – against some of their activities, such as affray, or breach of the peace. However, press representations of these figures achieved a condemnatory tone, not just – not even mainly – through disapproving illegal actions, but through disapproving the entire persons of the protestors. The Paulsgrove protests were condemned, not primarily through an explicit and principled objection to the women's actions, but through the markers of their habitus – their clothes, their bodies, their homes – all of which are assumed to reveal a deeper ignorance and stupidity. In other words, rules were invoked that were not the *explicit* 'rules of the game' (ie, the politics of protest) but were a set of rules around who can be recognized as legitimate political actors. In Nancy Fraser's (2001) terms, these women were not recognized: they were denied the status of full players in questions of distributive justice, because they belong to a group that is not *recognized* as having a parity with other, normalized groups to whom material and symbolic goods are deemed to rightfully accrue. There are less apparent 'rules' at work here – rules about who is, and who is not, authorized to speak at all – and these rules, in this case, hinge on class.

My argument here, then, is that formal rules or laws are not the only rules or laws operating within a particular field. Fields are always sites of struggle and part of this struggle centres on the struggle for legitimate ownership of various forms of capital, including the ownership of authority. This has impli-cations for how we theorize resistance.

120

Resisting authority

> People are not fools; they are much less bizarre or deluded that we would sponta-
> neously believe precisely because they have internalized, through a protracted and
> multisided process of conditioning, the objective choices they face (Bourdieu and
> Wacquant, 2002:130)

The white working class in Britain has increasingly come to be coded as 'backward', as embodying the very antithesis of New Labour's 'modernizing' project
(Haylett, 2001). Its supposed atavism works to set it outside of forces of
'progress'. I want to suggest that this coding of the white working class, together
with the ways in which 'resistance' or 'contestation' are usually conceptualized,
makes it difficult to frame actions such as these in terms of resistance. As Pamela
Fox (1994) argues, only some forms of contestation get to count *as* 'resistance';
and what gets to count as resistance tends to be what is approved by the bourgeois observer.

Fox argues that theories of resistance (and she is talking primarily about theories of class resistance) have tended to detach (progressive) 'resistance' from
'conformity' or 'incorporation'. Thus, she suggests, the complexity of working-
class people's lives can be reduced to simply one (or other) of its dimensions.
Fox herself wants to 'mark out a more expansive conceptualization of class
resistance' (1994:19), arguing that:

> [W]hat we identify as a 'conformist' attitude or position may be rooted in another
> kind of transgressive logic that is equally (if not more) compelling than the need to
> challenge capitalist or patriarchal ideologies directly (Fox, 1994:19).

Fox's analysis, importantly in my view, unsettles the conventional divide between
submission/incorporation and resistance.

Bourdieu, similarly, wants to alert his readers to the apparent paradox
embedded within relations of domination:

> When the dominated quest for distinction leads the dominated to affirm what distin-
> guishes them, that is, that in the name of which they are dominated and constituted
> as vulgar, do we have to talk of resistance? In other words, if, in order to resist, I have
> no other resource than to lay claim to that in the name of which I am dominated, is
> this resistance? Second question: when, on the other hand, the dominated work at
> destroying what marks them out as 'vulgar' and at appropriating that in relation to
> which they appear as vulgar (for instance, in France, the Parisian accent). Is this sub-
> mission? I think this is an insoluble contradiction: this contradiction, which is
> inscribed into the very logic of symbolic domination, is something those who talk
> about 'popular culture' won't admit. Resistance may be alienating and submission
> may be liberating. Such is the paradox of the dominated, and there is no way out of
> it (Bourdieu, 1994:155).

So, for Bourdieu, it is the logic of domination which means that submission and
resistance are interlinked in an apparently paradoxical relation. This characteristically bleak and pessimistic passage seems to confirm Bourdieu's determinism

and to conform to charges made against him that his work robs us of political imagination and vision (see Harker *et al* 1990). Yet it is clear that Bourdieu, every bit as much as Foucault, sees resistance going on along side domination (Bourdieu, 2002:80). It is not that people lack agency: rather, there is no 'innocent' position: no resistance that is not some way complicitous with power (cf. Bar-On, 1993). The complex relationships between habitus and fields may well lead people to behave in ways that are not considered 'progressive'. This is not because they are 'lacking' in any way, but precisely because 'people are not fools'. How liberating is it to have your clothes, your speech, your appearance vilified? On the other hand, how liberating is it to cast off these marks of difference and to adopt a normalized (middle-class) habitus?

However, and as Beverley Skeggs (1997) has pointed out, to cast off the markers of one's own domination poses no threat to the class system. There is a clear difference between individual forms of accommodation and resistance, and the overthrow of systems of domination. Yet this is what often gets lost in a current emphasis (both academic and political) on plasticity and change: if the putting on of, for example, middle class accents does not represent a threat to social relations, how far would affirming working-class existence do this?

Judith Butler *would* claim that markers of domination can be resignified. And she further suggests that this resignification can be the motor of social change. Against Bourdieu, Butler argues that the success or failure of authoritative performatives does not hinge on the (social) authority of the one who speaks. Although she grants that there is no *necessary* break between performative speech and its social context (as a Derridean view would suggest), she argues that there is always the *possibility* of such a break, so that 'imposters' can seize authority by speaking and acting 'as if' they owned authority. In this case, she asks, might there not be moments 'where the utterance calls into question the established ground of legitimacy, where the utterance, in fact, performatively produces a shift in the terms of legitimacy as an *effect* of the utterance itself?' (Butler, 1997:146–7). She continues:

> It is precisely the *expropriability* of the dominant 'authorized' discourse that constitutes one potential site of its subversive resignification. What happens, for instance, when those who have been denied the social power to claim 'freedom' or 'democracy' appropriate those terms from the dominant discourse and rework or resignify those highly cathected terns to rally a political movement? (Butler, 1997:157–8).

It is clear that there are political movements which have rallied in the way Butler suggests (achieving the resignification of 'Queer' or 'Black', for example). What is less clear is that the performative claiming of authority is *in itself* as efficacious as Butler suggests. Butler's argument analytically detaches linguistic authority from social authority, at least to the extent that those not socially 'authorized to speak' are still able to 'speak with authority'. At the same time, this linguistic seizing of authority can, for Butler, effect social changes, to the extent that they can overturn existing authority.

For Butler, this occurs because her theoretical framework demands that it must. The argument, in other words, is based on the formalism of her theory, rather than on empirical evidence. Although political changes have occurred that have involved dominated groups re-using and therefore resignifying the very terms by which their 'dominated' status is marked, Butler does not show (though she wants to claim) that these resignifications are the motor of such changes. It may be that resignification is only able to occur in specific social contexts.

Specifically, in relation to class, it is difficult to see how Butler's concept of resistance through resignification could work. As Mariam Fraser (1999) has argued, Butler's argument relies on a politics of visibility, in which oppressed groups rally under the sign of their oppression, and demand recognition of their identities. Work such as that by Beverley Skeggs (1997) shows that white working-class women engage in processes of *dis*identifying from their classed location. This is scarcely surprising, since to be working-class is to be represented in pathological terms. How, then, to reappropriate the signs of one's pathology? Butler would suggest that it is through such reappropriation that the pathology can be problematized and, ultimately, undone. Yet it is difficult to see how this could happen prior to some broader social changes that would provide alternative means of conceptualizing what 'working-class' means (especially for women). As Skeggs herself asks, 'Who would want to be seen as working-class? (Possibly only academics are left)' (Skeggs, 1997:95).

It is the *reception* to forms of resistance that is underplayed in Butler's work. If authority is instantiated in the habitus, then the gap Butler wants to introduce between 'speaking with authority' and 'being authorized to speak' is not at all clear-cut. Speech (authoritative or otherwise) goes on between the speaker and the listener. It is in this relationship, not in the speech itself, that authority either inheres or fails to inhere. Authority cannot simply be claimed by the speaker: it must also be granted by the listener. This is not a question of individual choice, but of doxic rules: there must be sufficient legitimation granted to the speaker.

The Paulsgrove women spoke in authoritative tones, but they were unable to 'speak with authority' because their speech was not authorized. This is not because it did not conform to ostensible rules, but because they were not authorized to be actors within the field of political protest. In this way, any authority they claimed was effectively de-authorized. In contrast, the protestors in Balham had no need to *claim* authority since it already inheres within their persons. The ways in which their gender is classed – 'educated' to the Paulsgrove women's 'ignorant', 'restrained' to their 'excessive', good mothers of good children to their bad maternity and abused children – are assumed to be appropriate to the field. Their social situation position renders them individuals whose actions are assumed to be straightforward, normal indicators of a normal (maternal) psychology. Their habitus, in other words, incorporates a 'feel for the game' that is already authorized. The aesthetics of *their* protest (from such deliberate elements as candlelit vigils to the non-conscious elements of their bodily hexis) was one which, not surprisingly, conformed to doxic understandings of 'real' women, and specifically, 'real' mothers. The Paulsgrove women could hardly achieve an aestheticized protest in this way, since the aesthetic itself is classed (Fraser, 1999).

It needs to be asked how far such resignification is even possible for working-class women, when across cultural, political and theoretical representations, their habitus is constituted only in negative terms. Even that most convention-ally feminine of positions – the devoted mother – was ruled out for the Pauls-grove women. Importantly, the signifiers used to mark these women as pathological are not explicitly the signifiers of class (they were not *explicitly* vilified for being working-class) but are a kind of second-order signifier that invokes an innate atavism, ignorance and lack. 'Class' was displaced on to indi-vidual and familial lack.

So, what I am suggesting here is that a conceptualization of 'resistance' only in terms of the (potential) overthrow of systems, *together with* a constitution of the white working-class as reactionary and backward – the very antithesis of 'progressive' – makes it difficult for white working-class people's acts of insub-ordination to count as contestation or resistance. But more than this, when the very existence of class divisions is either ignored or explicitly denied, how can people engage in acts recognized as classed contestations?

Conclusion

Bourdieu at times characterizes the working class as embracing a 'love of one's fate', and suggests that this is one means through which domination continues. But the Paulsgrove protests could be seen as one moment in which working-class women did not embrace their fate. They did not acquiesce to the 'calls to order' which would remind them 'that's not for the likes of us'. Rather, they claimed an authority to which they had no prior right. However, far from achiev-ing resignification, as Butler would suggest, their actions subsequently became annulled through a reassertion of the doxic understandings of their persons that 'forbade' their actions in the first place.

Bourdieu is often (rightly, in my view) characterized as pessimistic; and this pessimism is often (wrongly, in my view) characterized as determinism. The Paulsgrove women did not lack agency: their actions were not determined. Nevertheless, the story that emerges is not a happy one. For Gramsci (as for Foucault),[15] pessimism of the intellect is the motor for change: it demands that we pay attention to inequalities and injustices and rests on the belief that things do not have to be the way they are, and that they will not improve without inter-vention. Optimism of the will rests on the hope that things *could be* changed – though not without (collective) effort.[16] In the face of a contemporary political and theoretical emphasis on an easy plasticity and change, I think Bourdieu's work is important in reminding us that pessimism is not the same as determinism; that resistance takes many forms; and that, in any case, for many groups of people, change is very difficult to effect, no matter how much they resist. This is what it means to be dominated.

Acknowledgements

My thanks to Mariam Fraser, Paul Johnson, Celia Lury, and participants in the *Feminists Evaluate Bourdieu* Symposium, University of Manchester, for insightful comments on earlier versions of the paper.

Notes

1 Bourdieu himself sees this 'emptying out' of an essential human subject as part of the reason for the hostility to the concept of habitus. In this context, he argues that a sociology which conceptualizes the subject as social is another 'narcissistic wound' to be added to those evoked by Freud (the theories of Copernicus, Darwin and Freud himself). That is, it challenges the illusion of self-mastery (Bourdieu and Wacquant, 2002:132)

2 For Bourdieu, a field is a 'network, or a configuration, of objective relations between positions' (Bourdieu and Wacquant, 2002:97).

3 See Lovell's (2000) work on gender passing and Lawler (1999) for a discussion of 'disrupted habitus'.

4 Cf. Walkerdine and Lucey, 1989.

5 Interestingly, Walkerdine *et al* use this point to criticise Bourdieu, pointing out that class is about much more than the ownership of capitals: 'they are ways in which a kind of subject is produced, regulated, lived' (Walkerdine *et al*, 2001:39). However, they consider only Bourdieu's metaphors of capital, and not his concept of the habitus. It seems to me that what they are discussing is exactly what the concepts of habitus and field are designed to capture.

6 The research for this paper involved analysis of 52 reports from the websites of eight British 'broadsheet' newspapers: The *Times, The Sunday Times, The Telegraph, The Sunday Telegraph, The Guardian, The Observer, The Independent* and *The Independent on Sunday*. The URLs are: http://www.thetimes.co.uk/; http://www.portal.telegraph.co.uk/; http://www.guardian.co.uk/; and http://www.independent.co.uk/. *The Times* and *The Telegraph* are generally regarded as 'right wing' (or centre-right) newspapers, while *The Guardian, The Observer* and *The Independent* are broadly centre-left.

7 Although press coverage of subsequent trials indicates that men were involved in the protests, the focus of press attention was on women protestors.

8 The opposition is Vikki Bell's (2002).

9 The figures in this drama included members of the aristocracy, a magistrate a scriptwriter, and a worker 'in the arts'.

10 An interesting opposition: clearly the one (QCs, bank managers and City traders) is meant, by definition, to exclude the other (rioters). Conversely, the absence of QCs, bank managers and City traders among the Paulsgrove protestors might suggest that they could easily be characterized as rioters.

11 Hume 14/08/00. This story blames politicians, social workers and 'feminist academics' for stirring up the riots.

12 Bourdieu points to this contradiction when he says:

> [T]he embodiment of femininity is inseparable from an *embodiment of distinction*, or, to put it another way, from contempt for the vulgarity associated with plunging necklines, too-short

mini-skirts and too-heavy make-up (though this is generally perceived as very 'feminine' . . .). (Bourdieu, 2001:28. Original emphasis)

Clearly, this formulation positions women only as objects in masculine games of distinction. However, it can be reworked to draw attention to the ways in which 'excessive' femininity, coded as vulgarity, can position some women as at a distance from 'real' femininity.

13 And this, for Bourdieu, is an exercise of symbolic violence:

If there is any terrorism it is in the peremptory verdicts which, in the name of taste, condemn to ridicule, indignity, shame, silence . . . men and women who simply fall short, in the eyes of their judges, of the right way of being and doing; it is in the symbolic violence through which the dominant groups endeavour to impose their life-style (Bourdieu, 1986:511).

14 A reference to areas with high concentrations of young children.

15 I mention Foucault because he is so often seen as a theorist who emphasises freedom and change – and hence as an 'optimistic' theorist. Yet he wrote:

My point is not that everything is bad, but that everything is dangerous, which is not exactly the same as bad. If everything is dangerous, then we always have something to do. So my position leads not to apathy but to a hyper- and pessimistic activism. I think that the ethico-political choice we have to make every day is to determine which is the main danger (Foucault, 1983:343).

16 Gramsci wrote:

It should be noted that very often optimism is nothing more than a defence of one's laziness, one's irresponsibility, the will to do nothing. It is also a form of fatalism and mechanicism. One relies on factors extraneous to one's will and activity, exalts them, and appears to burn with sacred enthusiasm. And enthusiasm is nothing more than the external adoration of fetishes. A reaction [is] necessary which must have the intelligence for its point of departure. The only justifiable enthusiasm is that which accompanies the intelligent will, intelligent activity, the inventive richness of concrete initiatives which change existing reality (Gramsci, Remark 130 in Notebook #9, quoted in Gramsci, 1992:12).

References

Aaronovitch, D. (2000) 'Why I Am So Scared of Paulsgrove Woman' *The Independent* 11/8/00.

Bar-On, B-A. (1993) 'Marginality and Epistemic Privilege' in L. Alcoff, L. and E. Potter (eds) *Feminist Epistemologies*. New York and London: Routledge.

Bell, V. (2002) 'The Vigilant(e) Parent and the Paedophile: The News of the World Campaign 2000 and the Contemporary Governmentality of Child Sexual Abuse' *Feminist Theory* 3 (1): 83–102.

Bohman, J. (1999) 'Practical Reason and Cultural Constraint: Agency in Bourdieu's Theory of Practice' in R. Shusterman (ed.) *Bourdieu: a Critical Reader*. Oxford: Blackwell.

Bourdieu, P. (1986) *Distinction* (trans. R. Nice). London: Routledge and Kegan Paul.

Bourdieu, P. (1990) *The Logic of Practice* (trans. R. Nice). Cambridge: Polity.

Bourdieu, P. (1994) *In Other Words: Essays Towards a Reflexive Sociology* (trans. M. Adamson). Cambridge. Polity

Bourdieu, P. (1998a) *Practical Reason: On the Theory of Action*. Cambridge: Polity.

Bourdieu, P. (1998b) *Acts of Resistance: Against the New Myths of Our Time* (trans. R. Nice). Cambridge: Polity.

Bourdieu, P. (1993) *The Field of Cultural Production: Essays on Art and Literature* (ed. and introduced by R. Johnson). Cambridge: Polity Press.

Bourdieu, P. (2001) *Masculine Domination*. Cambridge: Polity.

Bourdieu, P. and Wacquant, L. (2002 [1992]) *An Invitation to Reflexive Sociology*. Cambridge: Polity.

Butler, J. (1997) *Excitable Speech: A Politics of the Performative.* New York and London: Routledge.

Colcutt, D. and Elliott, J. (2000)'Inside the Witch-Hunt' *The Sunday Times* 13/8/00

Dalrymple, T. (2000) 'The Sinister Ethos of the Baying Mobs' *The Telegraph* 13/8/00.

Dreyfus, H. and Rabinow, P. (1993) 'Can There Be a Science of Existential Structure and Social Meaning?' in C. Calhoun E. LiPuma and M. Postone, M. (eds) *Bourdieu: Critical Perspectives.* Chicago: University of Chicago Press.

Ferguson, E. (2001) 'The Unrepentant Vigilante' *The Guardian* 4/2/01.

Fiske, J. (1992) 'Cultural Studies and the Culture of Everyday Life' in L. Grossberg C. Nelson and P. Treichler (eds) *Cultural Studies.* New York and London: Routledge.

Ford, R. (2000) 'Mob Rule' *The Times* 11/8/00.

Foucault, M. (1983) 'On the Genealogy of Ethics: An Overview of Work in Progress', in P. Rabinow (ed.) *The Foucault Reader: An Introduction to Foucault's Thought.* Harmondsworth: Penguin.

Fox, P. (1994) *Class Fictions: Shame and Resistance in the British Working-Class Novel 1890–1945.* Carolina: Duke University Press.

Fraser, M. (1999) 'Classing Queer: Politics in Contradiction' *Theory, Culture and Society* 16(2): 107–131.

Fraser, N. (2001) 'Recognition without Ethics?' *Theory, Culture and Society* 18(2–3): 21–42.

Fuller, S. (1988) *Social Epistemology.* Bloomington: Indiana University Press.

Gillan, A. (2000) 'Chorus of Fear and Loathing Swells in the Streets of a Latter-Day Salem' *The Guardian* 12/08/00.

Gramsci, A. (1992) *The Prison Notebooks* (ed.) J. A. Buttigieg (trans. J. A. Buttigieg and A. Callari). New York: Columbia University Press.

The Guardian (2000) 'Angry, Axious and Ugly' (Leader Column) 11/9/00.

Harker, R. Mahar, C. and Wilkes, C. (eds) (1990) *An Introduction to the Work of Pierre Bourdieu: The Practice of Theory.* Basingstoke: MacMillan.

Haylett, C. (2001) 'Illegitimate Subjects?:Abject Whites, Neoliberal Modernisation, and Middle-Class Multiculturalism' *Society and Space* 19: 351–370.

Haug, F. (2001) 'Sexual Deregulation or, the Child Abuser as Hero in Neoliberalism' *Feminist Theory* 2(1): 33–78.

Hockey, J. and James, A. (1993) *Growing Up and Growing Old: Ageing and Dependency in the Life Course.* London: Sage.

Hume, M. (2000) 'The Vilest Mob Isn't in Paulsgrove, it's in Westminster' *The Times* 14/08/00.

Johnson, R. (1993) 'Editor's Introduction', in P. Bourdieu *The Field of Cultural Production: Essays on Art and Literature* (ed. and introduced by R. Johnson). Cambridge: Polity Press.

Lawler, S. (1999) 'Getting Out and Getting Away: Women's Narratives of Class Mobility' *Feminist Review* 63: 3–24.

Lawler, S. (2000) *Mothering the Self: Mothers, Daughters, Subjects.* London: Routledge.

Lovell, T. (2000) 'Thinking Feminism With and Against Bourdieu' *Feminist Theory* 1(1): 11–32.

McNay, L. (2000) *Gender and Agency: Reconfiguring the Subject in Feminist and Social Theory.* Cambridge: Polity.

Martin, N. (2000) 'Estate Mob Bays for Paedophiles' Blood' *The Telegraph* 10/08/00.

Martin, N. and Paterson, M. (2000) 'Judge Lets Paedophile Who "Suffered" Go Free' *The Telegraph* 11/08/00.

Midgley, C. (2001) 'A Very Polite Protest' *The Times* 18/01/01.

Milmo, C. (2000) 'Marathon Court Hearing Over Sex Offender Protests' *The Independent* 26/10/00.

Riddell, M. (2000) 'Salem Comes to Portsmouth' *The Guardian* 13/08/00.

Roberts, I. (1999) 'A Historical Construction of the Working Class', in H. Beynon and P. Glavanis (eds) *Patterns of Social Inequality.* London: Longman.

Sarler, C. (2000) 'Dads Are Not Demons' *The Observer* 26/11/00.

Skeggs, B. (1997) *Formations of Class and Gender: Becoming Respectable.* London: Sage.

Smart, C. (1989) *Feminism and the Power of Law.* London: Routledge.

Stanford, P. (2001) 'Nightmare in Nappy Valley' *The Independent* 19/01/01.

Strathern, M. (1992) *Reproducing the Future: Anthropology, Kinship and the New Reproductive Technologies.* Manchester: Manchester University Press.

Walkerdine, V. and Lucey, H. (1989) *Democracy in the Kitchen: Regulating Mothers and Socialising Daughters.* London: Virago Press.

Walkerdine, V. Lucey, H. and Melody, J. (2001) *Growing Up Girl: Psychosexual Explorations of Gender and Class.* Basingstoke: Palgrave.

Younge, G. (2000) 'Mobs and Monsters' *The Guardian* 14/08/00.

Habitus and social suffering: Culture, addiction and the syringe

Nicole Vitellone

The narratives of drug discourse do not proceed as simple discussions of 'fact', but instead assess the moral and symbolic value of particular paths and patterns of risk and blame. These stories must achieve the rhetorical effect of realism – 'facts' must overshadow the values and images they inflect (Nancy Campbell, 2000:38).

Introduction

Much has been written about Pierre Bourdieu's *The Weight of the World* (1999). Presented as a collection of interviews, the stories in this volume are understood to mark a shift in concern for Bourdieu, from a predicament with the taste practices of the respectable classes to the predicament of the socially marginalized. As Roy Boyne (2002:121) has suggested *The Weight of the World* marks a shift from concerns with social inclusion to exclusion. What characterizes the accounts of social suffering documented in *The Weight of the World* is the length of interview material presented and under-theorised interview data. Boyne suggests Bourdieu's tendency towards a descriptive account of the social lives of the inhabitants of French housing projects and his reluctance to theorise these spaces is strategic: 'He did not want to fix the meanings of these spaces in advance, since he knew they are places of kaleidoscopic experience, and so he did not always clearly say they are places of exclusion . . .' (2002:125).

Much of the impetus behind this methodological approach would appear to stem from Bourdieu and Waquant's critique of the use and misuse of the exclusionary and universalising concept 'underclass' in the US and Europe:

> . . . a fictional group, produced on paper by the classifying practices of those scholars, journalists and related experts in the management of the (black urban) poor who share in the belief in its existence because it is well-suited to give renewed scientific legitimacy to some and a politically and commercially profitable theme to mine for the others. . . . Inept and unsuited in the American case, the imported concept adds nothing to the knowledge of European societies (Bourdieu and Waquant, 1999:49).

But whilst the stories in *The Weight of the World* are understood to provide a more nuanced account of social suffering, avoid the trappings of cultural imperialism, and especially the 'imposition of a vision of a world' (Bourdieu and Waquant, 1999:50), Angela McRobbie argues in *The Weight Of The World* 'we are presented with the confident assumption of knowledge of the other' (2002:132). McRobbie suggests this is the case since Bourdieu does not analyse the social and cultural contexts in which the interviews take place, and as a consequence 'these testimonies exist merely as the stated truths of personal experience' (2002:131). With the exception of the chapters by Bourgois and Waquant on US crack using cultures, (which McRobbie considers to be 'more rounded and persuasive' as they 'are able to demonstrate their familiarity with existing scholarship on race and poverty' (2002:135)), McRobbie argues that for the remainder of the chapters 'on occasion the respondents appear to be exploited for their own grief' (2002:135). McRobbie sees the problem with *The Weight of the World* as resulting from Bourdieu's 'antipathy to cultural studies' (2002:136).

In their different ways, both Boyne and McRobbie suggest that to avoid the positioning of the socially excluded as other, as outside of the social, what is required is that these voices be heard *alongside* complex levels of theorising. In this chapter, I want to pursue this line of inquiry further and, in particular, address McRobbie's claim that such a critical balance is achieved in sections of *The Weight of the World*, specifically in Philippe Bourgois' groundbreaking ethnography on Puerto Rican crack dealers in East Harlem. By engaging with this much cited and award-winning ethnography, *In Search of Respect: Selling Crack in El Barrio* (1995), I address Bourgois' socio-structural analysis of crack and social suffering. I show how within his account of crack addiction, Bourgois produces an explicit form of empirical knowledge of illicit drug use as involving changing gender relations. However, in so doing, I argue Bourgois imposes a gendered vision of the social world onto his empirical data. Whilst Bourgois' theoretical intervention is called into question by Lisa Maher in her ethnographic observations of women drug users in Harlem, it is also, I will argue destabilized by recent feminist analyses of contemporary drug experiences as figured by medical discourses, drug policy and the media. What these discursive and textual analyses of addiction offer for understandings of the experience of drug use and social suffering is not so much knowledge of the other in the world but rather the cultural conditions and political and social effects of this othering.

By engaging with and moving beyond existing drug ethnographies of social suffering (and their critiques) this chapter draws attention to a further underlying assumption in Bourgois' work. Specifically, I address the division put in place by Bourgois between the culture of crack, on the one hand, and the nature of substances on the other. In so doing, I will suggest this division between the 'substance' and the 'social' evades the matter of crack and especially its relations with the materialisation of the social. Indeed, more generally, I will suggest that ethnography as a method evades the nature of substances, their embodied effects, and the relationship of substances to the social. The chapter therefore aims to show that the experience of social suffering cannot take for granted or indeed assume the matter of substances – particularly the use of crack and heroin – are simply effects of social exclusion, which can be measured via ethnographic observation. Rather I aim to address how it is that substances themselves have come to be inculcated in the social in ways that transform the nature of drugs, the experience of substances and the culture of addiction. Thus I will argue Bourdieu's notion of the habitus – as the embodiment of the sociocultural – should be extended to incorporate non-human matter such as crack and heroin. I will do so by examining British child poverty campaigns as well as recent British social realist films in which issues of heroin addiction are key. In so doing, I aim to create a reformulated notion of the habitus, which does not close off the matter of drugs but recognizes various substances and the techniques of their consumption as part of the embodied dispositions which make up the habitus. In addition I aim to show how such substances play a key role in the cultural production of the fictional group the 'underclass'.

The structure of crack

In his richly detailed ethnographic account of social suffering, Philippe Bourgois explains how crack use in the US inner city spaces concerns 'extreme forms of structural violence' (2003:32), with the highest proportion of crack addicts found amongst 'the most exploited population groups suffering from the most intense forms of systematic racial discrimination and spatial segregation' (2003:32). Bourgois' political economy perspective stresses the need to understand crack addiction as involving a shift from industrial to post-industrial service based economies, a shift that concerns structural unemployment and the withdrawal of government from urban US settings. The crack epidemic among African Americans, Latinos (especially Puerto Ricans) and working-class Lumpen whites, Bourgois argues, 'was the all-too-logical product of Ronald Regan's neo-liberal policies that dismantled the social welfare safety net and replaced it with the carceral dragnet' (Bourgois, 2003:36). Bourgois argues further that the infrastructural problems facing unemployed or drug addicted Puerto Rican men include a crisis in patriarchal social organization and control caused by rural urban migration, female empowerment and male economic feminisation. Moreover, this radically changing social structure is understood as having such a negative impact on masculine gender identities that a crisis of masculinity emerges in his ethnography dialogues 'as a central research focus' (1996:414). Thus it would appear that following Bourdieu, Bourgois finds 'the idea of masculinity is one of the last refuges of the identity of the dominated classes' (Bourdieu, 1993, in Fowler, 2003:469). As Fowler elaborates 'one of the chief distinctions of Bourdieu's theory of masculine domination is its capacity to grasp simultaneously both the purely subjective, *symbolic stakes* which preoccupy men when they experience struggles between each other for reputation, and the *economic/political interests* fuelling their actions' (Fowler, 2003:472).

In Bourgois' ethnography of crack use, structural transformations in economic relations are central to his account of the gendered experience of social suffering. Moreover, he argues 'the crisis of patriarchy in El Barrio expresses itself *concretely* in the polarization of domestic violence and sexual abuse' (1995:215, my emphasis). What creates the conditions for such violence, particularly violence against women both within and outside of the home is 'the complicated process whereby women are carving out a new public space for themselves' (Bourgois, 1996:424). In other words, according to Bourgois the mismatch between a masculine habitus and an increasing feminized public sphere produces a male crisis, one that takes expression in interpersonal physical violence. This power shift is illustrated well in his account of Primo, who was supported by a female crack dealer, Candy:

> After several months of the patriarchal role reversal of being economically supported by a woman and forced to satisfy her sexual desires upon demand, however, he attempted to recoup his personal sense of male respect by the only means immediately at his disposal: public physical violence. Years later, in crackhouse conversations, he emphasized his outrage over how his sense of masculinity was 'dissed' (disrespected) by Candy's violation of domestic roles (Bourgois, 1996:416).

Clearly, what stands out from Bourgois' Bourdieusian understanding of gender are a series of assumptions about social suffering as concerning alienation from a masculine gender identity, and a patriarchal socio-economic structure in crisis.

Gender in drug ethnographies

Following Bourgois commitment to ethnography 'as a key to understanding extreme social suffering' (Bourgois, 1999:62), Lisa Maher's ethnographic field work on the lives of drug using women in New York City takes up and challenges some of these assumptions regarding gender and social suffering. For instance, Maher's (1997) account of gender for homeless – mostly ethnic minority – women crack cocaine users in three Brooklyn neighbourhoods poses a rather different explanation of social suffering from that of Bourgois' in the sense that she does not assume a mismatch between habitus and field in her account of women's lives. Instead of seeing women's participation in an informal street-based drug economy as producing autonomous self interested agents or as positioning women as dependant victims of drugs and abusive men, Maher's observations of drug user's everyday interactions and exchanges – both violent and non-violent – are considered to be survival strategies. These include the mutual sharing of drugs, needles, valuable information, clothing and food (Maher, 1997:36). But Maher also questions Bourgois' depiction of the drug economy as male domain whereby economically marginal males 'reconstruct their notions of masculine dignity around interpersonal violence, economic parasitism, and sexual domination' (Bourgois, 1996:414). She argues:

> This account suggests that the 'backlash' against feminism has filtered through to the street-level drug culture where it gains expression in violence against women. Implicit is a desire to comprehend the perceived threat to 'hegemonic masculinity' presented

by women crack users. The validity of this argument is ultimately contingent on the degree to which one accepts that women crack users have challenged traditional gender roles and that patriarchal gender relations have been undermined as a result. While Bourgois' (male) informants may perceive this to be the case, *accepting such perceptions at face value may misrepresent* not only the position of women in the drug economy but the position of women more generally, and that of minority women in particular. A variant of the old 'she asked for it' theme, the notion of a male back-lash is neither unique to gender relations in the crack economy, nor does it provide an accurate representation of all such relations (Maher, 1997:14, my emphasis).

Even though over a third of her respondents had experienced physical violence whilst growing up, these women 'perceive themselves neither as powerless victims nor as emancipated and independent, nor – as their own accounts demonstrate – are they without agency and recourse to innovative forms of resistance' (Maher, 1997:19). By addressing the physical violence, economic hardship and social deprivation faced by women working in the street level drug economy as central to understandings of how power operates, particularly in terms of gender, race and class relations, Maher calls into question Bourgois' insistence that for his male respondents their experience of the drug economy is structured by class relations and in particular poverty and social marginalization. Such an account of social suffering Maher argues falls short since 'the privileging of class – or indeed race or gender – fails to provide an adequately nuanced explanation of the operations of systems of social stratification *in* the drug economy' (Maher, 1997:170, my emphasis). Maher therefore finds Bourgois' hegemonic account of masculinity troubling since it 'fails to elaborate the nature of women's participation in the drug economy and the ways in which their gendered status structures this participation' (Maher, 1997:13).

Bourgois' account of the structural transformation of the social and sociality as involving a feminization of the public sphere is complicated further by Lisa Adkins' critical analysis of detraditionalized accounts of the economy. In Adkins' analysis such readings of a feminised economic field are understood to involve not so much a 'failure to analyze and incorporate gender' (Maher, 1997:13) but a particular theoretical reading of Bourdieu's work on habitus. According to Adkins 'Bourdieusian-influenced accounts of transformations in gender in late modernity fail to register that . . . [a lack of fit between habitus and field] does not concern a liberal freedom from gender, but may be tied to new arrangements of gender' (Adkins, 2003:34). Interestingly this reconfiguration of gender emerges from Bourgois' (1995:278) fleeting analysis of the crack epidemic in the media and popular culture. Here he finds that public representations of crack users position women as not simply liberated from gender – through a patriarchal role reversal – but that the cultural narrative of crack in the mid 1990s becomes the very site for a re-traditionalized account of gender: 'The distinctive feature of the crack epidemic of the late 1980s and early 1990s . . . was that instead of an ethnic group or a social class being demonized for their proclivity for substance abuse, women, the family, and motherhood itself were assaulted. Inner city women who smoked crack were accused of having lost the "mother-nurture instinct" ' (Bourgois, 1995:278). Maher also touches on this particular story of crack in the media and popular culture. Specifically, Maher (1997:56) draws attention to press reports whereby 'women crack users have been held responsible for the creation of a "bio-underclass" of "crack babies", said to be lacking "the central core of what it means to be human" (*New York Times*, 17 September 1989)'. But Maher is quick to dismiss 'such partial representations [which] have served to obscure critical aspects of drug use behaviour' (1997:56). Indeed Maher is both critical of such media representations and firmly committed to the methodology of ethnography for telling the story of 'those who live at the margins of our own society' (1997:208). Consequently she argues against discursive and textual analyses, which 'evade issues of power, politics and participation' (1997:207–208), since 'textual cleverness side-steps power relations' (1997:207).

The obvious problems with textual and discursive analyses of crack, highlighted by Maher's study, concern questions of re-stigmatisation via a lack of engagement with complex networks of power relations in people's everyday lives. But similar criticisms have also been made of the construction of reality and empirical truths in some drug ethnographies, particularly in relation to gender. In *Using Women: Gender, Drug Policy and Social Justice* Nancy Campbell (2000) draws attention to what she sees as the problems of realism in many drug ethnographies. Campbell argues ethnographic studies run the risk of confirming stereotyped expectations of drug users as members of an underclass. In relation to gender, Campbell points out drug ethnographies often position drug use by men as normative, and part of male risk taking and a masculine identity, involving the street, violence and crime, whilst simultaneously positioning drug use by women as compromising family, domestic and parenting roles, thus reaffirming the common place view that drug taking behaviour in women concerns gender deviance. In many ways, Campbell's criticisms of drug ethnographies echo McRobbie's critique of *The Weight of the World*, especially the concern that such visions of the world fall short of a broader understanding of the historical and cultural contexts of social suffering.

'Crack' and its discursive effects

Campbell's project follows the discursive construction of drug use in US drug control policies and the political effects of such policies for women. And while Maher warns against the dangers of such a textual analysis, Campbell's project indicates that textual and discursive analyses of addiction need not necessarily evade issues of power and understandings of everyday social suffering. For instance, Campbell argues historically the discourses on women and drug use, including the recent US controversies around "crack babies" and "crack moms" 'exercise *material* effects that shape the experience and interpretation of addiction' . . . (2000:6, my emphasis). In the case of "crack moms", Campbell points out that the representation of crack as concerning the destruction of the maternal instinct extended well beyond the media and popular culture and 'was the commonly identified source of the [drug] policy problem' (2000:170). Moreover, the effects of locating the social problem of crack cocaine with women themselves not only involved the 'the deflection of responsibility for social problems' (2000:170) onto the figure of the 'crack mom', but also figured drug using women as 'produc[ing] the structural effects of economic erosion and neighbourhood disintegration' (2000:170). By making women appear to 'cause the effects of social inequality' (2000:171), Campbell shows how drug policy discourse simultaneously 'obscures social stratification' (2000:187) and 'displaced poverty as the chief cause of damage' (2000:169). Thus, in deflecting blame onto women crack addicts, 'policy-makers avoid addressing the larger structures, decisions, and policies that exacerbate our multiple drug problems' (Campbell, 2000:6).

Campbell's discussion of the social effects of US drug policy discourse clearly highlights the way in which official accounts of pharmacological addiction position women as responsible for the social reproduction of inequalities. Yet this particular narrative of poverty is not, as Campbell amongst others have pointed out, the case for all women. Rather it is African-American women who in the 1990s became positioned in US drug policy narratives as both biologically vulnerable to crack, and responsible for the making of the 'bio-underclass'. Whilst, according to Campbell, one outcome of the figuring of 'crack moms' as responsible for the biological reproduction of inequality was to conceal broader structural inequalities, another material effect was the coercive governing of (black) 'crack moms' (2000:187). To highlight 'the discursive pattern of causation at work' (Campbell, 2000:171) in public policy, Campbell addresses the hearings of the national drug prevention policy debated in the hearings and reports of the 101st Congress between 1989 and 1990:

> "Crack babies", according to then Senator Pete Wilson (r-CA), were "abandoned because of the particularly insidious effects of crack, the destruction of the maternal instinct". The "sickly, inattentive, and inconsolable 'crack baby'" became a focal point for neurobehavioral research focused on identifying cognitive deficiencies and intellectual outcomes. Researchers studied the subtle behavioural effects of cocaine exposure to discover "what kinds of interventions will work best . . . to soften the 'double whammy from nature and nurture' that these children have received". Responsibility for both "nature" and "nurture" fell to women. This position effectively absolved social policy from doing anything other than controlling women in order to break the "intergenerational transmission of the disease of addiction . . ." (2000:174).

In the attribution of deficiencies associated with crack babies to 'crack moms', drug-using women become solely responsible for producing a generation of children who have a predisposition to addiction, a predisposition which concerns the pharmacological structure of crack. The intergenerational logic of crack addiction produced by drug policy discourse thus presumes that the contemporary US crack phenomenon involves a biological reproduction of social suffering. Bourgois' account of the production of social suffering in the US is not able however to grasp either this discourse or its effects. This is because Bourgois claims that the 'pharmacological qualities of substances are virtually meaningless outside of the socio-cultural as well as political economic contexts' (2003:32). Thus he separates out substances from social-cultural contexts and therefore closes off an understanding of the constitution of social suffering, which takes into account the matter of substances including their insertion into discourse and their effects. This problem is compounded by Bourgois' insistence that the meaning of substances will only ever be grasped via the tools of ethnography.

Recent work on addiction, however, cautions against such relentlessly socio-logical readings of the meaning of drugs. According to Helen Keane (2000) such explanations, which seek to identify the social as producing both the conditions and effects for the meaning of the substance, are somewhat limited. This is the case since such understandings tend to close off and ignore the corporeal body and especially medical definitions of the addicted body. What is important regarding Keane's work in the context of my argument here is that her analysis radically destabilises the distinction between pharmacological substances and social-cultural contexts. Thus, rather than seeing the pharmacological qualities of substances as virtually meaningless outside of social-cultural contexts as Bourgois does, it could be argued that biological understandings of the addicted body also have social effects. Indeed following the work of Campbell we may ask to what extent are notions of social suffering framed by such biological understandings of the addicted body? As Keane argues the pharmacological term 'substance' works to create certain truths about the body. This is very different, she suggests, from the biological embodiment of substances, which re-work the corporeal rather than simply disrupts its 'healthy' configuration. Nevertheless Keane points out that the negative perception of drugs in the body is structured by the discursive juxtaposition of the 'pharmacological' with the 'corporeal':

> In particular, the words 'chemical' and 'substance' cannot be used to avoid the morally and politically loaded cultural category of drugs. The terms 'chemical' has its own powerful negative connotations, particularly when juxtaposed with a notion of the body as organic and natural. Natural versus chemical is a central conceptual dichotomy in addiction discourse, both medical and popular, and it can be argued that it provides a new home for the displaced moral dichotomy of good and evil. Defining drugs as substances other than those required for 'normal health' or to maintain 'normal biological processes' is a way of finessing this attribution of unnaturalness (Keane, 2002:18).

Keane's analysis has important implications for the 'crack-baby' crisis. In particular, it suggests that the terms 'crack-mom' and 'crack-baby' are themselves powerful in the war on drugs as they displace issues of poverty and social inequalities onto concerns about the contamination of the social body (babies and mum's) by the chemical substance 'crack'. This discursive effect of setting the chemical against the natural body not only calls into question the biological health and especially the neurobehavioral development of the crack-child but also suggests that the actual cause of child development problems concerns the pharmacological embodiment of substances. Put together, and used interchangeably, the unnaturalness of the popular medical concepts 'crack-baby' and 'crack-mom' set the terms for the social crisis around crack 'reproduction'.

Crack-babies

It is this reproductive logic of becoming (addicted) which has lead to both the criminalisation and prosecution of pregnant drug using women. As is well documented, the effects of the 'crack-baby' drug prevention policy resulted in a disproportionate number of poor African-American women being imprisoned in the US. Campbell reports on the alarming increase of women incarcerated for drug crimes between 1980 and 1994. 'The body count is highest among women of color – nearly half of imprisoned women are African–Americans, who are seven times more likely to be incarcerated than white women' (Campbell, 2000:5). Whilst more than 200 women faced criminal prosecution between 1985 and 2000 for using cocaine and other drugs during pregnancy (Oritz and Briggs, 2002:44), the logic behind these crack addiction convictions positions 'crack-babies' as occupying a somewhat contradictory relationship to childhood. For instance, Carol Mason points out that the 'fetuses labelled "crack babies" dwell in the impure domain' (2000:50). 'Undergrown, brain damaged and congenitally stigmatized, who as children would be unlovable, unadoptable, and unteachable' (Kandall, 1996:6, in Mason, 2000:50) 'crack-babies' and foetuses are presented as *innocent victims of crack moms*, 'hopelessly debilitated by their mother's drug use' (Mason, 2000:50). But at the same time 'crack babies are seen as perpetuating the impurities from which they come, burdening society with "a permanent sub-human biological underclass" . . .' (Mason, 2000:50). The effect of this contradiction is that 'black children are born guilty' (Mason, 2000:51). This finds expression in the foetal protection legislation established in South Carolina's Supreme Court in 1997. Although foetal protection law was set up to prosecute drug using women for posing a risk to foetal health, Mason argues legislators, along with pro-choice advocates (and anti-abortionists) do not want to protect foetuses 'perceived to be not healthy, normal, intact, whole, or "free from genetic or developmental abnormalities"' (2000:49). Mason thus suggests 'rather than a law aimed at prosecuting women [and protecting the unborn], it is as much a protection of society against degenerate black fetuses who will become burdensome black babies' (2000:51). Quite ironically, then, Mason argues foetal protection legislation protects society form unborn black kids by 'mak[ing] abortion *more attractive* to a pregnant black woman who can be prosecuted for her addiction' (2000:53).

Both the moral outrage over 'crack-babies' and the eugenicist push surrounding drug prevention policies and foetal protection legislation was critically called into question by developments in the medical sciences. Since the late 1990s the 'crack-baby' crisis has been found by a range of doctors and professional researchers including the original medic who launched the 'crack-baby' syndrome as not only inconclusive, but more seriously as erroneous:

> [W]hen the expected tidal wave of brain-damaged, unteachable monsters failed to materialize, a handful of thoughtful people started looking into some of the original assumptions. They discovered that the crack-baby epidemic, like the Nixon heroin scare, was a total fabrication – a blend of distorted data and sloppy journalism. The tiny infants trembling in their incubators were real enough – no question about that – but they were usually the victims of an older, more established ailment. What the cameras were capturing were the well-documented effects of malnutrition and poverty (Gray, 1998:108–109, in Mason, 2000:51).

Follow-up studies have questioned further the myth of the 'crack-baby' phenomena. Oritz and Briggs (2002:44) report on empirical findings from a 2001 study published in the *Journal of the American Medical Association*, which found no link between cocaine use by pregnant women and the making of a social "underclass". 'Crack-babies' did not become crack addicts and more still did not become children with developmental abnormalities, learning difficulties and delinquent tendencies.

Ultimately Oritz and Briggs (2002) find that the success of the racialising moral panic about 'crack-babies' concerned a shifting conceptualisation of poverty. This shift involved the passing of traditional modes of understanding poverty as concerning its social reproduction. Moving way from an intergenerational account of the socially disenfranchised, a model taken up by neoconservatives in the 1980s 'as concerning behaviours and beliefs learned in childhood' (2002:42), Oritz and Briggs argue poverty and its reproduction has been re-conceptualized as a biologized entity. Thus, unlike the culture of poverty thesis, whereby poverty is articulated in the embodied dispositions, actions and perceptions of the child, and is thus 'fundamentally about children and childhood' (Oritz and Briggs, 2002:43), they argue the 'pessimism about the culture of poor children [is now] turned into a concern about their biology' (Oritz and Briggs, 2002:44). Indeed this concern with the body of the child is most obvious in the 'biologized account of the growing impoverishment of urban communities of color' (Oritz and Briggs, 2002:48).

What seems important to note here in relation to Bourdieu's work on the habitus is that the embodiment of the social involves the matter of crack. Although Bourdieu does not appear to address such things as substances in his account of the habitus, taking up Lois McNay's (1999:99) account of the habitus as 'the incorporation of the social into the body' I want to suggest that for the 'newly biologized underclass', crack and its 'corporeal inculcation is an instance of what Bourdieu calls *symbolic violence* or a form of domination which is exercised upon a social agent with his or her complicity' (McNay, 1999:99). This is particularly evident in the case of the criminalization of 'crack-moms'. But it is also evident in the problematization of 'crack-babies'. For instance the corporeal inculcation of crack positions the body of the black child as 'intrinsically pathological and completely irredeemable' (Oritz and Brigg,s 2002:40). Although McNay (1999) cautions against interpreting the habitus in such a determinist fashion, that is as socially determining of lived experience, since, as she argues, Bourdieu's habitus introduces a 'temporal dimension to an understanding of the body' (1999:101),[1] in new biological accounts of poverty Bourdieu's 'notion of temporality as protentian – time as involving a 'practical reference to the future' (McNay, 1999:102)[2] is somewhat thwarted. For instance, Oritz and Briggs (2002) argue, 'popular scientific and lay discourses about children who have been traumatized portray them as unlikely to adopt the character traits of desired citizens as they grow to adulthood: they will always be "damaged goods" '(2002:41). In other words, 'crack-babies' do not realize their full embodied potential. And it is this un-realization of potential, caused by the perceived biological problems inflicted by intergenerational crack use, which is key for the reconceptualization of poverty, and in particular the figuring of the pathologized embodied 'underclass'.

Having little or no embodied potential makes for powerful claims about the social experience of childhood and the developing habitus of the child. For instance, it suggests that the agency, autonomy and future orientation attributed to the habitus, may not be universal. It also suggests that the perception of cultural commonalities within the 'underclass' concern issues of temporality. For instance, notions such as 'crack-babies' inscribe a temporal orientation onto the body of the child, one whereby the future – and potential – is suspended. According to Claudia Castaneda (2002) it is this particular conceptualisation of childhood *as a potentiality*, which gives the category of childhood great cultural value. Moreover Castaneda argues this potentiality of the child is constitutive of not just child-bodies but also broader ideas of adult nature and culture. By bringing 'the child into the center of discussions concerning the making of "facts" about human nature and culture' (2002:8), Castaneda is able to 'ask how figurations of the child are used to establish hierarchies of race, class, gender and sexuality as "facts" of the *natural human body*' (2002:9, my emphasis). In so doing Castaneda shows how the experience of childhood does not just concern the lived experience of the child in the world but crucially involves semiotic and material practices and especially their 'constitutive effects'. These effects themselves she argues are key to understanding social divisions and hierarchies.

Castaneda's compelling analysis is illustrated well by the 'crack–baby' crisis as here the medical and cultural figurations of childhood – as a racialized *non-potentiality* – established hierarchies of race and class as natural hierarchies of the child-body. Moreover, the configuration of the child–body as biologically flawed – rather than future orientated – suggests that questions of symbolic violence concern a degenerative habitus, whereby the corporeal inculcation of crack does not engender a positive relation between social time and social being but in fact stops time. Thus it is important not to assume or take for granted the temporality of the habitus as an embodied chronological experience. For as Castaneda explains 'should a given child either fail to possess or to realize its potential (as in the notion of "stunted growth"), he or she remains a flawed child and an incomplete adult' (2002:4). What the 'crack- baby' crisis illustrates is how substances themselves have come to be socially embodied as a failure of the potential of the child, as a failure of adult subjectivity, a failure that takes expression in the habitus of the urban 'underclass'.

Syringe-babies

My argument here about the inculcation of substances as producing a socially disrupted habitus is also evident in the British context. Recently in Britain there has been a series of child poverty awareness campaigns, which have centred on images of addiction and the child-body. Conducted by the children's charity Barnardo's, the April 2000 and November 2003 advertisements aimed to raise awareness of child poverty through a series of images. The November 2003 campaign ran for four weeks, in *The Guardian* and other daily national newspapers, and was axed after a record 466 complaints to the Advertising Standards Authority as its content was ruled to be too shocking. The campaign featured four separate photographs of newborn children, each lying down wearing only a nappy and hospital tag. What is startling about these full-page images is that three of these babies appear with objects violently inserted into, and/or protruding from their mouths. These objects include a giant cockroach (*The Guardian*:12/11/03) a life-size bottle of methylated spirits (*The Guardian*: 17/11/03), a large plastic disposable syringe with a half loaded barrel which also appeared in colour (*Observer Magazine*:23/11/03) juxtaposed with the final image of a very big, very white content blonde male baby with a silver spoon in his mouth (*The Guardian*: 24/11/03 and in colour *Guardian Weekend Magazine*: 6/12/03. See Figure 1).

These images are linked together through the 'Barnardo's' logo, which appears at the bottom left hand corner with the accompanying slogan 'Giving children back their future'. What also connects the first three images is the caption 'There are no SILVER SPOONS for children born into POVERTY' which appears in bold, large capitals alongside the first three photographs. This contrasts with the final message in the series, 'IF ONLY every child was born with a SILVER SPOON' (See Figure 1). All of the images include a small biography of the child. In the photograph of the syringe-baby the accompanying blurb reads:

> Baby Mary is three minutes old.
> Thanks to poverty she faces a
> desperate future. Poverty is waiting
> to crush Mary's hope and ambition
> and is likely to lead her to a future
> of drug use. We can't end poverty
> but we can provide the practical

Figure 1: Barnardo's: 'If Only Every Child Was Born With a Silver Spoon'.

> skills that Mary and thousands of
> others in the UK need to stop it
> predetermining their lives. Don't
> let poverty destroy a future.
> Call us. . . .

The campaign establishes some clear 'facts' about poverty. What is most apparent is the suggestion that poverty leads to a future of drug use, and in turn that drug use is caused by poverty. In addition, the advert asserts that children born into poverty have no future, since the potential (and indeed class privilege) embodied in the silver spoon, is replaced with the debilitating syringe. Moreover, in portraying intravenous substance use as *socially predetermined*, the degenerative habitus of the child-body (as having no future) is itself configured through the object of the disposable syringe. Thus, whilst in this particular advertisement poverty and its reproduction is configured in relation to the child-body, what stands out here is not so much a biologized account of social suffering as in the case of 'crack-babies' but social suffering as concerning the syringe and the technological embodiment of addiction. And yet, the striking claims made in the campaign, particularly regarding the social context of Mary's life is that these 'facts' are not based on the observation of heroin addicts in the world, that is an empirical study of intravenous drug users, but ways of seeing the syringe and the truth of such images. In other words, and to return to McRobbie's concern with the figuring of the other in *The Weight of The World*, what is missing here is not just a theoretical analysis of the social and cultural context of social suffering but also an *empirical* conceptualization, one which avoids ontologizing the syringe-user (Vitellone, forthcoming). What I am stressing here is the need to question the 'facts' about the social reproduction of inequalities as embodied in pharmacological substances such as crack and heroin and also the disposable object of the syringe. In addition I am suggesting that it is important to question the ways in which the notion of the habitus is taken up in the field of cultural production to account for social suffering.

Perhaps not coincidently the spoon and the syringe also appear in the previous Barnardo's campaign of April 2000. This advertisement, which ran in national daily newspers, received many complaints, with some newspapers refusing in the outcry to carry the ad. The advertisement also featured a photograph of young (white) boy in nappies. This time the child is sitting upright holding a loaded plastic syringe in his left hand with a tourniquet wrapped around his upper right arm ready to inject heroin. The tourniquet, a shoelace, is made tight by being pulled by the child with his mouth. This image appeared in A5 in *The Weekend Guardian* (25/11/2000). It is shot in colour and the child is sitting alone in the corner of room in what is clearly a dilapidated disused building. Next to the child is a spoon, this time not a silver spoon but an instrument used to cook up heroin. Above the rotated head of the child, which is tilted upwards and away from the right arm enabling a tightening of the tourniquet, is the name 'JOHN Donaldson. AGE 23'. In the right top hand corner the familiar 'Barnardo's' logo with the caption 'Giving children back their futures' and in the bottom right hand corner John's biography:

> Battered as a child
> It was always possible that
> John would turn to drugs
> With Barnardo's help
> Child abuse need not lead
> to an empty future

Unlike the previously mentioned 'Silver spoon' campaign, here the present is conceptualised in relation to the past. The image of an injecting-child is so shocking precisely because it suggests that the practice of injecting heroin and the technical skills required to do so, is an instinctual non-cognitive act, embodied in the child-body. Thus it suggests that the child unconsciously knows the techniques and practices of injection, and that this unconscious technically embodied knowingness is part of the habitus.

What also connects this technological habitus with the present is the narrative of childhood: 'Jon Donaldson age 23' – heroin addict – 'Battered as a Child'. Steph Lawler's (2000) work on childhood and class is significant here. Like Castaneda, Lawler suggests that the idea of childhood is not an ontological category but 'can be seen as a social *production*' (2000:36), both in terms of its textual production and social practices. Paying close attention to how the figure of the child is discursively constituted, Lawler argues 'childhood is made coherent through the emplotment and narrativization of lives' (2000:35). According to Lawler 'within this narrativization, later events are understood as a culmination and actualization of prior events. Hence childhood is the grounds and the foundation of adulthood, and adulthood is made coherent through invocations of childhood' (2000:35). Indeed, in John's story social suffering is made coherent through a retrospective emplotment and narrativization of his childhood. The habitus of the injecting-child is actualised by prior events – being 'battered as a child'. John's childhood trauma thus becomes the foundation for adulthood addiction and social suffering. This retrospective narrativization of intravenous drug use is made explicit in the Barnardo's caption 'Giving children back their futures'.

Social realism and heroin

This realization of the habitus through the emplotment and narrativization of childhood is further evident in contemporary British social realist films. Following the international success of *Trainspotting* (1995), drug use and in particular intravenous drug use has featured in many British films. Since the mid 1990s, films such as *Nil by Mouth* (1997) *Sweet Sixteen* (2002) and the less known *Pure* (2002) all feature heroin, heroin use and the heroin user. They do so to such an extent that that heroin and its use has become a significant visual and narrative technique in recent British social realist films.

Pure, directed by Gillies Mackinnon, is filmed in a London East End council estate and begins with Paul's tenth birthday. In the opening sequence a hit is prepared. The camera pulls into a close up of the spoon, matches, cooking up gear, drawing up off the spoon, and the loaded syringe. What is unusual about this practice is that a young boy in a school uniform performs it. The child places the syringe on a tray, which he then delivers to a sleeping woman in the adjacent bedroom. This woman is his mother. He then leaves the room and his mother injects the contents of the syringe. Before heading off to school Paul reminds his mother that it is his tenth birthday. In this opening sequence the viewer is confronted with a child who is skilled at loading the syringe, a practice he understands as caring for his sick mother who needs her 'medicine' to get out of bed. Whilst this act is unconscious and embodied, the child has no knowledge of the contents of the syringe, nor is he aware until much later in the film that his mother is indeed a heroin addict.

Paul's relationship to his mother's addiction ultimately infers a loss of childhood, a loss whereby Paul is catapulted from an innocent childhood to an adult world of addiction. Cinematically this loss is filmed using an observational camera shot that follows the child moving backwards and forwards to and from his home on his pushbike. The repetition of this shot indicates that for Paul, time, change and the future concerns an awkward backwards and forwards reversal. The camera style positions Paul as trapped within the process of being a child, and becoming adolescent and of a future thwarted by his association with heroin, including his mother's addiction, his mother's supplier and also a young pregnant addict who he befriends.

In many ways the story of heroin in *Pure* takes up what Julia Hallam and Margaret Marshment (2000) describe as the dominant concerns with the genre of contemporary social realism, which feature a dysfunctional family and the alienated youth living on the margins of affluent society. In *Pure* Paul's physical entrapment addresses a key concern in the contemporary social realist genre: to show the 'places where people are disenfranchised by poverty and lack of opportunity', and 'engage with socio-economic and spatial confinement of contemporary urban life' (Hallam and Marshment 2000:192). This is evident in the location of the film, the focus on everyday interactions within a family context, and the observation of people physically stuck and literally unable to move out of their immediate environment.

In the film *Sweet Sixteen*, directed by Ken Loach, Joe's coming of age is also set in a social landscape dominated by heroin. Filmed in a Glaswegian council estate, there is no outside of drug economy, no potential, no adolescence just a sharp jump from childhood to adulthood, an early development brought on by heroin. Moreover Joe's desire to stop what Ken Loach portrays as a particular cycle of poverty, ends tragically with Joe killing his mothers boyfriend, a dealer she is quickly re-united with after her release form prison. Joe's hopes of getting out of the estate and getting his mum clean never materialize. As Hallam and Marshment point out 'it is the refusal of the film to depict a fictitious resolution that is the source of its claim on reality' (2000:214).

In addition to the observational camerawork and social landscape creating a sense of the real, what also characterises the narrative and visual style of these reality films is the embodiment of heroin. Practices such as scoring, injecting, the euphoric rush and craving are visual events that create a chronological narrative, one that constitutes and is constitutive of the telling of the story and the narrating of individual biographies. *Pure* deals with the junkie-mom's increasing difficulty of surviving with/out heroin. It does so through an observation of everyday heroin dependence, a state of being reflected by a focus on the *body* of the addict and the physical environment inhabited by her young sons, who are eventually taken away by social services. The women's dilated eyes, her sweating forehead, the rush and brief euphoria from the hit, followed by nodding and a period of normality before symptoms of withdrawal feature heavily in the film. The close up observation of the body of the addict resonates with Keane's account of the medical discourse on addiction whereby she argues 'through concepts such as withdrawal, tolerance and craving, addiction is internalised in the body of the addict. Binding addiction to the addict's body gives the concept of addiction another form of ontological existence' (Keane, 2002:39). Filming the heroin addict in such a disordered corporeal state thus reflects the traditional medical definition of dependence syndrome, one which Keane points out 'reinforce[s] the idea that drug dependence is a different order of things from normal attachment to daily routines and habits, and normal preoccupation with certain activities' (2002:55).

In this sense ways of seeing the pharmacologically addicted body have indeed become part of the social realism genre as a claim to reality. Moreover, popular ways of seeing the embodiment of addiction in British social realist films in the 1990s suggests a synergy is taking place between the official medical gaze on drugs and the 'real'. For instance, watching heroin in *Pure* mirrors the sequential logic of the medical model of addiction involving 'predictable stages, (Keane, 2000:39) and a 'notion of temporal development' (Keane, 2000:40), a model which Keane points out is inscribed on the body itself. Interestingly, the embodiment of heroin contrasts with the final sequence of the film *Pure* whereby we witness the mother's successful recovery, and her ability to come clean, and be reunited with her children. This narrative also follows what Keane describes as a 'logic of reversal, from addiction back to normality' (Keane, 2000:13) here form the addicted-mother to the maternal body, and the syringe-child to an ideal childhood.

Conclusion

In analysing these social realist films and the Barnardo's campaign my aim has been to demonstrate how in a similar fashion to the ethnographies of social suffering – such as that produced by Bourgois – both make claims to capture the social reality or truth of social suffering via the use of the techniques of realism. Moreover in all three of the texts at issue here – ethnographic studies, media campaigns and social realist films – I hope to have demonstrated that the matter of drugs is crucial to the ways in which these texts make truth claims to understanding the social reproduction of social suffering. My analysis of the pharmacological habitus suggests that what is key in these texts is a particular cultural narrative of drug use as degenerative. In this narrative the social embodiment of drugs work towards the reproduction of social suffering and social exclusion because drugs will always take away the agency of users. But as I have shown Lisa Maher's ethnography resists this cultural narrative and this is the case because she recognizes that issues of class, race *and* gender are worked through (and are not outside of) the drug economy. In contrast, ethnographers such as Bourgois unproblematically accept and reproduce the assumption that drug use is simply structured by, or is the outcome of, socio-structural transformations.

I have argued further that the reproduction of this narrative by ethnographers such as Bourgois relates to the use of a substance/social distinction whereby substances are always understood to be outside of the social. Moreover the social/substance distinction leads to a failure to deal with how cultural narratives of drugs, their use and embodiment have social effects. I have suggested that these effects are both racialized and gendered, especially as they relate to issues of reproduction and the body of the child. On these grounds I have suggested that it is vital that the concept of habitus be revised to include the significance of substances and their embodiment. It is only when such a revision takes place can we see how cultural narratives on drug use *could* relate to issues of social suffering.

Notes

1 Which McNay argues 'establishes an active and creative relation . . . between the subject and the world' (1999:100).
2 Which 'thereby opens up the act of reproduction to indeterminacy and the potential for change' (McNay, 1999:102).

References

Adkins, L. (2003) 'Reflexivity: Freedom or Habit of Gender' *Theory, Culture & Society* 20(6): 21–42.
Bourdieu, P. (1999) *The Weight of the World: Social Suffering in Contemporary Society.* Cambridge: Polity Press.
Bourdieu, P. and Wacquant, L. (1999) 'On the Cunning of Imperial Reason' *Theory, Culture & Society* 16(1): 41–56.
Bourgois, P. (1995) *In Search of Respect. Selling Crack in El Barrio*. Cambridge: Cambridge University Press.
Bourgois, P. (1996) 'In Search Of Masculinity: Violence, Respect and Sexuality Among Puerto Rican Crack Dealers in East Harlem' *British Journal of Criminology* 36(3): 412–427.
Bourgois, P. (1998) 'Just Another Night in the Shooting Gallery' *Theory, Culture & Society* 15(2): 37–66.
Bourgois, P. (2003) 'Crack and the Political Economy of Social Suffering' *Addiction Research & Theory* 11(1): 31–37.
Boyne, R. (2002) 'Bourdieu: From Class to Culture. *In Memoriam* Pierre Bourdieu 1930–2002' *Theory, Culture & Society* 19(3): 117–128.
Campbell, N.D. (2000) *Using Women: Gender, Drug Policy and Social Justice*. London and New York: Routledge.
Castaneda, C. (2002) *Figurations: Child, Bodies, Worlds*. Durham and London: Duke University Press.
Fowler, B. (2003) 'Reading Pierre Bourdieu's Masculine Domination: Notes Towards an Intersectional Analysis of Gender, Culture and Class' *Cultural Studies* 17(3/4): 468–494.

Hallam, J. and Marshment, M. (2000) *Realism and Popular Cinema*. Manchester: Manchester University Press.

Keane, H. (2002) *What's Wrong with Addiction?* Melbourne: Melbourne University Press.

Lawler, S. (2000) *Mothering the Self: Mothers, Daughters, Subjects*. London and New York: Routledge.

Maher, L. (2000) *Sexed Work: Gender Race and Resistance in a Brooklyn Drug Market*. Oxford: Oxford University Press.

Mason, C. (2000) 'Cracked Babies and the Partial Birth of a Nation: Millenialism and Fetal Citizenship' *Cultural Studies* 14(1): 35–60.

McNay, L. (1999) 'Gender, Habitus and the Field: Pierre Bourdieu and the Limits of Reflexivity' *Theory, Culture & Society* 16(1): 95–117.

McRobbie, A. (2002) 'A Mixed Bag Of Misfortunes?: Bourdieu's *Weight of the World*' *Theory, Culture & Society* 19(3): 129–138.

Oritz, A.T. and Briggs, L. (2003) 'The Culture of Poverty, Crack Babies and Welfare Cheats. The Making of the "Healthy White Baby Crisis"' *Social Text* 21(3): 39–57.

Vitellone, N. (forthcoming) 'The Syringe, Junkies and Waste' *Cultural Studies*.

Mapping the obituary: Notes towards a Bourdieusian interpretation

Bridget Fowler

Introduction

An important strand of feminist practice has been the reconstruction of women's experience historically, using auto/biographical sources. This process has gone under the metaphorical banner of retrieving the hidden from history, bringing the invisible into visibility, giving voices to the silenced. The language of illumination and speech thus aligns such projects with a still vibrant Enlightenment project even as they draw attention to the ways in which the Enlightenment (and the Renaissance earlier) intensified women's marginalisation within Western bourgeois society.

One social mechanism that has been significant as a first stage towards remembering individuals has been the publication of an obituary on their death. A particularly influential form of collective memory, I want to claim, is derived from these literary memorials. Obituaries reveal and actively shape "how societies remember": indeed, in doing so, they parallel the school history textbook in shaping a whole generation's stock of knowledge. They do not do so neutrally. As Connerton remarks: 'The control of a society's memory largely conditions the hierarchy of power' (1989:1). Obituaries should not be seen merely as homage to individuals but as part of a wider play of symbolic power. Yet they have received very little attention either from sociology, feminism or Marxist cultural studies. The present essay is intended to develop an empirically-based approach to obituary narratives and to propose Bourdieusian theory, supplemented by the work of Paul Ricoeur, to understand this neglected form.

We might think of obituaries as commemorative pacts that help explain the inertia – the continuous reproductive re-enactment – of social structures (see, eg, Halbwachs, 1991). Of course, the obituary is a less cultic and more individualised form, unlike the ritualised institutions which other practices of social remembering, such as Armistice Day or May Day have taken. Yet, despite their appearance as a mere series of individual portraits, the written texts of the obituary possess a certain authority and their subjects receive from such accolades the stamp of legitimacy. Indeed, this social order of remembrance appears only to offer an anticipated bestowal of dignity on those who are in any case 'naturally' distinguished. Such an apparently obligatory social order allows us to see in the newspaper obituary something of the character of modern invented traditions (Connerton, 1989:63–64; cf. Hobsbaum and Ranger, 1983).

Yet where there is collective memory there is also organised forgetting. Thus one concern we might have is the question of who is deemed worthy of an obituary – are both genders, all nationalities and all ethnic groups equally represented? Are obituaries restricted to a traditional elite? Or are there specific obituary authors – analogous to Solzenitsyn, for the Gulag victims, and Toni Morrison, for slaves – who purposively stand out so as to rectify such collective oblivion? In such cases, we might say that they personally offer 'the struggle of their memory against forced forgetting' (Connerton, 1989). Examples might be the project of the M.P., Tam Dalyell, of contributing to the obituaries of Scottish political figures, or Philip Hobsbaum's sustained work of writing obituaries of poets. The sociological interest in the obituary as a realm of collective memory thus turns out to contain issues of cultural politics of canonisation (or cultural consecration), but also to spread a net wider than these.

Part of the fascination of the obituary is that it represents a contested space – between journalism and literature. That is to say, the obituary shares with journalism the imperatives of truth, to tell things how they really were, and with literature, the concern for form – or at least for a rarity and economy of expression. This literary defamiliarization of the obituary form emerges more in some national traditions than others, the French rather than the American, and especially in the obituaries for jazz singers and poets, more than those for other figures.

There is also the well-known tension between the claims of truth and elements shared by the obituary with religious rites de passage – the comfort to the survivors, the celebration of the life lived well. Thus the day of the obituary might be seen as a secularised judgement day on one's calling, the social equivalent to the figure of God weighing up one's sins and virtues in a divine settling of accounts. But it also raises crucial debates about the status of the obituary, whether as a genre of mere hagiography or, alternatively, as an instrument of realist honesty, and indeed, about the continuation of political battles within the obituary's newspaper columns.[1]

Bourdieu

Bourdieu is the trailblazer in the sociological analysis of obituaries. Indeed, Bourdieu, at his most cynical, regards some individuals as even able to elude death:

> Death, from the point of view of groups, is only an accident, and personified collectives organise themselves in such a way that the demise of the mortal bodies which once embodied the group – representatives, delegates, agents, spokesmen – does not affect the existence of the group [. . .] If this is accepted [. . .] then capital makes it possible to appropriate the collectively-produced and accumulated means of really

overcoming anthropological limits. The means of escaping from generic alienations include representation, the portrait or statue which immortalises the person [. . .] Thus it can be seen that eternal life is one of the most sought-after social privileges (Bourdieu, 1984:72).

The obituary is another such 'portrait' allowing the escape from some of the 'generic alienations' imposed by death.

Bourdieu's models help to illuminate the world of the dominants, the world that is being negotiated by editors when they make their more difficult and daring choices of obituary subjects. It is *The State Nobility* (1996b) which offers the best theoretical tools for a critical analysis of the obituaries in general. It is also this book which contains Bourdieu's own analyses of obituaries, using the poignant memorials of recently dead academics as evidence of different modes of university existence. More particularly, the concepts of *The State Nobility* can aid us in evaluating the frequent contention that an important, pioneering segment of this obituary newspaper field has now moved outside the 'old boys' 'circle of a 'parochial' 'Establishment' and become – in effect – democratized. This appeal to democratization and the alternative stress on a more meritocratic or varied criteria for memory are key features of modern newspaper obituaries. Take, as an example, James Fergusson's claims that *The Independent* obituary columns are now open to any one who has made their mark in the world in a significant, striking or surprising way:

> I think [. . .] of the multitude who might never have had obituaries written about them if the *Independent* [. . .] had not come along. Of all the photographers, monks, bookplate designers, chair makers, suffragettes, graffiti artists, jazz saxophonists, lexicographers, cartoonists, pulp publishers, puppeteers, mimes, weavers, ferrymen, schoolteachers and master plasterers; of Tom Forster, Britain's oldest working ploughman; Roly Wason, 91, Professor of Archaeology turned Hartlepool bus conductor [. . .], Mr. Sebastian, 63, body piercer and tattooist [. . .]; Winifred ('Winnie the Hat') Wilson, 88, fearless sometime picture dealer to Walter Sickert; . . . Donald MacLean, 66, for twenty-five years director of the Crieff Highland gathering and 'the greatest of all private collectors of the potato' (Fergusson 1999:159–160).

Bourdieu's extensive empirical analyses underpin a more disenchanted vision than that of Fergusson (1984; 1989, 1996). He thus offers what we might call 'an ethic of suspicion' with regard to such a democratic or universalistic claim.

The second reason for choosing Bourdieu as a major source for understanding obituaries is his theory that the dominant class has *changed its mode of legitimation*. He comments that the dominants' spiritual 'point d'honneur' was once religion: in its most famous Weberian version, such rationalisations depend on an assumption that those in a higher caste are there because they are closer to nirvana within the cycle of rebirths, or (in Calvinism) that the asceticism signifying election is divinely favoured by abundant profits. In other words, those most embodying the sacred ideal were recognized as exemplary models (Bourdieu, 1998). In contrast, Bourdieu's distinctive model of the transition from pre-capitalist to capitalist societies contains a theory of secularization.

On this account, the contemporary spiritual 'soul', has migrated to creative artists, with their characteristically non-economic actions, or to the aristocracy of culture, with their spiritual devotion or 'love of art'. Such a nobility of culture possesses an aesthetic attitude, which is principally revealed by a formalist commitment to beauty or style for its own sake (Bourdieu, 1984).

My own study shows that telling traces of these social changes appear in the sampled obituaries.[2] For example, in the earlier British obituaries of 1900, clergy and missionaries made up 8% of the total known occupations (*The Times*). In contrast, by 2000–1, they were only 2% in *The Times* and *The Guardian,* even fewer (1%) in *The Independent*. The numbers of those in the arts is vastly higher than it once was, having expanded in *The Times* from 12% in 1900 to the contemporary 30% and much more spectacularly in *The Guardian* and *The Independent* (both 51%).[3] Moreover, obituary subjects whose distinction lies outside the artistic field are now more often given additional seriousness and stature by reference to their love of art: 'he was a keen opera-goer' or 'he collected paintings' is a frequent significer of a magnanimous and sensitive character.

Thirdly, in a period some have labelled the 'auto/biographical society', Bourdieu offers a critique of an important 'biographical illusion' (1986; 1994: 81–89). In a sense his whole theory of practice offers an approach to this, especially its tight-rope passage between Sartrian voluntarism and mechanistic materialism. An article in *Actes* allows us to pinpoint more exactly his precise critique of commonsense life-histories, which is especially productive for those studying popular biographies or the newspaper obituary (compare, say, the earlier studies by Kracauer, 1995:101–7; and Lowenthal, 1961).

This *Actes* essay offers us a vantage point from which to criticise the atomized, pre-Freudian, unified self of liberal humanism, without abandoning altogether the notion of an authentic (Kantian) 'me'. In applying this to the obituary, I accept Bourdieu's view that we must avoid the seductive commonsense inherent in the unitary view of the subject. In clarifying what he calls the 'biographical illusion', Bourdieu discusses the 'contraband' of the 'mountain path view' of life's route. The 'rhetorical illusion' he suggests is that life makes up a homogeneous whole, a coherent, directed ensemble, which can be understood as the single arena of a subjective – or even 'objective' – intention. Signalled by terms like 'already', or 'from a very young age' this implies an:

> original project in the Sartrean sense . . . This life organized like a history unrolls according to a chronological order which is also a logical order, from a beginning, which is [. . .] a first cause, but also a raison d'être, to its final point, which is also its goal (Bourdieu, 1986:70).

Against this, Bourdieu argues, in an act of 'rhetorical revolution', that the biography could be better seen as Macbeth's 'tale, told by an idiot, a tale full of sound and fury, but signifying nothing' (Bourdieu, 1986:69–70). Yet his specific critique of the biographical illusion does not imply that subjects or agents are merely clusters of fleeting, refugee selves, caught up in an endless mobile flux created by contingency: the chaotic vision on which some recent writers put too much weight. Bourdieu's concept of the habitus saves us from total contingency, although we should constantly recall also that in his usage, the habitus represents durable dispositions, not an eternal destiny (Bourdieu and Wacquant, 1992; Bourdieu, 2002a). His general critique of the biographical illusion serves usefully to remind us that the 'life history approach' has been shaped overwhelmingly by the structuring mechanism of a steady progression within a career, coupled with the youthful anticipation of this. But this is an upward ascendancy which is more typical of an aristocratic or bourgeois élite than of the lower classes, whose less ordered experience makes their members forcibly more attuned to cyclical or even disrupted rhythms (cf Connerton, 1989:19; Maynes, 1989:105).

Such questions about time and the anticipation of the future are crucial to Bourdieu, as I have argued earlier (Fowler, 1997). The profound difficulty on the part of the subordinates in adopting a rational, future-oriented, progressive model of time is a matter of frequent insistence in both the early and very late work of Bourdieu (*Travail et Travailleurs en Algérie*, 1964 and *Pascalian Meditations*, 2000). Indeed, in the picture of the unemployed given in *Pascalian Meditations*, with its recognition of a Kafka-like fragility in the possession of a justified social existence, we have some of Bourdieu's most compelling and convincing writing.

In brief, as Bourdieu has taught us, when we confront the study of obituaries, we must be wary of those constructions that identify success too much with an individual's self-avowed objectives. Instead, we shall focus on *empowerment* as a result of birth into an élite or the *esprit de corps* within great public schools or Oxford and Cambridge (in France, within the grandes écoles) (Bourdieu, 1996b). Moreover, Bourdieu's sociological account of the art-world also appears a promising beginning to understanding the recent European and British obituaries. His approach to the 'world in reverse' inhabited by bohemian cultural producers and the position-taking available for the avant-garde, opens an under-explored new path for the qualitative study of the artistic biography.

The sociogenesis of the obituary

In order to understand any contemporary institution, we need to trace it back to its origins. Thus we shall explore briefly points in the genealogy of the obituary. In written form, the original British starting-point for the obituary is commonly thought to be John Aubrey's *Brief Lives* (1898 – originally 1669 and 1696). The newspaper form became current by the middle of the eighteenth century (O.E.D.). The official *History of The Times* refers to the inclusion of obituaries from its earliest days (1785) but the form was then already a standard element within all the daily newspapers (Anonymous, 1935, see also Grant, 1871). We therefore chose 1900, as a point at which the obituary was already well-established in a routinised and anonymous column of biographies. By that time the obituary was more than a bare announcement of death, but it was hardly ever as lengthy, elaborate and individuated as the genre that emerged by the mid-twentieth century.

The 1900 obituaries

The ranking of the dead in 1900 is still cast in terms of an estate society, where the obituaries of the higher species (royalty and the barons) have priority in terms of length and precedence over mere gentry and the plebeian strata. Of course there is some fusion of the old and the new in this form. The 'old' – the aristocrats of the Regiment and the Navy in particular, representing as many as 34% of the total – are now joined by the 'new' with the emergence of certain more modern figures, such as the 'electrician' (electrical engineer, Prof. D.E.Hughes, F.R.S.), who invented the telegraph or the chairman of a steamship company.

Women are curiously non-existent within these columns, appearing where they do principally as units of alliance in noble kinship networks. Thus it is extremely rare to read anything much about their individual distinction. The following – which gives a flavour of this whole category – is a complete (and typically stark) entry:

> Viscountess Newry died on Saturday at her residence, 98, Eaton Place, aged 80 years. Anne Amelia, Lady Newry, was the daughter of Gen. the Hon. Sir Charles Colville, and was married in 1839 to Francis, Viscount Newry and Morne, the eldest son of the second Earl of Kilmorey. She is the mother of the third Earl and was left a widow in 1851. [Note that *The Times* at this period finds it unnecessary to add 'London' to the Eaton Place address.]

There are only two 1900 exceptions to this. The Hon. Mrs. James Stuart Wortley appears as a 'one of the most interesting women of the epoch', while Mary Kingsley's obituary honours a short, but distinguished life as an anthropologist in Africa.

The men in the 1900 obituaries are all exemplary figures, many described in the language of medieval warriors. None descend into barbarism; none are brutalized by the closeness of violence. But the key point is surely this. If there was a fusion by 1834, of the middle class and aristocracy, blood and gold, this was a fusion that left aristocratic culture uppermost in many crucial forms (Mayer, 1981).

Industrial capital does not appear in the 1900 obituaries. There is one exception: an unprepossessing mine owner, who is symptomatically objectified in a manner similar now to the white working-class, in a language saturated with all the ambiguities of class racism:

> Though not a miner, but the owner of several coal-mines, Mr Cowan was not essentially different either externally or intellectually, from some of the rough, keen colliers of Northumberland today [who possess] a mental activity and a grasp rarely to be found among working people in other parts of the country. [. . .] Short in stature,

uncouth in dress and figure, and speaking a tongue the peculiarities of which are admired only to the manner born, he commanded in his early appearances anything but respect (*The Times* 19/2/1900).

Thus even in 'the age of capital', the merely 'regional' industrialists are put in their place.

There are occasional exceptions to the ideal-type warriors who dominated these columns. The second or third sons of aristocrats became Classics-trained clergyman. A minority of these led exemplary lives, living and working in the East End of cities. One such sacrificial figure is a Bristol vicar with a huge parish who died young, of a heart-attack.

Ruskin is another such exception. But with him we see the mould broken, for he is a heretical figure, even nicknamed "the Prophet of Brantwood". His death established a new way of seeing in the obituary. For it provoked not just a long regular obituary, but an accompanying obituary article, as well as an appreciation from the Chief Rabbi. Within these, Ruskin is heralded, as the inventor of a new artistic field, that of art criticism itself – 'Through him' says the main obituarist, 'a new life was infused into English art'.

Contemporary obituaries

There is a sense in which obituaries offer us not theodicies but sociodicies, accounts which serve to legitimate the social order (Bourdieu and Passeron 1979). They are tiny exemplary tales of our times. We expect these narratives to reveal the heroic individuals of our society, even while, as sociologists, we take our distance from them. But there are also negative biographies – those of anti-heroes, villains, call them what you will.

For example, in 2000–1, while post-colonial writing is celebrated, post-colonial politicians, unsurprisingly, may be castigated. Joe Modise can stand for the rest (*The Guardian* 29/11/01). His obituary charts his rise from street fighter to chief of the armed wing of the ANC, in which capacity he had the Communist, Chris Hani killed in the brutal Quattro camp. As Defence Minister he amassed £5.6 million in shares, but died decorated by Mbeki with the South African Grand Cross.

The obituarist progressively sows the seeds of doubt: his 'staggering brutality, extraordinary abuse of power' is followed by later by evidence of corruption. He ends using Shakespearean innuendo to reinforce Modise's critics: 'So his friends say, for all his sins, Joe Modise served the new South Africa well'. By this mustering of the evidence, the reader realises the verdict should not rest with his friends.

That the obituary is more geared to celebration rather than defamation appears most clearly when its 'rules' are flouted. This is the case with the prominent obituary of Lord Shore (Edward Pearce *The Guardian*: 26/9/01), which uses the impersonal gravitas granted to each individual obituarist for an unusually destructive judgement of the subject's entire personal reputation, a judgement that is underpinned, more evidently than is usual, by its author's antagonistic political agenda. The obituary savagely writes him off for 'dullmindedness', reassessing Shore's unsuccessful political odyssey in a series of barbed attacks on his radicalism, consistency and intellectual credibility:

> But Shore's political career involved a long dwindling without there ever having been quite a solid achievement to dwindle from. [. . .] He might even have had a reputation for magnificent independence like Tam Dalyell, but the melancholy truth was that undoubted courage, furious contradictions, and some force as a speaker were never enough to make Shore interesting [. . .]

The obituary includes words all the more savage for having the authority of a direct quotation: 'Wilson's comment to Richard Crossman was the more deadly for lacking anger: "I over-promoted him. He's no good"'. And much more. We might see this as the point-zero of the critical genre.

Obituary samples 2000–1

The decline of the aristocracy

In contrast with the remorseless procession of noble figures in *The Times* for 1900, we have to see the partial democratization of the obituary as the main feature of our own time. Some would call it a 'revolution'.

The obituary still represents the peerage who entirely populated the older columns – Lord Hailsham, Lord Catto, The Earl of Onslow, Lord Aldington, Princess Margaret. But it is conspicuous today for portraits which would have been unthinkable a hundred years ago. Take Emil Zatopek, the Czech marathon runner, for example, whose *Independent* obituary unfolded an extraordinary historical document in which the runner's micro world refracts in crystal-clear light the changes occurring on the world's stage, with regime changes and failed revolutions. This shoe-factory apprentice, a carpenter's son, ran in the manner of a country boy, grimacing and torturing himself, even practicing in Army boots through snow. Yet he became 'the man of legend – the greatest runner of all time'. Seen by some as mad, he won 18 World records and 3 events in the 1948 Olympics. His contrariness might have given Zatopek the resources to oppose the Soviet invasion of his country – for which he was confined to manual labour for seven years.

In this context, we might mention the less spectacular but equally sustained performances of Irene Thomas, the daughter of a gas-meter official and a seamstress. She had been to a grammar school but her parents could not afford University. She became Brain of Britain as well as Brain of Brains on the Radio Round Britain Quiz, despite having been rejected for seven years for the contest, and only eventually being permitted to take part in the absence of a suitable man. (*The Guardian* 4/4/01).

Again, there is the Nigerian-born London fitter, Michael Akintaro, who through this unusually lengthy piece gradually gains status as one who embodied the collective memory of immigrants. His obituary is absorbing not because of his competitive achievements but because of whom he was and whom he knew. He was counted by the legendary figure, George Padmore, as amongst the 'foot-soldiers in the fight against colonial rule' (*The Guardian* 7/10/00). It is therefore, something of a paradox that this foot-soldier of anti-imperialism was finally to be awarded an *Imperial Services Medal* for his work as a fitter from Whitehall to Buckingham Palace.

Yet it would be wrong in other ways for a sociologist to take at face-value this apparent transformation of élites. For the British equivalent of the State Nobility still dominate the obituary columns. There were *no* manual workers represented in the 2000–1 obituary sample of *The Daily Telegraph* and only 2% of those in *The Guardian*. And those with social origins in the manual working-class were still only a tiny proportion of the whole.

What we are witnessing is a shift towards occupations dominated by the possession of cultural capital rather than the old criterion of blood. Yet the dominant families are still able to retain their hegemony, although in changed terms. As evidence for this, one might simply note the educational origins of those featured. If the obituary were genuinely meritocratic and less geared to an Establishment, should we expect that 72% of the British figures in the 2000–1 British newspapers would have been to a public school? Or that 34% would have been to Oxford and Cambridge? These Universities, we argue, following Bourdieu, serve magically to consecrate the bearers of their degrees (1996b).

Class origins, 2000–1

The contemporary obituaries have an aura of upward social mobility about them, just as Trilling writes about the classic American novel as possessing, as its great masterplot, the individuals' unaided success (1961:247). The default mode, so to speak, of the obituary, is the anticipated tale of individual, hard-won success.

Yet the cultural reality of the obituary, between the lines, is actually divergent from this, and reveals instead the high likelihood of the continuing *reproduction*, or ossification, of the class order. Clearly, this does not mean a precise generational replication of a given occupation. Many patterns of overall class reproduction involve a change in class fraction. A conversion of economic capital into cultural capital, for example, occurs when a banker's son's refuses the bank so as to become an artist: as Bourdieu points out, a sense of novelty resonates from such subjectively risky choices. But given all those obituary portrayals where the parents' work or class position is also described, as many as 47 (64%) of *The Guardian's*, 30, or 58%, of *The Independent's* and 62% of *The Times'* subjects revolve around the inheritance of the class position of the parents in this broader sense. 23 (31%) of *The Guardian's* stories are of upward mobility – broadly similar to the 17 out of 52 (33%) in *The Independent* but contrasting with the smaller 15 (22%) in *The Daily Telegraph*. Downwards social mobility only occurs exceptionally: the total consists of in four cases in *The*

Times and two in *The Guardian*. Perhaps the most dramatic instance of such a fraught and anomic trajectory is the sad history of Benno Schultz, the boxer, who, having risen to prominence from the slums of Berlin, killed his wife in a fit of drunken jealousy at the height of his career and then sank, after prison, into the social 'living death' of poverty.

Migration

Perhaps the most startling revelation is the number of figures in the obituary landscape who had migrated across national borders. Migration was charted initially because of the importance of post-colonial theory, and especially because of the new phenomenon of writers from the Third World moving into the metropolises of the First World (Ahmad, 1991). But the correlation between the experience of migration and distinction appears to be more widespread than I had imagined, extending throughout many fields of British society. If élite or voluntary migration is included, then this category embraces 34% of the *Guardian* and *Independent*. In *The Times* and the *Daily Telegraph*, where the Forces or transnational diplomatic career feature particularly prominently, such migration includes as many as 45%. Even in the usual – more restrictive – sense of political exiles or economic migrants, 11 (10%) of *The Times* come into this category. The very telling presence of such a migrant minority most sharply differentiates the 2000–1 group from the 1900 subjects (0.8%).

Theorizing women's marginality within the obituary

Obituaries continue to be predominantly narratives of men. Nevertheless, one element within the selective democratisation of the genre since 1900 is the reduced marginalization of women, now 19% overall (cf. 11% in 1900). There is even a tiny minority of women whose deaths have been recorded in more than one newspaper, such as Barbara Cartland, or Lorna Sage, the literary critic.

When we begin to look more closely at those who do appear, one immediate generalization emerges: these women are distinctive collectively in having had very few children. From 1900 to the contemporary samples, over a third have not had children at all (36%) and a clear majority (53%), either one child only or none.[4] In *The Independent* of 2000–1, as many as 75% are stated to have had one or no children and 63% had been childless. It should not be assumed that such women always chose not to have children. These were the years of either a marriage bar or institutionalized anti-natalist policies for women employees. Professional motherhood had as its other side, compulsory spinsterhood: a historic concession by women in their subversion of male professional closure. As a consequence, it is difficult to establish the mixture of autonomous choice and structural pressures towards celibacy that were responsible for the childlessness of figures such as Brigadier Helen Meechie, Lieutenant-Commander Dame Anne Stephens, the journalist Muriel Bowen or Vera Atkins, the Assistant Head of the Special Operations Executive in the Second World War. We should not expect such childlessness in a later generation, where marriage bars have been swept away. Or should we? There is undoubtedly still a wider structural tension between women having children and what Bourdieu calls 'the male monopoly of noble tasks' (2001). I will consider this further later.

We need to pursue a closer, qualitative study of the obituaries of women to see what kind of interpretative analysis is given them. I shall offer this approach to women's obituary discourses through the prism of different genres. These are best approached by illustration, with ideal typical accounts of life histories. I shall then make some general explanatory comments on the rarity of women in the form.

Types of obituary for women

First, none of the obituaries for women have the grand heroic stature of those portrayals of the State Nobility, such as the full-page for Viscount Hailsham (*The Guardian* 15/10/01). Male figures, like Hailsham, lie in the most venerable tradition of the obituary, as we have seen. They represent old money, allied to noble tasks of domination: they are credited with untrammelled excellence of character. Even in the Centre-Left papers like *The Guardian*, their personalities are depicted as moulded like gloves for their offices. For these heroic figures, Bourdieu's words on the *State Nobility* and its training in the elite schools are memorable. They have both technical skills and the magic derived from office: both feed beneficially off each other.

1. The positive traditional obituary for women

There are obituaries which praise women who are exemplars of traditional femininity. One such was Lady Mary Townley, a Catholic, with seven children, married to Sir Simon Townley, a businessman and also the owner of an old Northern landed estate. She had no paid work but was a good wife, always extremely careful not to neglect her philanthropic work. Despite her love of riding, she insisted on undertaking all the menial tasks in the household, proof of an extraordinary and positive capacity for acts of self-abasement. This type of exemplary woman is extremely rare in the contemporary obituaries, although she had many predecessors earlier.

There is also a category of positive *vocational* obituary for women, that is to say, there are women who had an inner certainty of their virtuosity but who may also have had several children. One such is Noor Jehan (*The Guardian*), the Punjabi singer, whose extraordinary range combined Indian and Pakistani, high and low cultures. She excelled equally with popular songs, folksongs and works with modern settings by the great Pakistan poet, Faiz. Grief at her death, we learn, united the whole Indian subcontinent. In this category also appears the Wittgensteinian philosopher, Elizabeth Anscombe, of whom we read that she kept her name of *Miss* Anscombe, much to the discomfort of medical staff when she attended hospital for her sixth and seventh babies. Or there is the geneticist, Julia Bodmer, whose pioneering work at Oxford in the study of Hodgkins' disease gives her that rare distinction for a woman of being labelled 'brilliant'. With her husband, Walter Bodmer, she brought up three children, all of whom turned out well. Julia Bodmer is untroubled, free of conflict, moving with extraordinary harmony between the public and the private spheres.

2. The negative obituary

The negative obituary, rare for men, is even rarer for women. The obituary confers on such stigmatized individuals a certain niche within historical memory, but – as in the cases of Anne Lindbergh, the writer of space fantasies, or Lida Baarova, the Czech actress – as deeply flawed figures. Both were prominent collaborators with Naziism. Lindbergh, a feminist, was also a notorious patrician appeaser. She urged the Roosevelt Government in the 1930s to accommodate to the new German Government of a Hitler whom, she claimed, was *not* 'greedy for power' and whom Roosevelt should realise, was in any case 'unstoppable'. Lida Baarova, a beautiful Czech actress of great talent and presence, the well-heeled daughter of a civil servant, became Goebbels' mistress. By her fateful choice of complicity with Fascist power, she indelibly enhanced the aura of both Goebbels himself and the Nazis.

What is important in this category is that such women – clearly deservedly – are not ultimately 'one of us' but representatives of the Other. Like the obituaries of Laurent Kabila, the Congo leader, and the former Lebanese prime minister, Hadid Hélou, they had their opportunities and used them poorly. Nevertheless, one senses a certain reluctance to place women into this category. In the case of Diana Mitford, Oswald Mosley's wife, for example, it is conspicuous how charitable is the posture adopted in *The Independent* (13.8.2003) towards this pro-fascist devotee of the Hitler cult: here perhaps is the obituary's most clear-cut example of a fairy-tale re-enchantment lent by time and distance.

3. The ironic obituary

There is a category of negative obituary which is perhaps distinctive to women – not 'the other', but nevertheless sharply satirised, often in Flaubertian tones. Such women represent a style of life which, in terms of sexual and class doxa, has now become seen as outmoded, even ludicrous. Yet far from being interpreted as part of a destructive system of injustice, or class racism, they are seen in a comic mode. One example is Betty Kenward, the long-term writer of Jennifer's Diary in *The Tatler*. She was the living embodiment of a set of aristocratic rules, now dead, which extended to inventing linguistic markers of the social order:

> [S]he had developed her own rules about punctuation: charming, perversely logical, a mine-field for the sub-editors. Monarchs [...] must be hedged about with semi-

colons, the Duke of Edinburgh must always be protected with a comma. Otherwise both semi-colons and commas were rather scarce (*The Independent* 27/1/01).

4. The Tragic genre of obituary

Here are the women of noble families, traditional women, caught in a structural incongruity, which destroyed their happiness. These lives are dogged by reversals. Raised and elevated for great things, they embody the romantic sadness of those with legitimate hopes whose lives are brutally and unavoidably destroyed. The ex-queen of Iran, Soraya, is one such figure (*Independent*), whose future was irretrievably bound up with that of the Shah's Pahlavi regime. Thus, in matter-of fact tones, the obituary narrates the history of the Shah's access to power by force, through an Anglo-American manipulated *coup d'état*. Such manoeuvring wrested Anglo-Burma Oil from a democratic Iranian government, intent on nationalizing the oil. In this obituary, Soraya's collusion with the Pahlavis' illegitimate minority power is passed over as a mere background detail. Soraya is portrayed instead as a woman caught in an arbitrary Greek tragedy: her personal misfortune is her barrenness, leading to her divorce from the Shah she loved. Her subsequent unhappy nomadic exile, mainly in France, is summed up in the Parisian song 'Pleurez comme Soraya . . .'.

Another such tragic woman, Ruth Werner, the daughter of a prosperous German bourgeois family, was appalled to see dead babies littering the gutters of the street as the inter-war depression accelerated. She became an activist within the Communist Party, a stance for which the obituary author initially has sympathy. This sympathy is forfeited by her later actions, especially her assistance to Fuchs in passing Harwell atomic secrets to the Soviets. Werner's vital intermediary role led eventually to her rapid departure for East Germany. Her subsequent arid experience in the Eastern bloc is implicitly viewed as a punishment for her unwomanly and misguided activism earlier.

5. The celebratory, untraditional obituary for women

Compared with the obituaries of men, even the most celebrated of female figures have rarely had a regular career, appear more divided against themselves and were often no longer at home in their own countries. In brief, the obituary of women can come in the same 'mould breaking' shape that I described with Michael Akintaro, the Whitehall Nigerian fitter.

Take the long and vividly-written obituary of Joan Littlewood, the theatre director.[5] Her life does not take the pattern of a gradual upward ascent and such divergent experience thus indirectly illuminates what Bourdieu means by 'the biographical illusion'. Joan's international heyday was short, restricted to her 40s and 50s. Her trajectory in spatial terms was also highly unusual. Her odyssey was from a poor London district to RADA, then to Liverpool and the North, back to the East End of London again, but this time with crucial links to the West End. Defeated over funding at the height of her powers, she retreated to work with Soyinka in Nigeria and finally to France.

Yet it is not this which really distinguishes her, it is that she represents a type of modernism which flared briefly, being eclipsed in Britain by more politically-conservative and nostalgic forms (for example, of T.S. Eliot and Pound). Her theatre, which carried on the experimental innovations of Meierhold and German expressionism, was also a modernism which aspired to be accessible, democratic and popular. It is this which is so successfully at stake for her, in the collective production of *Oh What a Lovely War*.

Littlewood was an illegitimate child, who often felt ugly. When married to Ewen MacColl and penniless, she had an abortion. In brief she put her work first, at the cost of her life. Much later in the obituary, there is an inconspicuous reprise of this theme of children. The very last paragraph describes how her achievement was to have pioneered fringe theatre, pointing out that in London alone, when she died, there were 100 fringe groups. She commented near the end of her life: 'I have many children – all over the world'.

Tellingly, this obituary carefully deconstructs the language of genius. The accompanying obituary note, by Michael Billington, reverts to the old Romantic image of genius, but purloins it, by applying it to a woman. The main obituary breaks with it even more thoroughly by locating creativity in the social, quoting Littlewood direct: 'I really do believe in the community. [. . .] I really do believe in the genius of every person. And I've heard that greatness comes out of them, that great thing which is the people. And that's not romanticism, d'you see?' (*The Guardian* 23/9/02).

The stakes in the game

How then should we understand the obituary in general as a power-soaked, authoritative discourse? I want to expand Bourdieu's model of biographical illusion, taking into account his *Pascalian Meditations* on modes of anticipating the future. I shall consider especially the investment of time – as well as other stakes – in the illusio of professional fields: art, architecture, politics, science. Here I shall move on from his late works, like *The Rules of Art*, to a consideration of the games of art and science, both being characterized by their considerable scope for autonomy. Within these, Bourdieu perceives a sphere for indeterminacy, in the sense that the artist or writer is able to put into specific novels or poems a view of more than one social world, made possible through the writer's dream of social flying. Far from a reductively determinist view of the writer, etc. these late works – and especially *Science de la science* (2002b) – develop a view that succeeds in both objectivating the writer or scientist and in adopting a more generous interpretation of their potential for reflexivity (1996, 2000; Guillory, 1997). Indeed, Bourdieu here emphasizes the ways in which the professional world itself encourages such reflexivity (2002b).

One way to elaborate further on Bourdieu's notion of the vocational habitus is to take up, as McNay has done, Ricoeur's ideas about the phenomenology of time. This allows me to theorize further the transformative aspects of agency which may be disclosed in the obituary (McNay, 2000; Ricoeur, 1984).[6]

The key determinant of whether or not women receive obituaries is not just the question of how active they have been in the artistic or political field. Nor is it just a consequence of the filters used in interpreting their action: those interpretative practices of women obituarists or feminist men which enhance their historical visibility. My view is rather that the fundamental issue for women concerns their own perception of time and their involvement in a specific game. This is another way of approaching the thorny problem of canonisation, or, in Terry Lovell's concept, the notion of 'literary survival value' (Lovell 1987). It is also another way of returning to the fact that 36% of the women subjects overall do not have children.[7]

Bourdieu prompts us to ask: 'What stakes have women acquired in a game? To what degree has your fundamental sense of yourself and what you live for become tied up in that field?' Here he has some important points about the pre-reflexive 'protension' or imagining of the future, in which the future unfolds as part of the logic of the habitus, as in the case of the male State Nobility and their great worldmaking activities. In fact, as Bourdieu insists, it is only at a certain level of *distance from necessity* that *alternative projects for the future* can be anticipated: the future loses its doxic, taken-for-granted character and becomes a changed place, collectively achieved as in the classic trade-union imaginary or through individual practice (2000:216–7). Such active projects for the future – along with obligations to others – serve to distinguish those individuals with a 'justified' 'social existence' from those without. The power of 'symbolic baubles' (entry to *Who's Who*, honours etc) is to act *as a support for the social game*. That is, they act as buttresses for the decision to cope with one's own finitude or mortality, not by fleeing the world, but by seeking social esteem. This is the fundamental source of investment in a specific field:

> With investment in the game and the recognition that can come from cooperative competition with others, the social world offers humans that which they most totally lack, a justification for existing. (Bourdieu, 2000:239)

The possibility of a celebratory obituary could clearly count as one of the long string of 'symbolic baubles'.

Earlier, Bourdieu writes about the harsher face of competitive struggles – for example, when the surrealist, André Breton broke Pierre de Massot's arm in an argument about the future of art (1996:383). Now when we raise questions about women and time, it is to these kinds of phenomenological questions about the future that we should be turning. The issue raised by the surrealists' conflict is this: when does your artistic or craft effort seem so important that you will dedicate your whole life to it? Such an engagement is in part a question of not being caught up in other experiences of time: revolutionaries' 'disruptive' commitments, for example. In terms of those scientists or artists not so directly caught up, the passion with which you throw yourself into these disinterested fields or vocations is a key determinant of achievement. The performance of the work-in-hand becomes infused with an extraordinary importance. Undergoing *this* routine activity everyday, seeking, say, to understand cancer cells may be your way of changing the world . . .

Bourdieu writes of the doxa which preserves noble tasks for men. But women- or *any* carers – of very young children, cannot be involved in the same sense with the illusio of their work as a life and death struggle. Instead they are constrained to participate in other more pressing life and death struggles, such as their children's vulnerability to fatal illness or to ontological insecurity. Hence, one might write without any essentialist presuppositions, of their deficit of professional engagement, for they show, reluctantly, a suspension of effort.

What I have called here the necessary suspension of professional effort is neither lifelong nor found in all professional working women. Sarah Checkland, for example, writes vividly of Barbara Hepworth being accepted for a Venice Biennale, and of her husband Ben Nicolson – who had not been picked – enviously smashing her sculpted maquette. Hepworth's young triplets did not impede her artistic 'worldmaking activities', nor, indeed, her participation in the international constructivist group, the Circle, which enfolded both husband and wife (Checkland, 2000).

Bourdieu took from Husserl and Heidegger certain approaches to time which he went on to fuse with a more relationist historical sociology. Now Ricoeur has developed further one aspect of this earlier German phenomenology which may help theorise agency, as McNay also argues (McNay, 2000:85–96).

I note in particular Ricoeur's distinction between the contrasting experiences of 'linear, calendar time' and 'eternal time' (Ricoeur, 1984:25). Now we might call such 'eternal time', following Bourdieu, the time of posterity, the future in which the scientist or artist might make his or her mark. More interestingly, for feminism, Ricoeur has also stressed the effects of the imagination and utopia in freeing agency (1991:319–324). He has addressed Proust's long novel, *Remembrance of Things Past*, (tr. 1941) as a story about the author's oscillation between a vivid sensual understanding of the lost childhood time and the adult sense of disillusionment and knowledge of power, via his narrator, Marcel. The novel culminates in a commitment to vocational time as Marcel learns to unify these different worlds in order to become a writer (Ricoeur, 1985:144–5). Perhaps we can salvage something from this novel and go beyond its privileged milieu? Then this narrative might reveal for women on the ground more broadly the nature and dynamics of the engagement or illusion with modern fields of cultural production or the public sphere.

Now, from a critical perspective, the subjects of obituaries are often authority figures, linked more closely to what Ricoeur labels 'monumental' and 'official time' than to his 'eternal time' or Bourdieu's time of posterity (Ricoeur, 1985:106, 112). The obituary genre as a whole is wider than the depiction of original or distinctive achievements as in the meritocratic model, still being caught up with old forms of elitism. But with the narrowing of the gender difference in terms of a full engagement with the illusio of the field, the disparity between the numbers of obituaries for men and women will undoubtedly become less marked. Ricoeur's approaches to what he calls 'temporal refiguring', the enhancing of imaginative possibilities through the narratives in modernist novels, may turn out to clarify those forms of often transformative agency on which the modern meritocratic obituary typically draws (1988:274). But we would then have to remember that it is not simply the raising of consciousness that is at stake, but rather an activity as thorough and remorseless as 'involving repeated exercises [which alone] can, like an athlete's training, durably transform habitus' (Bourdieu, 2000:172).

Conclusion

Perhaps it is now possible to sketch further components of the obituary. First, holding economic capital on its own is only rarely a prerequisite for an obituary, at any point in the 100-odd year selection. Lowenthal – writing about such American 'heroes of production', in the early twentieth century – may be describing a distinctively American cast of biography (Lowenthal, 1961). The closest to this in Britain is *The Times* (2000) with still only 15% industrialists and bankers.

Second, I note the importance of art in the prophetic figure of Ruskin, in the 1900 *The Times*. In 2000–1 there has been a much greater increase in the arts-based occupations (see Appendix). This, and especially the turn to the popular arts, indicates the undeniable resonance with Lowenthal's 1960s analysis, and its stress on the growing significance of the 'heroes of consumption'. It is in this context that Bourdieu's recent diagnosis of contemporary practices in the arts is especially telling.

Finally, there has been a decline from 1900 in portrayals of hard-working, exemplary lives. Not only are there virtually no manual workers, but no teachers and nurses appear now. Since women particularly are linked with these professions, this may be related to their relative lack of representation. Given the importance of the obituary as an accolade and as a measure of valued activities, it is surprising that there are not more exemplary headteachers or self-sacrificing trade-unionists to stand alongside the outstanding achievements of the Hoyles, Anscombes, Bodmers and Quines.

Notes

1 I write after the death of Edward Said whose obituaries (and post-obituary notes) reveal with the utmost clarity the clash of perspectives which allowed some to celebrate him in the highest possible terms and others to engage in a systematic defamation of his actions or writings.
2 This study is based on a quantitative content analysis of a minimum of 100 sampled obituaries in each newspaper, from *The Times* in 1900 and 1948, to the 2000–1 British papers, *The Times*, *The Independent*, *The Guardian* and the *Daily Telegraph*; for comparison, *Le Monde* and *The New York Times* are also assessed. The qualitative analysis of obituary discourses includes, but goes beyond, these samples.

3 These overall figures for the arts include film critics and the media (journalists etc.).
4 These statistics include *The New York Times* and *Le Monde*.
5 *The Guardian* 23/9/02: 20.
6 There remains a certain tension between Ricoeur as the theorist of phenomenology and Bourdieu as the theorist of practice. It is important to note that I am not claiming here that the two sets of concepts are interchangeable: indeed Ricoeur is notably more prone to refer to the spiritual in some of his textual analysis than I would want to advocate. However, it is my view that Ricoeur does have an approach which permits us to fill out or supplement aspects of Bourdieusian theory, and this is at its most illuminating in his theory of the imagination.
7 This proportion varies sharply within the 2000–1 British newspapers, with between 16% of the recent *Guardian* female subjects, 24% of the *Daily Telegraph*, 44% *Times* and 63% *The Independent* having no children.

References

Primary sources

The Times, 1900, 1948 and 2000–1
The Guardian, 2000–1
The Independent, 2000–1
The Daily Telegraph, 2000–1.
H. Massingberd (ed.) (2001) *The Very Best of Daily Telegraph Books of Obituaries*. London: Pan.

Secondary works

Ahmad, A. (1991) *In Theory*. London: Verso.
Anonymous (1935) *The History of The Times: The Thunderer in the Making, 1785–1841*. London: The Times.
Aubrey, J. (1898 edition) *Brief Lives*. (ed. Andrew Clark.) Oxford: Clarendon.
Bourdieu, P. (1964) *Travail et Travailleurs en Algérie*. Paris and The Hague: Mouton.
Bourdieu, (1984) *Distinction*. London: RKP.
Bourdieu, P. (1986) 'L'Illusion Biographique' *Actes de la Recherche en Sciences Sociales* 62–63: 69–77.
Bourdieu, P. (1993) *The Field of Cultural Production*. Cambridge: Polity.
Bourdieu, P. (1994) *Raisons Pratiques*. Paris: Seuil.
Bourdieu, P. (1996a) *The Rules of Art*. Cambridge: Polity.
Bourdieu (1996b) *The State Nobility*. Cambridge: Polity.
Bourdieu, P. (1998) *Practical Reason*. Cambridge: Polity.
Bourdieu, P. (2000) *Pascalian Meditations*. Cambridge: Polity.
Bourdieu, P. (2001) *Masculine Domination*. Cambridge: Polity.
Bourdieu, P. (2002a) 'Habitus' in J. Hillier and E. Rooksby (eds) *Habitus: A Sense of Place*. London: Ashgate.
Bourdieu, P. (2002b) *Science de la Science*. Paris: Seuil.
Bourdieu, P. Chartier, R. and Darnton, R. (1985) 'Dialogue A Propos de l'Histoire Culturelle' *Actes de la Recherche en Sciences Sociales* 59: 86–93.
Bourdieu, P. and Passeron, J-C. (1979) *Reproduction, in Society, Education and Culture*. London: Sage.
Bourdieu, P. and Wacquant, L. (1992) *An Invitation to Reflexive Sociology*. Chicago: Chicago University Press.
Checkland, S. (2000) *Ben Nicolson*. London: John Murray.
Connerton, P. (1989) *How Societies Remember*. Cambridge: Cambridge University Press.

Fergusson, J. (1999) 'Death and the Press', in ed. S. Glover (ed.) *The Penguin Book of Journalism*. Harmondsworth: Penguin.

Fowler, B. (1997) *Pierre Bourdieu and Cultural Theory*. London: Sage.

Grant, J. (1871) *The Newspaper Press*. (Volume 2.) London: Tinsley Bros.

Guillory, J. (1997) 'Bourdieu's Refusal' *Modern Language Quarterly* December: 367–398.

Halbwachs, M. (ed.) (1991) *On Collective Memory*. Chicago: Chicago University Press.

Hobsbaum, E. and Ranger, T. (eds) (1983) *The Invention of Tradition*. Cambridge: Cambridge University Press.

Kracauer, S. (1995) *The Mass Ornament: Weimar Essays*. Cambridge, Mass: Harvard University Press.

Lovell, T. (1987) *Consuming Fiction*. London: Verso.

Lowenthal, L. (1961) *Literature, Popular Culture and Society*. Palo Alto, California: Pacific Books.

Maynes, M-J. (1989) 'Gender and Narrative Form in French and German Working-Class Autobiographies' in J. W. Barbre and The Personal Narrative Group (eds) *Interpreting Women's Lives*. Bloomington: Indiana U.P.

Mayer, A. (1981) *The Persistence of the Old Regime*. London: Croom Helm.

McNay, L. (2000) *Gender and Agency*. Cambridge: Polity.

Proust, M. (1941) *Remembrance of Things Past*. (12 vols.) London: Chatto and Windus.

Ricoeur, P. (1984; 1985; 1988) *Time and Narrative*. Volumes 1, 2 and 3. Chicago: University of Chicago Press.

Ricoeur, P. (1991) *From Text to Action: Essays in Hermeneutics, II*. London: The Athlone Press.

Trilling, L. (1961) *The Liberal Imagination*. London: Mercury.

Appendix

Table 1: *Obituaries (all samples, 1900–2000–1): Occupations and Gender*

	Male		Female		Total	
Artists	24	3.2%	3	2.1%	27	3.1%
Popular artists	4	.5%			4	.5%
Writers	41	5.5%	10	7.1%	51	5.8%
Popular writers	10	1.3%	5	3.5%	15	1.7%
Musicians – Jazz	14	1.9%	3	2.1%	17	1.9%
Musicians – Classical	27	3.6%	6	4.3%	33	3.7%
Musicians – rock/popular	12	1.6%	2	1.4%	14	1.6%
Musicians – Folk	6	.8%	1	.7%	7	.8%
Actors	27	3.6%	19	13.5%	46	5.2%
Dancers	3	.4%	2	1.4%	5	.6%
Popular dancers	2	.3%			2	.2%
Film/theatre directors/ cameramen/choreographers	12	1.6%	2	1.4%	14	1.6%
Artistic designers	2	.3%	4	2.8%	6	.7%
Architects	8	1.1%			8	.9%
Scientists	32	4.3%	4	2.8%	36	4.1%
Media	36	4.9%	8	5.7%	44	5.0%
Industrialists/entrepreneurs	54	7.3%	3	2.1%	57	6.5%
Bankers/financiers	18	2.4%			18	2.0%
Politicians	73	9.8%	3	2.1%	76	8.6%
Clergy	35	4.7%			35	4.0%
Academics	52	7.0%	6	4.3%	58	6.6%
Engineers	15	2.0%			15	1.7%
Sportsmen	22	3.0%	2	1.4%	24	2.7%
Army/Navy	89	12.0%	3	2.1%	92	10.4%
Doctors/Surgeons	33	4.4%			33	3.7%
Judges/lawyers/solicitors	15	2.0%	3	2.1%	18	2.0%
Civil servants/diplomats	41	5.5%	6	4.3%	47	5.3%
Farmers	5	.7%			5	.6%
Librarians/curators/teachers	13	1.8%	3	2.1%	16	1.8%
Sales assistants/managers	1	.1%	1	.7%	2	.2%
Manual	6	.8%	1	.7%	7	.8%
No paid work	2	.3%	32	22.7%	34	3.9%
Charity organisers/ campaigners	1	.1%	5	3.5%	6	.7%
Other	7	.9%	4	2.8%	11	1.2%
Total	742	100%	141	100%	883	100%

Table 2: *Obituaries (all samples, 1900–2000–1): Newspapers and Occupations*

	Artists	Popular artists	Writers	Popular writers	Musicians, jazz	Musicians, classic	Musicians, rock/pop	Musicians, folk
The Times 1900	2		5			4		
%	1.40%		3.60%			2.90%		
The Times 1948	3		4			3		
%	2.90%		3.80%			2.90%		
The Times 2000	1	1	5	3	2	5	2	
%	0.90%	0.90%	4.70%	2.80%	1.90%	4.70%	1.90%	
The Guardian	5	1	11	4	6	6	3	3
%	3.80%	0.80%	8.30%	3.00%	4.50%	4.50%	2.30%	2.30%
The Independent	5	1	6	4	3	4	8	1
%	5.10%	1.00%	6.10%	4.10%	3.10%	4.10%	8.20%	1.00%
Daily Telegraph	4	1	2	1	2	1	1	1
%	4.00%	1.00%	2.00%	1.00%	2.00%	1.00%	1.00%	1.00%
Le Monde	6		10		3	7		2
%	6.00%		10.00%		3.00%	7.00%		2.00%
New York Times	1		8	3	1	3		
%	1.00%		8.00%	3.00%	1.00%	3.00%		
Total	27	4	51	15	17	33	14	7
%	3.10%	0.50%	5.80%	1.70%	1.90%	3.70%	1.60%	0.80%

Dancers	Popular dancers	Actors	Film/ theatre direc/ camer	Artistic designers	Architects	Academics	Scientists	Media	Sportsmen
		1	1			4		4	1
		0.70%	0.70%			2.90%		2.90%	0.70%
		3			1	3	4	2	
		2.90%			1.00%	2.90%	3.80%	1.90%	
	1	6	1			8	2	5	4
	0.90%	5.60%	0.90%			7.50%	1.90%	4.70%	3.70%
2		13	4		3	11	5	10	3
1.50%		9.80%	3.00%		2.30%	8.30%	3.80%	7.50%	2.30%
2		7	2	1		9	8	6	5
2.00%		7.10%	2.00%	1.00%		9.20%	8.20%	6.10%	5.10%
	1	8		1		2	6	5	4
	1.00%	8.00%		1.00%		2.00%	6.00%	5.00%	4.00%
1		5	5		2	8	5	7	2
1.00%		5.00%	5.00%		2.00%	8.00%	5.00%	7.00%	2.00%
		3	1	4	2	13	6	5	5
		3.00%	1.00%	4.00%	2.00%	13.00%	6.00%	5.00%	5.00%
5	2	46	14	6	8	58	36	44	24
0.60%	0.20%	5.20%	1.60%	0.70%	0.90%	6.60%	4.10%	5.00%	2.70%

Table 2: *Continued*

	Industrialists/ entrepreneurs	Bankers/ financiers	Politicians	Clergy	Engineers	Army/ Navy	Doctors/ surgeons	Judges/ lawyers/ solicitors
The Times 1900	8	4	6	11	3	48	12	1
%	5.70%	2.90%	4.30%	7.90%	2.10%	34.30%	8.60%	0.70%
The Times 1948	7	4	4	7	2	17	4	5
%	6.70%	3.80%	3.80%	6.70%	1.90%	16.20%	3.80%	4.80%
The Times 2000	14	2	9	2	1	10	4	3
%	13.10%	1.90%	8.40%	1.90%	0.90%	9.30%	3.70%	2.80%
The Guardian	3	2	16	2	2	1	3	
%	2.30%	1.50%	12.00%	1.50%	1.50%	0.80%	2.30%	
The Independent	3		11	1	1	1	3	1
%	3.10%		11.20%	1.00%	1.00%	1.00%	3.10%	1.00%
Daily Telegraph	12	1	9	6	4	10		2
%	12.00%	1.00%	9.00%	6.00%	4.00%	10.00%		2.00%
Le Monde	5	1	14		1	2	7	
%	5.00%	1.00%	14.00%		1.00%	2.00%	7.00%	
New York Times	5	4	7	6	1	3		6
%	5.00%	4.00%	7.00%	6.00%	1.00%	3.00%		6.00%
Total	57	18	76	35	15	92	33	18
%	6.50%	2.00%	8.60%	4.00%	1.70%	10.40%	3.70%	2.00%

Civil servants/ diplomats	Librarians/ curators/ teachers	Charity organiser/ campaigner	Sales assistant/ managers	Farmers	Manual	Other	No paid work	Total
7	2			1	1		14	140
5.00%	1.40%			0.70%	0.70%		10.00%	100.00%
10	6		1		1	2	12	105
9.50%	5.70%		1.00%		1.00%	1.90%	11.40%	100.00%
7	3	2		1			3	107
6.50%	2.80%	1.90%		0.90%			2.80%	100.00%
6		2	1		4	1		133
4.50%		1.50%	0.80%		3.00%	0.80%		100.00%
1	1			1			2	98
1.00%	1.00%			1.00%			2.00%	100.00%
7		1		2		4	2	100
7.00%		1.00%		2.00%		4.00%	2.00%	100.00%
4	1					1	1	100
4.00%	1.00%					1.00%	1.00%	100.00%
5	3	1			1	3		100
5.00%	3.00%	1.00%			1.00%	3.00%		100.00%
47	16	6	2	5	7	11	34	883
5.30%	1.80%	0.70%	0.20%	0.60%	0.80%	1.20%	3.90%	100.00%

Section III:
Retheorizing the habitus

Agency and experience: gender as a lived relation

Lois McNay

Introduction

The division between material and cultural analysis has become somewhat entrenched in feminist thought, generating a series of theoretical impasses. The central point of contention is that cultural feminists feel that materialists rely on simplistic divisions such as base and superstructure, reality and representation in order to assert the primacy of economic forces in their analysis of women's oppression. Conversely, materialist feminists are critical of the effects of the 'linguistic' turn in feminist theory which, in their view, results in a narrowing down of the issue of oppression to the rarefied one of identity politics. In this chapter I argue for the importance of an understanding of gender as a *lived social relation* in mediating this impasse. The idea of gender as a lived social relation is opposed to an understanding of gender as a structural location which prevails in both materialist and cultural thought. In the former, gender is seen as a structural location within or intersecting with capitalist class relations, in a way that resembles early feminist debates over the relationship between class and patriarchy (Sargent, 1981). In the latter, gender is regarded primarily as a location within symbolic or discursive structures. By defining gender as a position within an abstract structure, albeit very differently conceived, both materialist and cultural feminists fail to recognize that such abstract forces only reveal themselves in the lived reality of social relations. In other words, it is through developing mediating concepts, in this case agency, that the determining force of economic and cultural relations upon daily life can be made visible and, in this way, the issue of identity can be connected to that of social structure.

Obviously, agency understood in this sense invokes some notion of experience which traditionally has been very problematic for feminist theory. By looking at the exchange between Judith Butler and Pierre Bourdieu on performative agency, I argue that an idea of experience is essential to an account of agency but that it must be understood in relational terms rather than in an ontological sense as the absolute grounds of social being. I develop this idea by drawing on Bourdieu's work on the phenomenology of social space.

© The Editorial Board of the Sociological Review 2004. Published by Blackwell Publishing Ltd, 9600 Garsington Road, Oxford OX4 2DQ, UK and 350 Main Street, Malden, MA 02148, USA

Determinism and agency

The differences between materialist and cultural feminisms have been played out in many different debates in feminist theory. Recently, several feminist theorists have made attempts to break out of the polemic by elaborating models to examine the interconnections of material and cultural power relations rather than seeking to assert the superiority of one over the other. Nancy Fraser's (1997 and 2000) work on redistribution and recognition is some of the most notable in this respect. She argues that feminist political theory has bifurcated between materialist analysis that views oppression as arising from unequal economic distribution and cultural analysis where it is viewed, in psychological terms, as a process of recognition and misrecognition. The problem with cultural models, on the one hand, is that, although they provide some genuine insights into the psychological effects of racism and sexism, they are essentially ahistorical because they disconnect questions of identity recognition from the context of access to economic resources and other types of social capital. On the other hand, a politics of redistribution can be economically reductive. Her point is that capitalism is so complex now that identity depreciation does not translate directly into economic injustice nor vice versa: 'markets follow a logic of their own, neither wholly constrained by culture nor subordinated to it: as a result they generate economic inequalities that are not mere expressions of identity hierarchies' (Fraser, 2000:111–12). Thus, against such dichotomised options, Fraser proposes what she calls a 'status model of subordination' which combines economic with cultural analysis. She argues that the ideas of redistribution and recognition do not refer to the two distinct societal domains of economy and culture but represent a 'perspectival dualism' which helps identify power relations that, in reality, are ineluctably entwined. This analytical tool yields an understanding of oppression as perpetuated through the two mechanisms of institutionalised subordination and maldistribution or denial of economic resources.[1] It also highlights, for example, the complex nature of gender oppression which is situated on the axes of both redistribution and recognition and has, therefore, a 'dilemmatic structure'.

In a response to Fraser's work, Iris Marion Young claims that, far from breaking down the opposition between economy and culture, the categories of redistribution and recognition in fact serve to reinforce it. By stating that the politics of recognition needs supplementing with a redistributional perspective, Fraser obscures the extent to which struggles over identity claims have never been simply about cultural issues but have always invoked material issues of redistribution. For example, Fraser categorizes the gay and lesbian struggle against heterosexism as an ideal type of the politics of recognition. Young points out, however, that even if the causes of homophobia can be classified as cultural, its oppressive effects are material and require remedies of redistribution as much as recognition: 'Whatever the 'roots' of heterosexism . . . this harm matters because those on the wrong side of the heterosexual matrix experience

176

systematic limits to their freedom, constant risk of abuse, violence and death, and unjustly limited access to resources and opportunities' (Young, 1997:157). Young makes the further criticism that Fraser's analytical dualism remains unjustified and 'brazenly dichotomous'. If social life is indeed permeated by multifarious power relations then it would make sense to deploy a plural categorization of oppression rather than the simplifying dualism offered by Fraser. Indeed, Young argues that Fraser's discernment of a dilemmatic structure within, say, gender oppression and politics, is purely the result of her bipolar analysis rather than being an actual contradiction; she 'finds contradiction where none exists' (1997:158). Young suggests an alternative typology where oppression is analysed along the five axes of exploitation, marginalization, powerlessness, cultural imperialism and violence: 'the purpose of elaborating a plural but limited categorization of oppression is to accommodate the variations in oppressive structures that position individuals and groups, and thus to resist the tendency to reduce oppression to one or two structures with 'primacy' (1997:151). Furthermore, this five-fold distinction can accommodate a political and legal aspect to social struggles which, in her view, is occluded by Fraser's bifocal analysis.

The debate between Fraser and Young illustrates the extent to which the material-cultural opposition is ingrained in feminist thought where even explicit attempts to get beyond the opposition are criticised for entrenching it further. My argument is that the opposition between material and cultural analysis appears to be insoluble because the debate between Young and Fraser stays at the abstract level of macro-structural analysis. Both theorists agree that symbolic and material power relations are intertwined yet irreducible to each other, but neither develops mediatory categories through which it is possible to map these imbrications. To put this in other terms, both theorists fail to recognize that structural forces only reveal themselves in the lived reality of social relations. Ellen Meiksins Wood makes precisely this point when she uses E. P Thompson's notion of experience against Althusserian definitions of class as an abstract structural location: 'since people are never actually 'assembled' in classes, the determining pressure exerted by a mode of production in the formation of classes cannot be easily expressed without reference to something like a common experience, – a lived experience of . . . the conflicts and struggles inherent in relations of exploitation' (Wood, 1995:96).

Wood's argument extends by analogy to other structures of oppression. Since individuals are never situated on a single axis of gender, racial or ethnic oppression then the only way in which the operations of these forces can be examined is from the level of social action. It follows that the idea of agency is a key mediating category through which the inter-connections between cultural and economic forces, identity formations and social structures can be examined. The material-cultural debate is, after all, a debate, in part, about the type of constraints that operate upon social action and how it may be possible to overcome these constraints. Even if it were possible to settle the question of whether it is the economy or culture that remains determining in the last instance, this would tell us little about why individuals act in some circumstances rather than others, and why it is some individuals rather than others who act in the same circumstances. In other words, agency cannot be deduced from abstract social structures. If, as Charles Taylor (1985) points out, the idea of agency refers, in some sense, to the individual's capacity for self-reflection and self-evaluation then it needs to be examined from some kind of hermeneutic perspective. Hermeneutic analysis necessarily involves the temporary abandonment of pure objectivism in order to examine the nature of social experience. This assertion that the analysis of experience is central to an understanding of agency is, of course, where the problems start for feminist analysis. The status that a category of experience should occupy in feminist theory has been widely debated and, as a consequence of the debate over essentialism, the category is often rejected because of its perceived excessive subjectivism. Yet, the problem remains that, even when alternative, 'anti-essentialist' theories of agency have been developed by, for example, post-Foucauldian thinkers such as Judith Butler, they remain conceptually etiolated. Arguably, they are not theories of agency at all but theories of structural indeterminacy (McNay, 2000). Thus, in the absence of any mediating categories, the impasse between material and cultural feminisms about determination remains. In order, therefore, to make the argument that it is necessary to recuperate some notion idea of experience for a 'generative' account of agency, I will consider in a more detail, the problems that the idea presents for feminist thought.[2]

The problems of 'experience'

Although, the uncovering and rediscovery of women's experience is central to the feminist project, the category of experience has been notoriously problematic on several counts. The concept of experience has been a crucial lever for criticizing the apparent objectivity of the natural and social sciences, yet the way in which it is deployed by certain feminist thinkers often reinforces rather than undoes dichotomies of objectivity-subjectivity. Against the objectivism of scientific knowledge, feminist standpoint theory, for example, asserts a counterveiling primacy of the subjective realm which privileges experience as the grounds of genuine knowledge. In this respect, experience is often associated with emotion and affect and imputed an authenticity that is counterposed to abstract male reason. (Scott, 1992:31). Experience, in this sense, is generally taken as a given, self-explanatory concept that each feminist specifies in her own way. Thus it is used to refer alternately to 'feelings, emotions, the personal, personality' (Lazreg, 1994:50). The granting of an epistemological privilege to experience in this way is a contentious strategy because it pushes feminism dangerously close to an unexamined empiricism which does not scrutinize the conditions that determine how experience relates to knowledge: 'To claim that women's experience is a source of true knowledge as well as the substance of the world to be known. . . constitutes the same 'epistemic fallacy' as the one encountered by classical empiricists' (see Lazreg. 1994:52). A final, well-rehearsed problem with the idea of experience is that it is often used to establish an arguably tendentious unity between women. The absence of definition allows it to 'create a sense of consensus by attributing to it an assumed, stable and shared meaning' (Scott, 1992:32). These unifying connotations have been subjected to extensive criticisms by feminists influenced by poststructuralism, such as Gayatri Spivak and Judith Butler (Butler, 1990:22–25; Spivak, 1987).

In her well-known article on experience, Joan Scott (1992) points out that some of the problems with the concept stem from the metaphor of visibility and invisibility that often governs the exploration of marginal experiences in historical analysis. While the project of making experience visible may bring to light the impact of silence and repression upon the lives of marginalized groups, it often prevents a more critical examination of the way in which categories of representation are historically constituted. The metaphor of visibility exposes the mechanics of repression along a vertical analysis of the explicit and the latent, the dominant and the marginal, but it does not have a horizontal analysis of the way in which these categories of representation are relationally constructed: 'Making visible the experience of a different group exposes the existence of repressive mechanisms, but not their inner workings or logics; we know that difference exists, but we don't understand it as constituted relationally. For that we need to attend to the historical processes that, through discourse, position subjects and produce their experiences' (Scott, 1992:25). To overthrow the metaphor of visibility is to consider experience itself as discursively constructed rather than to impute to it an incontestable authority. This process of historicization involves treating the emergence of concepts and identities not as unproblematic givens but as historical and discursive events, in the manner of, say, Foucault's (1978) analysis of the construction of a notion of 'perversion' in nineteenth century discourses of medicine and psychiatry. To analyse the construction of experience in this way is not, in Scott's view, to retreat to a form of linguistic determinism or to deny historical agency. As Scott puts it: 'Experience is a subject's history. Language is the site of history's enactment. Historical explanation cannot, therefore, separate the two' (Scott, 1992:34). It does, however, involve considering how the idea of experience is linked, as a legitimating principle, to the construction of truth and knowledge effects in any given era.

Despite Scott's claim that the analysis of experience as a discursive construction does not imply its absolute dissolution, the way in which this insight has been generalised in much poststructural work on subjectivity, has resulted in a form of linguistic determinism which often abandons the category altogether. Denuded of the idea of experience and attendant notions of self-hood, intention and reflexivity, poststructural work on subjectivity often finds itself without a workable concept of agency with which to animate its notions of resistance, subversion etc (see McNay, 2000). Agency refers to an individual's capacity for action and cannot be simply understood as a property of unstable discursive structures. Therefore, in order to understand some of the changes within sexual practices and gender norms that have occurred over the last forty years or so, an idea of agency has to be rethought around some kind of non-reductive notion of experience. In order to explain what this might look like, I will now consider the exchange between Judith Butler and Pierre Bourdieu on the idea of performative agency. Each thinker accuses the other of having an inadequate account of agency. In assessing this debate, I argue that Butler's idea of performative agency is not a viable theory of agency at all, but merely a structural abstraction. My main aim, however, is to show, that while there certainly are problems with Bourdieu's idea of agency, his idea of a phenomenology of social space has interesting implications for a relational analysis of experience. This, in turn, can be used to develop an understanding of gender as a lived social relation in contrast to Butlerian accounts where gender is understood primarily as location within discursive structures.

Butler and Bourdieu on the performative

The exchange between Butler and Bourdieu is focused around what constitutes the efficacy of a performative speech act. The essence of Butler's objection to Bourdieu's thought is that his concepts of habitus and the field are determinist in so far as they deny the possibility of radical change and, in the final analysis, reassert a reductive base-superstructure model. In *Excitable Speech*, Butler examines the problem of determinism which, in her view, is inherent to Bourdieu's understanding of the symbolic violence of performative speech acts. She argues that the concept of symbolic violence is problematic in that it ties the speech act too closely to its institutional context and misses the processes of temporal deferral and dissemination that are constitutive of the indeterminacy of the performative. It is this indeterminacy that is essential to understanding how it is that dominant norms may be appropriated and subverted by marginal groups. A similar lack of indeterminacy hampers Bourdieu's notion of habitus which, by stressing the extent to which there is an accommodation between dominant power relations and bodily dispositions, misses the ways in which the process of corporeal inculcation is never straight-forward or complete. This is because, despite his claims that there exists a relation of double conditioning between habitus and field, it is, in fact, the field that is attributed a pre-given objectivity and enshrined, therefore, as an 'unalterable positivity' (Butler, 1999:117). Whereas habitus may adapt to the objective demands of the field, there is no sense of a countervailing alteration of the field by habitus. The unidirectional causality ascribed to the field undermines any idea of the instabilities and resistances inherent to the process where social norms are drawn into the body. This is compounded by Bourdieu's deployment of a rather functionalist notion of adaptation in which habitus adjusts to the exigencies of the field and which reinscribes a dualism between the objective and the subjective where the former remains determining in the last instance. By producing an account of power that is structurally committed to the status quo, Bourdieu forecloses the possibility of agency emerging from the margins.

For Butler, the domains of the social and the linguistic, the material and the symbolic cannot be separated in such a distinct way because 'the discursive constitution of the subject [is] inextricable from the social constitution of the subject' (Butler, 1999:120). The repeated effects of racial slurs, for example, live and thrive in the flesh of the addressee. The performative interpellation of the subject in terms of race or gender is not dependent on a specific 'authorized' subject but is the effect of a generalized process of subjectification. The diffuse nature of the process of interpellation renders the effects of the performative potentially indeterminate and open to subversion. The performative utterance can not exclude the possibility of going awry, of being appropriated by marginal groups and being resignified with destabilizing effects. It is this reappropriation of the authorized position within language which serves to expose prevailing forms of authority. Bourdieu cannot explain the troubling effects of such indeterminacy because of the causal priority accorded to the social over the linguistic and the fixity of the subject over the utterance. In the final analysis, this undercuts claims about the generative nature of the habitus.

Bourdieu's only explicit response to Butler is contained in a few remarks made in *Pascalian Meditations* (2000), but his general view on her work can be deduced from his comments on 'linguistic universalism'. Bourdieu uses the term to denote a tendency within objectivist theory to annex and therefore deny the social actor's perspective. The economic and social conditions that underlie the scholastic world view are naturalized and universalised as impartial objectivity. In Butler's work, linguistic universalism operates by reducing the cluster of material inequalities and economic exclusions constitutive of gender hierarchies to the narrow issue of the symbolic construction of sexual identity. For example, Butler's claim that there are zones of social uninhabitability or spaces of 'abjection' is simply too undifferentiated to have much explanatory force (eg, Butler, 1993:xi). Arguably, the ability to participate in a performative politics presupposes a relatively privileged access to certain economic resources and cultural capital that is occluded in the blanket use of the term abjection. Bourdieu concludes that : 'it is naïve, even dangerous to suppose and suggest that one only has to 'deconstruct' these social artefacts in a purely performative celebration of 'resistance' in order to destroy them (Bourdieu, 2000:108). The imperialism of the universal that is implied in the over-extension of a linguistic model of identity formation is, in the final analysis, a form *par excellence* of symbolic violence perpetuated by 'enlightened' élites upon the practical activities of social actors.

The responses of each thinker to the other's work appear, on the face of it, to reproduce the theoretical split between material and cultural analysis. Yet, to some degree, this difference is overstated because of the polarising effects of polemic. Elsewhere in their work, both thinkers recognize the futility of trying to assert the primacy of a certain type of power relation over another and each develops an embodied account of agency which explicitly acknowledges the entwinement of material and symbolic power relations. In her article 'Marxism and the Merely Cultural' (1998), Butler rightly criticizes the resurgence of an orthodox Leftism which dismisses queer politics as an epiphenomenal fixation on identity and forestalls an analysis of a more fundamental politics of redistribution. Against this, Butler argues that not only is the distinction between the material and symbolic unstable, but also that redistributive issues lie at the heart of a politics of cultural recognition. Similarly, the centrality that Bourdieu accords the idea of symbolic violence in his theory of social reproduction, renders his work anything but materially reductionist. While he views material forces such as the division of labour and segregation within the work force are central to gender oppression, he regards the internalisation of symbolic gender norms within physical and psychological dispositions as the most important element in the reproduction of sexual division. For Bourdieu, the inextricable entwinement of material and discursive relations ('structure of positions' and 'space of possibles') is evident in all social realms and he uses the concept of the field to unpack these variable relations (see McNay, 2004).

The differences between the two thinkers lies, therefore, not in the misleading antithesis of material versus symbolic determinism but in the way in which they develop a concept of agency to think through the connections between discursive and material power relations. Essentially the problem with Judith Butler's account of performative agency is, as I have argued elsewhere, that it is not an account of agency *per se* but an account of the some of the discursive pre-conditions that must prevail for certain types of linguistic innovation to be possible (McNay, 2000:44–5). The possibility of linguistic agency is linked to the reiterative structure of language itself but this is a necessary and not sufficient account of agency. Butler posits agency as a property of language conceived as an abstract structure, rather than as a situated type of action or interaction. This conception of agency as an abstract linguistic potential is problematic because it does not adequately address central features of agency such as intention and reflexivity. Nor, because of the abstract nature of Butler's idea of discourse, does it address adequately enough how agency is determined by access to symbolic and material resources. Ultimately, the conflation of an idea of agency with the idea of instability within meaning systems results in a symbolic determinism which does not have the conceptual resources to differentiate discursive from other types of power relation.

If the central problem with Butler's account of agency derives from her tendency to subsume the social within the linguistic then, to some degree, it is the opposite problem that hampers Bourdieu's thought. Arguably, he significantly underestimates the autonomy of agents because of the tendency to reduce symbolic relations to pre-given social relations. This is evident in the conventionalism of his work on the performative – that language derives its symbolic force from the surrounding context – which underplays the extent to which the autonomy of language means that it can be used as a tool to subvert dominant power relations. It is certainly true that Bourdieu's account, in *Masculine Domination*,

of the way in which masculine and feminine identities are symbolically constructed lacks any notion of the complexities and instabilities within gender
identity that theorists like Butler have drawn attention to. Furthermore, as James
Bohman (1999) has pointed out, this conventionalism can lead to an exagger-
atedly instrumental idea of agency which blocks alternative accounts of the
interpretative and cognitive capacities displayed by social actors. Reflexivity is
a quality that Bourdieu seems to attribute only to the sociologist's reflection
upon her own activity at the expense of understanding it as a generalized capacity of social actors. Drawing on Habermas, Bohman argues that any account of
agency must not only consider ways in which actors are caught within structures
of power and domination, authorization and marginalization but must also
include an account of their capacity for practical reflection, as 'to give convincing reasons, to back up claims made in speech when challenged by other
speakers' (Bohman, 1999:140). By failing to attribute such a capacity to actors:
'the possibility of innovation and transformation becomes improbable and
dependent on external social conditions' (Bohman, 1999:141).

These criticisms certainly have force with regard to some of Bourdieu's
abstract comments on the behaviour of agents within fields (eg Bourdieu.
1993:73–4).[3] However, if we consider Bourdieu's ethnomethodological studies
of oppression and the way in which he situates these experiences within a 'phenomenology of social space', a very different account of agency emerges. In
order to sketch out what this might look like, I will now consider Bourdieu's
idea of a phenomenology of social space. The relational style of analysis
proposed in this idea suggests how a category of experience can be freed from
its essentialising connotations and used in an understanding of gender as a
lived social relation rather than, *pace* Butler, as a location within a discursive
structure.

Phenomenology of social space

In *In Other Words* (1990a), Bourdieu sets out the idea of a phenomenology of
social space in opposition to the objectivist and subjectivist approaches that he
regards as dominating in the human sciences. Bourdieu discusses the errors of
objectivism and subjectivism at length in *The Logic of Practice* (1990b) and his
arguments need only be summarized here. In short, the problem with objectivism is that its concern with social structures disregards the issue of agency
and questions of recognition and misrecognition. Subjectivism, on the other
hand, suffers from a 'substantialist illusion' and reduces the social world to
nothing but the representations of actors, recognizing no other reality other than
that which is available to direct intuition. If social action is to be properly understood, then it is important to analyse the representations that actors have of the
world and the way these inform action and interaction. Such representations
cannot be deduced from social structures. Nor, however, do they encompass
social reality in that they are determined by structures that are at one remove

from immediate experience: 'the visible, that which is immediately given, hides the invisible which determines it. One thus forgets that the truth of any inter-action is never entirely to be found within the interaction as it avails itself for observation' (Bourdieu, 1990:126–7).

In order to grasp the dialectical relation between structures and representa-tions, Bourdieu proposes a phenomenological analysis of social space. From the perspective of sociological analysis, spatial distances coincide with social dis-tances. Or, to put it in other terms, social space also functions as symbolic space (Bourdieu, 1990a:132). Actors occupy positions within social fields that are determined both by the distribution of resources within a given field and also by the structural relations between that field and others. By plotting social posi-tion as spatial position, the complex interaction between symbolic and mater-ial power relations, between immediate experience and invisible structures is elucidated. For example, social positions and distances are inscribed upon the body in the form of its pre-reflexive dispositions or habitus. Immediate corpo-real being contains within it the latent marks of abstract social structure. This process of inscription does not attribute determining priority to structures over representations because it is conceived of as a generative rather than determin-ing process. The 'semantic elasticity' inherent to the way in which objects (and subjects) of the social world are perceived and expressed render this phenome-nology of social space far from mechanistic: 'This objective element of uncer-tainty . . . provides a basis for the plurality of visions of the world . . . it provides a base for symbolic struggles over the power to produce and to impose the legit-imate vision of the world' (1990:133). Action and struggle are motivated by per-ception and representation not just by abstract social structures and economic forces.

It is Bourdieu's definition of his social phenomenology as relational that has interesting implications for a feminist analysis of gender as a lived social rela-tion. Its most significant implication is that it provides a way of placing experi-ence at the centre of social analysis without attributing to it some kind of apodictic or essential status. The idea of phenomenology as a relational rather than an ontological style of enquiry avoids the problem of the reification of 'experience' that hampers many kinds of interpretative analysis, feminist or oth-erwise. The essence of social being is not encompassed in experience itself but it does only begin to reveal itself through experience which must then be situ-ated in a broader context. This contextualization involves tracing the links between the phenomenal immediacy of experience and abstract systems of power that operate at one remove from every day activity. At the same time, the way in which actors negotiate these power relations cannot be derived from an abstract analytics of power. To explain agency, it is not possible to bypass an analysis of experience. But, the understanding of social experience does not offer us a complete perspective in itself. Indeed, the singularity of experience cannot be derived from a reliance upon 'a naively personalist view of the unique-ness of social persons' (Bourdieu *et al*, 1999:618). Rather, it is through the uncovering of immanent structures contained in the contingent that the singular complexity of actions and interactions can be understood. The use of a spatial metaphor to analyse experience compliments and extends the discursive analysis of experience that Scott speaks about by reminding us that discourse is a situated, rather than an abstract, medium where the situation itself is organized by invisible structures. It is this situated aspect of discourse that has been lost in the linguistic monism of constructionist work on gender identity. Defined in this way, Bourdieu's idea of relational phenomenology resembles the idea of the situation developed in the work of Simone de Beauvoir and the late Sartre where the generality of social forces is regarded as an absent but structuring presence within social interaction (Sartre, 1976:94).

I will now go on to consider some of the implications of Bourdieu's idea of a phenomenology of social space for an understanding of gender as a lived social relation. Bourdieu himself does not consider gender in this way.[4] He sketches out what a relational phenomenology looks like largely with respect to forms of class dispossession in for example, *The Weight of the World* (1999). I will begin by considering the different view that emerges about the reproduction of normative identity if the experience of gender is considered as a lived social relation rather than as a location within a discursive structure.

Gender as a lived relation

The focus on experience that underpins a relational phenomenology brings to the fore conflicts inherent to the reproduction of normative forms of gender identity that are obscured in discursive models of identity formation like Butler's. In the latter, stress is placed on the inherently complex nature of all identities but, by and large, this is regarded as an effect of the relational nature of language and is elaborated largely in relation to the formation of non-heterosexual identities. An effect of regarding gender identity largely as a question of position within language and not as a lived social relation is that the dominant is left unproblematized. The lack of any substantive notion of agency means that the reproduction of normative types of gender identity is construed in terms of an exogenous imposition of gender norms, rather than as a process that involves some degree of negotiation on the part of subjects. The conflicts underlying such processes of negotiation are obscured because they can only be perceived from the perspective of experience. Of course, as Judith Butler points out, there is a compulsory element to the acquisition of gender identity and, in this regard, voluntarist theories of agency as performance or choice are inappropriate and naïve. It is an error, however, to assume that hegemonic heterosexuality passively exists as a form of dominance, rather it 'has continually to be renewed, recreated, defended, and . . . also continually resisted, limited, altered, challenged by pressures not at all its own' (Williams, 1977:112). On this view, the reproduction of normative identities cannot be understood simply as a question of positioning within language but as a lived social relation that necessarily involves the negotiation of conflict and tension.

   Such conflicts and tension can be illustrated by Beverley Skeggs's (1997) study of the ways in which working-class women position themselves and are positioned by dominant conceptions of femininity. Skeggs argues that, as a consequence of their locations of class and sexuality, the women occupied a series of contradictory subject positions. On the one hand, working-class women have an uneasy relation to dominant norms of femininity because these have evolved historically from idealized notions of bourgeois womanhood. Traditionally, working-class women have been positioned as the Other of such norms; against bourgeois ideals of elegance, refinement and controlled eroticism, they have been defined as common, bawdy and sexually promiscuous. This uneasy relation to the middle-class norm of femininity is negotiated, in part, through the idea of 'respectability' that provides an interpretative trope for them to construct their own version of femininity distinct from stereotypes of the working class slattern. The idea of 'glamour' is another trope that also provides a particularly effective tool in enabling them to hold together femininity and sexuality in a 'respectable' performance. Skeggs's point is that the idea of respectability is used by these women as a means to accrue some symbolic value to their devalued and vulnerable class position. To become respectable or to 'pass' as middle-class, working-class women make strong investments in bodies, clothes, consumption practices, leisure pursuits, homes etc. And yet, at the same time, they remain wary of many middle class dispositions and values, retaining a strong sense of the injustice of their social and economic positioning. In short, the women both identified and dis-identified with their class position and lived these ambivalences as the 'hidden injuries' of shame, awkwardness and the sense of being judged by others (see Sennett and Cobb, 1977).

   Skeggs's study is a powerful illustration of the uncertainties and negotiations that accompany the reproduction of normative gender identity. In discursive theories of identity formation, such as Butler's, feminine identity is indeed problematised, but from a Saussaurian point of view of the relational nature of meaning and the consequent impossibility of achieving any kind of fixed identity. As the devalued position within a phallocentric order, femininity becomes an impossible place to occupy because it is based on a fundamental negativity. The problem with this type of explanation is that it lacks any kind of social or historical specificity by imposing an abstract, self-same logic where any and all identity is posited as unstable. In contrast, by analysing what the assumption of identity means at the level of a lived social relation, Skeggs's study highlights that femininity is a difficult place for certain women to occupy not because of semantic or psychic instabilities, but because of class dynamics. To put it bluntly, for many working-class women, it is because their prospects of achieving respect through educational achievements, occupational success or any other indices of social prestige are minimal that they invest so heavily in themselves. In the absence of economic and social capital, the only capital in which they have to invest is their own body and appearance. Yet, despite this heavy investment, many of these women feel like interlopers in their enactment of femininity because it is associated with an unattainable middle class elegance and '*savoir faire*'. Furthermore, they cannot take themselves too seriously in case they are 'seen' as taking themselves too seriously and, by implication, as betraying their class origins. It is their class position that also generates a refusal of feminism which is regarded as the discourse of privileged women and irrelevant to their lives. Indeed, from their perspective, the feminist critique of conventional femininity undermines one of the few ways open to them to achieve any kind of social recognition, as fleeting and unstable as it might be. These complex identifications are occluded in predominant discursive models of identity formation whether they be psychoanalytic or discursive. While the latter may produce psychically and linguistically complex models of identity formation, they lack social depth and cannot explain the intersection of gender with other structures of power.

A relational phenomenology suggests, for example, a way of acknowledging the centrality of emotions in social being without treating them as an end in themselves or reducing them to symptoms of an inescapable indeterminacy of identity. By analysing emotions as a form of social interaction it is possible to see how they are both shaped by latent social structures and also the vehicle through which invisible power dynamics are made present within immediate everyday experience. This kind of treatment corresponds to that suggested by Raymond Williams' idea of structures of feeling where the affective elements of consciousness and relationships are not reified as a permanent form of indeterminacy but are treated as structured formations that can 'exert palpable pressures and set effective limits on experience and on action' (Williams, 1977:132). If certain types of social experience possess an unfinished or open-ended quality, it is because they may be historically emergent (or residual) or pertain to the experiences of socially 'muted' groups. Although these experiences may be marginal, they are not ineffable but are explicable through the analysis of contextual power relations. In other words, contrary to the ontological status that constructionist work grants to ideas of indeterminacy and flux, it is possible to acknowledge the often uncertain and confused present of lived experience without relinquishing the possibility of tracing its connections to social structures.

The libidinalized model of identity and language that prevails in constructionist work does not allow connections to be made between emotions and social structure because its focus is upon the internal workings of 'desire'. An example of this is Butler's work on melancholia which traces the emotional sources of agency back to a primary disjunction between psyche and society (see McNay, 2000:130–33). The problem with this narrowing of emotion to a certain delimited concept of desire is that it reinforces an ego-logical understanding of the subject detached from any social context.[5] By analysing the grounds of emotion within social interaction rather than in the psyche, it is easier to trace the way in which subject positions are mediated through abstract relations. In *Profit and Pleasure* (2000), Rosemary Hennessy argues, for example, that class dynamics are always present, in an explicit or latent form, in the antagonisms and conflicts of daily experience. Class relations remain the 'kernel of human relationships' in so far as they structure emotions and legitimate or 'outlaw' need but in ways that are indirect rather than causal. Thus, as Simon Charlesworth (2000) has demonstrated, in his study of a working-class community in Rotherham, abstract processes of deindustrialization and class dispossession manifest themselves primarily through the intensely felt emotions of boredom, inchoate anger and a sense of powerlessness.

Thus, against the cultural feminist concern with the ambivalences of desire, a socio-centric concept of experience allows a systematic examination of the contradictory forms of identification and affective force that underlie these ambivalences and connects them to fundamental social structures. For example, Skeggs's study shows that the 'passionate attachment' of working-class women to a certain notion of femininity is not the result of a melancholic process of foreclosure but rather is a kind of emotional compensation for their marginal social standing. Similarly, Rosemary Hennessy (2000) describes how embracing hetero-normativity through marriage can offer an emotional 'compensation' for social discrimination. Marriage gives many non-white workers an 'imaginary compensatory psychological wage of normalcy' which may offset economic exploitation and racial discrimination. Compensations may be imaginary or material but they both 'keep those who benefit and those who lose from seeing their wider common interests' (Hennessey, 2000:92). Of course, such emotions have psychic underpinnings which can be explored through ideas of desire, foreclosure and melancholia but, because of their egological orientation, these categories do not get us very far in understanding the socially specific nature of oppression. It is not that such accounts are not valuable, but they are of a different order, and do not throw much light on the complex and historically varied ways that the lived realities of identity, gender or otherwise, connect to abstract social structures of oppression.

Conclusion

The above discussion is not intended as an assertion of the determining primacy of class over other types of power relation. It is, however, to demonstrate the different types of insight that emerge from a phenomenological analysis of experience that treats gender identity as a lived social relation. These insights are not available from a constructionist position because its dissolution of any idea of experience weakens the concept of agency which is required to examine the way individuals make sense of the often submerged conflicts that structure their lives. It is also to demonstrate how a reworked notion of phenomenology that treats experience as a relational entity, rather than as an end in itself, can begin to reconnect questions of identity formation to a context of visible and latent power relations. To return to the starting point of this paper, it sketches out a possible way in which the impasse between material and cultural styles of analysis may begun to be overcome.

Notes

1 To understand misrecognition from a status perspective means that it is neither a psychic defor-
mation nor a free-standing cultural harm but an institutionalized relation of social subordination. To be misrecognised is not to be thought ill of or devalued in other's attitudes but to be
denied the status of a full partner in social interaction as a consequence of institutionalized patterns of value that deem certain individuals less worthy of respect and esteem than others. It takes
the form, for example, of legal sanctions against same sex partnerships, welfare policies that
stigmatize single mothers, and policing practices such a racial profiling that perpetuates the
prejudicial association of race with criminality.
2 For a fuller account of what I mean by a generative concept of agency see my *Gender and Agency*
(2000), especially chapter one.
3 At first sight, it might seem obtuse to accuse Bourdieu of failing to develop an adequate account
of agency given that his oeuvre is so explicitly directed towards a theory of praxis. In many
respects he is one of the main inheritors of French phenomenological thought, exemplified in
the work of Sartre, Merleau-Ponty and de Beauvoir, where a praxeological account of agency
is a central concern. Indeed, I have argued elsewhere (McNay, 2000) that his theory of habitus
provides a fuller and more generative account of the underpinnings of subjectivity and agency
than is available in the poststructural negative paradigm of subject formation. At a general
level, this remains the case. Bourdieu's elaboration of Husserl's notions of retention and proten-
tion provide a useful account of the temporal conditions that generate agency. Similarly, the
habitus-field couplet provides a non-reductive account of power relations in which to situate
agency.
4 His only sustained consideration of gender in Masculine Domination (2001) is rather simplistic
and also objectivist in that it lacks any interpretative element.
5 They miss, for example, the ways in which a certain notion of desire is compatible with the com-
modification of social life, as Rosemary Hennessy puts it: 'These more open, fluid, ambivalent
sexual identities . . . are quite compatible with the mobility, adaptability, and ambivalence
required of service workers today and with the more fluid forms of the commodity. While they
may disrupt gender norms and challenge state practices that are indeed repressive, they do not
necessarily challenge neoliberalism or disrupt capitalism' (Hennessy, 2000:108–9).

References

Bohman, J. (1999) 'Practical Reason and Cultural Constraint' in R. Schusterman (ed.) *Bourdieu: A
Critical Reader*. Oxford: Blackwell.
Bourdieu, P. (1990a) *In Other Words: Essays Towards Reflexive Sociology*. Cambridge: Polity Press.
Bourdieu, P. (1990b) *The Logic of Practice*. Cambridge: Polity.
Bourdieu, P. (1993) *Sociology in Question*. London: Sage.
Bourdieu, P. (2000) *Pascalian Meditations*. Cambridge: Polity Press.
Bourdieu, P. (2001) *Masculine Domination*. Cambridge: Polity Press.
Bourdieu, P. *et al* (1999) *The Weight of the World: Social Suffering in Contemporary Society*.
Cambridge: Polity Press.
Butler, J. (1990) *Gender Trouble: Feminism and the Subversion of Identity*. London: Routledge.
Butler, J. (1993) *Bodies that Matter: On the Discursive Limits of 'Sex'*. London: Routledge.
Butler, J. (1997) *Excitable Speech: A Politics of the Performative*. London: Routledge.
Butler, J. (1998) 'Marxism and the Merely Cultural' *New Left Review* 227 : 33–44.
Butler, J. (1999) 'Performativity's Social Magic' in R. Schusterman (ed.) *Bourdieu: A Critical Reader*.
Oxford: Blackwell.

Charlesworth, S. (2000) *A Phenomenology of Working Class Experience*. Cambridge: Cambridge University Press.

Foucault, M. (1978) *The History of Sexuality: An Introduction*. Harmondsworth: Penguin.

Fraser, N. (1997) 'Heterosexism, Misrecognition, and Capitalism: A Response to Judith Butler' *Social Text* 15(3–4): 279–89.

Fraser, N. (2000) 'Rethinking Recognition' *New Left Review* 3: 107–20.

Hennessy, R. (2000) *Profit and Pleasure: Sexual Identities in Late Capitalism*. London: Routledge.

Lazreg, M. (1994) 'Women's Experience and Feminist Epistemology: A Critical Neo-rationalist Approach', in K. Lennon and M. Whitford (eds) *Knowing the Difference: Feminist Perspectives in Epistemology*. London: Routledge.

McNay, L. (2000) *Gender and Agency: Reconfiguring the Subject in Feminist and Social Theory.* Cambridge: Polity Press.

McNay, L. (2003) 'Out of the Orrery? Situating Language' *Journal of Political Ideologies* 8(2): 139–56.

McNay, L. (2004) 'Situated Intersubjectivity' in A. Witz and B. Marshall (eds) *Engendering Social Theory*. Maidenhead: Open University Press.

Sargent, L. (1981) *Women and Revolution: A Discussion of the Unhappy Marriage of Marxism and Feminism*. London: Pluto Press.

Sartre, J.P. (1976) *Critique of Dialectical Reason* (vol. 1). London: New Left Books.

Scott, J. (1992) ' "Experience" ' in J. Butler and J. Scott (eds) *Feminists Theorize the Political.* London: Routledge.

Sennett, R. and Cobb, J. (1977) *The Hidden Injuries of Class*. Cambridge: Cambridge University Press.

Skeggs, B. (1997) *Formations of Class and Gender: Becoming Respectable*. London: Sage.

Spivak, G.C. (1987) *In Other Worlds: Essays in Cultural Politics*. London: Routledge.

Taylor, C. (1985) *Human Agency and Language: Philosophical Papers 1*. Cambridge: Cambridge University Press.

Williams, R. (1977) *Marxism and Literature*. Oxford: OUP.

Wood, E.M. (1995) *Democracy Against Capitalism: Renewing Historical Materialism*. Cambridge: Cambridge University Press.

Young, I.M. (1997) 'Unruly Categories: A Critique of Nancy Fraser's Dual Systems Theory' *New Left Review* 222: 147–60.

Reflexivity: Freedom or habit of gender?

Lisa Adkins

Introduction

The increasing significance of Bourdieu's social theory in the social sciences and humanities has been noted by a number of writers (Fowler, 1997; Painter, 2000; Shusterman, 1999). In this chapter I am concerned to map this influence in recent accounts of gender in late modern societies. More specifically, I aim to map this influence on a specific thesis which is common (either implicitly or explicitly) to a number of contemporary feminist analyses of gender transformations. This thesis draws on Bourdieu's arguments about social transformation and especially his arguments regarding the constitution of a critical reflexive stance towards formerly normalized – or at least, taken-for-granted – social conditions. More particularly, this thesis draws on the Bourdieusian argument that such reflexivity is constituted in circumstances where there is lack of 'fit' between the habitus (the feel for the game) and field (the game itself), that is, when synchronicity between subjective and objective structures is broken. More particularly still, this thesis involves the argument that in late modernity there is a lack of fit between habitus and field in certain public spheres of action via an increasing transposition or movement of the *feminine* habitus from private to public spheres. For those deploying this thesis two further stages of argument usually flow from this proposition. The first is that this transposition constitutes a heightened critical awareness vis-à-vis gender and the second is that this transposition is linked to specific forms of gender detraditionalization. In short, this thesis concerns a three-fold argument in regard to gender which links feminization, critical reflexivity and detraditionalization.

But while in this chapter I map the characteristics of this thesis, I am also concerned to highlight its limits. In particular, and by drawing on alternative accounts of reflexivity to that of the critical reflexivity found in Bourdieu's account of social transformation, as well as recent ethnographic studies of the workplace, the easy association made between reflexivity and detraditionalization is questioned. I will argue that reflexivity should not be confused with (or understood to concern) a liberal freedom to question and critically deconstruct the rules and norms which previously governed gender. Indeed rather than detraditionalizing, it will be suggested that reflexivity is linked to a reworking or refashioning of gender, indeed that reflexivity is perhaps better conceived as a habit of gender in late modernity. This exploration of the limits of the Bourdieusian styled thesis linking feminization, critical reflexivity and social transformation will in turn lead to a critical discussion of Bourdieu's ideas regarding social transformation. In particular it will be asked, why, when thinking about social change does Bourdieu tend to abandon his own principles regarding practice? And how might practice be rethought to move away from problematic notions of liberal freedom of the sort found in contemporary accounts of reflexivity and social transformation? To begin it is necessary that I provide a very brief commentary on recent debates on reflexivity.

Reflexivity and detraditionalization

One of the most influential ideas in contemporary social theory is that a range of aspects of social life are both characterized by and increasingly require reflexive forms of conduct. Indeed the claim that contemporary social life demands reflexive forms of action has been and continues to be strongly debated in the social sciences (Alexander, 1996; Boyne, 2002; Lichtblau, 1999; Pellizzoni, 1999) and is the centrepiece of a thoroughgoing framework for understanding late modern societies, that of reflexive modernization or reflexive modernity (Beck, Lash and Giddens, 1994). Beck neatly sums up the thrust of this framework when he writes 'the more societies are modernized, the more agents (subjects) acquire the ability to reflect on the social conditions of their existence and to change them accordingly' (Beck, 1994:174). Such increased capacities for reflexivity have been understood to be linked to – and constituted by – a decline in the significance of socio-structural structural forms of determination. As a consequence of the retrocession of the structural, agency is understood as being progressively 'freed' or unleashed from structure. Hence it has been claimed that reflexive modernization is a theory 'of the ever increasing powers of social actors, or 'agency' in regard to structure' (Lash, 1994:111), and it is this process which is understood to provide the conditions for increased reflexivity, that is for critical reflection on prevailing social arrangements, norms and expectations.

But the 'freeing' of agency from structure is understood not only to provide the conditions for the emergence of reflexivity but also for the undoing of what are sometimes termed as 'traditional' rules, norms, expectations and forms of authority associated with modernity, including those organized along axes of gender, class and status. Beck and Beck-Gernsheim have, for example, commented that 'people are being released from the constraints of gender . . . axes of (socially organized) difference, such as class, gender and sexuality (even life and death), are more of a matter of individual decisions (Beck and Beck-Gernsheim, 1996:29). Thus with the disintegration of modes of life associated with modernity, external forms of authority are replaced by the authority of the individual. Indeed, individualization intensifies in the context of detraditionalization since individuals are now constantly compelled to create themselves as individuals. So strong are tendencies towards individualization that Beck has claimed that in the contemporary world the individual 'is the reproduction unit of the social in the lifeworld' (Beck, 1992:90).

Situating reflexivity in-the-world

While the framework of reflexive modernization enjoys wide-ranging currency, it is certainly not without its critics. One powerful line of critique is that the conception of reflexivity deployed in this framework is far too realist and cognitive in orientation (see eg. Crook, 1999; Dean 1998; Lash, 1993; 1994; Lichtblau, 1999; Pellizzoni, 1999). Thus it assumes that subjects somehow exist outside of social worlds and cognitively and objectively reflect on that world in a realist fashion. It tears subjects away from life-world contexts (Lash, 1994) assuming that self-conscious (reflexive) forms of conduct are somehow separate from such life-worlds. While not denying that late modern societies call for greater reflexivity, a number of writers have therefore suggested that reflexivity needs to be understood not in a realist or objectivist fashion, but needs to be situated in-the-world (Lash, 1994; May, 1998). That is, to break with the problematic objectivism of Beck and Giddens, other writers have forwarded a more hermeneutic understanding of reflexivity. And in providing this alternative account, a number of writers have turned to and extended the social theory of Bourdieu, and especially Bourdieu's understanding of practice.

As is well known, Bourdieu's social theory breaks with the dualisms (objectivism versus subjectivism, structure versus action) characteristic of much classical social theory via an account which integrates an explanation of both the regularity and generative character of social action or practice. For Bourdieu social action is neither entirely determined nor entirely arbitrary. The notion of habitus is crucial here. The habitus concerns a dynamic intersection of structure and action: it both generates and shapes action. Composed of durable, transposable dispositions and competencies that shape perception and actions, the habitus is a 'system of lasting, transposable dispositions which, integrating past experiences, functions at every moment as a matrix of perceptions, appreciations and actions' (Bourdieu, 1977:83). The habitus thus produces enduring (although not entirely fixed) orientations to action. But while the habitus structures and organises action it is also generative. Specifically, the habitus is productive of individual and collective practices; practices which themselves are constitutive of the dispositions of the habitus.

But more than this, on Bourdieu's conception, the habitus operates within specific fields. Bourdieu understands the social world to comprise of differentiated, but overlapping, fields of action, for example, the economic field, the political field, the legal field and so on. Each field has its own logic, and it is the field which both informs and sets certain limits on practice. Although habitus and field are not entirely locked together, nonetheless, for the most part Bourdieu sees a compatibility between the two. Indeed, it is such compatibility which ensures the viability of institutions.[1] Specifically, institutions (for example, economic, legal) are only fully viable if they are durably embedded in the dispositions of agents operating within the field (Bourdieu, 1977). Yet agents are not simply the benign carriers of the rules and norms of particular fields. For while the field sets certain limits on practice, nonetheless the actions of agents also shapes the habitus of the field and hence the field itself. Thus within fields distinct 'games' are played. In the artistic field, for example, players contend for the various goods and resources which are considered and recognised to be of value within this specific field of action. In so doing players both shape the habitus of that field and the forms of action which are constitutive of that field.

This however is not done consciously. For the most part players will not be aware of the constitutive role of their actions in terms of the fields of action in which they operate. This is because Bourdieu understands practice – competencies, know-how, dispositions, perceptions – not to be fully consciously organized. They operate below the level of consciousness and language through a 'feel for the game'. That is, social practice often works through an unconscious practical mastery. As Williams has put it 'Most of us, most of the time take ourselves and the social world around us for granted, we do not think about what we do because, quite simply, we do not have to' (Williams, 1995:581). The feel for the game is therefore a pre-reflexive, non-cognitive form of knowledge which often cannot be explicitly articulated. Driving a car is an example of such knowledge. It is something that is practised and learnt but which becomes for the most parts instinctual, pre-reflexive and non-cognitive. The techniques and competencies of the highly skilled athlete are also illustrative of such knowledge. Such skills may be learnt and practised over many years, yet for the athlete are a matter of instinct and non-cognitive habit.

It is this Bourdieusian understanding of practice – as unconscious and pre-reflexive[2] – which has informed the development of a more hermeneutic understanding of reflexivity. For following Bourdieu's understanding of practice, as well as his injunction that '"communication of consciousnesses" presupposes community of "unconsciouses" (ie, of linguistic and cultural competences)' (Bourdieu, 1977:80), reflexivity cannot be understood to concern an objective, cognitive reflection on structure. Indeed, reflexivity cannot be understood to be cognitive at all, since knowledge of the world never concerns an external knowing consciousness. As Bourdieu puts it, agents engaged in practice,

> [know] the world . . . in a sense too well, without objectifying distance, [s/he] takes it for granted, precisely because he [sic] is caught up in it, bound up with it; he inhabits it like a garment . . . or a familiar habitat. He feels at home in the world because the world is also in him, in the form of habitus (Bourdieu, 2000:143).

Following this understanding of practice, reflexivity must therefore be understood to involve reflection on the unthought and unconscious categories of thought, that is, the uncovering of unthought categories of habit which are themselves *corporealized* preconditions of our more self-conscious practices

(Lash, 1994). In short, reflexivity entails reflexivity and understanding of unthought categories and shared meanings, what Lash (1994) has termed a hermeneutic or aesthetic reflexivity. Lash discusses post-traditional economic communities involved in knowledge intensive production to illustrate such reflexivity. In such communities reflexive production is guided by communal exchange relations, involving personalized trust relations and symbolic exchanges of, for example, shared identities. Such communities are therefore characterized by an ethics of commitment and obligation, not to the self, but to a community. Everyday activities in such communities concern the routine achievement of meaning, that is the production of substantive goods 'guided by an understanding . . . of what is regarded as substantively good by that community' (Lash, 1994:157). The substantively good is not however somehow torn away from the everyday, rather it is already present in the world of meanings and practices which are learnt, but become 'unconscious as if inscribed on the body' (Lash, 1994:157). In such communities reflexivity is, in other words, not 'in' the subject or 'in' the self, but in shared background practices, that is in Bourdieu's habitus, in the durable yet transposable set of embodied dispositions and competencies which (unconsciously) shape perceptions and actions.[3]

Bourdieu's social theory of practice leads, therefore, not to an objectivist reflexivity but to a situated reflexivity, a reflexivity which is not separated from the everyday but is intrinsically linked to the (unconscious) categories of habit which shape action. The significance of extending Bourdieu's theory of practice to understand reflexivity does not however simply lie in the manner that it challenges the objectivism of writers such as Beck and Giddens via situating knowers in their life-world. It also lies in the way it breaks with the assumption found in the reflexive modernization thesis that reflexivity goes hand in hand with individualization. In Lash's account of hermeneutic reflexivity, for example, there is a break with the view that reflexivity is intrinsically linked to individualization. Thus, unlike Beck and Giddens, whose accounts foreground radical individualization (I am I) and leave little room for collectivity, in Lash's account reflexivity has a collective dimension. In particular, such reflexivity, based as it is in the *shared* background practices of economic agents involved in knowledge intensive production, is collective in scope, indeed is characteristic of post-traditional economic communities. In short, in extending and elaborating upon Bourdieu's social theory, Lash is able to account for the existence of collective identities in the context of the retrocession of the socio-structural.

Reflexivity and social transformation

While Lash develops the social theory of Bourdieu to critique the objectivism of Beck and Giddens and to arrive at a hermeneutic understanding of reflexivity, nonetheless at least one question may be asked of this analysis. How is it that situated knowers in post-traditional communities come to reflect on the unconscious and unthought categories that shape action? Why are there

195

reflexive communities in some places and not others?[4] Put another way, while this analysis rightly critiques objectivist modes of thinking regarding reflexivity, it does not attend to the issue of the constitution of situated reflexivity. This issue is also raised by Alexander (1996) in a discussion of Lash's hermeneutic reflexivity. Specifically, Alexander asks, where does this account leave reflexivity? The problem as Alexander sees it is that looking to sources of reflexivity via the social theory of Bourdieu leads to a theoretical dead end. In particular he suggests this move cannot get at 'the kind of critical reflexivity that differentiates contemporary democratic, multicultural and civil societies from earlier more authoritarian, homogeneous and anti-individualistic regimes' (Alexander, 1996:137). Alexander claims that to be able to account for this kind of critical reflexivity requires connecting ideas about community situated ethics to the idea that critical thinking depends on the existence of more abstract, universalistic systems of reference. Such a move cannot, he suggests, be made via the social theory of Bourdieu, as this is precisely what it does not do since it embeds meaning making in historically delimited institutional fields and geographically specific communities. In short, Alexander is suggesting that an analysis of hermeneutic reflexivity cannot account for the kind of reflexivity that characterizes the contemporary condition. Beck and Giddens, he argues, are at least aware that there is something in the contemporary condition that is different and new, and that this newness has something to do with an increased capacity for critical reflexivity.

But Bourdieu's social theory *does* contain an account of social change and moreover this account links social transformation to heightened capacities for the kind of critical thinking to which Alexander refers. While this aspect of Bourdieu's work is less developed than his account of social organization,[5] indeed, as I will go on to illustrate, in certain crucial respects this aspect of Bourdieu's writing breaks with his theory of practice, nonetheless his social theory does address issues of social transformation and moreover links social change to increased capacities towards critical reflexivity (what Bourdieu sometimes refers to as an 'awakening of consciousness' (Bourdieu, 1977:83). Furthermore, this account is integrated into Bourdieu's overall social theory, that is, is integrated into his account of habitus and field. Specifically, for Bourdieu social change and heightened capacities towards critical reflexivity are understood to be potentially at issue when there is a lack of fit between habitus and field, that is when there is discord between the previously routine adjustment of subjective and objective structures: a dissonance between the feel for the game and the game itself. While, as noted above, for the most part Bourdieu sees compatibility between habitus and field,[6] this unity is, however, neither fixed nor inevitable. The habitus for example has a transposable character – a mobility which may disrupt the routine adjustment of subjective and objective structures. In addition, changes in objective structures (fields of action) may disrupt the synchronicity of habitus and field. Such changes may not necessarily lead to either social transformation or increased tendencies towards critical reflection since there is an inertia, or what Bourdieu terms a hysteresis of the habitus

(Bourdieu, 1977:83; Bourdieu and Wacquant, 1992:130). But nonetheless, when the adjustment between habitus and field is broken increased possibilities may arise for critical reflection on previously habituated forms of action. Indeed, in such contexts agents may secure what Bourdieu terms a 'symbolic mastery' of the principles of the habitus and transforming practices may emerge:

> . . . transforming practices and the 'awakening of consciousness' takes place by the direct or indirect possession of a discourse capable of securing symbolic mastery of the practically mastered principles of the class habitus (Bourdieu, 1977:83).[7]

Bourdieu does not elaborate in any systematic sense on the conditions of the latter. Indeed it is unclear why some changes in objective structures may lead to increased possibilities for the development of transforming practices and others do not. But nonetheless, for Bourdieu, when shifts in objective conditions precipitate a lack of fit between objective and subjective structures there are increased possibilities for both critical reflexivity and social change. Indeed this kind of reflexivity, constituted in the specific conditions of a lack of fit between the feel for the game and the game itself, must itself be understood as a transforming practice.[8]

Gender reflexivity in late modernity

It is this specific aspect of Bourdieu's social theory, in particular the view that possibilities for critical reflexivity and social transformation are heightened in the context of a lack of fit between subjective and objective structures, which has been taken up by a number of feminist social scientists and especially feminist sociologists in accounts of transformations of gender. What is at issue in such accounts is the broad idea that within late modernity there has been a restructuring of gender regimes, particularly in regard to the public sphere, evidenced it is claimed particularly in the economic field of action, especially in the movement of women into the labour market, including movements into professional and high status occupations previously coded as masculine. For those following this line of reasoning these changes in the gender ordering of public fields of action are conceptualized in a Bourdieusian fashion as undoing the previous synchronicity of habitus and field, and hence as leading to the possibilities for critical reflection on the (previously unconscious and unthought) norms, rules and habits governing gender, indeed to a possible transformation of gender. While this line of reasoning clearly has certain resonances with theories of reflexive modernization (especially in the equation of reflexivity with detraditionalization), nonetheless for those following this line of reasoning, and with the accounts of hermeneutic reflexivity discussed above, the broader social theory of Bourdieu, especially Bourdieu's theory of practice, is understood to place certain caveats on the framework of reflexive modernization. However, here the issue is not so much that Bourdieu's broader social theory can be extended to move away from a cognitive and overly individualized understanding of reflexivity, but that it may be mobilized to correct a perceived over-emphasis in the reflexive modernization framework on possibilities for a self-conscious fashioning of identity, particularly gender identity.

Discussing theories of reflexive modernity broadly, but especially the work of Giddens (1991; 1992), Lois McNay (1999; 2000), for example, has argued the idea that identity is an issue of reflexive self-transformation fails to fully consider issues concerned with gender identity. She suggests that an examination of questions related to gender (and sexuality) reveal aspects of identity that renders it less amenable to reflexive processes of re-fashioning. Indeed, in stressing the potential for a self-fashioning of identity in late modernity, McNay suggests that theories of reflexive modernization run the risk of re-instating the disembodied and disembedded subject of masculinist thought and leads to a tendency towards voluntarism. As a corrective to the overemphasis on self-fashioning, McNay turns to the general social theory of Bourdieu. But while as noted above, writers such as Lash have turned to Bourdieu to break with the objectivism of Beck and Giddens and to forward a more hermeneutic understanding of reflexivity, McNay turns to Bourdieu to highlight embedded and embodied aspects of identity which she suggests render certain aspects of identity less open to reflexive interpretation – even hermeneutic or aesthetic interpretation. For McNay it is the recognition of the unconscious, pre-reflexive and non-cognitive understanding of practice (and the incorporation of the social into the corporeal) in Bourdieu's social theory which is central here. Specifically for McNay this understanding underscores how rather than as a self-conscious practice, gender identity is in important respects enacted at a pre-reflexive level (McNay, 1999:101). In terms of the understandings of identity found in theories of reflexive modernization this conceptualization of identity has a number of important implications. In particular, and as McNay makes clear, it points to aspects of embodied experience which, although not entirely fixed, may be less amenable to reflexive interpretation.

To illustrate these more entrenched aspects of gender identity McNay points to the ways in which men and women may have entrenched 'often unconscious investments in conventional images of masculinity and femininity which cannot easily be reshaped' (McNay, 1999:103). In addition, she discusses the ways in which, despite women's entry into the labour force, certain conventional arrangements of gender have not necessarily been dismantled and indeed may have become more entrenched. For example, McNay argues such moves have not freed women from the burden of emotional responsibilities (McNay, 1999:103). Instead they have made the process of individualization for women more complex since the ideal of performing an individualized biography – 'living one's own life' – is in sharp conflict with the conventional expectation of 'being there for others'. For McNay this kind of unevenness in the transformation of gender relations illustrates how an emphasis on strategic and self-conscious self-monitoring overlooks more enduring aspects of identity. She also points to sexual desire and maternal feelings as examples of unconscious, pre-reflexive, entrenched aspects of identity which question the process of identity transformation highlighted by writers such as Giddens. And importantly McNay also notes that the entrenched nature of gender identity concerns the ways in which other social distinctions – such as those of class – may be played out through the categories of gender. McNay suggests that such unevenness in the transformation of gender is again indicative of how Bourdieu's general social theory is of relevance for theorizing gender. In particular this unevenness is understood to illustrate Bourdieu's claim that the habitus may continue to work long after 'the objective conditions of emergence have been dislodged' (McNay, 1999:103), that is to illustrate the inertia of the habitus.

Detraditionalization, gender, mobility and social fields

As this suggests, while McNay finds the emphasis on self-fashioning in the theory of reflexive modernization wanting, this is not to say that she does not agree that in late modernity there have been certain transformations of gender. Specifically, while critical of the idea of a straightforward, self-conscious transformation of identity, McNay accepts there is an ongoing – albeit uneven – detraditionalization of gender. McNay posits that such detraditionalizing processes are currently expressed in women's entry into the workforce; the opening up of negotiations regarding marriage and the gendered division of labour; and current conflicts between achieving (or choosing) an individualized and a more traditional biography for women. Moreover, and again drawing on the social theory of Bourdieu, but in this instance, Bourdieu's specific ideas regarding social transformation, McNay proposes that this detraditionalization of gender may be fruitfully understood and analysed as concerning the transposition or movement of the *feminine* habitus into different fields of action. Thus she suggests that women's entry into the workforce (that is into a field previously coded as masculine) may be understood in these terms. But more still, and again following Bourdieu's ideas regarding social transformation, McNay argues that such movements of women into 'traditionally non-feminine spheres of action' (McNay, 1999:107) may be understood as meaning that in late modernity there is a lack of fit between gendered habitus and field. Indeed, McNay suggests that it is crucial to give attention to this lack of fit for understanding gender in late modern societies since it is this lack of synchronicity which she claims is leading to uneven detraditionalizations of gender, that is to an undoing of certain rules, norms and habits vis-à-vis gender. Moreover, McNay suggests this Bourdieusian influenced understanding of social change – as involving a lack of fit between gendered habitus and field – provides a further avenue to assess claims concerning the increasingly reflexive nature of gender identity. In particular, she argues that such claims need to be assessed in the light of Bourdieu's understanding of critical reflexivity (the 'awakening of consciousness'): that such reflexivity is constituted when the routine adjustment between subjective and objective structures is broken. In short, while critical of the idea of a kind of self-driven notion of social transformation, McNay is suggesting that in late modernity a lack of fit between gendered habitus and field has lead to heightened possibilities for both critical reflexivity and social transformation vis-à-vis gender.

To substantiate these claims McNay considers the example of women entering the workforce after child rearing. Such women, she argues, may experience difficulties since their expectations and predispositions (constituted largely through the experience of the domestic field) may sit rather uneasily with the 'objective requirements of the workplace' (McNay, 1999:110). Such dissonance may however lead to greater critical awareness of the shortcomings of a patriarchally defined system of employment. McNay's point here is that the emergence of critical reflexivity towards gender is based on what she terms a 'distanciation of the subject with constitutive structures'. Thus critical reflexivity towards gender – for example, a questioning of conventional notions of femininity – is understood to arise from the tensions in negotiating a lack of fit between habitus and field, in this case the tensions inherent in the negotiation of increasingly conflictual female roles. Indeed McNay suggests that such reflexivity can only emerge from distanciation provoked by the conflict and tension of social forces operating within and across specific fields. Reflexivity is therefore understood by McNay not to be a generalized, universal capacity of subjects but to arise unevenly from subjects' embeddedness within differing sets of power relations. Thus she suggests any recent shifts in conventional notions of masculinity and femininity are best understood as arising from the 'negotiation of discrepancies by individuals in their movement within and across fields of social action' (McNay, 1999:111). In following Bourdieu's understanding of social change, McNay therefore tends to view critical reflexivity (however unevenly manifest) as a transforming practice. Indeed, while placing certain important caveats on the framework of reflexive modernization, nonetheless she tends to agree that reflexivity vis-à-vis gender is detraditionalizing.

Other writers have taken up a similar Bourdieusian style thesis regarding social change, critical reflexivity and gender. In a discussion of Bourdieu's analysis of critical reflexivity Christopher Bryant (1995), for example, also draws attention to the transposable character of the habitus and how movement across and within fields of action may 'lead to clashes or prompt reflection' (Bryant, 1995:74). He argues, 'patriarchy at home . . . might clash with educational opportunity for girls and women at school and university' (Bryant, 1995:74). Thus for Bryant, like McNay, critical reflexivity in regard to gender is understood to arise via the negotiation of discrepancies in the context of movements across fields of action, particularly movements for women from private to public fields. Such mobility is, therefore, understood to be productive of the kind of discrepancies and conflict through which a critical awareness vis-à-vis gender may arise. But also like McNay, Bryant's analysis implies that such reflexivity is made possible because of a kind of *feminization* of the public sphere that is the transposition of a feminine habitus into public spheres of action. Thus for Bryant while 'patriarchy [exists] at home', school and university offer girls and women opportunities.

With McNay, Bryant's analysis therefore also suggests that it is a transposition of the feminine habitus into different fields of action that is central to the constitution of critical reflexivity towards gender. Thus it is the feminization of public spheres of action which is at issue in regard to the lack of fit between habitus and field, movements across fields of action (specifically from private to public fields of action), and the constitution of reflexive awareness towards gender (a distanciation of the subject with constitutive structures). Indeed, a number of recent accounts of gender in late modernity either implicitly or explicitly subscribe to this line of reasoning and more specifically link a feminization of public sphere fields to a detraditionalization of gender. Arguing for a positive engagement between Bourdieu's social theory and contemporary feminist theory, Lovell (2000) has for example argued that femininity as a form of cultural capital is beginning to have broad currency in what she claims are unexpected ways. In particular she discusses a general increase in demand for feminine skills in the labour market (Lovell, 2000:25). Lovell suggests this increased demand may mean that femininity may begin to have a competitive market advantage compared with the attributes of traditional masculinity, a shift which 'may have profound effects on "la domination masculine"' (Lovell, 2000:25). Thus Lovell, like McNay, implies that a transposition of the feminine habitus into public sphere fields of action is detraditionalizing of gender. In her recent study of medical doctors in Australia and the UK, Pringle (1998) follows a similar line of reasoning. Specifically she suggests that within the medical profession there is an increasing demand and recognition of feminine skills, indeed that there is a shifting habitus in regard to gender in medicine. She writes, 'doctors have been compelled to take on a more feminine style, more holistic, and more concerned about communication' (Pringle, 1998:8). Pringle locates this shift as being part of what she sees as a more general repositioning of gender and work within late modernity involving shifting relations between public and private fields of action.

A similar line of argument is also put forward by Illouz (1997), who in an analysis of recent transformations of the workplace suggests the emergence of the service economy (which demands an orientation towards persons rather than commodities) compelled workers 'to incorporate . . . in their personality . . . so called feminine attributes such as paying attention to emotions, controlling anger and listening sympathetically to others' (Illouz, 1997:39). Drawing on Bourdieu's general social theory, Illouz suggests that in service economies such feminine attributes are defined as forms of capital to be traded, a trade which was made possible via the articulation of a new language of selfhood.[9] Thus Illouz too suggests that work in service economies is feminized, involving the breakdown of the distinction between public and private spheres which she argues 'tends to blur distinctions of gender and gender roles' (Illouz, 1997:51), a blurring which Illouz understands to have led to an increasingly prominent model of selfhood characterized by androgyny. The feminization of the economic field is therefore not only widely understood to constitute new forms of power for women through a re-valuing of the skills of femininity at work, but also to signal a reworking of gender identities and gender relations. Indeed this reworking of gender identities is widely understood to concern a detraditionalization of gender in late modernity, with a reworking of traditional notions of public and private and the emergence of a reflexive attitude towards gender typically taken as substantive illustration of such a detraditionalization.

Reflexivity as habit of gender

But should such shifts be so easily understood as concerning a detraditionalization of gender? Should critical reflexivity and more specifically the emergence of a reflexive attitude towards gender be bracketed off from other forms of social action which are understood to be more habitually rooted and hence as tied in to the constitution and reproduction of the norms, expectations and habits of gender? That is, is it possible to differentiate between reflexive and non-reflexive action in the way that such accounts presume? My suggestion is that such assumptions are doubtful. Indeed, it is my suggestion that rather than detraditionalizing, reflexivity is tied into the arrangements of gender in late modernity. That is, it may be said that rather than detraditionalizing or providing a freedom from gender, a critical reflexive stance towards gender is increasingly characteristic of gender in late modernity – a habit of gender in late modernity.

I take as my cue here recent ethnographic studies of the workplace, particularly ethnographies of service sector workplaces and especially those managed in accordance with a performance based culture. While such studies are not explicitly concerned with the issues I am interested in here, nonetheless they have noted how in the economic field workers are increasingly taking up a critical, reflexive stance towards a whole array of aspects of economic life (Martin, 1994; Hinchcliffe, 2000), including a critical stance towards gender at work. Such studies show how management practices, for example, training techniques, attempt to incite such reflexivity. Emily Martin's study of the emergence of the flexible body as a new workplace ideal (1994) underscores this point well. Here, Martin describes training techniques which attempt to shift away from the idea of gender as a taken-for-granted characteristic of workers to create a critical awareness and recognition of gender at work, to the extent that workers are encouraged to 'scramble characteristics usually associated with males and females' (Martin, 1994:213). Thus such training exercises establish gender not only as a matter of reflexivity and also as a matter of performativity. Further still, Martin notes how training techniques attempt to establish reflexive 'scrambling' as central to corporate growth and success. Studies of interactive service work have in particular highlighted the take up of this reflexive, performative stance towards gender. Here it has been noted that for both men and women gender is increasingly taking the form of a self-conscious artifice which can be managed, strategically deployed and performed. In Linda McDowell's (1997) ethnographic study of financial service workers in the City of London, for example, workers displayed high degrees of reflexivity toward their workplace performances of gender to the extent that they would attempt to adapt their gendered style for different audiences (especially for different customers). Thus one respondent in this study commented 'it depends who I am going to be seeing. Sometimes I'll choose the 'executive bimbo look'; at other . . . [a plain but very smart tailored blue dress] looks tremendously, you know, professional' (McDowell, 1997:198).

While such studies have recorded that reflexivity vis-à-vis gender is increasingly routine – even habitual – across a range of workplaces, nonetheless they warn against a simple elision of such reflexivity with detraditionalization. This is particularly evident in regard to the issue of the exchange of such reflexive gender performances into forms of workplace capital. Specifically, while such studies have noted that such reflexive performances of gender may be converted into forms of workplace capital, they also suggest that this process is by no means straightforward and this is especially so for the case of performances of femininity for many women. Women's performances of femininity at work are often defined as not concerning reflexive skills or competencies, but rather as 'natural advantages' (McDowell, 1997:154) which should not receive workplace recognition and rewards such as, for instance, promotion. Thus, many women workers are not recognized as taking up a reflexive stance towards gender since the relationship between women and femininity is made immanent. In short, and in contradistinction to those following the Bourdieusian styled thesis of the feminization of the economic field, the emergence of gender reflexivity as characteristic of the economic field may not lead to a straightforward critical deconstruction of the norms, habits and rules of gender and therefore to detraditionalization (for instance to new forms of economic power for women). Indeed it seems that reflexivity may be linked to (gendered) positions of privilege and exclusion – to gendered (and as Featherstone, 1992, has shown classed) processes of categorization and classification in late modernity.

What this suggests is that the idea of feminization and especially the idea of the transposition of the feminine habitus 'into' the economic field, which leads to a lack of fit between habitus and field, the take-up of a reflexive stance towards gender, and a process of detraditionalization, may be a less than adequate conceptualization of the reconfiguring of gender and gender identities in late modernity. In particular, it suggests that this thesis blocks out of view the ways in which reflexivity concerns not so much a straightforward detraditionalization of the norms, habits and expectations of gender but may be tied into a *reworking* of gender in late modernity, a reworking characterized by positions of reflexivity and immanence (Adkins, 2002b), indeed that reflexivity may be bound up with modes of classification and with specific forms of power and inequality post (sociological) structure. In short it suggests that the Bourdieusian influenced accounts of transformations in gender in late modernity fail to register that reflexivity does not concern a liberal freedom from gender, but may be tied into new arrangements of gender. But what this also implies is that the theoretical tools being used in recent accounts of transformations of gender and gender identities in late modernity derived from Bourdieu's account of social transformation are also less than well suited to come to grips with this task. Specifically, the coupling of critical reflexivity with detraditionalization and the unproblematic understanding of reflexivity as involving reflection and critique of previously habituated social conditions which then leads to social transformation (indeed that reflexivity itself is a transforming practice) appear to be inadequate assumptions for exploring the relationship between reflexivity and gender in late modernity.

Indeed, if we turn to recent discussions of Bourdieu's social theory, there is some critical commentary on his assumptions regarding reflexivity and social transformation. In particular critical commentary on the way in which when it comes to social change Bourdieu's social theory tends to overwhelmingly associate both critical reflexivity and social transformation with a thinking consciousness and disconnect such forms of action from more habituated, unconscious, corporealized forms. Crossley (2001), for example has argued that the problem with this set of assumptions is that it underestimates the extent to which reflexivity may routinely enter into everyday life as a matter of course, a point underscored by the Merleau-Ponty-ian motif that thought and the body are indissoluble. Indeed, and echoing aspects of Lash's analysis of hermeneutic reflexivity, Crossley notes that considered from a more phenomenological point of view, rather than separate from habitual, unconscious forms of action, reflexivity must itself be understood to be rooted in the habitus.[10] In short, even when it comes to the issue of social change reflexivity may not be as thoroughly disconnected from the realm of habituated forms of practice as Bourdieu's writings on social transformation appear to imply.

This point has a number of implications for the analyses of transformations of gender I have outlined in this chapter. In particular it suggests that in separating out critical reflexivity from more habitual forms of action, such analyses may be greatly underestimating the ways in which reflexivity is part of everyday habit and hence overestimating the possibilities for gender detraditionalization in late modernity. Thus, as I indicated in my more substantive discussion of reflexivity, situated men and women in their life-worlds routinely enact reflexive forms of action in regard to gender. Indeed, in a review of recent studies of social divisions, Boyne (2002) has noted that this is the case not only for gender but for a whole range of social identities. He argues that a number of such studies show how 'structural contexts such as class, ethnicity, gender, age, medical status, are now routinely and reflexively incorporated into conceptions of self-identity' (Boyne, 2002:119). Class cultures are for example now marked by reflexive attitudes: 'rueful, ironic, envious, reflectively proud' (Boyne, 2002:119). And I would add to this, at least in the case of gender, that such reflexive practices may be said to be so habituated that they are part of the very norms, rules and expectations that govern gender in late modernity, even as they may ostensibly appear to challenge these very notions.

Even those analyses such as McNay's which have mobilised Bourdieu's theory of practice to critique the idea that identity is increasingly a matter of reflexive self-fashioning and to set certain limits on the reflexive modernization thesis, may have also greatly overestimated the possibilities for gender detradition-alization in late modernity. In particular, by following Bourdieu's assumptions regarding social change and critical reflexivity, especially the assumption that critical reflexivity is a transforming practice which is separate from the every-day world of habit and more specifically in assuming that reflexivity is dif-ferentiated from the norms and habits of gender, McNay's analysis ironically ends up reproducing the very problem which she seeks to redress in the reflex-ive modernization thesis. That is, McNay along with the analysts of transfor-mations of gender and gender identity in late modernity considered in this chapter, overstate the possibilities for detraditionalization vis-à-vis gender in late modernity.

Bourdieu, reflexivity and social change: rethinking action

In this chapter I have suggested that reflexivity needs not only, as Lash has argued, to be decoupled from individualization, but also from detraditionaliza-tion. Indeed I have suggested that the relations between reflexivity and detradi-tionalization or social transformation can in no way be taken for granted. But while this is so, the problems I have identified with the Bourdieusian-derived feminization thesis common to a number of recent accounts of gender trans-formations in late modernity prompt some perhaps more serious questions in regard to the social theory of Bourdieu, particularly his assumptions regarding critical reflexivity and social transformation. Why is it, for example, when think-ing about the issue of social transformation, that Bourdieu abandons the principles he develops in regard to action? That is why, when it comes to social change, does Bourdieu tend to disembody actors and understand action as a matter of thinking consciousness? Why does social change end up being about consciousness when most of his social theory attempts to get away from this view of social action and of the human subject? In other words, why does Bour-dieu move towards the prevailing model of power within sociological thinking – as a 'system of concepts, values and beliefs, *ideology*, that primarily effect con-sciousness' (Grosz, 1990:62, emphasis in original) – and enact the conventional philosophical dualism between everyday life and critical reflection (Felski, 2000) – when the vast majority of his work critiques this view both theoretically and methodologically?

Of course, and as mentioned above, it is widely rehearsed that Bourdieu's social theory does not contain a developed account of social change and his work is often critiqued on these grounds. For the most part, however, most critics do not see this as a problem of his wider conceptualization of the social (as comprising habitus and fields), yet it is my belief that this is where the problem resides. The problem, as I see it, is that when it comes to social change Bourdieu is forced into a position of abandoning his understanding of practice since he ultimately tends to understand the field as an 'objective' structure which determines – or at least sets crucial limits on – practice. True. this practice is embodied; true, habitus and field are in dynamic interplay. But for the most part, and as Butler (1997;1999) has recently pointed out, for Bourdieu the relation between habitus and field is understood as an 'encounter' or event, that is as an encounter with an *external*, objective phenomena, an understanding which assumes that the field is a precondition of the habitus and that the habitus will always submit to the field. That is, Bourdieusian social theory tends to assume that the habitus will adapt or accommodate itself to the field and that the habitus cannot alter the field because of the external, objective status that is attributed to the field. Moreover Bourdieu assumes that the habitus always encounters the field in this way. As a consequence of this understanding of the relation between habitus and field, and again as Butler makes clear, not only is the habitus always inclined to adapt to the field, but agents are always inclined towards submission – since inclination or adaptation is part of the very set of dispositions and competencies which are part of the habitus. In short, Bourdieu assumes a mimetic relation between field and habitus, object and subject, a mimesis that produces congruence between habitus and field. Indeed Bourdieu assumes that mimesis itself concerns a process of adaptation.

This determinism of the field in Bourdieu's social theory has been pointed out by many sociologists but few have considered alternative understandings of mimesis to think through correctives to this determinism. Indeed, most simply argue that a stronger account of social change is required and therefore stay both within a traditional sociological structure-action problematic and close to Bourdieu's own understanding of mimesis (see eg Howson and Inglis, 2001). But what is particularly germane here is recent work on subjectivity and subject formation, which provides a rather different orientation to this issue (Bell, 1999). The key motif of this body of work is that subjects never fully occupy or identify with norms (see eg Fraser, 1999; Haraway, 1991; Skeggs, 1997) indeed that there is an *ambivalence* at the very heart of inclination.[11] Ambivalence must, in other words, be understood to be at the very heart of mimesis. As Butler herself has put it,

> ... the mimetic acquisition of the norm is at once the condition by which a certain resistance to the norm is also produced; identification will not 'work' to the extent that the norm is not fully ... incorporable (Butler, 1999:118).

Understanding mimesis in this way requires an emphasis on the *temporality* of action on, for example, iteration and citation, for instance, on how identifications as well as social positions are subject to a logic of iteration (and not simply a singular process of adaptation or accommodation), a logic which explains both how and why possibilities of instability, ambivalence and interruptability are at the core of mimesis or inclination.[12] In short, what such work underscores is that the logic of ambivalence at play within mimesis demands an understanding of instability not as external to but as internal to the operation of norms themselves. As Campbell and Harbord (1999) have discussed, Homi

Bhabha's (1994) account of mimicry and the colonized subject underscores this point well. Rejecting the view of such mimicry as a simple identification with and adaptation to the dominant colonial subject and colonial power, Bhabha suggests that the practice of mimicry is far more ambiguous, indeed that it is characterized by ambivalence. Thus while mimicry may signal an identification with the dominant, it may also as Campbell and Harbord note 'mask the language of the other, raising the spectre that this seeming 'identification' may indeed be a parody' (Campbell and Harbord, 1999:236).

This view clearly questions the tendency in Bourdieusian social theory to assume that incorporation and mimesis 'work': that the encounter between habitus and field involves an adaptation of the habitus to the field. Indeed it highlights the ways in which because Bourdieu understands norms to be generally incorporated he closes off any ability to think through ambivalence and hence social transformation within his understanding of practice.[13] Thus he must always place ambivalence outside of the realms of practice. This, for me, explains why Bourdieu's understanding of social transformation and critical reflexivity is so incongruous with the rest of his social theory. In short, because Bourdieu understands norms to be incorporated (since agents are generally understood to identify with norms or, perhaps better said, an agreement between the dispositions of agents and the demands of a field is generally assumed) he has to abandon his understanding of practice and resort to a more problematic sociological understanding of action (as conscious, cognitive and disembodied involving a system of concepts, perceptions, values and beliefs) when he wants to talk about social transformation. This contradiction will not be resolved, however, by making Bourdieusian social theory more sociological but via a conceptualization of mimesis which understands norms as never fully occupied and via an emphasis on the temporal aspects of practice. Such procedures would, moreover, allow a move away from problematic notions of liberal freedom of the sort found in recent sociological accounts of reflexivity and social change, indeed from the very dilemma of determinism versus freedom which in his social theory Bourdieu himself sought to overcome (Bourdieu, 2000:131).

Notes

1 This compatibility is neither fixed nor inevitable indeed, and as I will go on to discuss, in times of crisis the synchronicity between habitus and field may be undone.
2 It is worth pointing out that for Bourdieu the unconscious is 'the forgetting of history which history itself produces by incorporating the objective structures it produces in the second natures of the habitus' (Bourdieu, 1977:78–9).
3 A number of writers have challenged the assumption that reflexivity resides in the self. See for example, Adkins (2002a), May (1998), Probyn (1993), Vitellone (2002).
4 While Lash recognizes that there are reflexivity winners and losers, nonetheless he does not directly attend to the question of how such unevenness vis-à-vis reflexivity is constituted.

5 It is widely recognized that Bourdieu's social theory has much more to say about social reproduction than social change see eg Calhoun, 1993.

6 Thus Bourdieu notes that for differentiated societies 'a whole series of social mechanisms tend to ensure the adjustment of dispositions to positions' (Bourdieu, 2000:147).

7 Bourdieu does not spell out how it is exactly that agents may come directly or indirectly to secure such symbolic mastery, that is he does not discuss the relations between such discourses, the habitus and the field.

8 It is interesting to note that more broadly speaking Lash situates his analysis of hermeneutic reflexivity in the context of social change, specifically, a shift from a mode of production to a mode of information, that is, the emergence of what Lash terms the information field. What appears to be at issue in the constitution of hermeneutic reflexivity in Lash's account is therefore the very same issue we find in Bourdieu's account of social change and reflexivity, that is, a change in objective conditions, in this case the emergence of the information and communication field. But for Lash the latter does not comprise of the familiar social structures of sociological analyses (economic, political, ideological), but non-social cultural structures.

9 Illouz suggests that this new language of selfhood was articulated primarily via psychological expertise (see Rose, 1990).

10 While this suggests that phenomenological and/or hermeneutic understandings of reflexivity offer some important resources for the theorization of gender in late modernity, it is important to stress that there may be certain limits to such understandings. Indeed while it is the case that a number of feminist theorists for the past decade or more have drawn on the phenomenology of Merleau-Ponty, particularly in the theorization of sexual difference and intercorporeality (Grosz, 1990; Weiss, 1999), this has not taken place uncritically. In particular feminists have critiqued the universalism of Merleau-Ponty's phenomenology of the body. Thus his notion of body-subjects and the implication that the body *is* the subject and the subject *is* the body can be critiqued for its assumption that all body-subjects are lived in the same way (Ahmed and Stacey, 2000). Indeed while the notion of reflexive habit with its emphasis on in-the-world corporealized reflexivity acts as an important corrective to claims that gender is radically detraditionalizing, nonetheless what appears to be missing from this account is a sense of the ways in which such in the world corporealized reflexivity may be bound up with the articulation of differences. Thus it does not seem to be able to attend to the point highlighted in my discussion of reflexivity, gender and economy, that such reflexivity is bound up with particular arrangements of gender characterized by positions of reflexivity and immanence, and that such positions involve relations of privilege and exclusion.

11 While via the development of the theory of practice Bourdieu clearly rejected the notion of the social actor as rule follower or norm respecter, nonetheless his understanding of mimesis tends to undermine such claims.

12 Interestingly, Bourdieu's social theory has often been praised for its emphasis on temporality (see eg McNay, 2000), especially its emphasis on the temporality of practice. However Bourdieu tends to understand time as deriving its force or efficacy via the structured spaces of positions operating in social fields. Thus he writes, we know 'how much advantage the holder of a transmissible power can derive from the art of delaying transmission and keeping others in the dark as to his ultimate intentions' (Bourdieu, 1977:7). In Bourdieusian social theory temporality is therefore read off from social positions (indeed is held to be in a mimetic relation to the field) and hence concerns a map of social power. Temporality is thus conceived as only ever reproducing this map of power.

13 For some the move I am suggesting here – that recent work on subjectivity and subject formation may complement and profitably extend Bourdieu's social theory, and in particular that this work will allow for a fuller account of action particularly in regard to questions of social change – may appear problematic. For many have seen in such analyses an inexcusable emphasis on the linguistic which is held to unable to account for the specificities of the socio-historical. However, even if one is concerned with language quite literally, Butler (1999) has shown how speech is performed bodily and hence how citation and iteration are social logics.

Bibliography

Adkins, L. (2002a) 'Reflexivity and the Politics of Qualitative Research' in T. May (ed.) *Qualitative Research: Issues in International Practice*: London. Sage.

Adkins, L. (2002b) *Revisions: Gender and Sexuality in Late Modernity*. Buckingham: Open University Press.

Ahmed, S. and J. Stacey (2000) 'Introduction: Dermographies' in S. Ahmed and J. Stacey (eds) *Thinking Through the Skin*. London and New York: Routledge.

Alexander, J. (1996) 'Critical Reflections on "Reflexive Modernization"' *Theory, Culture and Society* 13(4): 133–138.

Beck, U. (1992) *Risk Society: Towards a New Modernity*. London: Sage.

Beck, U. (1994) 'The Reinvention of Politics: Towards a Theory of Reflexive Modernization' in U. Beck, A. Giddens and S. Lash, *Reflexive Modernization: Politics, Tradition and Aesthetics in the Modern Social Order*. Cambridge: Polity.

Beck, U. and E. Beck-Gernsheim (1996) *The Normal Chaos of Love*. Cambridge: Polity.

Beck, U., A. Giddens and S. Lash, (1994) *Reflexive Modernization: Politics, Tradition and Aesthetics in the Modern Social Order*. Cambridge: Polity.

Bell, V. (1999) *Feminist Imagination*. London: Sage.

Bhabha, H. (1994) *The Location of Culture*. London and New York: Routledge.

Bourdieu, P. (1977) *Outline of a Theory of Practice*. Cambridge: Cambridge University Press.

Bourdieu, P. (2000) *Pascalian Meditations*. Cambridge: Polity Press.

Bourdieu, P. and L. Wacquant (1992) *An Invitation to Reflexive Sociology*. Cambridge: Polity.

Boyne, R. (2002) 'Bourdieu: From Class to Culture' *Theory, Culture and Society* 19(3): 117–128.

Bryant, C. (1995) *Practical Sociology: Post-empiricism and the Reconstruction of Theory and Application*. Cambridge: Polity.

Butler, J. (1997) *Excitable Speech: A Politics of The Performative*. London and New York: Routledge.

Butler, J. (1999) 'Performativity's Social Magic' in R. Shusterman (ed) *Bourdieu: A Critical Reader*. Oxford: Blackwell.

Calhoun, C. (1993) 'Habitus, Field and Capital: The Question of Historical Specificity' in C. Calhoun, E. LiPuma and M. Postone (eds) *Bourdieu: Critical Perspectives*. Chicago: The University of Chicago Press.

Campbell, J. and J. Harbord (1999) 'Playing it Again: Citation, Reiteration or Circularity' *Theory, Culture and Society* 16(2): 229–239.

Crook, S. (1999) 'Ordering Risks' in D. Lupton (ed) *Risk and Sociocultural Theory*. Cambridge: Cambridge University Press.

Crossley, N. (2001) 'The Phenomenological Habitus and Its Construction' *Theory and Society* 30: 81–120.

Dean, M. (1998) 'Risk, Calculable and Incalculable' *Soziale Welt* 49: 25–42.

Featherstone, M. (1992) 'Postmodernism and the Aestheticization of Everyday Life' in S. Lash and J. Freidman (eds) *Modernity and Identity*. Oxford: Blackwell.

Felski, R. (2000) *Doing Time: Feminist Theory and Postmodern Culture*. New York and London: New York University Press.

Fowler, B. (1997) *Pierre Bourdieu and Cultural Theory*. London: Sage.

Fraser, M. (1999) 'Classing Queer: Politics in Competition' *Theory, Culture and Society* 16(2): 107–31.

Giddens, A. (1991) *Modernity and Self-Identity: Self and Society in the Late Modern Age*. Cambridge: Polity.

Giddens, A. (1992) *The Transformation of Intimacy: Sexuality, Love and Eroticism in Modern Societies*. Cambridge: Polity.

Grosz, E. (1990) 'Inscriptions and Body-Maps: Representations and the Corporeal' in T. Threadgold and A. Cranny-Francis (eds) *Feminine/Masculine/Representation*. St Leonards: Allen and Unwin.

Haraway, D. (1991) *Simians, Cyborgs and Women: The Reinvention of Nature*. London and New York: Routledge.

Hinchliffe, S. (2000) 'Performance and Experimental Knowledge: Outdoor Management Training and the End of Epistemology' *Environment and Planning D: Society and Space* 18: 575–595.

Howson, A. and D. Inglis (2001) 'The Body in Sociology: Tensions Inside and Outside Sociological Thought' *The Sociological Review* 49(3): 297–317.

Illouz, E. (1997) 'Who Will Care for the Caretaker's Daughter? Toward a Sociology of Happiness in the Era of Reflexive Modernity' *Theory, Culture and Society* 14(4): 31–66.

Lash, S. (1993) 'Reflexive Modernization: The Aesthetic Dimension' *Theory, Culture and Society* 10(1): 1–23.

Lash, S. (1994) 'Reflexivity and its Doubles: Structure, Aesthetics, Community' in U. Beck, A. Giddens and S. Lash, *Reflexive Modernization: Politics, Tradition and Aesthetics in the Modern Social Order*. Cambridge: Polity.

Lichtblau, K. (1999) 'Differentiations of Modernity' *Theory, Culture and Society* 16(3): 1–30.

Lovell, T. (2000) 'Thinking Feminism With and Against Bourdieu' *Feminist Theory* 1(1): 11–32.

Martin, E. (1994) *Flexible Bodies: Tracking Immunity in American Culture – From The Days of Polio to the Age of AIDS*. Boston MA: Beacon Press.

May, T. (1998) 'Reflexivity in the Age of Reconstructive Social Science' *International Journal of Social Research Methodology* 1(1): 7–24.

McDowell, L. (1997) *Capital Culture: Gender at Work in the City*. Oxford: Blackwell.

McNay, L. (1999) 'Gender, Habitus and the Field: Pierre Bourdieu and the Limits of Reflexivity' *Theory, Culture and Society* 16(1): 95–117.

McNay, Lois (2000) *Gender and Agency: Reconfiguring the Subject in Feminist and Social Theory*. Cambridge: Polity.

Painter, J. (2000) 'Pierre Bourdieu' in M. Crang and N. Thrift (eds) *Thinking Space*. London and New York: Routledge.

Pellizzoni, L. (1999) 'Reflexive Modernity and Beyond: Knowledge and Value in the Politics of Environment and Technology' *Theory, Culture and Society* 16(4): 99–125.

Postone, M., E. LiPuma and C. Calhoun (1993) 'Introduction: Bourdieu and Social Theory' in C. Calhoun, E. Lipuma and M. Postone (eds) *Bourdieu: Critical Perspectives*. Chicago: The University of Chicago Press.

Pringle, R. (1998) *Sex and Medicine: Gender, Power and Authority in the Medical Profession*. Cambridge: Cambridge University Press.

Probyn, E. (1993) *Sexing the Self: Gendered Positions in Cultural Studies*. London and New York: Routledge.

Rose, N. (1990) *Governing the Soul: The Shaping of the Private Self*. London and New York: Routledge.

Skeggs, B. (1997) *Formations of Class and Gender: Becoming Respectable*. London: Sage.

Shilling, C. (2001) 'Embodiment. Experience and Theory: In Defence of the Sociological Tradition' *Sociological Review* 49(3): 327–344.

Shusterman, R. (ed) (1999) *Bourdieu: A Critical Reader*. Oxford: Blackwell.

Vitellone, N. (2002) '"I think it more of a white persons kind of awareness": condoms and the making of a white nation in media representations of safer (hetero)sex' *Feminist Media Studies* 2(1): 19–36.

Weiss, G. (1999) *Body Images: Embodiment as Intercorporeality*. London and New York: Routledge.

Williams, S. (1995) 'Theorising Class, Health and Lifestyles: Can Bourdieu Help Us?' *Sociology of Health and Illness* 17(5): 577–604.

Anamnesis and amnesis in Bourdieu's work: The case for a feminist anamnesis

Anne Witz

Introduction

Feminists tend on the whole to 'selectively appropriate' (Moi, 1999) elements of the Bourdieun conceptual armoury in order to inform an analysis of gender and of its relationship to class. These elements most commonly comprise the concepts of capitals (Reay, 1998; Skeggs, 1997), symbolic violence (Krais, 1995; McNay, 2000; Moi, 1999), habitus (Krais, 1995; Lovell, 2000, 2003) and field (McNay, 2000). There is something approaching an emerging consensus amongst some feminist commentators that the Bourdieun concept of gender habitus is a potentially fertile one for feminist theory (Krais, 1995; Lovell, 2000, 2003; McNay, 2000; Moi, 1999). Rarely, however, do feminists buy into Bourdieu's own analysis of masculine domination (Bourdieu, 1990b, 2001), preferring instead to distance themselves from this work (see for example Krais, 1995; Lovell, 2000). Whilst there is nothing necessarily reprehensible about this strategic use of Bourdieun theory by feminists, Bourdieu's own analysis of masculine domination deserves more scrutiny.

In his sustained, book length study of *Masculine Domination* (2001) Bourdieu aims to effect an *anamnesis* of the hidden constants of androcentrism, particularly what he terms the androcentric unconscious. Effecting such an anamnesis entails using his Kabyle fieldwork from the 1950s and 1960s as the means of accessing traces and fragments of an androcentric unconscious, thereby reappropriating 'a knowledge (*connaisance*) both possessed and lost from the beginning' (2001:55). In *The Logic of Practice* (1990a), written 20 years earlier, he similarly returned to his Kabyle material, but this time to effect an anamnesis of the hidden constants of his own intellectual labour since his Algerian days because, as he acknowledged, this labour tends 'to remove its own traces' (Bourdieu, 1990a:1).

Here I shall argue that, before we can selectively appropriate and put elements of Bourdieu's conceptual armoury safely to use within feminist analysis, we similarly need to effect a *feminist anamnesis* of the hidden constants of Bourdieu's own thinking on the gender habitus. Such a feminist anamnesis involves the recovery of traces and fragments of Bourdieu's *own* hidden anthropological labour of intellectual construction, particularly a dubious anthropology of gender.

A feminist anamnesis reveals, amongst other things, how Bourdieu's concept of habitus is forged out of both a phenomenological *and* an anthropological labour of construction, although traces of the latter have tended to be erased. A feminist anamnesis is of relevance, then, not only to feminist debates about the utility of Bourdieu's theory, but also to more general debates concerning the ability of Bourdieu's theory of practice, with its conceptual centrepiece of habitus, to either theorise agency (eg Butler, 1997, 1999; Calhoun, 1995) or embody sociology (eg Crossley, 2000, 2001; Howson & Inglis, 2001).

Anthropological and phenomenological labours of intellectual construction in Bourdieu's work

A more careful scrutiny of Bourdieu's *Masculine Domination* (2001) reveals more than simply a less than satisfactory analysis of male domination in contemporary society or a cavalier treatment of contemporary feminist theory, which are the grounds on which this work is normally criticised by feminists. Bourdieu's tendency to overstate the doxic order of gender relations is a point well made (see Lovell, 2000; McNay, 2000; Mottier, 2002). I want to probe this tendency further and move closer towards identifying the roots of those elements of Bourdieun analysis that feminists find irritating. I distinguish between two labours of intellectual construction underpinning Bourdieu's gender analytic and, more diffusely throughout all his works, the concept of habitus. One is anthropological. The other is phenomenological. My focus here is on the anthropological labour of construction because this is particularly fateful for Bourdieu's understanding of gender.

By effecting an anamnesis of the anthropological labour of construction we find those vestiges of canonical structuralism with its foundational gender binaries that Margolis (1999) alerts us to in Bourdieu's thought. The traces and fragments of this anthropological labour of construction compromise not only his analysis of masculine domination but also potentially, as Margolis (1999) cautions, his entire sociology with its conceptual centrepiece, habitus. Some grist to the mill of Margolis's contention is provided by a feminist anamnesis, which reveals how the intellectual labour of construction of the concept of habitus combines and condenses a phenomenology of embodiment, on the one hand, and a structuralist anthropology of specifically gendered embodiment, on the other. Traces of its anthropological labour of construction are clearly evident in *The Logic of Practice* (1990a), where it is the gender binaries which saturate the Kabyle world view that provide Bourdieu with the substantive material that he finds so good to think with to elaborate his powerful analysis of the bodily incorporation of the durable dispositions of the habitus and the very definition of habitus as 'embodied history' (1990a:56). Yet these traces of an anthropological labour of construction, replete with foundational gender binaries, are subsequently erased by Bourdieu and his commentators, for whom the concept of habitus becomes mired, to all intents and purposes, in an exclusively phenomenological labour of intellectual construction.

Bourdieu and his readers, then, have selectively removed traces of Bourdieu's own intellectual labour of construction of the concept of habitus, effecting an *amnesis* of the anthropological labour of its construction. As the concept that reigns the body in from the edges of the social to place it at its very core, generating an embodied ontology of social being, it is applauded (or criticized) primarily insofar as it is a concept mired in phenomenological philosophy (eg Crossley, 2000, 20001; Dreyfus & Rabinow, 1995; Howson & Inglis, 2001). Its miring in a dubious anthropology of gender that relies heavily on binary structuralism is rarely confronted or even noted, the major exceptions here being Margolis (1999) and feminist Bourdieun's, notably Fowler (1997), Krais (1995), Moi (1999) and Mottier (2002).

In *The Logic of Practice* (1990a) Bourdieu undertakes a labour of reconstruction of his own intellectual labour by 'doubling-back' to the point where he started – to the Kabyle material and his Algerian days. Likewise, a feminist anamnesis of the hidden constants of Bourdieu's intellectual labour can be done by doubling-back from Bourdieu's later texts such as *Pascalian Meditations* (2000) and *Masculine Domination* (1990b, 2001) to *The Logic of Practice* (1990a) written 20 years earlier. Claims made in *The Logic of Practice* (1990a) are reiterated 20 years later in *Masculine Domination* (2001) and these are of particular interest from the point of view of a feminist anamnesis, for these are traces and fragments of Bourdieu's own androcentrism. Here I focus on two aspects of the hidden anthropological labour of construction. One is a methodological constant concerning the standpoint of the knower and the necessity for reflexivity, whilst the other is an analytical constant to be found in Bourdieu's reliance on the notion of the collective androcentric unconscious.

The anthropological labour of construction:
from *The Logic of Practice* (1990a) to *Masculine Domination* (2001)
and *Pascalian Meditations* (2000)

In *The Logic of Practice* Bourdieu declares that anthropology or ethnology is a 'particularly powerful form of socio-analysis' (1990a:146). Yet he is also keenly alert to the *dangers* of ethnology in so far as the ethnological description of practices can be construed as essentialist, whilst its thick description of these practices could be seen to be simply reinforcing racist representations. Ethnologists, then, must maintain a constant vigilance to mitigate reinforcing racist representations and justifying the colonial order which amount to 'a particularly scandalous form of ethnocentrism' for Bourdieu (1990a:3). This discussion occurs in the context of Bourdieu's retrospective contextualisation of his Kabyle material within what he himself describes as the highly *emotional* (Bourdieu, 1990a:2) intellectual and political context of doing ethnology, albeit tempered with the new scientific humanism of Levi-Strauss's structuralist anthropology, in the Algeria of the late fifties and early sixties. Nonetheless, the power of ethnology is boldly re-asserted in *Masculine Domination* (2001) whilst the dangers of naive ethnocentrism that accompany its careless use in *colonialist* political and intellectual contexts are claimed by Bourdieu to be obviated in *feminist* political and intellectual contexts. This is because Bourdieu believes that he is just being brave enough to tell it *as it is* although he might *seem* to be reinforcing sexist representations of women. Bourdieu's work *Masculine Domination* (2001) thus warrants further scrutiny. Thus in his analysis of masculine domination, ethnology is the methodological constant of nearly half a century, running as it does all the way from Algeria, through *The Logic of Practice* (1990a) to *Masculine Domination* (2001). Ethnology is highly symptomatic of Bourdieu's anthropological labour of construction of the concept of gender habitus. Bourdieu does seem to have learnt one thing from his own critical reflections on its political dangers in *The Logic of Practice* (1990a), which is the need to *pre-empt* the same criticisms being made by feminists of his use of this very same method (and indeed Kabyle material) to analyse masculine domination at the end of 20th century.

The collective androcentric unconscious is another hidden constant. In *Masculine Domination* (2001) Bourdieu sets about recovering fragments and traces of this, ie, effecting his anamnesis of its hidden constants. This he does by evoking ethnological descriptions of the Kabyle androcentric world view immediately followed by evocations of gender binaries similarly at work in contemporary society. It is this hidden *anthropological labour of construction* that renders Bourdieu's analysis in *Masculine Domination* (2001) so seriously deficient. It is the constant slippage backwards and forwards between anthropological and sociological registers that produces a contradictory work, at one and the same time demonstrating the indubitable utility of Bourdieun concepts for an analysis of the contemporary gender order, whilst littered with arbitrary and irritating interruptions drawn from his Kabyle ethnology.

Bourdieu and the feminists

In *Masculine Domination* (2001), as well as *Pascalian Meditations* (2000), Bourdieu treats feminist writers in much the same way as he treats all writers – in a thoroughly self-serving manner (see Robbins, 2002). If there's a dualism to be obviated, a binary to be busted, or a scholastic dilemma to be resolved, then Bourdieu's your man. If there's bad news, then you can be sure that Bourdieu's got the good news. Feminism, it seems, has generated more than its fair share of scholastic dilemmas and mistaken beliefs.

In *Pascalian Meditations* (2000) Bourdieu has bad news for feminists, which is that they are mistaken in thinking that the power of reason can make any serious dent in the symbolic machinery of male dominance – so consciousness-raising was a politically naive strategy (Bourdieu, 2000:180, 172). This is because masculine domination is a symbolic form of domination *par excellence* and submission to the doxic order of genders is secured through symbolic violence, which has the qualities of a social super-glue, durably and deeply inscribing schemes of perception and appreciation in the bodies of the dominated. Symbolic violence cannot be overcome with the weapons of consciousness and will (Bourdieu, 2000:172; 2001:39). The weapon of reason with which feminists arm themselves cannot wake women from their 'doxic slumber' (Bourdieu, 2000:173). This is only effective against wrongheaded Kantian notions of cognitive structures as forms of consciousness. But the goods news is that Bourdieu has what feminism lacks and needs: 'a dispositional theory of practices' (Bourdieu, 2000:172).

In the meantime, Bourdieu has more bad news for feminists. This is that one of the most powerful mechanisms maintaining the symbolic order of masculine domination is *twofold naturalization* which 'combines and condenses two operations: it legitimizes a relationship of domination by embedding it in a biological nature that is itself a naturalized social construction' (Bourdieu, 2001:23). Mercifully, however, Bourdieu has a weapon that makes it 'theoretically possible to neutralize the effects of naturalization' (Bourdieu, 2000:182). This weapon is historicization. The snag, though, is that it may not actually be very effective in the face of that devious, epistemological smokescreen which the process of naturalization triggers in order to render itself immune from critical attack. This epistemological smokescreen consists of 'presuppositions and limitations on thought which, being embedded in the body, are beyond the reach of consciousness' (Bourdieu, 2000:181). Consequently we are all caught in something of an epistemological double-bind because:

> Being included, as man or women, in the object that we are trying to comprehend, we have embodied the historical structures of the masculine order in the form of unconscious schemes of perception and appreciation (Bourdieu, 2001:5).

A number of male thinkers, including 'even the most alert of analysts (Kant, Freud, Sartre and even Lacan)'(Bourdieu, 2001:115), are cited as guilty of unreflexively drawing on the gendered unthought, using as the instruments of knowledge the very schemes of perception and thought that ought to be treated as objects of knowledge. Significantly, though, Bourdieu does not indict himself but instead prides himself on exercising an unusual degree of *reflexivity* in his analysis of masculine domination.

Bourdieu also seems to think that he has made a better job of engaging with the problem of masculine domination than feminists have. Whilst the ability of male thinkers to think outside of patriarchal categories of understanding is dubious, the tendency of feminists to let their politically interested stance get in the way of an appropriately 'reflexive analysis' and to produce 'bad science' is regrettable (Bourdieu, 2001:113–117). The relationship of 'sympathetic externality' to his subject matter that Bourdieu arrogates to himself grants him precisely the kind of appropriately reflexive engagement that somehow eludes feminists, who eschew 'the real' and instead produce idealized representations of the oppressed. In short, feminist objectivity is compromised because they are afraid that by documenting the negative effects of domination they would appear '. . . to justify the established order by bringing to light the properties through which the dominated (. . .), as domination has made them, may contribute to their own domination' (Bourdieu, 2001:114). This discussion is characteristically self-serving, as Bourdieu is pre-emptively striking back at feminist criticism of his analysis of symbolic violence with its compliant, slumbering women for blaming the victim by shifting the burden of responsibility for women's oppression from men to women themselves (Bourdieu, 2001:114–5).[1] He is mobilizing an epistemological justificatory strategy in order to pre-empt criticism of how his ethnological methodology predisposes him to thick description, the danger of which (as he is perfectly aware) is to be seen to be reinforcing sexist representations of the dominated 'as domination as made them'.

So women are deep in a doxic slumber, feminists are misguided, and male thinkers are epistemologically lazy. Yet Bourdieu can claim a special relationship to all that he surveys – sympathetic externality, as well as a particular mode of engagement with his subject matter – a reflexive one. It is *reflexivity* that clears the epistemological fog of androcentrism, whilst historical critique or historicization is the 'major weapon of reflexivity' (Bourdieu, 2000:181). What you would never guess from Bourdieu's epistemological justificationary strategy is that, since the 1980s, feminists have been busily debating whether there are distinctive epistemological *standpoints* so as to render male, female and feminist knowers more or less enthralled or enchanted by schemes of perception and appreciation or categories of knowledge that derive from an androcentric world-view *and* whether or not it is necessary to *embody* knowers (Harding, 1986; Rose, 1994). Bourdieu simply bypasses these debates.

In *Masculine Domination* (2001) Bourdieu deploys his historicist weapon to reach those aspects of androcentrism that women are blissfully unaware of, feminists have misrecognised and male thinkers just wouldn't even think of looking for.[2] The historical labour of dehistoricization obscures the process of two-fold naturalization referred to above. In particular, it obscures the operations of symbolic power and violence that convert 'as if by magic' a social law into an embodied law, working on and through the body by depositing dispositions 'like springs, at the deepest level of the body' (Bourdieu, 2001:38). Thereby women are lulled into a state of 'enchanted submission'. By using his magical reflexivity to 'reconstruct the history of the historical labour of dehistoricization' (Bourdieu, 2001:82), ie, by revealing as socially constructed that which is magically contrived to appear natural, Bourdieu becomes a highly reflexive *sorcerer*.

Bourdieu the sorcerer

Bourdieu himself seems equally enchanted by the *permanence* of masculine domination. His sorcery becomes particularly evident when he conjures up *as if by magic* the notion of as androcentric unconscious (Bourdieu, 2001:5, 54) to

216

account for its obduracy. At first sight, to resort to a notion of a collective unconscious appears somewhat curious for a theorist who will have no truck with Freudian psychoanalytic theory. Bourdieu reassuringly insists that the androcentric unconscious is an historical unconscious '. . . linked not to a bio-logical or psychological nature, like the difference between the sexes according to psychoanalysis, but to a specifically historical labour of construction . . .' (Bourdieu, 2001:45). Yet it does still seem akin to a Jungian collective uncon-scious when Bourdieu refers to 'the infinitesimal traces and scattered fragments of the androcentric worldview' (Bourdieu, 2001:54). Equally, it belies traces of a Levi-Straussian structuralism.

How, then, is Bourdieu to access these traces and fragments? The meth-odological tool chosen by Bourdieu in order to construct what he terms his 'ar-chaeological history of the androcentric unconscious' (Bourdieu, 2001:54) is ethnological description. He treats ethnographic analysis of Kabyle society as the basis of a 'socioanalysis of the androcentric unconscious' (Bourdieu, 2001:5). By looking at a society entirely saturated with and constructed around an androcentric worldview, Bourdieu claims to reappropriate a knowledge both possessed and lost from the beginning, effecting an anamnesis of the hidden constants of androcentrism. So Bourdieu's analysis of masculine domination, like his reading of Virginia Wolf's *To The Lighthouse*, is conducted 'with an eye informed by the Kabyle vision' (Bourdieu, 2001:5 fn. 1). His analysis of the doxic gender order of Kabyle society – 'a particularly well-preserved androcentric society' (Bourdieu, 2001:vii) – furnishes him with the methodological and ana-lytical tools through which he claims to understand what might be called the deep structure of gender relations today – ie 'the best concealed aspects of what those relations are in the economically most advanced societies' (Bourdieu, 2001:vii). The effect of this is that Bourdieu fails to shift from an anthropolog-ical or ethnological to a sociological register in his analysis of gender relations and masculine domination. A Kabyle tunnel vision truncates Bourdieu's grasp of the complexities of the modern gender order in differentiated, as distinct from relatively undifferentiated, societies such as the Kabyle.

If, as he suggests in *The Logic of Practice* (1990a), he was 'haunted' by the 'hyperbolic realization of all male fantasies' discernible in Kabyle society, then in *Masculine Domination* (2001) he seems to have become enchanted by the Kabyle world view, which predisposes him to see continuity and permanence, to overstate the doxic order of gender, and to underestimate not only the histori-cization or changing structure of male dominance but also its modern day, het-erodoxic features (Moi, 1999; Lovell, 2000; McNay, 1999, 2000; Mottier, 2002).[3] Although noting forces for change that 'help to break the doxa and expand the space of what is possible' (Bourdieu, 2001:85), Bourdieu is continually over-whelmed by the permanence of the symbolic order of genders and its durably doxic qualities. Symptomatic of this is Bourdieu's insistence that, whatever women's position in social space and notwithstanding their newly-won rights of participation in a variety of social fields where men have traditionally played their competitive games of honour, simply being a woman entails a diminution of symbolic capital as women continue to be 'separated from men by a negative symbolic coefficient' (Bourdieu, 2001:93). The problem here is with the overemphasis on the doxic order of genders, *not* with the analysis of homologies between gendered practices and logics of practice in social fields, which is a fruitful line of analysis for feminists.

Neither is the problem to do with what is indeed an astute recognition of the symbolic order of masculine domination. It has more to do with how Bourdieu's truncated Kabyle vision continually predisposes him to *overstate* his point. For example, he declares that 'In fact, it is not exaggerated to compare masculinity to a nobility' (Bourdieu, 2001:60). Well, actually, it *is*, especially when Bourdieu propels us back to Kabyle material to underscore this point. Furthermore, the slippage between anthropological and sociological registers is evident here as he then segues into an almost entirely speculative analysis of gender struggles over labour market skills in modern industrial society. This analysis is oblivious to modern feminist work which has not only *historicized* the relation between gender and skill but also demonstrated how this relation has been a contested one and the site of struggle*s* that *secured*, in the terms of Bourdieu's own theory, homologies between the dispositions of a gender habitus and position in a social field (see Cockburn, 1983; Phillips and Taylor, 1986; Pringle, 1998; Walby, 1986; Witz, 1992). Moreover, the text *Masculine Domination* is littered with arbitrary evocations of gender binaries – the analytical force of which is little more than a 'here's a binary I prepared earlier'.[4] For example, when talking of body parts and their valuation, Bourdieu observes how men tend to be critical of parts of their bodies that are 'two small', whilst women tend of be critical of parts of their bodies that are 'too big'. It seems to me that, in the age of cosmetic surgery, *breasts* throw a spanner in the works of *this* particular gender binary – or at least confound our ability to evoke gender binaries so straightforwardly.[5]

A feminist anamnesis, then, reveals how traces and fragments of the Kabyle thought style litter *Masculine Domination* (2001). Ethnology and the concept of the androcentric unconscious are two traces or fragments that belie a hidden anthropological labour of construction that underpins his gender analytic.

Some comments on gender, habitus and bodies in Bourdieu

At the centre of Bourdieu's 'dispositional theory of practices' is the notion of embodied dispositions. This term is currently being burdened with far too much meaning. We need to be alert to the different registers in which Bourdieu evokes bodies and the anthropological and phenomenological labours of construction that underpin these. I would argue that, although Bourdieu may invoke the particular example of gendered bodies in the context of discussions of habitus conducted in a phenomenological register, often to underscore the point of the deep and durable inculcation of the dispositions of the habitus in bodies and implying at the same time that this is *particularly* so in the specific case of gender, it is traces of an anthropological labour of construction that are driving this idea of the particularly deep or durable investment of gender in bodies.

It is this combination and condensation of a phenomenology of embodiment, on the one hand, and a structuralist anthropology of specifically gendered embodiment, on the other, that I think makes a feminist sociological appropriation of the Bourdieun concept of habitus so difficult. Traces of the labour of structuralist anthropology in constructing the concept of habitus are, to all intents and purposes, removed or downplayed from Bourdieu's later reiterations of the concept of habitus and its relation to field, having been displaced by a phenomenological labour of construction. Whilst we can welcome Bourdieu's use of the phenomenological concept of habitus to reign the body in from the edges of the social and place it at its very core, populating the sociological imaginary with mindful bodies or embodied agents, nonetheless, we must also exercise caution with respect to Bourdieu's bodies, especially insofar as vestiges of structuralist anthropology might obfuscate the relation between the cognitive and the corporeal aspects of embodied dispositions.[6] Here we must be particularly alert to the tendency of structuralist binary taxonomies underscoring classificatory operations to be referentially grounded, in the last instance, in a binary of binaries: bodies, notably anatomically differentiated male and female bodies. This becomes abundantly clear in the following quote from *The Logic of Practice*:

> The division of sexual labour, transfigured in a particular form of the sexual division of labour, is the basis of the *di-vision* of the world the most solidly established of all collective – that is, objective – illusions. Grounded first in biological differences, in particular those that concern the division of work of procreation and reproduction, it is also grounded in economic differences, in particular those which derive from the opposition between labour time and production time and which are the basis of the division of labour between the sexes (Bourdieu, 1990a:146).

The problems with this binary thinking become acute in delineating the relation between the cognitive and the corporeal in the case of the embodied dispositions of the *gender* habitus. Although practices are necessarily embodied, it seems as if reflexive practices, for example, are heavily mindful (Adkins, 2003) whilst gender practices are heavily corporeal.

It seems to me that the concept of *symbolic violence* becomes central to Bourdieu's own attempt to rid his thinking of the vestiges of binary structuralism vis-à-vis gender, and thereby remove its traces from both his general sociology and his analysis of masculine domination. He therefore uses the symbolic to do the work of gender differentiation and domination and, I would argue, to mask any residual naturalistic evocations of male and female bodies. In his later works, however, he evokes a particularly embodied depth to the symbolic operations of masculine domination compared to other forms of symbolic domination, referring to 'the paradoxical logic of male domination, the form par excellence of symbolic domination, and of female submission . . .' (Bourdieu, 2000:170–71). Here Bourdieu is distinguishing masculine domination from other *relatively less somatized* power relations. Ostensibly removing traces of his own binary structuralism, he evokes the operations of a 'twofold naturalization' as one of the most powerful elements in the operation of all forms of symbolic power, which inscribes the social in things *and* in bodies (Bourdieu, 2000:181), thereby constituting the dominating or dominated habitus (for both parties are equally enchanted by the operations of symbolic power). This is a solidly social constructionist view of gendered embodiment along with all forms. And it is a view of gendered embodiment that Bourdieu strives to articulate and struggles to hang onto in *Masculine Domination* (2001, see especially 9–33) where he rehearses the familiar social constructionist view which seeks to evacuate the bodies of gender of any lingering vestiges of biological determinism, essentialism or naturalism. Yet his social constructionist analysis of gender is continually interrupted by the re-emergence of the hidden anthropological labour of construction, such as in his extended discussion of the collective androcentric unconscious with its heavy miring in structuralist anthropology.

As I have already argued, it is this 'doubling-back' to the anthropological register of the specifically gender habitus that makes *Masculine Domination* (2001) such an unsatisfactory work of sociology. If we pause on our journey between *The Logic of Practice* (1990a) and the later works, *Pascalian Meditations* (2000) and *Masculine Domination* (2001) to take in *Distinction* (1984), then it is instructive how here Bourdieu does not double back to his anthropological material to articulate the concept of *class habitus* with its 'class bodies', which are instead theorised and substantiated through (for its time) contemporary data on consumption practices in France. In *Distinction* (1984) we find the most straightforwardly sociological purchase on bodies as not simply the taken-for-granted fleshly 'shell' of a disposition, as in phenomenology, but as actually existing, fleshly manifestations of cultural and social practices that materialize class specific bodily *hexis* and, at the simplest level, leave their traces on our corporeality – our body size, shape, level of fitness, ways of walking and eating, health chances and so on. It is here in *Distinction* (1984) that Bourdieu provides a sociological handle on *the bodies we are* and the processes whereby these have materialized in specific and discernible ways within the context of social and symbolic practices. These are the bodies that have social roots, social lives and social consequences. These are not the embodied dispositions evoked at the level of abstraction of phenomenological philosophy (Howson and Inglis, 2001) to delineate the necessarily embodied social agent. Rather these are the embodied dispositions of social actors, the lived, practically accomplished bodies of everyday practices.

I think it is telling that the concept of *somatization* assumes more prominence in Bourdieu's concept of the gender habitus. Thus when discussing masculine domination Bourdieu will talk repetitively of a *somatization* of the social relations of domination (2001:23) whilst it would appear that the concept of *materialization* drives his analysis of the class habitus and classed bodies. Hence in *Distinction* Bourdieu states, for example, 'that the body is the most indisputable materialization of class taste' (Bourdieu, 1984:190). We might see the concept of the materialization of class bodies as signalling how these emerge *out of practices*. Hence social and cultural practices leave their mark on (or inscribe) bodies.[7] The concept of somatization, however, although this is by no means used exclusively in relation to the gender habitus, evokes more of a feeling that gender practices are always, already heavily *mired in bodies*. This general tendency of Bourdieu to mire gendered dispositions too deeply in bodies *per se* suggests caution in the face of claims (Krais, 1995; McNay, 2000) that Bourdieu's key contribution to feminist theory is that he somatizes gender relations.

Conclusion

As Margolis (1999) has cautioned, Bourdieu grounds and might indeed be *risking* his entire sociology on a deep, generative binarism of the sexes, which in this chapter I have suggested becomes particularly evident if we 'double-back' to *The Logic of Practice* (1990a) with its miring in Kabyle material. So *is* this acceptable or not? Or is it only feminist Bourdieuns who need to worry away at this, whilst general Bourdieuns circulate Bourdieun theory amongst themselves, conveniently overlooking its vestiges of canonical structuralism and its lingering commitment to foundational binaries between the sexes?

I have argued here that we do need to be alert to the vestiges of canonical structuralism which can be discerned in what I have termed an anthropological labour of construction. I have suggested further that feminist appropriation of Bourdieun sociology will be facilitated by first effecting an anamnesis of this hidden anthropological labour of construction in Bourdieu's work generally, but particularly when he mobilises illustrative examples that turn on gendered embodiedness or addresses the topic of masculine domination.

Hence if we harbour ambitions to make productive use of the Bourdieun conceptual armoury for feminist analysis then we must first recover and dispense with the traces and fragments of Bourdieu's own androcentric world view, of which his enchantment with his Kabyle material is, as I have argued, symptomatic. Such a feminist anamnesis reveals how Bourdieu adopts precisely the same methodological procedures in *Masculine Domination* (2001) as he did in Algeria nearly half a century earlier and how his reflections on the dangers of ethnocentrism, racism and essentialism that accompany ethnological description do not prevent him from applying exactly these same methodological tools to the study of masculine domination 20 years after *The Logic of Practice* (1990a) and nearly half a century on from the heady days of Algerian fieldwork and political struggle. The sensitivity he shows to the political dangers of ethnocentrism in the context of mid 20th century colonial anthropology is not matched by a similar sensitivity to the political dangers of sexism in the context of late 20th century feminist sociology.

One of my main points of contention in this chapter has been that it is useful to make a distinction between anthropological and phenomenological labours of construction in the formation of Bourdieu's concept of habitus. Furthermore, it is necessary to be alert to a hidden anthropological labour of construction in Bourdieu's treatment of the specifically gender habitus. By doing so feminists might be able to better disentangle the good bits from the bad bits in Bourdieu, running with the former whilst dispensing with the latter.

Notes

1 Had Bourdieu taken the time to engage with Simone de Beauvoir's work, then he might also have drawn some comfort from the fact that she too describes the negative effects of domination, and has similarly come in for criticism from feminists for seemingly painting disparaging portraits of the female character. Bourdieu does note and draws some comfort from the fact that even feminists such as Catherine MacKinnon get accused of being condescending to women (Bourdieu, 2001:115).

2 See Probyn (1990) for an excellent discussion of the way in which the concept of misrecognition is problematic for feminist theory.

3 Running through from *The Logic of Practice* (1990a) to *Masculine Domination* (2001) is the claim concerning the truth of the collective androcentric unconscious. In the *Logic of Practice* (1990a) Bourdieu offers the following example of the potent demystificatory power of ethnology:

> ... it forces one, for example, to discover, in the hyperbolic realization of all male fantasies that is offered by the Kabyle world, the truth of the collective unconscious that also haunts the minds of anthropologists and their readers, male ones at least (Bourdieu, 1990a:146).

Here, the reader is automatically *assumed* to be male, an assumption belied by the hasty qualification 'male ones at least'. Yet a similar claim concerning the alleged 'truth of the collective unconscious' is made 20 years later in *Masculine Domination* (2001), a book that is far more likely to be consumed by feminist readers than those allegedly haunted male readers of *The Logic of Practice*.

4 Crossley (2000) also tends towards this binary thinking when discussing issues of gender and sexuality.

5 At another point, Bourdieu's (2001) Kabyle tunnel vision leads him to offer – as if he has discovered a hidden constant of the andocentric unconscious – an example of the constant *embodied* labour of gender dissymmetry in the Kabyle binary construction of the swelling of a (male) penile erection and a (female) stomach due to gestation. Now is this evoked to demonstrate how gender dissymmetry works through bodies *or* what biologically different bodies bring to gender dissymmetry? The former would be a Laqueurian reading of the discursive construction of the 'truth' of male and female bodies; the latter an example of the foundational binary of binaries evoked in *The Logic of Practice* (1990a).

6 For a more general argument regarding the problems inhering in the recuperation of bodies within sociology, see Witz, 2000.

7 See Hayles (1999) for a discussion of the distinction between inscription and incorporation which loosely corresponds to my distinction between how Bourdieu will treat the classed body on the one hand and the gendered body on the other.

References

Adkins, L. (2002) *Revisions: Gender and Sexuality in Late Modernity.* Buckingham and Philadelphia: Open University Press.

Adkins, L. (2003) 'Reflexivity: Freedom or Habit of Gender' *Theory, Culture and Society* 20(6): 21–42.

Bourdieu, P. (1984) *Distinction: A Social Critique of the Judgement of Taste.* London: Routledge.
Bourdieu, P. (1990a) *The Logic of Practice.* Cambridge: Polity Press.
Bourdieu, P. (1990b) 'La domination masculine' *Actes de la Recherche en Sciences Sociales* 84: 2–31.
Bourdieu, P. (2000) *Pascalian Meditations.* Cambridge: Polity Press.
Bourdieu, P. (2001) *Masculine Domination.* Cambridge: Polity Press.
Butler, J. (1997) *Excitable Speech: A Politics of the Performative.* London: Routledge.
Butler, J. (1999) 'Performativity's Social Magic' in R. Shusterman (ed.) *Bourdieu: A Critical Reader.* Oxford: Blackwell.
Calhoun, C. (1995) 'Habitus, Field and Capital: The Question of Historical Specificity' in C. Calhoun, E. LiPuma and M. Postone (eds) *Bourdieu: Critical Perspectives.* Cambridge: Polity.
Cockburn, C. (1983) *Brothers: Male Dominance and Technological Change.* London: Pluto Press.
Crossley, N. (2000) *The Social Body.* London: Sage.
Crossley, N. (2001) 'Embodiment and Social Structure: A Response to Howson and Inglis' *Sociological Review* 49(3): 318–26.
Dreyfus, H. and Rabinow, P. (1995) 'Can There Be a Science of Existential Structure and Social Meaning?' in C. Calhoun, E. LiPuma and M. Postone (eds) *Bourdieu: Critical Perspectives.* Cambridge: Polity Press.
Fowler, B. (1997) *Pierre Bourdieu and Cultural Theory: Critical Investigations.* London: Sage.
Hayles, N. K. (1999) *How We Became Posthuman: Virtual Bodies in Cybernetics, Literature, and Informatics.* Chicago, Ill.: The University of Chicago Press.
Harding, S. (1986) *The Science Question in Feminism.* Milton Keynes: Open University Press.
Howson, A. and Inglis, D. (2001) 'The Body in Sociology: Tensions Inside and Outside Sociological Thought' *The Sociological Review* 49(3): 297–317.
Krais, B. (1995) 'Gender and Symbolic Violence: Female Oppression in the Light of Pierre Bourdieu's Theory of Social Practice' in C. Calhoun, E. LiPuma and M. Postone (eds) *Bourdieu: Critical Perspectives.* Cambridge: Polity Press.
Lovell, T. (2000) 'Thinking Feminism With and Against Bourdieu' *Feminist Theory* 1(1): 11–32.
Lovell, T. (2003) 'Resisting with Authority: Historical Specificity, Agency and the Performative Self' *Theory, Culture and Society* 20(1): 1–17.
Margolis, J. (1999) 'Pierre Bourdieu: *Habitus* and the Logic of Practice' in R. Shusterman (ed.) *Bourdieu: A Critical Reader.* Oxford: Blackwell.
McNay, L. (1999) 'Gender, Habitus and the Field: Pierre Bourdieu and the Limits of Reflexivity' *Theory, Culture and Society* 16(1): 95–117.
McNay, L. (2000) *Gender and Agency.* Cambridge: Polity Press.
Moi, T. (1999) *What is a Woman? And Other Essays.* Oxford: Oxford University Press.
Mottier, V. (2002) 'Masculine Domination: Gender and Power in Bourdieu's Writings' *Feminist Theory* 3(3). 345–359.
Phillips, A. and Taylor, B. (1986) 'Sex and Skill' in Feminist Review (ed.) *Waged Work: A Reader.* London: Virago.
Pringle, R. (1998) *Sex and Medicine: Gender, Power and Authority in the Medical Profession.* Cambridge: Cambridge University Press.
Probyn, E. (1990) 'Travels in the Postmodern: Making Sense of the Local' in N. Fraser and L. Nicholson (eds) *Feminism/Postmodernism.* London: Routledge.
Reay, D. (1998) Class *Work: Mothers' Involvement in Children's Schooling.* London: University College Press.
Robbins, D. (2002) 'Sociology and Philosophy in the work of Pierre Bourdieu, 1965–1975' *Journal of Classical Sociology* 2(3): 299–328.
Rose, H. (1994) *Love, Power and Knowledge.* Cambridge: Polity Press.
Skeggs, B. (1997) *Formations of Class and Gender.* London: Sage.
Walby, S. (1986) *Patriarchy at Work.* Cambridge: Polity Press.
Witz, A. (1992) *Professions and Patriarchy.* London: Routledge.
Witz, A. (2000) 'Whose Body Matters?: Feminist Sociology and the Corporeal Turn in Sociology and Feminism' *Body & Society* 6(2): 1–24.

Shame in the habitus[1]

Elspeth Probyn

Introduction

It's September 11, 2002. I awake listening to the news. I'm in Australia, so we've arrived early to this day of memorializing. On the other side of the dateline, the rest of the world is preparing to deal with a welter of emotion. On the radio a somewhat incoherent man in New York talks about how he'll drink a lot of 'brewskis' tomorrow. The interviewer is sympathetic. Bodies do strange things under stress. They act out. Like plants, our bodies are tropic, and twist and turn in reaction to different stimuli. Think of those reports from New York of 'terror sex' and the surge of interest in singles' bars. All those bodies madly moving, seeking and turning to other bodies, like so many flowers orienting themselves towards the light. The warmth of another body, being held and holding – a momentary balm for frayed nerve endings. Bodies in embrace burning out the fear in the dim light of a bar.

Perhaps it worked for a while. But then bodies broke apart. Specialists in trauma tell us that trauma is the overwhelming feeling of too much feeling. 'Affect-flooding'[2] causes our bodies to want to shut down, to turn away. Too much feeling. Every minute change in stimulus causes the body to shift, and 'it moves as it feels and it feels itself moving' (Massumi, 2002:1). More movement, more feeling. Brian Massumi describes the way that 'the slightest, most literal displacement convokes a qualitative difference, because as directly as it conducts itself it beckons a feeling, and feelings have a way of folding into each other, resonating together, interfering with each other, mutually intensifying, all in unquantifiable ways apt to unfold again in action, often unpredictably' (2002:1).

So a tiny movement, perhaps so slight a shift that other parts of the body remain unaware, sets off sensors that register in feeling another feeling. It's all so small. The densely worded explanations defy meaning, squeeze it out. Or maybe meaning reappears in unfamiliar places.

In the world changed forever, feelings are thrown around blithely and they too cease to have much meaning. Ordinary people and men of distinction can only repeat the words. Writing in *The Guardian*, Jay McInerney, talks about his feelings of anger, depression, compassion and revenge. Edward Said speaks of fear, shock, horror, outrage and sorrow. What we don't get is any sense of what these words describe. What did they feel?[3]

It's an interesting paradox: for once, we all have free rein to talk of feelings, but the words don't mean much. Fear, compassion, sorrow, outrage – the words float off from any anchor. Our talk of feelings is vacuous revealing a void in our comprehension of the ways bodies are supposed to make meaning.

My concern here is not directly related to the events of September 11th. It is much smaller. Compared to that event, my objective is embarrassingly pedantic. I want to think about a way of talking about a modality of an emotion. The emotion that interests me is notable for its absence within all the talk of feelings. Shame was certainly not high on the list of the pro-American feelings, nor did the critics of the West, even as some cheered loudly express it.[4] Of course, it's hard to delineate strictly where one emotion ends and another starts. Anger and rage can be closely tied to shame, attempting to displace the more painful feeling of shame. Shame can also bleed into sorrow. Shame is born in interest.

What I'm calling white shame is a twist within emotion. It is also an affect, and I'll try to indicate why it is at times important to distinguish between the two. While I'll engage with analyses positioned on one side or the other, I'm more interested in how the theories, as well as the actual affects and emotions continuously inform each. I want to see whether distinct ideas and experiences can, like Massumi's description of feelings, fold into each other, resonate together, interfere with each other, and mutually intensify.

Rather than simply listing different approaches to emotions and affect, I'll use Bourdieu's concept of the habitus as a heuristic device to position emotion and affect. This is more than just a handy conceit. Bourdieu himself is rather vague on the place of emotion within the habitus. His attention to the physicality of the embodied habitus does, however, promise a way of thinking about emotion and affect as simultaneously social and physical. This attention to the feeling body, which is foregrounded by Marcel Mauss' use of the habitus, goes against much of the appropriation of Bourdieu's thought by those who now feel the need to make a passing reference to the body. This produces clunky uses of the body, that secure and promote the supremacy of other more 'serious' concerns. Such uses hastily move away from the body and onto surer matters. Bodies get lost in abstraction, including those of class or gender.[5] By using the concept of the habitus against and with radically other notions about the body, affect and emotion perhaps we can inject some life into it.

But first I turn to an example. I'll use it as a small instance of experimentation. It doesn't stand in for anything. It is idiosyncratic: etymologically, a private admixture; eccentric in the lines it may throw out. In Massumi's argument, 'experimentation activates detail', and the success of examples hinges on their detail (2002:18). Personally I don't think that stories can have too much detail, although perhaps theories can.

Getting to Uluru

As many will know, at the heart of Australia there's a big rock. It's really big, and sort of red. It is, apparently, the world's biggest monolith and made of arkosic sandstone. It's 9.4 km in circumference, 345 metres high, 3.6 km long and 2 km wide. It's thought to extend downwards several kilometres. Known still by some as 'Ayers Rock', its Aboriginal name Uluru has become increasingly common usage. It is symbolically central to many groups. Most legitimately, it is at the heart of the beliefs of the Anangu, the Aboriginal peoples who have lived in the vicinity of Uluru for some 22,000 years or more. It is also at the heart of white Australia's imagining of the country, although many have not been – it's an expensive enterprise to get to the Centre from the east coast where much of the population lives. This doesn't stop the masses of foreign tourists for whom 'Ayers Rock' is a central destination. They pique our envy as they flash around so easily our cut-price dollar.

The Anangu are now the legally recognized custodians of the rock and the park, and Uluru-Katajuta is a World Heritage cultural landscape, or more precisely 'an associate cultural landscape'. This testifies to 'the combined works of nature and of people, and manifesting the interaction between people and the natural environment'.[6] This recognition has been immensely important for the Anangu and for Aboriginal people more widely. The mainly Aboriginal Board of Management was also rewarded the 1995 UNESCO Picasso Gold Medal for their outstanding management and conservation. All of these awards do not stop a surprising number of tourists from respecting the Anangu's gentle request that people not climb the rock.

For the Anangu, Uluru is the site of the energy called Tjukurpa, a Pitjant-jatjara word that encompasses their history, religion and law. In the words of Yami Lester, the chair of the Uluru-Katajuta Board of Management, 'In the past some people have laughed and called it dreaming but that Tjukurpa is real, it's our law, our language and family together'.[7] The Tjukurpa can be said to map the relationships and the travels and activities of the ancestral beings who inhabit the land. Uluru is a busy place, with dozens of sacred sites both for women and men.

In the very dead of winter, we[8] made our way to Uluru. Elliot's phrase made us smile as we descended down from Darwin. The really hot days were behind us, and the sun would now be on our backs until we turned west at Alice Springs, 1600 kilometres south of Darwin. The rhythm of time changed slightly as we hit the Stuart Highway. In the back, against the bags, my feet out the window, my body slowed and became all eyes to take in the subtly changing landscape. 'Nature stops' and tea breaks gear-shifted the smooth flow of time and space. I wondered again and again at the marvel of a billy boiling in minutes, perched on a nest of twigs. The dryness is pervasive, the land yields up a sigh when I swat to pee. At night we sleep on foamies – a luxurious version of the swag, little rectangles under the stars.

We turned right at Alice and after stopping in the ghost-drenched former mission of Hermannsburg, continued onto a rough track through the Finke Gorge. The riverbed was a dry as could be, but debris from the last time it flooded was left high in the branches of the great river gums. The four-wheel drive clambered up and down sand dunes and rocks. Sometimes you could walk faster but I didn't want to leave the vehicle and my companions – it had subtly become home. It's easy to explain how such a radically different configuration could feel like home: a secure human and nonhuman capsule upon which my life depended. It's harder to know why it so displaced my real home. I caught those whiffs of feeling before thought sets in, when the reference of home would not compute: Sydney, Montreal, Naramatta, Llandewi; city, quartier, or Land Cruiser – how do we home in on home?

On the road to Uluru we found a track into the mulga and made camp far away from the noise of the big tourist buses. It was crepuscule, or as one of companions said in Australian, 'crepuscular'. Jack climbed a dune and came back to say that we could see the rock. The dark had fallen and by the light of the gas lamp I read my book. The rock could wait.

The next day we broke camp faster than usual. We had a destination. We had plans. For all that the image of the rock burned in my sense of Australia, I was less excited than my companions who had seen it many times before. Vague feelings of discomfort lingered as I sat in the back. Maybe I wouldn't like it, or worse, maybe I wouldn't have the right feeling. Could I read my novel if I got bored with Uluru?

After the undulations of the previous country, the land was undeniably flat. A wide-open flatness that does the heart good. And it's red, well more than red can convey. We drove with no sign of change to the land. How could something that big disappear, or fail to appear?

Then there it was. Awe-inspiring, mind-bogglingly there. Wow – a useless word; but Wow. Complying with a request from their daughter, my companions played her favourite song for the sighting of the rock: 'Beds are Burning' from Midnight Oil's *Diesel and Dust*. As we got closer – movement in slowed time – I breathed in an elation that seemed to be the result of a million things resonating. Then as I breathed out the quivering were transposed into sobs – great, big, ugly ones. Peter Garrett and the boys sang over them. The anthem of good white Australia dissipated out the window and into the red dust: 'The time has come to say fair's fair/To pay the rent, to pay our share/The time has come, a fact's fact/ It belongs to them, let's give it back' (1986).

Like a child I cried myself out and felt that sleepy, empty calm. In a daze I walked around the rock, registering somewhere its magnificence. We drove to Yulara, the Ayers Rock Resort, where I picked a fight with the white waitress. Our travels continued but I'll leave us there, filling the water tanks and picking up supplies. And I'll try to turn this travelogue into something that might resemble an academic discussion.

What struck me forcefully about my small cloudburst of emotion was the way in which it was seemingly a moment of pure affect. Struck by intensity my body acted, forming expressions that had really nothing to do with the awkward terms I could put upon them. My immediate cognitive thought, when I started thinking, was 'well wasn't that weird'. In the confined space of the car, my companions had been mostly unaware, and then seemingly unconcerned, or at least not in the way that people are concerned by expressions of sadness, grief, or anxiety. They hadn't caught any of those feelings, certainly not because they were unfeeling, but because my sobs were not of that order.

Another thought was: I'm not going to write about this. I have written through myself too much not to know the dangers of experimenting on and with oneself. Sometimes you inflict damage on yourself, and while there is certain heroism in dredging up pain, sometimes it just hurts. Part of the impetus of this chapter and of my forthcoming book (Probyn, 2005) is to recognize what we do when we plunge into affect: what, as writers, we do to our bodies, and what our writing may do to the bodies of our listeners and readers. I also know that attaching me to that moment is likely to meet with the usual reactions from serious scholars. Often it's sheer incomprehension, but equally it can be nervousness and embarrassment. Whatever its source or expression, a certain disdain can greet so-called personal writing. This feeling is catching, and too often my interlocutors' squeamishness brushes off on me and I feel ashamed of what I've done. Then there is a deeper sense of shame. The shame that writers very rarely speak about, because it is so shameful: the shame of being more interested in the writing than in its putative object.

I am, however, going to experiment with that moment. But in order to ease any feelings of queasiness, I'll now turn to the question of how various concepts of the body in emotion might help us understand the passage of affect.

Before I attend to some of the more recent theory on emotion and affect, let's review the salient aspects of Bourdieu's version of the concept of the habitus. His is, of course, not the only version and later I'll discuss Marcel Mauss' use of the term. For Bourdieu, the concept primarily seems to serve two functions. On the one hand, it is narrowly epistemological, and on the other it has a wider function within the epistemology of engaged sociology (*la sociologie engagée*). On the first level it is so narrowly epistemological that one could say that it is a methodological principle within Bourdieu's 'fieldwork in philosophy'. Here habitus serves to correct the two tendencies within the social sciences that Bourdieu spent much of his life fighting: objectivism, and more pointedly subjectivism. On this point, here is what he had to say in *The Logic of Practice*:

> [T]he concept of the habitus, which is predisposed by its range of historical uses to designate a system of acquired, permanent, generative dispositions, is justified above all by the false problems that it eliminates, the questions it enables one to formulate better or to resolve, and the specific scientific difficulties it gives rise to. (1990:53fn)

In this vein, the concept serves as an epistemological check and also as generative of its own possibilities. The concept provides a way out of the twin perils of objectivism which 'universalizes the theorist's relation to the object of science', and subjectivism which 'universalizes the experience that the subject of theoretical discourse has of himself as subject' (1990:45–6).

These philosophical/methodological arguments then coincide with the project of accounting for practical knowledge. Hear, for instance, in the following quotation the way in which habitus, as a warning to the researcher, shifts into habitus as generative:

> One has to situate oneself *within* "real activity" as such, that is in the practical relation to the world, the preoccupied, active presence in the world through which the world imposes its presence, with its urgencies, its things to be said and done, things made to be said, which directly govern words and deeds without ever unfolding as spectacle. (1990:52)

The critique of the underlying assumptions that structure the field and fieldwork have, of course, been made time and again – although it is always a little surprising to hear in the excited voice fresh from a stint of fieldwork how quickly acknowledgment of the critiques has vanished. As a tangent, perhaps we need to attend to the sources and mechanisms of that excitement, a project that Don Kulick (1995), amongst others, has suggestively raised.

But let us return to 'the infinite yet strictly limited generative capacity' of the concept (Bourdieu, 1990:55). Generative is an important term in Bourdieu's argument about what the habitus does (we'll leave aside for the moment that concepts are by their nature generative). The habitus as a description of lived realities is that which generates practices, frames for positioning oneself in the world, and indeed ways of inhabiting the world. And analytically it acts as an optic into that world. These two sides come together in his catchy phrasing of the habitus as 'a metaphor of the world of object, which is itself an endless circle of metaphors that mirror each other ad infinitum' (1990:76).

The way in which Bourdieu makes the habitus both an object of study and an analytic is repeated throughout his work. The search for a hinge, or for different hinges that will render evident the coinciding of the objective and subjective worlds of sociality is after all at the heart of the Bourdieusian enterprise. In one of the many lovely phrases that tend to get lost in his prose, Bourdieu states that 'the habitus – embodied history, internalized as second nature and so forgotten as history – is the active presence of the whole past of which it is the product' (1990:56). Elaborating on this, he argues that

> The habitus, a product of history produces individual and collective practices – more history – in accordance with the schemes generated by history . . . [the habitus] ensures the active presence of past experiences, which, deposited in each organism in the form of schemes of perception, thought and action, tend to guarantee the "correctness" of practices . . . more reliably than all formal rules and explicit norms. (1990:54).

In this way, and before the current resurgence of interest in how bodies are produced materially (which of course goes back at least to Marx), Bourdieu argues that institutions and privileges 'produce quite real effects, durably inscribed in belief' (1990:57).

There is, I think, something quite poignant about Bourdieu's insistence and his persistence in following through on this crucial insight. Finally, the concept of the habitus delivers a history that is 'both original and inevitable' (1990:57).

Poignant though this may be, Bourdieu does not wax lyrical about emotions. On one reading, he seems almost dismissive:

> Emotion . . . is a (hallucinatory) "presenting" of the impending future, which, as bodily reactions identical to those of the real situation bear witness, leads a person to live a still suspended future as already present, or even already past, and therefore necessary and inevitable – "I'm a dead man, "I'm done for" (1990:292fn).

Here emotion projects the habitus' tendency to continually frame and adjust between the unlikely (possibility) and the likely (probability). This can be clearly heard in Bourdieu's description of how 'agents "cut their coats according to their cloth" and so to become the accomplices of the processes that tend to make the probable a reality' (1990:65). In this depiction of the rather dour state of the habitus, emotion shades the process by which aspirations come to be severely tailored to reality. Either hallucinatory or fatalistic, emotion seems to return to haunt the body in its adjustment of anticipation to 'the present of the presumed world, the only one it can ever know . . .' (1990:65).

It's hard to categorize which emotion produces the statement, 'I'm done for'. At once it is the cry of fear. But equally it could express the realization that there's nothing left to fear but fear itself – a reaction to terror that paralyses. It's certainly not a positive feeling and in Bourdieu's scattered comments on emotion, there's not a lot of joy. The sense of emotion as anticipation/resignation before the worst is joined elsewhere by an aside to Freud's conception of hysteria. Hysteria, says Bourdieu, 'takes expressions literally, really feeling the heart-rending or the smack in the face to which the speaker refers to metaphorically' (1990:293fn). These are shocking examples. They summon a narrative of being heart-rended *and* smacked in the face. It's such a femininized tale of abuse. This is not to say that Bourdieu exclusively genders emotions as feminine, as the phrase and the emotive charge of 'I'm a dead man' demonstrates.

Nonetheless one wonders why Bourdieu has taken up this classic example of emotion that is located literally in the woman's womb – the *hustera*. Certainly being named as hysterical haunts women; that moment when a woman expresses emotion only to be dismissed as hysterical. Whether or not Bourdieu is imputing a sexual division of emotion, his example could not be more obviously rooted in the body. The implicit gendering of emotions in this example of hysteria becomes even more intriguing in relation to Bourdieu's discussion of how the 'fundamental oppositions of the social order . . . are always sexually overdetermined' (1990:72). He supports this with an example about the 'lowering or bending of the head or forehead as sign of confusion or timidity, and also shame and modesty'. His conclusion is: 'Male, upward movements and female, downward movements . . . the will to be on top, to overcome, versus submission.' It is '*as if* the body language of sexual domination and submission had provided the fundamental principles of both the body language and the verbal language of social domination and submission' (1990:72, my emphasis).

In this manner, the body's expressions – including that classic one of shame, the hanging the head – act as metaphor for the wider structures of social domination. Within this schema, emotions seem to act as synecdoche for the body. The body, these 'acts of bodily gymnastics', root 'the most fundamental structures of the group in the primary expressions of the body . . . as is clearly seen in emotion' (1990:71).

The role of emotion and where it is placed becomes somewhat clearer in Bourdieu's exposition of belief and the body. 'Practical belief', he argues, 'is a state of the body' (1990:68). Furthermore, 'enacted belief [is] instilled by the childhood learning that treats the body as a living memory pad' (1990:68). This learning ensures that values are 'made body', and instills a 'whole cosmology'. Belief – what he calls 'the almost miraculous encounter between the habitus and the field – is then crucially linked to emotion's role in animating the body. Emotion and bodily gymnastics are central to the fact that 'it is because agents never know completely what they are doing that what they do has more sense than they know' (1990:69). It is the simple act of 're-placing the body in an overall posture which recalls the associated thoughts and feelings' (1990:69). These acts of the body in emotion then are key to the work of symbolic capital, arguably the most valued of the forms of capital in Bourdieu's well-known theory of distinction:[9]

> Symbolic power works partly through the control of other people's bodies and belief that is given by the collectively recognized capacity to act in various ways on deep-rooted linguistic and muscular patterns of behaviour, either by neutralizing them or reactivating them to function mimetically' (1990:69).

From this encapsulated picture of where emotion fits into Bourdieu's world, it's clear that emotion is far from simple. Nor is it easily understood given the ways in which Bourdieu, more often than not, subsumes emotion to other concerns. To draw him out, emotion is part of the body's knowledge. In the body's privileged role as productive of practical sense, emotion seems to work to amplify or reduce instilled tendencies. However, given Bourdieu's vagueness about which emotion he is discussing, this description of emotion could be called affect. This is not semantic quibbling. Massumi, for instance, distinguishes affect as intensity and as 'irreducibly bodily and autonomic' from emotion, which he sees as 'subjective content, the sociolinguistic fixing of a quality of experience' (2002:28). Certainly in Bourdieu's description, emotion is not directly cognitive although its effects may initiate cognition.

This becomes more pointed in Bourdieu's argument about the role that mimeticism plays in the reproduction of any number of beliefs, structures, values – in short, in reproducing the habitus. And again, the role of emotion, while seemingly incidental, emerges as crucial:

> The body believes in what it plays at: it weeps if it mimes grief. It does not represent what it performs, it does not memorize the past, it *enacts* the past, bringing it back

to life. What is "learned by the body" is not something that one has, like knowledge that can be brandished, but something that one is (1990:73).

This idea of the body as what 'is' sits uneasily with Bourdieu's argument about 'hallucinatory' role of emotion. As we saw, emotion '"presents" an impending future'; it causes the body to adjust to the inevitability of the future as past. Bourdieu's phrasing of this is 'I'm a dead man', 'I'm done for'. Earlier I queried the resignation that this expresses – a sort of sociological equivalent of 'sod's law', things will go bad if they can. In this description, emotion presages and confirms finality of the habitus. To replay Bourdieu's description, the habitus produces a history that is both original and inevitable. In line with this, as exemplified in the above quotation, the body enacts the past. Listening carefully to the sequence of events described, the body feels, enacts an emotion, and then brings into being the past. It is therefore the feeling body which has the consequence of summoning the past – a spectral past as future.

In some regards this is quite plausible: it describes, for instance, the feeling of *déjà vu*. Where it is problematic, however, is in the ordering of feeling to emotion: the body mimes grief and it weeps. Here Bourdieu imputes cognition to the body, followed by feeling, or to use another language, emotion followed by affect. In this argument the body cannot brandish knowledge, but emotions can – they are ineluctably structured and structuring. While of course this is the very principle of the habitus, it rests on shaky ground. We might accept that emotion as fully socialized can play this role. But where does that leave the body's affective expressions? Sometimes we weep and are caught within grief and joy. The role of the habitus may well be to sort out that confusion, to reproduce the feeling of inevitability. However, there may also be times when the feeling shakes up the habitus; when the body outruns the cognitive capture of the habitus.

Maussian assemblages

In this way, Bourdieu's use of emotion seems to close down the possibilities for the body that his own theory authorizes. The separation of the feeling body and emotion, and the implicit role of the latter as a cognitive adjustment mechanism, conceptually means that the body is captured in and by the social. As I've mentioned, this is at odds with Bourdieu's admission of the physicality of the body, which he clumsily contains within a vaguely termed emotion. At the very least, this attests to a paucity of conceptual vocabulary with which to figure the different operations of the body with the habitus. At an important level, it tends to disembody the habitus, which is after all a crucial cornerstone in Bourdieu's theory.

I now turn to Marcel Mauss' use of the habitus which may clarify the issues at stake, and extend more clearly the nebulous role of emotion that I've described above. Mauss' attention to the physiological nature of the habitus provides another way of thinking about the feeling body, beyond it being always and already social, or inversely impossible to describe. While it seems that Bourdieu never explicitly took Mauss' work into the heart of his own, he was of course cognizant of Mauss' place in the field of French sociology. Bourdieu after all held the Chair of Sociology in the College de France which Mauss had occupied in 1930. Bourdieu also published three volumes of Mauss' work in his series, *Le sens commun*. As Marcel Fournier – Mauss' preeminent bibliographer – comments, Bourdieu seemed to find Mauss less rigid than Mauss' uncle, Emile Durkheim. In Fournier's estimation, there are several profound links between Mauss and Bourdieu especially in terms of their acute attention to the logic of practice and the rigorous understanding of the discipline and the role of the sociologist as politically engaged through sociological practice.[10] For all these connections, the linkages between Mauss and Bourdieu tend to go unattended. There is also little acknowledgement of Mauss' legacy and how it is reworked and 'straightened out' in Bourdieu's thought.

According to Wendy James (1998), Mauss was the first to coin habitus as a sociological concept. She also mentions that originally the term was used medically to describe the outward appearance of the face and the boy in relation to its internal state of health or sickness (1998:20). Habitus is an important tenet in Mauss' striving to comprehend 'l'homme total', a vision of a sociological accounting for totality that joins 'the local connectedness of form and content, . . . the tangible aspect of human life . . . in relation to the body and its material experience, the techniques of work, and the rhythmic enactment of ritual and symbolic performance' (James, 1998:15). Nathan Schlanger describes Mauss' work as 'a fieldwork of modernity' (1998.193), in which we can hear a precedent to Bourdieu's 'fieldwork in philosophy'. In Bruno Karsenti's description, Mauss' project concerned nothing less that 'an enquiry into the principles on which the human being is "assembled" . . . a reorientation of the conceptualization of the social' (1998:76).

As Mauss candidly put it, 'after having of necessity divided things up too much, sociologists must strive to reconstitute the whole . . . The study of the concrete, which is the study of completeness is possible' (1990:80). Mauss' challenge included the detailed analysis of the parts as well as the task of figuring how to make them re-connect. In some ways, it is totality from below, one that works through example and detail. For Mauss, it is through the triple analysis of the physiological, psychological, and the societal that one might arrive at an understanding of the total man. In this, the practical, living body was key: Through the body' physiology, 'the coordination of articulated motions by which it functions and by which it embodies and conveys meaning . . . these efficacious bodily acts [education, fashion, prestige] confirm the social nature of the *habitus*' (Schlanger, 1998:198–9).

Along with the sheer breadth of Mauss' project, there is also something very appealing about the man. In ways that must have been quite shocking at the time, and that remain refreshing, Mauss allowed for human foible within his sociology of humanity. That humans habitually do things wrong or clumsily, that our actions and techniques attest to trail and error, mistakes and sometimes plain stupidity was not only accepted by Mauss but often corroborated by examples from his own experience. In his exposition of body techniques, he recounts, for example, how his swimming techniques were a product of a time when 'swimmers thought of themselves as a kind of steamboat' (1979:99), and depicts himself pushing though the water spouting great streams of water. And what to say of a thinker who on presenting his work – and his challenge – to the *Société de psychologie*, remarks that he was inspired in his thoughts about swimming when he came into contact with someone 'whose initials I still know, but whose name I can no longer remember'. Apparently the article was excellent, but says Mauss, 'I have been too lazy to look it up' (1979:98).

While the mixture of the anecdotal, the accidental and the humorous may now be admitted within academic work (albeit grudgingly), for the time it seems incredible that a sociologist within the College de France, and Durkheim's nephew and enthusiast to boot, should be so cavalier. Equally, and less surprising, much of Mauss' ideas about the body and its techniques were infused with his experiences within the trenches of WWI. As is detailed in Fournier's biography, 'Besides his grief at the loss of friends and colleagues, Mauss also discussed the sentiments of fear and panic he had to endure, and his recognition of the physical and moral force of instinct, which animates or on the contrary discourages and isolates the individual during extreme moments' (in Schlanger, 1998:209fn).[11]

While Mauss was rather scathing about a theory of the emotions per se, he wasn't shy about using his own emotional experiences. For instance, in regards to the war he recalls how 'I have also experienced fear, and how it is reinforced by panic to the point that not only the group, but also the individual will itself, even the brute instinct of self-preservation, dissolve all at once' (1979:14). In response to psychological theories of sthenia and asthenia (courage or weakness towards life), Mauss refers again to the tripartite integration of the physiological-psychological-sociological. Within this complex, instinct is a driving force which in some regards exceeds man's symbolic capacities. Humans might communicate with symbols, but the only reason that we have symbols and can communicate with them is that we have instincts: 'The exaltations and ecstasies which create symbols are proliferations of instinct' (1979:16). As Karsenti argues, Mauss' conception of the connection between the corporeal and the psychic was 'not a causal relationship that keeps one outside the other' (1998:76). In relation to this body-psychic linkage, the social cannot be seen as merely that which is imposed or internalized. In the search to grasp the collective totality of our being, the social needs to be understood as 'truly internal, natural in the strong sense of the word' (Karsenti, 1998:77).

The striking thing about Mauss' model, along with its combination of strangeness and commonsense, is the way in which totality is understood through the intersection of quite distinctive singularities. When one aspect threatens to overtake the totality, Mauss then returns to it an autonomous yet articulated role. Hear, for example, the number of things going on in Mauss' description of totality.

> [W]e converge with physiology, the phenomena of bodily life, for it seems that between the social and the bodily the layer of individual consciousness is very thin: laughter, tears, funerary laments, ritual ejaculations, are physiological reactions just as much as they are obligatory or necessary or suggested or employed by collectivities to a precise end, with a view to a kind of physical and moral discharge of its expectations, which are physical and moral too. (1979:10).

Compared to Bourdieu's equivocation about the body and emotion, Mauss goes straight to the pervasiveness of physiological convergences. And in contrast to the way that the social seems to close down the body in the Bourdieusian habitus, Mauss is careful to highlight the very thin layer that exists between the physiological and the social. Moreover that layer is inhabited and disturbed by the feeling body – its tears, laughter and ejaculations. Unlike Bourdieu, these do not have to be contained as emotion, which as we've seen plays a crucial role in securing the inevitable operations of the habitus. While Mauss also links the body's feelings to 'a precise end', he retains an emphasis on the very physiology which animates their moral discharge. The consequent social expectations are charged by their own physical and moral discharges. In this we have a very different picture of embodiment wherein the body does not fall away before the social, or become mere support for its static existence. The social here is charged by physicality.

Mauss' comments were made in the context of arguing for collaboration between sociology and psychology. In part he was conceding to psychology the realm of the emotions, at the same time that he seems to be claiming the affective body for sociology. As he puts it, 'whatever the suggestive power of the collectivity, it always leaves the individual a sanctuary, his consciousness, which is yours' (1979:10). Underscoring this gesture is the fact that he reserves for sociology 'a few exclusively social grand facts: value, the scared, articulated time, marginal and central spaces, techniques, etc.' (1979:12). Despite his magnanimous concession, it is clear now that in fact Mauss kept the most interesting bits for sociology. Psychology can have the emotions, but sociology gets the affective body, the key to both individual and collective feelings.

The affective habitus

Unfortunately, sociology has not done as much as it could with the object that Mauss secured for the discipline. In fact, it has squandered the resources that he gathered. Perhaps most precious is the precision of his analysis of the physiological, along with its place, its convergence with the psychological and the societal. Fearful of losing its hold on the social, sociology has distanced itself from the innate, the biological, the instinctual and the affective. And while the body is claimed, it is a body devoid of any interest except as a screen for the social.

This has had important consequences. As Michèle Barrett has argued, 'sociology is conspicuously inadequate . . . Physicality, humanity, imagination, the other, fear, the limits of control; all are missing in their own terms, in their own dynamic' (2000:19). Barrett's comments are made in the context of honouring Stuart Hall. And while they certainly do point to Hall's contribution, they also reveal a wider lacuna: the inability to produce insights which are 'imaginative, sensual even, in that they speak to experience, which includes the senses rather simply cognition' (2000:19). Her conclusion is that 'sociology has become boring' (2000:19).

They are large claims, but they are substantiated by much sociological research on the body and the emotions. It's quite a feat to make these areas boring, but by force of guarding against the intrusion of the nonsocial, and policing its boundaries, the body has become predictable. In part this tendency is presaged by the shift from Mauss' understanding of the habitus to Bourdieu's. Or rather, given Bourdieu's acknowledgement of the body's sheer presence, it may be more the result of how he has been taken up. Even if Bourdieu's argument is sketchy on this point, there is a recognition of the way that the body *is* which allows for a glimmer into its physicality, its own logics. As Norman Denzin, a pioneer in the contemporary sociology of emotion, aptly puts it, 'the body does not call out interpretations' (1984:25). Denzin is rare in his insistence that 'the physiological and neurological substrate of emotions must be taken into account before psychological accounts or theories can be built' (1984:22). But even this acknowledgment is quickly qualified by the argument that such theories and accounts will be a 'level above the physiological level of analysis'.

In terms of distancing the body's physiological and emotive unruliness, Bourdieu's habitus is repeatedly brought in to make sure that we know that it is the social that rules. For instance, in Terry Lovell's framing, the habitus' greatest value seems to be the way in which it ensures that 'cultural arbitraries' win out over 'the natural and the immutable' (2000:15). For Lila Abu-Lughod, Bourdieu's notion of the body hexis allows for 'ways of thinking about the fact that emotion is embodied without being forced to concede that it must be "natural" and not shaped by social interaction' (1990:12). Abu-Lughod does in fact follow through on ideas about body techniques, yet her discussion is framed by the need to protect emotions as 'cultural products' and as discursive. In Rita Felski's (2000) discussion of shame and the lower middle classes, there is no mention of how bodies in their physiology might influence the experience and expression of emotion. Given how visceral, physiologically evident and painful shame is, this omission is astonishing.

Felski prefaces her discussion of shame and the lower middle class with something of a tirade against 'personal writing', and then goes on to say that her essay is a 'semiautobiographical reflection on the problems of writing autobiographically' (2000:35). Strangely, she implies that speaking about emotions is of necessity speaking the self. This reveals the odd place emotion occupies: it is cultural, discursive, or conversely interior to the self. Setting aside the disdain with which Felski covers 'speaking the self', her understanding of shame doesn't extend far beyond the obvious – that, at least in the texts she privileges, lower middle class culture is bounded by shame. As such she strips the intricacy with which Bev Skeggs (1997) deploys her Bourdieusian analysis of the mechanisms of respectability within female working class culture. The only emotion that emerges clearly from Felski's argument is that of anger and resentment against cultural studies' love of 'the image of a vital, sensual, popular body', and its ignorance of lower middle class culture (2000:36). Fair enough, but where is the body in its physiological twists and turns caught within 'the constant struggle to keep up appearances on a low income'? (Felski, 2000:37).

As Felski demonstrates in her literary/cultural analysis, the bracketing of the feeling part of emotions and the reticence to engage with a bodily description of how different emotions feel is not unique to sociology. Several years ago in their introduction to the ideas of Silvan Tomkins, Eve Sedgwick and Adam Frank (1995) made a pointed argument about the ways in which affect tends to be used in literary and cultural criticism. To sum up their intricate argument, affect gets taken as a homogenous category with little or no attention to the modalities of different affects. There is, as we've also seen in sociology, a seeming necessity on the part of cultural critics to affirm that affect is cultural, discursive, not natural – in sum, to bracket it tightly away from the physiological, the biological and indeed the affective. Attesting to a prevailing emphasis on the cognitive, 'the space for discursive social construction of affects seems guaranteed by the notation that (since we are not "animals at heart") the raw material of our arousal is *infinitely* malleable by a fully acculturated cognitive faculty' (1995:19). Drawing on Tomkins' insights accrued through his experimentation, they point out that 'regardless of whether this cognitive account of emotion is *true*, what we want to emphasize is that it is not *less essentialist* than an account . . . that locates in the body some important part of the difference among different emotions' (1995:19).

What Sedgwick and Frank identify as attempts 'to detoxify the excesses of the body, thought and feeling' exacts a heavy price in terms of contemporary social and cultural theory. While certainly there are now a few individuals who counter this established tendency (Massumi, 2002; Connolly, 2002; Wilson, 1998; Gibbs, 2001; Adamson and Clark, 1999), as yet they are few and far between. With the exception of Anna Gibbs and in a different vein, William Connolly, and of course Sedgwick, those who do find inspiration in different non-cognitive models do not necessarily reconnect with older or forgotten traditions within the social sciences and humanities. Conversely those who have rediscovered distinct philosophies of emotion and affect (Redding, 1999; Nussbaum, 2001) do not feel the need to venture far beyond the boundaries of their field. Nor should they necessarily do so.

My own project is less an attempt to right my own field(s), than it is to encourage and extend experiments that may have become bogged down, sometimes caught by their own momentary success. This is for instance the case of the body.

237

In its contemporary emergence, interest in the body was fueled by feminist desires to understand different connections – the body and power, the relation of the psychoanalytic to the workings of gender, the refusal to be captured within a dominant conception of biology, etc. The exigency of these engagements (and let's not forget that at least in the public realm certain, perhaps erroneous, biological arguments are routinely used against women) may have resulted in a retreat into and a celebration of the cultural. Equally, while we may now acknowledge that the repetition of 'the discursive' and 'resistance' has become rather tired, the original terms of Foucauldian discourse analysis did offer a powerful tool for the analysis of power.

Unfortunately there has been a tendency to view everything – all levels of life – as within the grip of discourse. The attention to discourse and the sense that the cultural has to be defended against an onslaught of the biological doesn't necessarily play out in precise analyses of different levels. Within these terms, how could it? And in this lack of precision, many precious insights have been lost.

One of the ephemeral yet terribly necessary things that we may have misplaced is the exuberance of approaches such as Mauss'. Of course, his was a different time when funding wasn't considered a problem, when the sciences of man were less rigid in their proprietorship, and therefore were less defensive to each other. We can look back and consider this a golden age when bodies weren't as tired and worn down. But we can only do this by ignoring Mauss' account of the battles he waged within and outside sociology, by forgetting the terrible toll of two world wars. Despite this context the energy of his theory is appealing: as a description and as an analytic it abounds with high spirits, and is just so very fertile.

As I've mentioned, Mauss' style may have shocked more than a few, and it may be one of the reasons that he has been relatively forgotten. By style I mean more than the actual form of writing. Style encaptures a way of doing research, modes of experimentation. Mauss' mind ranged widely over very different fields and areas, shamelessly taking up examples from fieldwork conducted by others in several different parts of the world. And sometimes he got it wrong, or at least in the detail. Ben Brewster (1979), the translator of *Sociology and Psychology*, notes that Mauss has the Seri living on the Madeleine Peninsula in California when in actual fact they live on the island of Tiburon and in the Sonora province of Mexico. This doesn't make a great deal of difference to Mauss' argument. While I'm not advocating sloppiness, his example of gathering together so many sheer interesting facts is refreshing. His desire to raise the physiological from its place of ignominy plays out in thousands of small and large examples. These were not displayed to prove his erudition but were put to work in furthering Mauss' grand passion of promoting the study of the total man.

These days we don't often see such passion, at least within the social sciences and humanities. It does still seem to animate other areas, especially those concerned with understanding why, how, and where we feel. The few places where passion, excitement and interest show up is in arguments that grapple with what the scientific passions might mean if translated into the humanities. As Massumi candidly says of his work in this area, it is a 'shameless poaching from science'. But unlike some of the dogs' breakfasts that resulted from high postmodern pastiche, one of the crucial rules that guide this poaching is respect: a poaching that 'betrays the system of science while respecting its affect, in a way designed to force change in the humanities' (2002:20). In a similar vein, William Connolly's recent work engages with current neurological theories in order to advance or renew thinking within the humanities. For Connolly, work such as Joseph LeDoux's *The Emotional Brain* (1998) can be made to reverberate with Deleuzian philosophy. He locates their proximities at the level of findings on how the brain works and the role of affect within it, and not as mere metaphor. This research, as is evident from much of the work on the emotions and the affects, requires that we bracket the need to immediately impose cognition. Connolly takes to heart that pause, and sees in it the space of interest, enjoyment and awe. From a different yet compatible universe, Deleuze's insistence is germane: that there might be 'something mute in the world that has not yet been translated into the register of thought' (in Connolly, 1999:23). In consort with Deleuze, Connolly uses the interest provided by very different research to promote an ethical sensibility: 'a constellation of thought-imbued intensities and feeling', the stuff of new techniques of thinking (1999:27).

At first blush, it might seem that shame is hardly a subject associated with passion, and if it is a sensibility then surely it is only a painful and uneasy one. Shame is undoubtedly painful, in part because it activates so many sensations. In Tomkins' argument, shame is 'a single bodily-based affect capable of differentiating into a variety of cognitively differentiated emotions – shyness, embarrassment and guilt'. As he famously puts it, shame is the experience of the self by the self, and can at its hottest be felt as a 'sickness of the self' (Tomkins in Sedgwick and Frank, 1995:136). But shame does more than sensibilize us to the vast variety of sensations that inform life; it also proposes a sensibility at once practical and ethical: 'the appropriate reaction to one's own shame is a type of self-transformation', as Paul Redding summarizes Nietzsche's view (1999:2).

From the perspective of our bodies, madly trying to deal with immense amounts of sensation, the most salient point about shame right now is that it is always conceived of in interest. Shame is our bodies' way of telling us that we are interested: that we were interested, and that we will continue to be despite shame's painful interruption. Shame produces a somatic temporality, where the future of being again interested is felt in the present pain of rejection. My wager is that shame is intimately involved in the passions of interest. In its basic manifestation, 'without positive affect, there can be no shame: only a scene that offers you enjoyment or engages your interest can make you blush' (Sedgwick and Frank, 1995:22). As Sedgwick and Frank also point out, the physiological attitude characterized by shame, 'the lowering of the eyelids, the lowering of the eyes, the hanging of the head is the attitude of shame, it may also be that of reading' (1995:20). From the physiological to its social and psychological manifestations, shame returns us to the primacy of interest.

In my forthcoming book (Probyn 2005) I draw out the different ways in which shame makes interest matter again – interest in our collective and individual histories marked by trauma, interest in the academic matters of how to respond, interest in writing and listening, interest in living ethically. The white of white shame refers at one level to the ongoing exigency to develop the project that Paul Gilroy (2000) so interestingly outlines: a pragmatic, planetary humanism. White shame here is not to be solidified as an identity, a speaking position, or a subjectivity. It is to be used as an impetus to make what Gilroy calls 'the predicament of fundamentally fragile, corporeal existence into a key to a version of humanism' (2000:17). If the classic example of shame is the blush, it's not for nothing that it appears so much more clearly on white faces. But in line with Gilroy's argument about breaking down raciology's defensive modus operandi, white shame evoked cannot turn into guilt. The affects, and the body's sensations that get named shame or guilt are, in any case, quite different. So too must be the hijacking of the affect into distinct politics or ethical engagements.

The white in white shame also refers to the feeling of white hot; of sheer bodily intensity. As I've argued, recognition of the body in its physiological matter has tended to disappear under the weight of its cultural importance. As I've also tried to indicate in the examples of Bourdieu and especially Mauss, there are traditions of thought within the social sciences that have attended to the physiological, and have seen in it a necessary component to understand the total human (perhaps a conceptual forebear of Gilroy's planetary humanism). At a fundamental level, it is in the physiological, the somatic, that the body is interesting because it is there that the body reveals its interest. Without that basic interest, all our theories fall flat. Writing about shame as an impetus in an alternative understanding of what theory is about, Sedgwick and Frank argue that shame provides a different gestalt:

> [A] switch point for the individuation of imaging systems, of consciousness, of bodies, of theories, of selves, an individuation that decides not necessarily an identity but a figuration, distinction, or mark of punctuation (1995:22).

In this way, the white hot sensation of shame may allow for a different type of shading of theory than is the norm. While the link between a literary theorist like Sedgwick and the sociological perspective I've described may seem tenuous, the refusal of theory as an on/off, digitalizing process of distinction interestingly draws them together. While Bourdieu may have begun to harden into *a* theory, enlivened by Mauss, we can perhaps return to the habitus and see in it one way of figuring the body and its beliefs, customs, practices and cultural meanings as analog layerings of different kinds of distinction.

And what of that example left so rudely all these pages ago? Now that the moment of affect has faded, how to get back into that emotional body sitting in the back of a Land Cruiser, choked on the sight of a huge rock? I look at my reprints of photos taken by one of my companions. The colours on mine aren't as vivid as hers. Which photographs are true?

This fading of emotion and of affective intensity is the toughest thing to deal with. Of course, when they really hurt, you're glad that the heat blanches out from the memories. Conversely, in some theories and depending on the intensity and repetition of the affect, grooves get worn into bits of the brain (Nathanson, 1996:16). In the case of trauma (a specialized case of, as I've mentioned, overwhelming affect-flooding) the recursive nature of traumatic experience has long been recognized. As Bessle van de Kolk argues, following Janet and Pavlov, 'after repeated aversive stimulation, intrinsically non-threatening cues associated with the trauma (conditional stimuli – CS) become capable of eliciting the defensive reaction by themselves (conditional response – CR)' (1994:1).[12] As van der Kolk summarizes research into post-traumatic stress syndrome, 'the highly elevated physiological responses that accompany the recall of traumatic experiences that happened years, and sometimes decades before, illustrate the intensity and timelessness with which traumatic memories continue to affect experience' (1994:2). He furthers contends that in some cases severe stress interferes with the placement of mediated memories in the hippocampal localization system, the part of the brain where memories are thought to be stored and categorized. In these events, 'it is likely that some mental representation of the experience is laid down by means of a system that records affective experience, but that has no capacity for symbolic processing and placement in space and time' (1994:8).

This is all interesting stuff; does it mean that some affective experiences are recorded somewhere but our brains have forgotten where? In more normal cases, the mechanism for assigning meanings to experiences, filing them away, and then remembering where they are seems to run pretty smoothly considering the complexity. Van der Kolk describes how some researchers think it works: 'the amygdala assigns free-floating feelings of significance to sensory input, which the neocortex then further elaborates and imbues with personal meaning' (1994:8). Straight forward really, except for when the system gets knocked for a loop by stress or by too much affect, an 'unmodulated affective amplification of terrible density' (Nathanson, 1996:16).

Affect theorists such as Donald Nathanson put a slightly different spin on what happens in less intensified affective situations. Most would concur that 'so much is going on in the brain that nothing gains attention unless it triggers an affect'. It's 'that which gains affective amplification [that] gets into the limited channel we call consciousness' (Nathanson, 1996:12). Children seem to be better at more randomly picking up various triggers, by the time we are adults relatively few triggers achieve recognition. Nathanson, a biologist turned psychotherapist and a disciple of Tomkins, has formulated a three-part explanation of what happens. His terms are a bit geeky, but maybe that's their appeal. At the level of 'hardware', he identifies the structural wiring and data handling of the central nervous system, the skin and muscles of the face, and assorted chemicals and hormones in the body. The drives and affects are located at the level of 'firmware'. 'Software' is the what he calls the experience of life, of family background, etc. Others, such as Basch (1996), argue that affect is a biological phenomenon, and emotion 'represents the assemblage of any affect with our previous experience of that affect'. As Nathanson sums it up: 'affect is biology, while emotion is biography' (1996:13).

Wouldn't it be something if the long debates over nature and nurture could be so winningly phrased? It's certainly clear, at least in some circles, that the convergence of the biological and the cultural/social is really not as insurmountable as it has been made out to be. For the affect theorists, we are born with innate affects. Tomkins categorized these as: interest-excitement; enjoyment-joy – these are the positive ones; surprise-startlement (which he called neutral); and the negatives ones of fear-terror; distress-anguish; anger-rage; shame-humiliation; dismell; disgust (Nathanson, 1996:12). These are, says Nathanson, the palette each of us gets; it's in their experience-affect combinations that we experience both individual and collective emotions.

Interesting, but I've again strayed from my example. These ideas from another scientific realm may help with understanding where affect and emotion fit together within the habitus. Of course, we're not constrained to a language of hardware and software. For instance, this passage from a memoir/novel, *Craft for a Dry Lake*, describes in another shade what happens when the physiological and biographical converge:

> Crossing the border back into the Territory, my childhood rushes to meet me. The colours begin to intensify, the light sharpens. I begin to feel something in my bones and nerves and viscera. I would not describe it as an emotion. It is more like a chemical reaction, as if a certain light and temperature and dryness triggers a series of physical and nervous realignments. . . . My pulse is up, everything takes on a hallucinatory clarity (Mahood, 2000:35).

Later Mahood again describes her affective reaction to the land as more than an ensemble of mental images: 'it is something else too, a set of visceral alignments over which the intellect has no jurisdiction' (2000:174). Mahood's book is ostensibly in honour of her father's memory and her voyage back to her family's station in the Tanami – a vast track of land between the Simpson Desert and Western Australia. It's also an account of her affective experiences, told in the terms of her physiological realignments to the land, set against a refusal of emotion. Her father, we're told, was deeply suspicious of emotion: 'He described it as *spilling your guts* or, ironically, *expressing your innermost feelings*' (2000: 224). Mahood agrees with her father, although he was, she says, extreme in his 'terror of exposing himself'. At one point she apologizes to her dog for her overt expression of emotion (2000:194). Is it important she travels alone with her dog? In the assemblage of human/nonhuman and land and space that emerges, it seems to be.

Her father took to drink, and in banal way we could surmise that Mahood's own emotional response to this was shame. But that would be to flatten her more interesting affective experience. In her separation of affect from emotion we hear with clarity expression of that experience. Her writing is deeply relational. A sense of how this is the case comes across in Massumi's definition of relational as 'intensively cross-referencing disparate planes of experience' (2002:20 fn). Mahood writes as a white women in relation to the land which was her family's and the ground of her childhood. She equally writes of her relation to a singular Aboriginal relationship to the land. And when she is invited to a big women's business ceremony,[13] she finds herself automatically following the Aboriginal tradition of setting camp in the direction of that land, 'that country that my father turned into a cattle station' (2000:124). The relations of relation multiply seemingly indefinitely. As a child she was given a skin name by the local Aboriginal women on the station, 'a formality which places [whites] in a category of relationships and behaviour'. She now acknowledges the ambivalence: 'It's as if I have come by a secret password by dishonest means and have hoarded it against the moment when it might open a magic door' (2000:125). And in trading in her words, don't I feel the same.

To map all the relationships among the affects Mahood expresses would take a long time. At once she is shy, embarrassed, proud. But is she ashamed? Not in the usual sense, and she pushes back the obvious emotional expression of white shame that she has experienced in the city in relation to urban folk filled with romanticism. When she speaks of her use of her relation to Aboriginality, 'her unearned title', as creating a frisson in urban society, it's hard to tell if the shame is on her or on them – her urban colleagues.

I'm not interested in pigeon-holing – the question of who is shamed or ashamed is already a shameful endeavour. Rather it is the multiplicity and ubiquity of the lines that interest me. As a reader I want to be laced in by these lines. At one moment there is a fleeting possibility of a mutual interest that might tie me in with her to this land. She's reading Deleuze and Guattari's *Nomadology* (1986) and I lean into the page, only to be rebuffed when she kind of ridicules them. Or maybe it's just the words are out of joint. That moment of interest curtailed, I inwardly blush: I went to wave at a friend who turned out to be a stranger. Her description of Aboriginal Australia's relationship to the land draws out 'a harsh sexuality', that both quashes white myths and places her, as a white woman, on the sidelines. She estranges those myths of comfort, and herself.

> The primordial landscape is scattered with the evidence of ancestral acts of rape, copulation, dismembering. It is about a physical encounter with the land itself, a wounding, a letting of blood, a taking of the country into oneself, of taking oneself into the country (2000:195).

In contrast to this unfathomably deep relationship, the non-Indigenous seem to flounder. 'Whites who live here struggle to articulate an attachment over which they have no control' (2000:195). 'They leave and return, resentfully, full of anger and indigestible griefs'. These white experiences are 'scratches on the land'[14] that cannot be understood without an appreciation of the 'price the homage this country extracts'. 'Acceptance' is possible, 'predicated on limited ambition: a moment by moment focus on the job to be done, the life to be lived'. It seems unendurable, just as it seems amazing that whites keep at it, rearing livestock in conditions where there may be one steer per 100s of acres. It also contains, as Mahood clearly wants us to know, 'a narrow and deeply grounded wisdom' (2000:195).

Mahood's account points to a different sense of white shame than that more familiar to those who grew up as city-dwellers. The white shame I sense in Mahood's account is predicated on interest – the type of interest that's hard to come by unless it's deep within your habitus. In her description of her father and those who stayed on, now as managers on Aboriginal-owned land, there is a sense of the affective complex of anger-rage, and shame-humiliation. The clinical description of anger-rage – the frown, clenched jaw, red face – uncannily captures the image of the tough laconic white Australian on the land. To live, to continually return, to live a life circumscribed by 'limited ambition' is to be placed within the ambit of interest interrupted – of shame.

As a cipher for the larger history, Mahood's physiological reactions again and again speak of interest, and interest foiled. This cannot be understood outside of her habitus. Here the physiological is the psychological and the social. The body is. And the body is its reactions to the dryness, the light, the history which is enfolded fully within that particular habitus. White shame is in the habitus: the body expresses such interest, and then registers that the interest cannot be fully followed through on. This is not, however, a tragic tale; it is not the romanticization of shame that is played at an emotional level. Nor is a condemnation of a generalized white history. It's harder than that. It's not a shame that can be relieved by apology.

Neither heroic, nor scandalous, this white shame is deeply interested and interesting in ways that cannot be easily described. It is not purely social (that would make it easier to eradicate). Nor cannot it be written into some general account of a white psychology. The physical and visceral acting of affect disturbs such pigeon-holing. It does recall strongly Mauss' assemblage – the physiological-psychological-sociological intersection – and maybe that language may begin to shed light on the delicacy of white shame. If, as the affect theorists put it, we're born with a basic palette of affects, how, where, and when they move us also needs to be understood in different shades of terms. If the social is natural in the strong sense (Karsenti, 1998), let's make our descriptive language as muted as the colours of the land.

And again, what of my own little example? The constant deferral already speaks of shame. The moment that I described of seeming pure affect certainly did translate into shame; or more precisely two different kinds of shame coincided. One was of a different order than the white shame I see in Mahood's habitus. My shame was certainly born in interest. The exaltation before and in the sight of Uluru can be precisely described as interest-excitement, and enjoyment-joy. There may also have been some of the neutral affect Tomkins calls surprise-startle. The eyebrows up, eyes wide open and blinking, smiling and looking and listening: I couldn't quite believe I was there. And then the near simultaneous movement to sobbing, head down, fingers covering my face. Well, yes these are the classic facial displays of shame.

In that moment, or that tensing together of sensation, there was a splitting of shame. As Massumi's has argued, the difference between emotion and affect can also be described as a bifurcation in response, where 'language functions differentially to intensity' (2002:25). The fact that Midnight Oil was playing cannot be forgotten, their words cannot be ignored. 'How can we sleep while out beds are burning', how can we exalt before the sight of Uluru, metonym of Aboriginal Australian, taken away, grudgingly given back? 'The time has come to say fair's fair'. At that cognitive level, the shame I expressed was straight-forward: one good white crying with other good whites. Shading into guilt, it loudly asks for absolution.

This is undeniably one shade of white shame, but it's not the only one nor is it the most generative definition. For the sake of argument, we could call it emotional shame. The other white shame, so much harder to name, is bred in the bone, whispers in the habitus. Because of our histories, differently em-bodied it goes without saying, I have a very different capacity to experience Mahood's form of affective white shame. But not an incapacity. As I describe in *Blush* (Probyn, 2005), ancestral shame is fully part of my habitus, and perhaps those of others. The intricacy of the habitus does not permit any easy match-ing of experiences. It does, however, remind us that the affective patterns that are our bodies and histories dictate interest. My brief experience of weeks of travelling in country, of body become eyes and fingers and open pores, even that briefest of experience awakened my interest. It also awakened a visceral sensing of this affective shade of white shame.

When I returned to Sydney I felt bereft. My senses seem to lack object. This feeling of feeling nothing passed, and everyday life took over again. But I remained curious about those shifts of affective interest. The emotional level of white shame is more widespread in the city, revealed in newspaper stories about the continuing scandal of a twenty year difference in mortality rates for Abo-riginal Australians and the rest of us. But that emotional sensing of shame moves quickly onto new sites. It's fuelled by a different type of interest: the sen-sational, the new, the mediated. Concern about Reconciliation seems to have dropped out of our collective interest. In its place are other questions. What to do with the refugees detained in the middle of the country, who sew their lips together in protest? What to do about the shame heaped on Australia from abroad by human rights groups?

These are important instances of shame-making, but they are not of the same order as the affective white shame in the habitus that I've been trying to draw out. They operate on a cognitive level, what Connolly calls the 'supersensible' level. In his argument, this level is regulated by 'a command model of morality' (1999:21). Against this juridical framing of morality, his call is to foster the 'infrasensible', the realm of affective interests. 'An ethic in which visceral attach-ment to life and the world provides the preliminary soil from which commitment to more generous identities, responsibilities and connections might be cultivated' (1999:21).

Of course it's foolhardy, and indeed should be shame-producing, to make hard and fast distinctions about how people feel. My two shades of white shame often overlap. But the public climate again and again hardens into black and white: those who would promote a politics of shame and guilt, and those who steadfastly will not admit a bar of it. Morality gets played two ways and squeezes out the interest necessary for an ethics of the type that Connolly proposes. For me, the challenge is to promote and explore models that can more comprehensibly understand feelings and interest. A sociology of humanity.

Notes

1 This is a slightly different version of an argument presented in my book, *Blush* (2005). My thanks to Lisa Adkins, Nicole Vitellone and Bev Skeggs for their hospitality in Manchester and their generous feedback on the presentation on which this chapter is based.
2 My thanks to Anna Gibbs for pointing this out, and for her invaluable knowledge about affect shared so generously.
3 Jay McInerney, *The Guardian*, September 18, 2001; Edward Said, *The Observer*, September 16, 2001.
4 Were the parents and family of those who went over to fight with the Taliban ashamed of their sons? In a piece published during the buildup to whether the US would go to war against Iraq, Thomas Friedland wrote in the *New York Times* about the ways in which young Islamic men were filled with humiliation faced with the disparity of what Islam promises and 'the poverty, ignorance and repression' of their home countries. It is 'this humiliation' says Friedland, 'this poverty of dignity – that drives them to suicidal revenge'. Reprinted in the *Sydney Morning Herald*, 20.902.
5 Jean-Michel Berthelot (1992) has cogently argued that this movement away from the body to other domains is a feature of any attempt at a sociology of the body. As he has also put it, class for all its importance, is an abstraction: when was the last time you encountered physically a class? This points to the fact that we need more concrete analyses of classed bodies, such as Skeggs (1997).
6 http//:www.geollab.jmu.edu/fichter/IgnRx/Introigrx.html (12/9/02).
7 As cited on http://www.thesalmons.org (12/9/02).
8 My warmest thanks to my travel companions, Robyn and Jack Durack.
9 Bourdieu distinguishes between cultural capital which is the 'encorporation' (the making body) of objective markers of social distinction from symbolic capital which is the 'world-making and changing' ability that he states is the possession of artists and writers (Bourdieu, 1986). See also Hage (1998) for an interesting application of Bourdieu's ideas.
10 My thanks to Marcel Fournier for these comments. For the most complete positioning of Mauss' work see Fournier (1994).
11 Mauss' experience of WWII was perhaps even more traumatic, although by then he was writing much less. W. S. F. Pickering (1998) remarks that Mauss, who did not hide his Jewishness clearly marked in his second name of Israël, may have stepped down in 1940 from his position of director of Ecole Pratique des Hautes Etudes (5th section) because of Nazi pressures.
12 http://www.trauma-pages.com/vandeerk4.htm (19/9/02).
13 Aboriginal law dictates that there are separate women's and men's spiritual roles and duties.
14 The reference is to Mary Louise Pratt's groundbreaking book about women travelers (1992).

References

Abu-Lughod, L. and Lutz, C. A. (1990) 'Introduction: Emotion, Discourse and the Politics of Everyday Life' in C. A. Lutz and L. Abu-Lughod (eds) *Language and the Politics of Emotion*. Cambridge: Cambridge University Press.

Adamson, J. and Clark, H. (1999) (eds) *Scenes of Shame: Psychoanalysis, Shame and Writing*. New York: SUNY Press.

Barrett, M. (2000) 'Sociology and the Metaphorical Tiger' in P. Gilroy, L. Grossberg and A. McRobbie (eds) *Without Guarantees: In Honour of Stuart Hall*. London: Verso.

Basch, M. F. (1996) 'Affect and Defense', in D. Nathanson (ed.) *Knowing Feeling: Affect, Script, and Psychotherapy*. New York: W. W. Norton.

Berthelot, J. M. (1992) 'The Body as a Discursive Operator: Or the Aporias of a Sociology of the Body' *Body and Society* 1(1): 13–23.

Bourdieu, P. (1986) 'The Forms of Capital' in J. G. Richardson (ed.) *Handbook of Theory and Research for the Sociology of Education*. New York: Greenwood Press.

Bourdieu, P. (1990/1980) *The Logic of Practice*. Cambridge: Polity.

Butler, J. (1999) 'Performativity's Social Magic' in R. Shusterman (ed.) *Bourdieu: A Critical Reader*. Oxford: Blackwell.

Connolly, W. (1999) 'Brain Waves, Transcendental Fields, and Techniques of Thought' *Radical Philosophy* March/April: 19–28.

Connolly, W. (2002) *Neuropolitics: Thinking, Culture, Speed*. Minneapolis: University of Minnesota Press.

Deleuze, G. and Guattari, F. (1986) *Nomadology: The War Machine*. New York: Semiotext(e).

Denzin, N. K. (1984) *On Understanding Emotion*. San Francisco: Jossey-Bass.

Felski, Rita. (2000) 'Nothing to Declare: Identity, Shame and the Lower Classes' in R. Felski *Doing Time: Feminist Theory and Postmodern Culture*. New York: New York University Press.

Fournier, M. (1994) *Marcel Mauss*. Paris: Fayard.

Gibbs, A. (2001) 'Contagious Feelings: Pauline Hanson and the Epidemiology of Affect' *Australian Humanities Review*. Issue 24, Dec 2001-Feb 2002 http://www.lib.latrobe.edu.au/AHR/

Gilroy, Paul. (2000) *Against Race: Imaging Political Culture Beyond the Color Line*. Cambridge: Harvard University Press.

Hage, G. (1998) *White Nation: Fantasies of White Supremacy in a Multicultural Soci*ety. Annandale: Pluto Press.

James, Wendy. 1998) ' "One of Us": Marcel Mauss and "English" Anthropology' in W. James and N. J. Allen (eds) *Marcel Mauss: A Centenary Tribute*. New York: Berghahn Books.

Karsenti, Bruno. (1998) 'The Maussian Shift' in W. James and N. J. Allen (eds) *Marcel Mauss: A Centenary Tribute*. New York: Berghahn Books.

Kulick, D. (1995) (ed.) *Taboo: Sex, Identity and Erotic Subjectivity in Anthropological Fieldwork*. London: Routledge.

LeDoux, J. (1998) *The Emotional Brain*. London: Weidenfeld and Nicolson.

Lovell, T. (2000) 'Thinking Feminism With and Against Bourdieu' *Feminist Theory* 1(1): 11–32.

Mahood, K. (2000) *Craft for a Dry Lake*. Sydney: Anchor/Random House.

Massumi, B. (1996) 'The Autonomy of Affect' in P. Patton (ed.) *Deleuze: A Critical Reader*. Oxford: Blackwell.

Massumi, B. (2002) *Parables for the Virtual: Movement, Affect, Sensation*. Durham: Duke University Press.

Mauss, M. (1979) *Sociology and Psychology*. Translated by Ben Brewster. London: Routledge & Kegan Paul.

Mauss, M. (1990) *The Gift: The Form and Reason of Exchange in Archaic Societies*. New York: Norton.

Midnight Oil. (1986) *Dust & Diesel*. Sony: Australia.

Nathanson, D. L. (1996) (ed.) *Knowing Feeling: Affect, Script and Psychotherapy*. New York: Norton.

Nussbaum, M. C. (2001) *Upheavals of Thought: The Intelligence of the Emotions*. Cambridge: Cambridge University Press.

Pickering, W. S. F. (1998) 'Mauss' Jewish Background: a Biographical Essay' in W. James and N. J. Allen (eds) *Marcel Mauss: A Centenary Tribute*. NY: Berghahn Books.

Pratt, M. L. (1992) *Imperial Eyes: Travel Writing and Transculturation*. New York and London: Routledge.

Probyn, E. (2005) *Blush: Faces of Shame*. Minneapolis: University of Minnesota Press.

Redding, P. (1999) *The Logic of Affect.* Melbourne: Melbourne University Press.

Sedgwick, E. K, and A. Frank. (1995) 'Shame in the Cybernetic Fold: Reading Silvan Tomkins' in E. K. Sedgwick and A. Frank (eds) *Shame and it Sisters: A Silvan Tomkins Reader*. Durham: Duke University Press.

Sedgwick, E. K. and Frank, A. (eds) *Shame and it Sisters: A Silvan Tomkins Reader*. Durham: Duke University Press.

Schlanger, N. (1998) 'The Maussian Shift: A Second Foundation for Sociology in France' in W. James and N. J. Allen (eds) *Marcel Mauss: A Centenary Tribute*. New York: Berghahn Books.

Skeggs, Beverley. (1997) *Formations of Class and Gender*. London: Sage.

Van der Kolk, B. (1994) 'The Body Keeps the Score: Memory and the Evolving Psychobiology of Post Traumatic Stress'. http://www.trauma-pages.com/vanderk4.htm.

Wilson, E. A. (1998) *Neural Geographies: Feminism and the Microstructure of Cognition*. New York and London: Routledge.

List of contributors

Lisa Adkins is Reader in Sociology at Manchester University and has researched and published widely in the areas of social and cultural theory and the sociologies of economy, gender and sexuality. Her latest book is *Revisions: Gender and Sexuality in Late Modernity* (Open University Press 2002). She is currently writing a book on feminism and contemporary social theory.

Bridget Fowler is Reader in Sociology at the University of Glasgow, where she has been lecturing, mainly on the sociology of culture and social theory since 1966. She is the author of two books, *The Alienated Reader: Women and Popular Romantic Literature in the Twentieth Century* (Harvester Wheatsheaf 1991) and *Pierre Bourdieu and Cultural Theory* (Sage 1997), together with various articles, particularly on the sociology of Pierre Bourdieu. She also edited *Reading Bourdieu on Society and Culture* for Sociological Review Monographs (Blackwell 2000). At present she is engaged in extending the essay in this volume into a book on obituaries, a project for which she is grateful to have been aided by a Leverhulme Award.

Stephanie Lawler is Lecturer in Sociology at the University of Durham. She has published in the areas of social theory; the sociology of class and gender; class, representation and recognition; and social methodology and epistemology (particularly narrative research). Her most recent book is *Mothering the Self: Mothers, Daughters, Subjects* (Routledge 2000) and she has articles published in *Feminist Review*, *Feminist Theory* and *Social Epistemology*.

Terry Lovell is a Professor Emeritus in the Department of Sociology at the University of Warwick, where she has lectured in sociology, women's studies and cultural studies since 1972. Her publications include *Pictures of Reality: Politics, Aesthetics and Pleasure* (BFI Publications 1980), *Consuming Fiction* (Verso 1987), and *A Glossary of Feminist Theory* (with S. Andermahr and C. Wolkowitz (Edward Arnold 2000)). She has written extensively on feminist social theory and the sociology of culture. She has published two papers on Bourdieu, in *Feminist Theory* 1(1) 2000 and *Theory, Culture and Society* 20(1) 2003.

Lois McNay is Reader in Politics at Oxford University and fellow of Somerville College. Her last book was *Gender and Agency* (Polity 2000). She is currently working on a book on intersubjectivity.

Angela McRobbie is Professor of Communications at Goldsmiths College, London. She is author of several books and many articles on young women and popular culture, the fashion industry and cultural economy. Her most recent books are *The Uses of Cultural Studies* (Sage 2005) and *Feminism and the 'TV Blonde': The Displacement of Sexual Politics* (Sage 2005).

Elspeth Probyn has taught media studies, sociology, and literature in Canada and the US, and is now the Professor of Gender Studies at the University of Sydney. Her work focuses on questions of identity, sexuality and bodies. She has been constantly interested in what people think and do with their bodies from eating, sex, to emotions. Elspeth has published several books in these areas, including *Sexing the Self* (Routledge 1993), *Outside Belongings* (Routledge 1996), *Carnal Appetites* (Routledge 2000) and *Sexy Bodies* (Routledge 1995). Her latest book is *Blush: Faces of Shame* (Minnesota University Press 2005). She is also interested in ethics, the media and popular culture, and recently co-edited *Remote Control* (Cambridge University Press 2003), a book on media ethics, and new forms of television such as reality TV and food shows.

Diane Reay is Professor of Sociology of Education at the Institute for Policy Studies in Education at London Metropolitan University. She has published widely in the areas of gender, social class and ethnicity. Her most recent book – *Choices of Degree: Social Class, Race, Gender and Higher Education*, with Stephen Ball and Miriam David (Stylus Press 2005) – uses Bourdieurian theory to explore higher education access.

Beverley Skeggs worked at the Universities of Keele, York, Lancaster and Manchester before joining the Department of Sociology at Goldsmiths College, London. She has worked in the areas of Women's Studies and Cultural Studies as well as Sociology. Her main publications include *The Media* (1992), *Feminist Cultural Theory* (1995), *Formations of Class and Gender* (Sage 1997), *Transformations: Thinking Through Feminism* (Routledge 2000); *Class, Self, Culture* (Routledge 2004), *Sexuality and the Politics of Violence and Safety* (Routledge 2004) (from an ESRC funded research project on violence, sexuality and space, with Les Moran, Paul Tyrer and Karen Corteen). She has also published on areas of popular culture, social theory, race and methodology. She is a series editor of the *Transformations: Thinking Through Feminism* book series (with Routledge) and is working on a new ESRC funded project (with Helen Wood) on *Making Class and Self through Televised Ethical Scenarios*.

Nicole Vitellone is Lecturer in Sociology and Cultural Studies at Manchester Metropolitan University. Her research interests are in the areas of material culture, AIDS and technological embodiment. She is currently working on an empirical project of IV drug use and the object of the syringe. Her articles on the syringe have appeared in *Body & Society* and *The Journal for Cultural Research*.

Anne Witz is Reader in Sociology at the University of Leicester and author of *Professions and Patriarchy* (Routledge 1992), co-author of *Gender, Careers and Organisations* (Macmillan 1997) and co-editor of *Gender and Bureaucracy* (Blackwell 1992), *For Sociology: Legacies and Prospects* (Sociology Press 2000) and *Engendering the Social: Feminist Encounters with Sociological Theory* (Open University Press 2004).

Index